Secret Alliances

NEW HORIZONS IN INTERNATIONAL RELATIONS

Series Editor: Patrick James, *Dornsife Dean's Professor, School of International Studies, Dana and David Dornsife College of Letters, Arts and Sciences, University of Southern California, USA*

New Horizons in International Relations is a book series that embraces the wide range of topics, theoretical frameworks and methods that combine to produce the field of International Relations. The series welcomes studies that are paradigm-based, studies that emphasize a visual approach and also those that fit within the new tradition of analytic eclecticism. In addition, this book series is well-disposed toward interdisciplinary research. Items with a pedagogical focus are welcome along with those that might be characterized more purely as works of theory or empirical analysis.

With oversight from the Series Editor, Patrick James, the Dana and David Dornsife Professor of International Relations at the University of Southern California, the book series is seeking out projects from scholars at all career stages. As a former President of the International Studies Association, the Series Editor hopes to include a wide range of subject matter, theoretical outlooks and methods among the books that appear. The volumes under the auspices of New Horizons in International Relations will be essential reading for professors and students, along with those in the policy world.

For a full list of Edward Elgar published titles, including the titles in this series, visit our website at www.e-elgar.com.

Secret Alliances
Why States Make, Keep, and End Them

Matthew Millard

Assistant Professor of Strategy and Security Studies, Department of Strategy and Security Studies, Global College of Professional Military Education, Air University, USAF, USA

NEW HORIZONS IN INTERNATIONAL RELATIONS

Edward Elgar
PUBLISHING

Cheltenham, UK • Northampton, MA, USA

© Matthew Millard 2025

All rights reserved. No part of this publication may be reproduced, stored in a retrieval system or transmitted in any form or by any means, electronic, mechanical or photocopying, recording, or otherwise without the prior permission of the publisher.

Published by
Edward Elgar Publishing Limited
The Lypiatts
15 Lansdown Road
Cheltenham
Glos GL50 2JA
UK

Edward Elgar Publishing, Inc.
William Pratt House
9 Dewey Court
Northampton
Massachusetts 01060
USA

Authorised representative in the EU for GPSR queries only: Easy Access System Europe – Mustamäe tee 50, 10621 Tallinn, Estonia, gpsr.requests@easproject.com

A catalogue record for this book
is available from the British Library

Library of Congress Control Number: 2025937333

This book is available electronically in the Elgaronline
Political Science and Public Policy subject collection
https://doi.org/10.4337/9781035326884

ISBN 978 1 0353 2687 7 (cased)
ISBN 978 1 0353 2688 4 (eBook)
ISBN 978 1 0353 7033 7 (ePub)

Printed and bound in Great Britain by TJ Books, Padstow, Cornwall

Contents

List of figures		vi
List of tables		vii
Acknowledgements		viii
1	Introducing secret alliances: an under-studied aspect of conflict	1
2	Nobody knows what goes on behind closed doors: targeting, division of goods, and secret alliances	33
3	Never meant to last: violations and why secret alliances are not institutionalized	55
4	Let's just be friends: secret alliances and political similarity	93
5	However it ends, it ends: reputation, norms, the long shadow of the future, and secret alliances	130
6	The best friends are enemies: the Molotov–Ribbentrop Pact	161
7	Trouble in the Suez: the British–French–Israeli plan for war	180
8	Big state, little state: apartheid, domestic opinion, and the South Africa–Swaziland agreement	203
9	Conclusion and the future of secret alliances	227
Appendices		241
References		255
Index		275

Figures

2.1	Issue indivisibility, multi-player games, and secret alliances	38
2.2	Division of goods and targeting in secret alliances point estimates, Model 1 (95% CIs)	47
2.3	Division of goods and targeting in secret alliances marginal effects, Model 1 (99% CIs)	48
2.4	Division of goods and targeting in secret alliances marginal effects, Model 2 (99% CIs)	50
3.1	Survival estimates, public/secret alliance	75
3.2	Survival estimates, public, partially secret, fully secret alliance	78
4.1a	Marginal effects plots (Models 1–2)	119
4.1b	Marginal effects plots (Models 3–4)	120
4.2a	Marginal effects plots (Models 5–6)	121
4.2b	Marginal effects plots (Models 7–8)	122
4.3a	Marginal effects plots (Models 9–10)	125
4.3b	Marginal effects plots (Models 11–12)	126
5.1a	Kaplan-Meyer survival estimates (Models 1–2)	148
5.1b	Kaplan-Meyer survival estimates (Models 3–4)	149
5.2a	Proportional hazards (Models 1–2)	150
5.2b	Proportional hazards (Models 3–4)	151
A3.1	Point estimates, H2 95% CIs	244
A3.2	Point estimates, H3 95% CIs	245
A3.3	Point estimates, H4 95% CIs	246
A3.4	Point estimates, H5 95% CIs	247
A3.5	Point estimates, H6 95% CIs	248

Tables

2.1	Variables	43
2.2	Descriptive statistics	44
2.3	Secret alliance observations	45
2.4	Division of goods and targeting in secret alliances	46
2.5	Hypotheses confirmed/rejected	51
3.1	Time to violation (hazard ratios)	74
3.2	Institutions and secret alliances (terminated and ongoing)	76
3.3	Secret alliances and adding members	80
3.4	Secret alliances and specific length mentioned	83
3.5	Secret alliances and military contact	86
3.6	Secret alliances and military contact	88
3.7	Hypotheses confirmed/rejected	90
4.1	Variables	107
4.2	Political similarity (year prior) and any secret alliances (logistic model)	113
4.3	Political similarity (year prior) and any secret alliances (rare events model)	114
4.4	Political similarity (year prior) and fully/partially secret alliances	115
4.5	Hypotheses confirmed/rejected	128
5.1	Variables	147
5.2	Effects of secret/termination on future alliances (Cox models)	152
A1.1	Secret alliance list	241
A4.1	Descriptive statistics	249
A5.1	Effects of secret/termination on future alliances (clustered standard errors)	250
A5.2	Effects of secret/termination on future alliances (Weibull models)	252

Acknowledgements

Writing a book is never easy. Doing so while being a department chair makes it considerably more difficult. As such, I must first acknowledge and express my sincerest gratitude to everyone from the Strategy and Security Studies department at the Global College of Professional Military Education, including both past and present members: Lieutenant Colonel Pete Brunke, Lieutenant Colonel John Walker, Lieutenant Colonel Dave Calderon, Major Chris Zummo, Major Arturo Urquieta, Dr Augustine Meaher, Dr Carl Watts, Dr Robert Clemm, Dr Brad Podliska, Dr Charlie Thomas, and Dr Nate Gonzalez. Without their patience, understanding, and advice, this book would not have been possible.

I would also like to especially thank Dr Brett Ashley Leeds and Dr Erik Gartzke. Both provided some excellent advice and, while usually glaringly obvious, I sometimes failed to notice the contradictory incentives in why states make secret alliances. Their advice, both at conferences and in more informal settings, certainly helped make this book what it is.

The impetus for this book emerged from discussions at conferences and several journal rejection letters. Often, the editors or anonymous reviewers would offer: "Why are you talking about why alliances form?" "You should talk about how they end!" "Or you should talk about why they don't institutionalize!" While those are all interesting areas of research covered in this book, they could not be covered in a single journal article. That is when I came to the realization that there had never been a thorough study of secret alliances and their life cycle. In fact, the outline for the chapters in this book was scrawled out frantically in a single afternoon on a whiteboard in an office I shared with Lieutenant Colonel Brian O'Leary, to whom I also extend my gratitude. While the project had developed a few years earlier with input both from my time at Saint Louis University and UC San Diego, I also extend a heartfelt thank you to one of my graduate students at Saint Louis University, Trevor Bachus.

I would also like to extend thanks to my copywriter/editor Peter Gross. While he did not have the opportunity to review the entire book because of my short notice, his inputs, suggestions, and alterations certainly improved the flow and organization of the book. His imprint is clearly visible in the chapters he helped edit.

I would also like to acknowledge the entire team at Edward Elgar, especially Nina Booth and Alex Pettifer. They certainly were incredible to work with and were an essential part of the process. I would also like to thank the anonymous reviewer who provided excellent feedback on the proposal for this project. This reviewer provided five pages of single-spaced notes on just the proposal. This indicated to me that the research was being taken seriously and that the publisher was able to receive reviews from the scholarly community that were thoughtful, informative, and, above all, helpful. While I received several offers from other publishers, this anonymous reviewer's feedback was perhaps the greatest factor in deciding to publish with Edward Elgar.

Naturally, I would also like to thank my family for putting up with me: Mom, Dad, Jill, Andy, Daniel, Katy, Sam, and Luke. Thank you for listening to an academic talk about, well, academic things. I know it is tedious, but I appreciate your patience.

In conclusion, I would just like to offer a bit of advice to graduate students and young faculty: rejections are only the beginning. Rejection letters did not kill this project. They just helped me understand that something as complicated and important as the life cycle of secret alliances could not be accomplished in a single 10,000-word journal article. When academia gives you a rejection letter, take it and make a book!

1. Introducing secret alliances: an understudied aspect of conflict

In October 1956—on the eve of the Suez Crisis that would last until November—Israeli Prime Minister David Ben-Gurion made a hasty trip to the Parisian suburb of Sèvres. After a secret 17-hour flight on a French plane, he met with British and French diplomats in an isolated chateau that had been used by the Resistance during World War II (Bar-On 2006, p. 173). Ben-Gurion and his entourage, which included Director-General of Defense Shimon Peres and Israeli Defense Force (IDF) Chief of Staff Moshe Dayan, met to discuss war with French Foreign Minister Christian Pineau.[1,2] The British, much to their disgust and the unexpected delight of Ben-Gurion, arrived after the French and Israelis had already begun discussions (Bar-On 2006, p. 177; Troen 1996, p. 126) The three states quickly commenced negotiations to plan a joint military operation that would address Egyptian President Gamal Abdel Nasser's nationalization of the Suez Canal.

Israel was concerned about being seen as an aggressor, despite repeated border incursions from Egypt (Bar-On 2006, pp. 179–80). The British and French were focused on securing access to the canal and undercutting Nasser. Over three days, including two days of negotiations between the French, British, and Israelis, the three countries developed a plan to advance their shared interests. The proposal was known as the Challe Scenario: Israel would attack Egypt along the Suez Canal, with IDF paratroopers inserting along the Mitla Pass (Bar-On 2006, p. 181). The French and British, after calling for a ceasefire, would land near the canal zone and demand Egyptian and Israeli withdrawals of ten miles (Troen 1996, p. 131). Under the agreement, the French would provide naval and aerial cover for Israel, selling them at least two squadrons of Mirage aircraft manned by French aviators (Bar-On 2006, p. 181).

British Foreign Minister Selwyn Lloyd received his country's approval after briefly returning to London and consulting with Prime Minister Anthony Eden. Documents were prepared, as was the standard custom for diplomatic agreements, and all three states signed on to the plan.[3] The French hoped to remove Nasser, who had been supplying arms to the Algerian resistance (Troen 1996, p. 125). The British wanted to denationalize the Suez Canal and contain the spread of Nasser's pan-Arabism in the Middle East, without being seen as taking sides. The Israelis, surrounded by hostile neighbors and with their backs to the sea, also hoped to snuff out Nasser's pan-Arabism while securing their country after a mere eight years of independence, and carving out a niche as a regional great power. At the end of the conference, bottles of champagne were produced to toast a new era of politics in the Middle East (Shlaim 1997, p. 525).

However, all was not well back in London. After he learned of signed copies of the agreement, Eden ordered Lloyd to request, and even demand, the return of those copies to be destroyed (Troen 1996, p. 124). Ben-Gurion and the French declined (Shlaim 1997, p. 526). Eden is reported to have personally destroyed the British copy (Shlaim 1997, p. 526), although the exact details of its destruction remain disputed. Bar-On (2006, p. 184; וןא־רב 1997) states that Ben-Gurion did not trust the British, which is corroborated by Ben-Gurion's own diary entries (Troen 1996, p. 129). It was Ben-Gurion who insisted that all parties sign the agreement (Troen 1996, p. 127). Before leaving Sèvres, Ben-Gurion folded the Israeli copy of the treaty and put it into his vest pocket (Bar-On 2006, p. 185). To this day, the only remaining copy resides in the Ben-Gurion Heritage Institute in Kiryat Sade Boker (וןא־רב1997, p. 94).

As Helmuth von Moltke observed, plans do not survive first contact with the enemy. In this case, the secret agreement between France, Britain, and Israel did not survive first contact with global public opinion or the realities on the ground. The arrangement rapidly fell apart, and France, Britain, and Israel were viewed as aggressors in a conflict that threatened to draw in the United States and the Soviet Union (Troen 1996, p. 128). Although few people knew of the secret agreement outside of its actual signatories, many suspected that it existed. With the ink barely dry, rumors of a secret meeting in Paris began to spread quickly (Shlaim 1997, p. 526).

In meetings at the United Nations Security Council in New York, the plan was widely condemned, and the French and British withdrew their forces after barely a week. The Israelis did not withdraw until March 1957, after securing Egyptian concessions regarding access to the Straits of Tiran (Dinstein 2017). The episode was an embarrassment that resulted in the fall of the Eden government. It also created friction within the French Fourth Republic, affecting the ongoing war in French Algeria and France's humiliating 1954 withdrawal from Indochina.

Oddly enough, the Israelis were the only signatories that emerged looking somewhat respectable. One wonders what Ben-Gurion was thinking as he folded the formal declaration and tucked it into his vest pocket. Surely the tiniest, weakest, and newest state involved in the agreement would not be the most gleeful—in just a few hours, Israeli troops would be engaging in combat. But Ben-Gurion now enjoyed the status of being a regional great power. More importantly, he had an insurance policy.

Why would states make formal secret agreements in the first place? After World War II, with growing norms and legal doctrines discouraging wars of aggression, it would be poor practice to document such an activity (Dinstein 2017). Secret agreements are also a threat to operational security, risking leaks from diplomatic sources. However, they do address one concern: defection. Ben-Gurion's insistence on a signed copy, which he kept on his person and refused to return or destroy, tacitly reveals his lack of trust in his newfound allies. It also represents a degree of cunning that other seasoned negotiators in the room may not have understood.

One participant who recognized the threat of the physical documents was Eden, a former foreign minister and minister of Churchill's War Cabinet. His experience in World War II had established that secret agreements were a political "hot potato" that should not be held when the music stopped. Eden went to great lengths to ensure that the British copy was destroyed, and he unsuccessfully attempted to have the French and Israeli copies returned and destroyed. But why would Eden be afraid of a written record? What harm could come from open, frank diplomacy between allies? And why risk a new alliance with calls to destroy the treaty? Such questions, along with the reasons why states make, keep, and end secret alliances—as well as what happens after—are the focus of this book. Secret alliances are riddles of international diplomacy. They were most prevalent from 1870 to 1916 (Kuo 2020), but they continue to be employed in modern international relations. Scholars need a better understanding of why they happen and what the prospects are for the future. Although this book primarily focuses on formal secret alliances, the lessons obtained from scholarly inquiry may apply to informal alliances made between states in the modern era.

The book is divided into two substantive sections. The first looks at four central questions: Why do states make alliances? Why don't states institutionalize secret alliances and are such alliances more or less enduring than public ones? Do secret agreements happen between states that share similar alliance networks or interests? And what happens to the reputation of states that make secret alliances? The second section consists of three case studies to analyze these effects on individual historical cases, chosen specifically for variation across several important variables.

ALLIANCES AND INTERNATIONAL RELATIONS

There are generally only two ways to prepare for war: building up arms or making alliances (Colaresi and Thompson 2005; Senese and Vasquez 2008). States can adopt either approach or a mix of both to ensure their security interests. North Korea, for example, has a well-known policy of autarky and self-sufficiency, developing "juche" as a driving political philosophy (Sŏ 2013, p.

3). While the term is often translated in the West as "self-reliance," a better translation involves "being the master of revolution … (and) rejecting dependence on others" (Sŏ 2013, p. 3). The country has purposefully pursued a policy of domestic military strength without reliance on outside alliance networks—its only formal alliances have been with the USSR (followed by limited agreements with Russia and a recently negotiated pact in 2024), China, and Cuba (Leeds et al. 2002).

Other states are more interested in pursuing alliance networks. After renouncing violence as a legitimate means of foreign policy in 1951, Japan relied heavily on its US ally. Japan's pacifist constitution and national prohibitions on military spending have discouraged it from building up arms, but the country has more US military bases and service personnel than any other country outside the United States (Hussein and Hadad 2021). This presence sends strong signals of the credible US commitment to Japanese security interests.

Although alliances and arms buildups have benefits and drawbacks that can be mitigated by pursuing a mixed strategic approach, states are more likely to favor one approach over an equal mix of both.

The Advantages and Disadvantages of Alliances

Alliances can best be understood as a "quick" way to secure a state—the Anglo–Polish Agreement of 1939 came a mere two days after the Molotov–Ribbentrop Pact. Although it was unsuccessful, the fact that an agreement could be negotiated and formalized so quickly illustrates the speed with which alliances can be brought to bear against security threats.

However, in relying on alliances, states are vulnerable to allies failing to uphold their obligations. Countries can renege on their obligations for many reasons, such as changes in the international or regional security environment, administration changes within their governments, military commitments elsewhere, developments that occur before the alliance is fully ratified, or side agreements with other states that may be hostile to an ally. An allied nation's military prowess may also atrophy over time, making the country unable or unwilling to mount an effective defense of an ally in need. The nature of what type of promises are made in formal alliances (Leeds 2003) also dictates to what degree a state is willing to commit to another, with agreements being carefully crafted to minimize risk to an allied state (Chiba, Johnson, and Leeds 2015). These problems are explored in two bodies of interrelated literature: credible commitments and reputation. This literature addresses alliance formation and continuation along with the prospects of future conflict involving one or more alliance partners.

Credible commitments

The credible commitment literature maintains that allies must have "skin in the game" for an alliance to seem credible. One state's pronouncements to defend or to engage in a policy of nonaggression with another are merely "scraps of paper" (Morrow 2000) and "cheap talk" without evidence of a commitment. An abundance of evidence shows states failing to meet their obligations (Sabrosky 1980), but other scholarship suggests that alliances are more likely to be successful when backed up by public commitments. Fearon (1994) finds that democratic regimes are more likely to credibly commit, and their leaders are punished for backing down. Leeds (1999) finds that mismatched regime dyads are less able to deter one another because of differing preferences and credibility. Morrow (1994) argues that the costs of alliances are carried during times of peace.

As Stein (1990) notes, the nature of a commitment is more important than a formal alliance. Theoretically, a state placing forces on another state's soil or publicly promising to send military assistance could result in behavioral changes from hostile parties, even without a formal alliance. However, history has many valid counterexamples, such as British Prime Minister Neville Chamberlain's public pronouncements of support for Poland from the floor of Parliament. Even a formal treaty between the British and Poles in late August 1939 was not enough to deter Germany, although the agreement lacked a credible deployment of forces or equipment to Poland.

This illustrates a complex problem in credible commitments: the nature of commitments can vary, from weak public pronouncements to strong troop deployments in allied countries. Although public pronouncements from democratic regimes are likely to be more substantial than pronouncements from autocrats, they still do not guarantee credible commitments. Public statements are often dismissed as "cheap talk" while physical commitments of goods or forces exhibit greater resolve. The United States often pursues a mixed approach, with forward deployment of troops and the staging of equipment in regions to demonstrate a willingness to become involved in a conflict along with the capability to react. However, democracies are also noted to carefully design alliances such that they offer minimal commitments to allies in order to ensure maximum flexibility in choosing how to respond to a threat (Chiba, Johnson, and Leeds 2015).

Reputation

Reputation is another important factor for states to consider in making alliances. Alliance reputation literature shares some similarities with—and is, in fact, rooted in the understanding of—reputations in arms race literature (Huth 1988; Schelling 2020). For a state to be secure and to be taken seriously, its past and present behavior builds a reputation that is acknowledged by other actors. Reputations are, in fact, owned by their subjects but constructed by their peers.

Some scholars claim that the importance of reputation is overblown (Downs and Jones 2002), but most maintain that prior actions (or inactions) develop a state's reputation outside the narrower confines of an immediate crisis or dispute (Weisiger and Yarhi-Milo 2015). And while scholars have largely focused on the claim that reputation matters, they have ignored questions regarding when, how, and where reputations matter (Dafoe, Renshon, and Huth 2014), or how reputations may differ between actors.

In defining reputation, scholars often frame it as inherently linked with a state's resolve, or "the extent to which a state will risk war to achieve its objectives" (Mercer 2010, p. 1; Weisiger and Yarhi-Milo 2015, p. 474). A state's reputation for resolve "refers to others' perception of that state's willingness to risk war" (Weisiger and Yarhi-Milo 2015, p. 474). Since states do not exist in a vacuum, they form ideas about other states based on their own and other states' prior interactions. Even in the theory of firms in business scholarship, a firm's reputation depends not only on its relationship with a potential acquirer or acquisition target, but also with other firms (Das and Teng 2002). Thus, perceptions of a state's willingness to "risk it all" are that state's reputation. As Weisiger and Yarhi-Milo (2015) point out, a steadfast reputation does not mean that a state will always fight. Instead, it indicates that other states would be well advised to pursue a policy of moderation.

In the alliance literature, scholars have found that a state's reputation is an important factor in which states are chosen as alliance partners. Some scholars assert that allied states only become involved in conflicts 25 percent of the time (Siverson and King 1980). However, Leeds, Long, and Mitchell (2000) find that when one examines the actual promises in alliance agreements, fulfillment of treaty obligations jumps to 75 percent.

Crescenzi et al. (2012) contend that "the expected reliability of future partners is also a component of an alliance seeker's decision calculus" and that "states form alliances for multiple reasons. Behind these reasons lies an assumption of reliability" (p. 260). While a state may not form an alliance for reliability alone, it remains an important part of the process. Specific examples show alliances breaking down due to the loss of confidence in a state's resolve to live up to its commitments, such as the Anglo–German alliance that terminated in 1901 (Crescenzi et al. 2012, p. 260). At least in the case of Britain and Germany, it appears that a state's interactions with others and its attempts to live up to commitments will affect alliance formation and termination. If states pursue alliances for security, it makes sense to seek a reliable partner.

Gibler (2008) echoes the importance of reputation in forming alliances. He states that living up to alliance commitments not only affects the alliance but also the narrower disputes that test alliance ties. Gibler finds that reputation matters in alliance formation, particularly as the "relative worth" of the alliance commitment increases, and that states are less likely to be targeted by third parties when they have defensive alliances with states known for living up to their commitments (Gibler 2008, pp. 432–3).

Literature on credible commitments and reputation are closely linked. A state willing to deploy troops and equipment sends signals to its allies (and potential adversaries) that its relationships are important. These commitments are part of a state's reputation, and they can affect confidence in current alliances and calculations for future ones. Forces or equipment moved away from an ally can signal a state's changing security objectives, an anticipation of greater challenges elsewhere, or a change in the level of commitment to an ally. (Such movements can also indicate that the state in need of an ally has shifted its policy to provide for its own security needs.)

Advantages and Disadvantages to Arms Buildups

Arms buildups come with their own challenges. Paramount among these is the security dilemma: a state's actions to increase its own security can provoke reactions that make it less secure. Scholars have debated whether the best defense is to prepare for war (Diehl 1983) or whether the escalatory nature of arms buildups is counterproductive (Wallace 1979), largely concluding that these buildups do increase the probability of war (Sample 1997). However, others have suggested that arms buildups merely indicate underlying tensions between states instead of driving them (Senese and Vasquez 2008). And although the security dilemma is a real concern, a state that is determined to engage in conflict is less likely to be deterred by the costs of facing a better-armed opponent.

While arms can provide maximal freedom to determine whether a state engages in a conflict, they also require a substantial amount of resources. Building up arms, particularly in an era where technology and precision often dictate the outcome of battle, takes time. Ramping up domestic manufacturing or even securing external sources for weapons and raw goods is no easy task. The symbiotic relationship between Weimar Germany and the Soviet Union during the 1920s is one such example: Germany needed cover to develop its weapons and the raw materials that the Soviets could provide. The Soviets lacked the technical expertise to develop and effectively deploy weapons systems. Ironically, the extensive knowledge and expertise that Germany and the USSR gained from such exchanges were used to fight against each other in World War II.

SECRECY IN INTERNATIONAL RELATIONS

In his "Fourteen Points" address to Congress, US President Woodrow Wilson warned of the risks posed by secret treaties. Instead, he argued for "open covenants of peace," asserting that public disclosure decreases the risk of miscalculation and the problems posed by asymmetric information (Bas and Schub 2016). Secret alliances can be problematic for international peace because they are likely to involve "salient stakes" that nations consider worth fighting for. Public disclosure of agreements involving those stakes—when the agreements are made at the expense of states that have been excluded—could trigger preemptive attacks to defend against the loss of the salient stake.

As Tadjdini (2015) notes, secret alliances or agreements technically violate international law. The practice was banned under Article 18 in the Charter of the League of Nations and Article 102 of Chapter XVI in the United Nations Charter (Tadjdini 2015). The Vienna Convention on the Law of Treaties, first proposed in 1969 and ratified in 1980, also bans such practices; it requires all treaties, subject to certain criteria, to be deposited with the United Nations. These are the legal realities, but states may classify alliances as non-treaties or find other reasons to avoid filing these agreements that end up becoming informal alliances. It is assumed that this would even pertain to alliances that were forged in secret. The most obvious way to circumvent this reporting requirement is simply to ignore it. Given that the opposition to secret alliances is a relatively recent norm, the repercussions for such a transgression might be minuscule or short term. The horizontal nature of international law means that a state failing to deposit a secret treaty at the United Nations is unlikely to face any immediate repercussions.

Article 10 of the Convention also states that for a document to be considered a valid treaty, it must discuss the procedure for its ratification in the body of the treaty or include signatures by authorized state representatives from the treaty signatories (United Nations 1969, pp. 5–6). Theoretically, states could formalize a secret agreement while also avoiding the registration requirement if both sides agree to the agreement's contents without having the documentation include signatures or a discussion of ratification. (This may not violate the text of the Convention, but it does seem at odds with the spirit of the law, and it does little to prevent states from backing out of such agreements.) An unsigned document is not prima facie evidence of collusion between two or more states, and Prime Minister Anthony Eden's reaction to the signing of the Protocol of Sèvres rested precisely on this distinction—the written plan had been signed by his personal representative to the conference.

While the distinction between a formal and informal alliance is murky at best, informal alliances can be seen as a form of "gentleman's agreement," where states have committed to a particular course of action without an explicit written record. The obvious drawback to such an arrangement is that it is no more enforceable in international relations than a gentleman's agreement would be under contract law; changing geopolitical landscapes or government regimes may make such agreements null and void. However, the relative lack of consequences for failing to uphold such agreements can be appealing to the states that make them.

Secrecy remains vital to international relations. According to Newman (1948), "diplomacy is traditionally supposed to be secret—and the few attempts to make it 'open' have been dismal failures" (p. 42). However, there is an inherent tension between the illegality of making secret alliances and the secrecy shrouding states involved in diplomatic negotiations.

Secrecy provides many advantages. It allows states to reveal their true preferences, making them more likely to negotiate in "good faith." It provides domestic cover for politically unpopular decisions, which is valuable in democracies and regimes without strong autocrats. Secrecy also provides international cover and the potential to avoid public backlash that might undermine coordination efforts. Finally, secrecy prevents countervailing coalitions or states from formulating policies that undermine the negotiations. However, a chilling effect—where states are reluctant to reveal their true preferences because their private conversations may become public—can undermine the expectation of secrecy between actors in the long term. This must be included in the considerations made by states during their negotiations.

One such example is Bradley Manning's unauthorized disclosures of classified US government information, which allegedly had a "chilling effect" on US government relations with other states (Committee on Oversight and Governmental Affairs 2011; Fenster 2011; Ramstack 2013; Springer et al. 2012). The US government was unable to demonstrate that Manning's disclosures were directly related to the deaths of US personnel, but it repeatedly asserted that the leaks damaged future relationships between the United States and other countries. Some have claimed that such a chilling effect would be short term at worst (O'Brien 2023), but it is challenging to validate either set of claims because of the difficulty in identifying secret negotiations that have been harmed by the potential for future unauthorized disclosures.

On the other hand, some evidence of a similar chilling effect is readily available and quantifiable. After Edward Snowden's unauthorized 2013 disclosure, scholars found that traffic to Wikipedia's privacy-sensitive articles decreased (Penney 2016). Opinion remains divided on the severity of chilling effects, but such behavior remains a real concern for governments around the world.

WHAT IS AN ALLIANCE?

The definition of what constitutes an alliance has focused on formal and informal alliances. Quantitative evidence primarily relies on the observation of formal alliances, for obvious reasons. Formal alliances almost invariably concern security issues, but some informal security agreements also address security issues, which means that they are at risk of being overlooked by scholars conducting quantitative analysis.

This distinction between alliance and agreement is not merely semantic. Informal alliances hold less legal weight, are more easily broken, and can cover different topics. They can also be made at the non-principal level of exchange between states. Alliances, on the other hand, require the accession of the entire state, rather than *part* of the state (such as a single ministry). An alliance is a commitment made by a sovereign entity;[4] informal agreements can be made by sovereign or non-sovereign entities and can be broken more easily. Lipson (1991) does not discuss alliances specifically, but he maintains that agreements "are promises about future behavior" that entail "reciprocal promises or actions" and they are informal "if they lack the state's fullest and most authoritative imprimatur" (p. 498).

Lipson (1991) details the value of informal agreements in international relations. Many non-security-related informal agreements address mundane areas such as floating exchange rates in the wake of the collapse of the Bretton Woods agreement (p. 495). Tacit understandings and informal agreements between the USSR and the United States addressed security issues during the Cold War (p. 496), but calling such agreements "alliances" illustrates the problems associated with these definitions. "Alliances" often equate to security-related issues, particularly among "friends" in international relations—laymen often equate alliances with friendships, rather than mutually advantageous alignments of interests. These unclear definitions have likewise meant that scholars have been less likely to study informal agreements (Lipson 1991, p. 502).

Informal agreements can occur along two axes: (1) the level of government at which the agreement is made, and (2) the form taken by the agreement (Lipson 1991, p. 498). Forms can include formally written documents, joint communiqués, oral agreements, or tacit understandings (Lipson 1991, p. 498). The shape and degree of approval for such agreements can vary. The value of informal agreements, then, is "as a device for minimizing the impediments to cooperation at both the domestic and international levels" (Lipson 1991, p. 500). Thus, while they do not constitute the same level of cooperation as formal agreements, they are necessary tools for international diplomacy. This is especially true for governments where the formal approval process for foreign agreements is more onerous, due to more numerous veto players involved in the process.

Democracies often encounter the greatest domestic impediments to international cooperation; autocratic regimes can circumvent barriers to approval more easily. International agreements are two-level games—with leaders negotiating at an international level while managing constituents at a domestic level—and both levels must be satisfied for an agreement to legally apply domestically and under international law (Putnam 2017). When a democratic state cannot formally approve an agreement (e.g., the ratification of the Trans-Pacific Partnership), it may still follow the spirit of such an agreement internationally. However, the legal grounds for such activities would best be described as shaky.

There are four reasons why informal agreements may be necessary: (1) the desire to avoid formal visible pledges; (2) the desire to avoid the ratification process; (3) the ability to renegotiate or modify as circumstances change; and (4) the need to reach agreements quickly (Lipson 1991, p. 501). But maintaining an accurate record of informal agreements and the topics that they cover, even when they are not secret, is highly problematic. Courts generally refuse to honor undocumented "gentlemen's agreements" for similar reasons: the facts of their existence cannot easily be verified.

To delimit the parameters of a formal alliance, the scope of its definition must categorize and account for the fullest possible sample[5] existing within a given timeframe. Quantitative definitions are an effective means of identification because quantitative conflict processes identify and categorize important variables related to conflict. Two of the most widely utilized datasets are the Correlates of War (COW) alliance dataset (Gibler 2009; Singer and Small 1966) and the Alliance Treaty Obligations and Provisions (ATOP) dataset (Leeds et al. 2002). There is a substantial amount of overlap in the cases covered by these datasets, but each set has distinct advantages and disadvantages. Both of them use the term "alliance" to describe "formal alliances" of a security nature rather than economic agreements or other considerations.

Scholars have spent decades working with the COW alliance dataset. In its most recent form (Gibler 2009), it relies on the original definition of "formal alliance" that Singer and Small developed (1966). Instead of starting with a definition of formal alliances that identifies the sample of cases (deductive approach), they take a more inductive approach and work from the sample of cases to explore the general phenomenon of alliances. Considerable attention has been dedicated to how this contrasts with the deductive approach familiar to most social scientists (Singer and Small 1966, p. 2).

Singer and Small relied on three primary sources to catalogue all foreign alliances existing in the original timeframe (1816–1939). First, the League of Nations treaty repository was their primary source of agreements made during the inter-war years. Second, foreign ministry publications from the major powers were another source during this timeframe and earlier. Third, they also relied on historical monographs, which were inherently problematic (Singer and Small 1966, p. 1).

To be included in the dataset, alliances needed at least two signatories that were sovereign states. Signatories had to commit to defensive, offensive, neutrality, or entente policies. Agreements also needed start dates and required a degree of "seriousness" between states engaging in an alliance (Singer and Small 1966, pp. 2–3). Singer and Small (1966) also address the problems associated with formal and informal alliances: they acknowledge, "we do not assume that all meaningful bonds between nations are expressed by, or codified in, written treaties; nor do we imply that the only—or even the most-significant coalition is the formal alliance" (Singer and Small 1966, p. 4). They find value in analyzing formal alliances because "the formal treaty of alliance is an extremely common mode by which nations join together and divide in pursuing their self-defined interests, and that as such it is worth systematic interest" (Singer and Small 1966, pp. 4–5). The willingness to write down an agreement indicates a state's sincerity in giving up some of their sovereignty in exchange for security.

The ATOP dataset (Leeds et al. 2002), in contrast, precisely defines what constitutes a formal alliance. They begin with Toscano's (1966) definition of formal alliances: "those acts which authorized organs of the respective states exchange with each other in their reciprocal contacts in the name of, and on behalf of, the states as members of the international community" (p. 21). For Leeds, Ritter, Mitchell, and Long, alliances are "formal agreement(s) among independent states to cooperate militarily in the face of potential or realized military conflict" ("Alliance Treaty Obligations and Provisions (ATOP) Codebook" 2022, p. 6). In their dataset, alliances must have legal force, be signed by official representatives between independent states, and concern military cooperation or promises to provide such security or cooperation (Leeds 2022, pp. 6–7).

Apart from the different approaches, there are other important distinctions between the two datasets. ATOP's primary advantage is its depth and breadth, covering the same timeframe as the COW dataset but including more variables of interest to scholars, allowing them to examine questions that otherwise might go unanswered.

Outside of these datasets, confusion surrounding the definition of "partner" and "ally" is not confined to historical or scientific analysis. Such terms are often used interchangeably by journalists, laymen, and others, obfuscating the commitments between the United States and other countries around the world. The US Department of Defense (2019) identifies the primary difference between partners and allies and acknowledges varying levels of commitment:

the strongest support goes to allies, and more limited support is provided to partners. Despite this distinction, allies can be partners and partners can be allies, depending on the circumstances or the nature of cooperation. The difference between the two is not purely academic; Poast (2023) and Metz, Davidson, and Linetsky (2023) have pointed out that conflating them has consequences affecting foreign policy.

Some agreements described as "alliances" by laymen or the media can be broken with less severe consequences because they do not involve the force of international or domestic law. The COW dataset identifies a militarized interstate dispute (MID) as a "threat, display or use of force" authorized by the central government (i.e., clear, directed intent from a state). In the case of alliances, especially when forged to address MIDs, they must be formally approved by state mechanisms.

Toscano (1966, p. 21) defines a formal alliance as "those acts which authorized organs of the respective states exchange with each other in their reciprocal contacts in the name of, and on behalf of, the states as members of the international community" (Leeds 2022, p. 6). These are not informal "handshake" agreements between unauthorized government officials. This means that for this definition as well there must be clear, directed intent from the state itself, rather than radical agents acting independently of the state. In the case of alliances, they must be formally approved by the mechanisms in place within the state itself. Within some states, this may be a high hurdle. For instance, within the United States, formal treaties must be approved by the US Senate and then sent to the President for approval. Other such agreements, which the media or laymen may describe as "alliances," would thus be more easily broken because they do not involve the force of both international and domestic law (though some agreements may have other obligations under the force of domestic law, such as with the requirement for the United States to sell weapons to Taiwan).

Given that alliances are sometimes considered to be "cheap talk" (Mercer 2010), there is value in writing down the specifics of an alliance and formally approving it as an agreement between two nations. These agreements provide a public understanding of shared security interests, and they are difficult to abandon.

Although a theory of firms approach is often used in studying international relations, it makes problematic assumptions about the enforceability of contracts between states. With sovereign equality, the enforceability of contracts is difficult or non-existent, even when one considers the power differentials between actors (Lake 2011). Since states find it difficult to recover the costs of an alliance that was abandoned by their peers, reputation can impose a long-term cost on states attempting to capture short-term advantages by reneging on their agreements (Crescenzi et al. 2012, p. 261; Lipson 1991). The costs of domestic and international public embarrassment over the long term can provide enough leverage to make short-term defection unpalatable.

While these dynamics are evident in public alliances, the mechanism for retaliation in secret alliances takes a different form. A signatory of a secret alliance that reneges on their commitment is more likely to face public embarrassment by having their partners reveal the existence of the agreement. This both affects the long-term reputation of a state (arguably more so than if it had defected from a public alliance) and it thwarts the short-term goal that was to have been achieved by the secret agreement. In fact, placing the fruits of a secret alliance just outside the grasp of an ally may be enough to keep them from defecting in the first place. The denial of a secretly promised good is likely to be more of a setback to signatories than future reputational damage. Nonetheless, such short-term defection is likely to harm both a state's public and private reputation.

Informal agreements between heads of governments can be seen as commitments, but subsequent government leaders may not be obligated to honor them. A prominent example is the discussions between US Secretary of State James Baker and Soviet Premier Mikhail Gorbachev agreeing not to extend the North Atlantic Treaty Organization (NATO) eastward into a newly unified Germany (Taubman 2017, pp. 546–52). Debates surrounding the meaning and validity of this agreement abound, but NATO ultimately expanded to include former communist states and the newly reunited Germany. By that time, Gorbachev's Soviet Union no longer existed, the discussions had taken place with only a single NATO member, that member's head of state was not involved, and the US head of state at the time of the agreement was no longer president when the former Eastern bloc states were added to NATO. Informal agreements are, by design, easier to escape from.

A series of informal agreements occurred between Japan, the United States, and (to a lesser extent) Canada in 1907–08. Japan agreed to refrain from issuing passports for its citizens working in the United States, and in exchange, the United States agreed to protect rights for Japanese workers that were more in line with the protections afforded to White laborers (Hajimu 2015). This agreement broke down after the signing of the US Immigration Act of 1924 (Hajimu 2015). The act, which was signed by Congress and the President, superseded the informal arrangement. Other informal agreements abound in international politics. The 1975 Helsinki Accords, signed by 35 nations, do not represent legally binding commitments to peace in Europe (Schachter 1977), which is illustrated by the ongoing war in Ukraine. In fact, the US delegation's lead negotiator, Harold Russell, did not intend for the accords to be legally binding, and neither did other negotiators present at the event (Schachter 1977, p. 296). As Schachter (1977) points out, "international lawyers generally agree that an international agreement is not legally binding unless the parties intend it to be" (p. 296).

WHY FORMAL SECRET AGREEMENTS?

Alliances send signals and allow coordination between states in the international system (Gibler 2009). These signals can indicate when a state is willing to support or make peace with other states. Public declarations can also send signals to a state's other allies and to the new ally itself. Such signals can be meant for potentially aggressive states, conveying information regarding a state's values, levels of commitment, and dedication to defending or supporting allies. Public pronouncements detail what potential foes and friends can expect if they exhibit aggressive behavior toward an ally. As such, alliances are important mechanisms for transmitting information in international relations.

States can also make alliances to coordinate broader geopolitical activities. Such agreements can serve as a formal division of labor to identify what will be done under specific circumstances, determining who is responsible for what types of actions and how forces may be allocated for training or defensive purposes. These uses are not mutually exclusive; alliances can be tools for signaling and coordination simultaneously.

Secret alliances are not generally used as signaling mechanisms, because that would undermine the point of secrecy. However, there are two different kinds of secret alliances: fully secret and partially secret. With the latter type of agreement, secret arrangements are generally attached to a publicly acknowledged treaty, such as with the Molotov–Ribbentrop Pact of August 1939. The public component of these arrangements may be fully disclosed, or the pact can merely be publicly acknowledged, which makes it possible for partially secret alliances to send signals. Although fully secret agreements can send signals, the only states that receive them are the other signatories.

Any rapprochement or agreement between the signatories of a fully secret agreement is not publicly acknowledged. This lack of public acknowledgement can be problematic from a social science point of view, and it is definitely a problem for scholars who cannot access the contents of the agreements. In both the COW and ATOP datasets, there are many instances in which scholars do not have direct public access to alliance documents. The ATOP dataset contains 589 total alliances, and 20 of them come from secondary sources ("Source" variable) because the primary document is unavailable. These secondary sources are used for a mere 3.4 percent of alliances in the ATOP dataset, but the lack of detail remains a concern.

Scholars may be unable to access secret agreements for several reasons: the documents may no longer exist; the state—or, more probably, the regimes that signed the document—may no longer exist; or the alliance may be classified, even if acknowledged publicly, making its details unavailable to the public. The last possibility is particularly concerning, not only for scientific inquiry into secret alliances but also for any study of alliances. It is likely to mean that related censorship has affected all available alliance data, particularly for alliances that remain in effect. There are political incentives to conceal active secret alliances, especially when there is an odious intent.

However, Deeks (2019) has found that secrecy can be beneficial. States may use secret agreements to facilitate trust between otherwise belligerent parties. Such secret agreements mean that states do not have to publicly disclose potential sources of embarrassment and that they can be better understood as negotiating from a position of good faith.

There are largely two reasons why a state would want to classify an agreement as secret (which is covered more thoroughly in Chapter 2). First, formal secret alliances are likely to cover salient stakes, such as contested territory or threats to regime stability discussed in secret (Rider 2013, p. 581). Second, secret alliances are more likely when domestic or international public opinion is fragile or otherwise unsupportive, which is most likely to occur within democratic states. In such states, the selectorate is larger (Bueno De Mesquita, Koch, and Siverson 2004a) and those selectorates are less likely to benefit from conflict. In autocratic regimes, the need to conceal agreements has less to do with public opinion and more to do with the fact that revealing such alliances can undermine their objectives.

In the Protocol of Sèvres, all three states were full democracies (Marshall and Gurr 2020). This incentivized them to avoid publicizing the text of their agreement and led to further efforts, particularly within Britain, to conceal the agreement long after it was invalid. Another example is the 1982 South Africa–Swaziland pact, which was kept secret because its disclosure would have been politically problematic and embarrassing for ruling elites in both states.

Some alliances are kept secret to protect a state's international reputation. For instance, the disclosure of the Sykes–Picot Agreement in late 1917 demonstrates some potential consequences. After the French and British intent to claim Ottoman territory became public knowledge, the Ottomans were incentivized to continue fighting rather than to negotiate peace agreements. Arab individuals in Ottoman territory were similarly discouraged from cooperating with the British or French because they were unwilling to end up in circumstances that were identical to those they endured under the Ottoman Empire. The Protocol of Sèvres shows how these dynamics can play out in the era of international organizations: enormous pressure in the United Nations and the lack of support from allies such as the United States meant that Britain, France, and Israel were eventually forced to back down in the Sinai.

Formal secret alliances can be useful during a crisis. The private nature of such agreements makes them less likely to trigger domestic disagreements regarding the convergence of interests between two or more states. This can facilitate two-track diplomacy (Putnam 2017) that allows parties to reach agreements that satisfy domestic and international stakeholders before crises or disputes spread further.

Scholars should analyze formal secret alliances because "big events are likely to be known, small events are less likely to be known" (Price and Ball 2014, p. 11). It is difficult—if not impossible—to hide the influence of major formal secret alliances, such as the partition of Poland by the Soviets and Nazis. The Soviets argued that they invaded Eastern Poland due to "political instability" created by Poland's governance vacuum (Roberts 1989),[6] but none of the major diplomatic corps in Western capitals are known to have believed this was the case. The Soviet occupation of the Baltic states throughout the spring of 1940 was equally suspicious, along with the military occupation of Bessarabia and North Bukovina, which both had high concentrations of ethnic Volksdeutch who were vital to Berlin.

Similarly, few believed that British and French involvement in the October 1956 conflict along the Suez Canal was not collusion ahead of time. The quick deployment of British and French troops, especially when the French were otherwise engaged with the uprising in French Algeria, was highly unusual and indicative of advance planning. The apparent 1982 rapprochement between Swaziland and its more powerful neighbor South Africa is another example. Given events that were happening throughout southern Africa and the heavy criticism of South Africa's apartheid government and outright support for the anti-apartheid African National Congress, such a reconciliation seemed atypical. Knowledge of the secret Swaziland–South Africa pact was made public two years later (Davies and O'Meara 1985, p. 200), but their rapprochement—especially after the offer to return two South African Bantustans to Swaziland—was difficult to ignore. It indicated that there must be a private agreement between the two states (Griffiths and Funnell 1991, p. 51). While these changes are difficult to hide, smaller changes to the international environment that are less consequential are easier to hide and, theoretically, less impactful to international security.

THE PROBLEM WITH SECRET ALLIANCES

Secrecy itself is the problem with knowing about secret alliances and their impact on events (Scoville 2020). As an example, Scoville (2020) used Freedom of Information Act requests to identify 61 new secret agreements in the United States alone. Some 5–15 percent of all executive agreements in the United States are classified as top secret. While secret treaties are classified,

Scoville (2020) has observed that the metadata associated with the signing of such agreements is not required to be classified. And while these agreements are classified, the issues involved in them are unlikely to carry the same geopolitical weight as formal alliances.

US executive agencies frequently fail to transmit agreements to the State Department after making them with foreign governments, despite it being required by the 1972 Case-Zablocki Act (Scoville 2020). This act was designed to provide Congress with oversight over informal agreements made not just between the United States and other states but also between US agencies and their foreign counterparts (Johnson and McCormick 1977). Neither are these agreements filed with the United Nations, perhaps because they are considered to be executive agreements that do not legally qualify as treaties.

Although the specifics of secret agreements are difficult to ascertain—particularly when states are incentivized to hide their actions—some states are more receptive to the idea of disclosing a prior administration's secret machinations, as was the case with the 1916 Sykes–Picot Agreement. Although the British and French were dividing up territory from the Ottoman Empire, their negotiations required assent from Italy and Russia. After the 1917 Bolshevik Revolution, the czar's secret negotiations went public in *Pravda* and *Izvestia*. It was then picked up by the British press in November of that year.

The reason why scholars and laymen know about many of these secret agreements is through observation of their effects rather than through direct access to the treaty itself. As Tadjdni (2015) points out, some countries' classification laws bar the release or even acknowledgement of such agreements for anywhere from 20 to 50 years. Some of the formal public agreements found within the COW and ATOP datasets cite documents that are not publicly available. This may be due to continued domestic classification of the treaty or a loss of the agreement (which was alleged to have happened to the French copy of the Protocol of Sèvres). In other instances, it is kept secret due to agreements between the signatories, which appears to be the case with one of the most recent and consequential active agreements: the Sino-Russian agreement publicly announced on February 4, 2022.

Singer and Small (1966) identified this problem with secret formal alliances at the outset of their quantitative study. They acknowledged that their sources have "one major failing (in) the absence of secret treaties whose existence only comes to light years or decades later" (Singer and Small 1966, pp. 1–2). Secrecy can be problematic for the study of all alliances, and not merely the secret ones.

However, it is worth taking a closer look at the second half of Singer and Small's (1966) statement: they indicate that secret agreements do eventually come to light. There is a degree of optimism in this claim—the idea that actions done in the dark will eventually come to light might provide some form of reassurance to scholars. Scholars and practitioners alike recognize the value of secrecy in foreign policy, but secret agreements have disadvantages from asymmetrical information (Bas and Schub 2016). Shlaim (1997) has pointed out that the Protocol of Sèvres is not only the best-known war plot but also the best documented, which may be due to the fact that its signatories were democracies (p. 510).

WHY DO STATES RECORD SECRET AGREEMENTS?

It is not possible to know whether agreements are more likely to be formalized between close friends or antagonistic rivals. Scoville (2020) provides two scenarios in which states are unlikely to acknowledge secret alliances. First, secret agreements may be more common between closer allies because of ongoing interactions between those states. Alternatively, secret agreements may be more common between antagonistic states because of the nature of their relationship or the lack of transparency in those regimes. Because of this lack of trust, states may be more likely to document their illicit alliance as an "insurance policy" against defection. The secrecy of such agreements makes it difficult to determine which scenario more accurately reflects reality.

It is problematic for a state to credibly commit to a secret alliance partner because, in doing so, a state may reveal strategic goals that created the agreement. Credible commitments are primarily intended for two audiences: allies and potential foes. However, using a secret alliance to send signals of credible commitment to states outside of that alliance would be antithetical to the entire purpose of secrecy.

As Morrow (2000, p. 65) points out, alliances always come at a cost. In most cases, the trade-off involves lost sovereignty (Morrow 1987, 1991). However, secret alliances not only involve the loss of sovereignty that comes from maintaining the agreement, but they also risk losing reputation, domestic stability—particularly in democratic regimes—and even the objective of the agreement if their secrecy is lost (Chiba, Johnson, and Leeds 2015). In formal secret alliances with the highest stakes, the agreements are more likely to be written down to protect against defection that could reveal the existence of the secret. (This is not to say that defection is impossible; the Molotov–Ribbentrop Pact is an obvious example of defection among secret allies.) Formal written agreements make it more costly to defect from secret alliances.

The issue of making credible commitments in a secret alliance, showing both commitment to the allies and commitment to secrecy, can be addressed with a formal agreement. Participants have placed themselves in a "prisoner's dilemma" situation: if one party reveals the existence of an agreement, they may be spared the harshest public judgment. If all parties publicize the agreement, they suffer equal (but less severe) effects. If every participant cooperates to maintain secrecy, they all receive the benefits. States forging secret alliances are incentivized to write down their agreements (Morrow 2000) because—as seen with Ben-Gurion in 1956—formal recognition of the agreement makes it less likely other participants will defect. This dilemma can be understood as both a prisoner's dilemma and a Stag Hunt game.

In a Stag Hunt game, every actor working together nets a benefit for the entire group, while individuals working solely for their own gain will ruin the collective effort. In secret alliances, states can make side deals or agreements with other states to either directly or indirectly betray the secret alliance. Under the Molotov–Ribbentrop Pact, both states were explicitly required to consult each other prior to signing any agreement with another state. A similar requirement existed in Article 1 of the 1936 Anti-Comintern Pact between Germany and Japan (which expanded to include other countries), requiring consultation with Japan before making any agreements with the Soviet Union. The agreement was technically broken by Germany's alliance with the Soviet Union.

The issue of trust is the reason why it is important for secret agreements to involve written contracts detailing the existence, limitations, and obligations of the signatories. As Lipson (1991) notes, domestic courts generally do not honor undocumented "gentlemen's agreements" because it is difficult to establish either the obligations of such agreements or their very existence in the first place. In security-related issues, where the stakes are highest—and particularly when they involve salient stakes—written formal agreements are vital for recording the obligations understood to be inherent in the agreement. The existence of the documents also tacitly acknowledges that the signatories do not trust one another. The evidence can be presented to the public (as in the United Kingdom, with the fallout from the Protocol of Sèvres) or in international forums (as with the Bolshevik revelation of the Sykes–Picot Agreement) to demonstrate the unreliability of an alliance partner that defects.

CHOICE OF QUANTITATIVE DATA

Two generally acceptable and equally impressive data collections can facilitate a quantitative analysis of secret alliances: the Correlates of War (COW) program (Gibler 2009) and the Alliance Treaty Obligations and Provision (ATOP) data (Leeds et al. 2002). There is a large overlap between the datasets, but the ATOP information contains additional variables that are useful to scholars. It is claimed that "the ATOP project stands alone in combined depth and breadth of coverage, providing systematic detailed information" (Leeds 2022, p. 5).

The ATOP dataset was compiled partly to provide greater depth in addressing specific obligations and what those provisions look like in alliances (Leeds 2022, p. 5). Scholars resolved debates around alliances almost immediately after the data was released, settling discussions around alliance-making that had largely mirrored earlier debates regarding arms races and the probability of conflict.

Some scholars have argued that arms races increase the risk of conflict (Wallace 1979). Others, such as Diehl (1983), claim that arms buildup does not increase the probability of conflict. Sample (1997; 1998) states that these contradictory findings can best be explained by coding decisions made while conducting analyses, asserting that arms races do marginally increase the probability of conflict. Similarly, some scholars (e.g., Gulick 1955; Morgenthau 1948; Waltz 2010) maintain that alliances decrease the probability of conflict. They argue that states should make alliances to benefit from deterrence that can prevent war. Other scholars find that alliances increase the probability of conflict (Siverson and Starr 1991; Vasquez 2009).[7,8] Their reasoning holds that the presence of allies reduces the perceived cost of conflict or makes the target state more nervous and provokes preemptive strikes. Leeds (2003) helped resolve this debate by pointing out that different types of alliances perform different functions. A defensive alliance—when clearly articulated as such and backed up with credible commitments (Morrow 1994)—likely decreases the probability of war. An offensive alliance is more likely to result in conflict because it provides different information to other states.

A more nuanced debate has considered alliance-making behavior and the probability of conflict. Smith (1996a) finds that states are more likely to intervene in a conflict when they have an alliance. Others disagree, claiming that these states were merely preparing for war. Vasquez (2009) and Senese and Vasquez (2008) point out that there are both immediate and underlying causes (read correlates) of war, a point further argued by Sample (2021). These findings claim that in trying to establish the hazard ratio of an increased probability for conflict, some steps are more likely to aggravate the underlying issues that precede outright combat.

ATOP has been more direct in answering whether alliances increase or decrease the probability of conflict; the debates on alliance-making behaviors needed a greater depth of understanding for individual alliances. From its fine-grained approach, scholars could make general claims about how alliances affect conflict and peace. Leeds, Ritter, Mitchell, and Long (2002) coded whether alliances were public, partially secret, or fully secret, making it possible to develop a greater understanding of secret alliances' mechanisms and effects. This balance of depth and breadth makes the ATOP dataset invaluable for the questions in this book.

SELECTION EFFECTS AND BIAS

The quantitative study of alliances and secrecy immediately encounters a problem: Is systematic bias built into the data? To answer that question, we must make the distinction between systematic and non-systematic bias, how it could affect the dataset examined in this analysis, and what strategies may be used to mitigate such concerns. Non-systematic bias is not problematic for social scientific research, but systematic bias results in poor explanations because the researcher does not know what the true population looks like as the sample may be systematically biased.

Systematic bias (sometimes called selection effects) exists when a selection of data points is not sufficiently random. King, Keohane, and Verba (1994) assert that random selection is important because it satisfies three assumptions: (1) that the process of assigning values to the explanatory variables is independent of the dependent variables (i.e., there is no endogeneity problem); (2) that selection bias is absent; and (3) that omitted variable bias is also absent (p. 94).

Concerns over the effects of systematic bias exist in the study of international relations. Jones, Bremer, and Singer (1996) traced the history of the Militarized Interstate Dispute dataset, analyzing the coding procedures and the potential omission of relevant cases. Gibler, Miller, and Little (2016) later examined each case in the MID dataset, suggesting cases that were chosen inappropriately or failed to fit the original coding procedures of the project. Here, the authors identified 251 cases (10 percent of the data) that did not conform to the coding rules, 234 disputes that contained major coding errors, and 1009 cases that required minor changes. In a rejoinder, Palmer et al. (2020) agreed with 76 percent of the changes, but they found that some of the suggestions "are not due to their data, but rather to the strategies they employ for replication" (p. 469).

The 2016 analysis by Gibler, Miller, and Little—and the 2020 rejoinder from Palmer et al. (2020)—are about more than the cases themselves. They illustrate biases or coding errors that can and do exist in event datasets used in the study of international relations. Jones, Bremer, and Singer (1996) acknowledge:

> As we and others began to analyze the first version of the Militarized Interstate Dispute (MID) data set and to examine the relationship between these disputes on one hand and their precursors and outcomes on the other, it became evident that our search, diligent and costly as it was, had not yielded the full population of cases. (p. 167)

Disputes between scholars have fueled a search for alternative measurements of conflict that can address biases affecting the quantitative study of conflict processes. Gibler, Miller, and Little (2016) argue that inappropriate cases, such as those related to the Tanker War and World War II, are inappropriately listed as separate disputes between states, which violates the coding rules and objectives of the MID project. But this does not address cases that have been excluded from the MID dataset. The question remains whether such exclusions occur systematically or non-systematically.

MID data may also be biased against cases that do not occur in Europe or North America because lesser-known cases between developing states are less likely to be discussed in contemporary English news media. This problem is compounded by time; cases from the early 1800s are less likely to be picked up than those of more recent vintage. These cases may be relatively minor and may not have developed into war, but there is no assurance that more modern cases rising to the level of war would be excluded from the dataset at the same rate.

Such datasets may systematically exclude non-Western cases—or those occurring between polities that are not recognized as members of the international system—or cases that occurred many years ago. It may also be difficult to ascertain whether disputes were initiated by a central government or whether they were "mistakes on the ground" instigated by a low-level commander.

Finally, there is the selection of cases tied to the recognition of states themselves. Many international relations datasets begin in 1816, immediately after the end of the Napoleonic Wars. However, the most important cases explaining state formation for many of the "core" states in the international system are excluded from such databases. This potentially biases against states in the early years of state formation and may explain state behavior among non-European/non-Western states that emerged from a post-colonial world. Thus, systematically excluding such states is problematic for all conflict research because not all states in the sample have the same starting point.

Selection bias is an endemic problem affecting the large-n study of many issues within international relations and conflict. Scholars have noticed its presence in the literature on deterrence (Danilovic 2001; Fearon 2002), decisions to engage in "big" or "small" wars (Bueno de Mesquita 1990), human rights abuses and policymaking (Price and Ball 2014), the urban/rural divide in conflict reporting (Price and Ball 2014), Eurocentrism and the democratic peace (Sabaratnam 2013), and alliance reliability (Smith 1996a). In fact, selecting cases for large-n study is problematic because cases can be included or excluded at will, depending on how the coding rules are written, which can result in intentional or unintentional bias.

Regarding these concerns, Gibler (2008) notes that states strategically select into alliances, and the analysis of qualities such as reputation is inherently difficult to measure. This strategic selection means that scholars cannot necessarily see instances of states with poor reputations making alliances. Because some states have poor reputations, sometimes for reasons apart from their ability to adhere to prior alliance commitments, one can never know whether they would be a reliable partner for an alliance. Other components of reputation are important along with the factors that determine why states make alliances.

A well-known axiom is that "politics makes for strange bedfellows." Many alliances throughout history have initially seemed odd; the Molotov–Ribbentrop Pact between Nazi Germany and the Soviet Union was an alliance between two otherwise belligerent powers. The late 19th-century alliance between Germany and Britain was also noteworthy for its mismatch of goals and political values. Both illustrate that there is more to an alliance decision to ally than a state's reputation. Likewise, in knowing about secret alliances, Newman (1948) unequivocally states that "while diplomatic secrecy is never absolute, its 'leakages' are often spasmodic. In particular, the whole truth about events leading to war emerges slowly, and in fragments."[9,10] It is possible for scholars to know much about secret alliances, even when secrecy clouds some information and cases. However, care must be taken for a proper scientific study of such phenomena.

Selection effects have long been known as problematic for scholars (Fearon 1997; 2002; Smith 1996b; 1998); they recognize that it is inherently difficult to know when a state selects into a specific behavior or what processes motivated their decision. If the decision to make a formal secret alliance is different from the decision to make an informal secret alliance or even a public alliance, scholars must understand why. In developing that understanding, quantitative methods are inherently problematic when the inclusion of those decisions into such datasets would bias the results of a study. One way of dealing with such a problem involves a mixed-methods approach, examining cases from a dataset that includes secret alliances. Choosing cases that vary across important causal mechanisms may also be useful, because it allows scholars to demonstrate how the mechanisms underlying such behaviors can vary across important dimensions.

However, Gibler (2008) points out that case studies have been problematic in some areas of research. Specifically, he finds reputational case studies to be less than convincing in deterrence literature. Here, scholars have largely found more practical situational variables that are more likely to affect the outcome of a crisis or dispute (Gibler 2008, p. 431).

Unfortunately, this problem is predominant in any scenario where researchers rely on sampling rather than an entire population of events (Johnson and Joslyn 1995, p. 189). A sample is a convenient way to measure larger phenomena, but it is an inherently imprecise instrument. The question should not be whether the data are correct but whether the data are useful and free from systematic biases that might undermine the analysis. To otherwise ignore such distortions is to choose blissful ignorance over honest effort.

It is also problematic to assume that an entire population can be known. In the case of secret alliances, it is not possible for scholars to know what the entire population looks like due to a variety of factors, including disparate definitions of what constitutes an alliance and when secret agreements are made. However, these phenomena have been essential components of major and minor conflicts, which is why they are crucial to an understanding of how, when, where, and why conflict may be more likely to occur.

Smith's (1996b) work on alliance reliability shows the mechanism by which bias may be introduced: it finds that a state's decision to initiate conflict is inherently linked to whether it has allies it can call on. The measurement of reliability in conflict is unreliable because the states that would be more likely to engage in combat when they have allies are unlikely to do so unless they have allies in the first place. This indicates two selection problems: the decision to engage in conflict and the reliability of an alliance partner. Any assessment of the decision to make an alliance must address these self-selection problems.

Another concern is temporal bias. Scoville's (2020) research on secret alliances created by the United States from 1994 to 2018 has demonstrated that the largest volume of US secret alliances was created in the 1990s. However, he points out that some documents cannot be acknowledged because of their secrecy. If active, ongoing alliances cannot be counted because of their secrecy, then any attempt to measure the population of secret agreements will suffer from selection effects. This discussion of the problems associated with data collection in conflict and international relations more generally is not intended to be a criticism of such data but a recognition of the problems in collecting it. As Price and Ball (2014) have stated, "incompleteness is not a criticism of data-collecting complete or representative data under conflict conditions is generally impossible" (p. 10). The primary responsibilities for researchers are to know that such problems exist and to mitigate against them.

The debates around conflict data and selection effects revolve around the completeness of available data. Few scholars assume they can account for *every* instance of conflict, alliances, arms races, human rights abuses, or the like. In many cases, the incompleteness can result in the accumulation of new data attempting to reconcile the omissions.

Within secret alliance-making, there are two dimensions along which systematic bias is most likely to occur: success or failure and the temporal domain. Below, I address both of these concerns.

Success or Failure: the Most Likely Culprit

Some argue that secret alliances are relics of the past. Kuo (2020) illustrates that 80 percent of all alliances made between 1870 and 1916 were either fully secret or partially secret, which implies that secret alliances have declined precipitously in the modern era. However, this assumes that states submit records of their alliances to the United Nations, though we know that states routinely do not submit all treaties to this repository. Although formal secret alliances may be less likely in the modern era, there are several potential avenues for states to make agreements that they want to keep secret and at least five reasons why secret agreements may remain undiscovered.

First, states may simply be better at hiding formal secret alliances. State collapse is less likely today than at any other time in recent history, which means that fewer secret agreements are disclosed by either succeeding governments or victorious armies, as was the case with the Molotov–Ribbentrop Pact. An argument might be made that communications technology and the proliferation of media outlets provide ample opportunity for disclosures, but that brings us to the next possibility.

A second reason for fewer formal secret agreements could be that as norms against secret diplomacy and alliances have become more common, states have refrained from formally recording their cooperation. This is precisely what shocked Anthony Eden in October 1956. Instead, such coordination could be kept slightly below the level of a formal alliance, relying on informal measures and agreements to achieve specific goals. However, the risk is that such informal, unrecorded agreements increase the risk of defection, but they are likely to be honored among states that have a high degree of issue convergence because international relations is an iterated game.

A third reason (related to the second) is that the number of democracies has dramatically increased in recent decades. If the first two points are correct, it poses a systemic explanation for fewer formal secret alliances. These democratic regimes are likely to group geographically, and for most states, alliances are likely to be beneficial in their geographic proximity, making formal secret alliances less necessary. Democratic states are also said to be more trusting of one another (Maoz and Russett 1993), meaning that any concerns regarding the breakdown of informal agreements can be resolved at the negotiating table rather than settled on the battlefield.

When democratic states are more likely to trust each other, public alliances are less problematic; "hiding" such agreements from the public seems unlikely in open regimes. Although one strand of literature claims democracies are more likely to make secret agreements to avoid domestic blowback (see Baum 2004; Gibbs 1995; Schuessler 2010). Small (1995) claims that democracies are reticent to make secret agreements. As Kuo (2020, p. 64) points out, this may be partially explained by the turn against secret diplomacy or because democratic states are more trusting of one another or that issues best addressed by secret diplomacy—such as territorial gains—have been "selected out" by democratization.

Instead, democracies and autocracies may make secret alliances for different reasons. Democracies answer to larger selectorates (Bueno de Mesquita 1990; Bueno de Mesquita and Siverson 1995), which may lead them to conceal controversial foreign policies. This was the case for the British, French, and Israelis drafting the 1956 Protocol of Sèvres agreement (Chapter 7). Autocrats are incentivized to keep agreements secret to avoid the loss of benefits that would occur if the agreement became public. Autocrats are most likely to make secret alliances over non-negotiable "salient stakes" that can invite a preemptive attack from rival states that feel threatened by the agreement.

The fourth reason why fewer formal secret agreements have been identified in the present day is that states with strong regimes are able to keep them classified for longer periods. Formal legislation and bureaucratic procedures for classifying state secrets have become more prevalent under the administrative states that have developed in many parts of the world, particularly among democratic states. As the world has grown more interconnected and information is shared more rapidly, it may also be easier for states to punish individuals who disclose secret information. In the same way that forensic technologies such as DNA analysis have identified and apprehended criminals more rapidly, security technology is continually changing the dynamics between states and individuals, making it harder for security breaches to occur. Even with alternative outlets for disclosing information, such as pseudo-journalistic outlets like Wikileaks or social media platforms such as Discord, the ever-present surveillance state has become more effective at tracking, identifying, and apprehending individuals who share classified information.

Fifth, the increased alignment of interests and alternative opportunities for resolving disputes have made formal secret alliances less necessary. Dispute resolution systems like the United Nations or regional security organizations may have made secret alliances obsolete. However, this does not account for the most salient of stakes, such as Russia's 2022 invasion of Ukraine. It is already well known that a formal secret agreement exists between Russia and China. It is likely such agreements also exist between Russia and Belarus and probably between Russia and North Korea (including the recent public alliance), or even Iran. It could be that some issues can only be resolved through secret diplomacy.

Similar arguments can be made for changes in the volume of formal secret alliances at comparable points in history. As Singer and Small (1966) have pointed out, different alliance types seem to prevail in various historical eras. During the period from 1878 to 1919, defense treaties reigned supreme. The major powers all but eschewed the practice from 1919 to 1939, when nonaggression and neutrality pacts abounded (Singer and Small 1966, pp. 21–2). The deciding factor for the alliances pursued in these different timeframes was the systemic distribution of power. As the international system became more multipolar, defensive treaties abounded. Kuo (2020) notes that this was a time in which secret alliances also blossomed. With a return to great power rivalries and competing nodes of power (most visible between the United States and China, but to a lesser degree with Russia and the European Union), it is likely that secret alliances will return to foreign policy toolkits around the world, if they are not present already. While they are less likely to be the formal alliances of the past, informal secret agreements are likely to become more prevalent in an increasingly interconnected world. Scholars may look back on the 2020s as a time in which states returned to alliance structures from previous eras. Though we cannot know the successes or failures of secret alliances in the current day, we can study the fate of secret alliances from the past. Their outcomes can help us better understand the secret alliances of tomorrow.

The data indicate that Kuo (2020) is correct; undoubtedly right-censoring occurs in secret alliance-making. Secret alliances are unlikely to last as long as public alliances (Chapter 3), but scholars and the general public are less likely to know about ongoing secret agreements—or even secret agreements that were recently terminated.

This book uses a mixed-methods approach to alleviate concerns surrounding the potential for systematic bias in quantitative data. Such an approach allows for a more in-depth analysis of cases that provide interesting points of convergence and divergence, providing unique opportunities to add breadth and depth to the understanding of secret alliances.

CASE SELECTION OF QUALITATIVE DATA

This book examines three specific cases for various reasons, but most importantly because of their major variations across all variables that could potentially play a role in secret alliance formation, termination, issue alignment, and their reputational effects. It is not possible to examine states that considered secret alliances and declined to pursue them—in the same way that one cannot know which states considered public alliances without following through (Gibler 2008), or states that considered deterrence and ultimately backed down (Fearon 2002)—but it is important to examine the historical record. Although the examination of these cases does not strictly vary along the dependent variable, there is variation across the dependent variable in terms of fully secret or partially secret alliances. The three cases consider states that chose to make secret alliances and likewise vary across important independent variables.

By looking at states that pursue a strategy of secret alliances, we can better understand how they came to that decision. The cases contained in this book vary along several important metrics and demonstrate the diverse population of states that select into secret alliance-making.

One area of variation is major power status. Nazi Germany and the Soviet Union were major powers when they signed the Molotov–Ribbentrop Pact. France and the United Kingdom were major powers in 1956, when the Protocol of Sèvres was signed, but Israel was not a major power. And in the case of the South Africa–Swaziland pact, neither state was a major power. This provides variation across the cases and within them: one involves solely major powers, another has only minor powers, and the third is mixed.

Quantitative methods in conflict processes are often criticized for bias against cases that did not occur in Europe or North America. Scholars in recent decades have worked to remedy this problem, and this book looks to present regional variation across the cases it examines. The Molotov–Ribbentrop Pact takes place in Europe, although it ultimately had global consequences. The Protocol of Sèvres was made between two European states and one from the Middle East, and it concerns Middle Eastern affairs that affected Europe. The South Africa–Swaziland pact involved states in Africa's southernmost region.

A third important variation involves the goods discussed in negotiations and the objectives of the alliances. With the Molotov–Ribbentrop Pact, the Nazis hoped to avoid a two-front war while also obtaining territory in Poland. Germany also gained economic benefits from trade with the Soviet Union, which was part of the deal and earlier economic agreements. The Protocol of Sèvres sought to return the Suez Canal to private ownership and remove Egypt's president from power (or otherwise curb his influence over other Arab states), resulting in Israel's temporary occupation of the Sinai. Finally, the secret South Africa–Swaziland pact hoped to pressure Swaziland into closer ties with apartheid South Africa, which would ease considerable political and economic constraints. The South Africa–Swaziland agreement was problematic for South Africa's controlling White minority and in the Black-controlled areas promised to Swaziland in exchange for greater cooperation with South Africa's regional and domestic policies.

Fourth, the cases also vary across regime type. Findings show that democratic regimes interact differently with each other and with other regimes, making variation across regime type an important consideration. Both regimes involved in the Molotov–Ribbentrop Pact were autocracies. All three signatories to the Protocol of Sèvres were full democracies. As for the South Africa–Swaziland pact, South Africa is coded as a "4" in Polity IV and did not reach full democracy until the end of apartheid and the beginning of majority rule in 1992. Swaziland was not a democracy, either.

Fifth, varying uses of force are also involved in the alliances being studied. This is important because different alliances promise different things that may or may not require the use of force. In the Molotov–Ribbentrop Pact, Germany and the USSR invaded Poland, and the USSR went on to invade Bessarabia, occupying and incorporating the three Baltic states. The Protocol of Sèvres had Israel invading the Sinai, with France and Britain staging a sham military intervention to separate the combatants. The South Africa–Swaziland pact involved support for South Africa's regional program and aggression against non-state actors but no formal invasions of a third-party state.

Sixth, these cases include variations in the aims of the secret agreements. Just as Leeds (2000) has found differences in what alliances promise more generally, the same holds for secret alliances. In the Molotov–Ribbentrop Pact, both states agreed to "spheres of influence" that they occupied until turning on one another. The Protocol of Sèvres sought to reprivatize the Suez Canal, creating a buffer zone around the canal and allowing Israel to control the Sinai, while also limiting Nasser's growing public appeal in the Arab world. The agreement between South Africa and Swaziland proposed a trade of land for Swaziland to support South Africa's regional aims and sought to eliminate African National Congress (ANC) safe havens in Swaziland.

Seventh, these cases also consider success and failure, which are difficult to operationalize when the goals of alliances are different. Just as Fearon's (2002) work on deterrence has established that one can never know if deterrence worked, we can never know if an alliance was considered but not pursued. In the case of secret alliances, we can more clearly understand success and failure, but it is more problematic to identify short-term versus long-term success.

The Nazis successfully occupied Poland with the signing of the Molotov–Ribbentrop Pact, and the Soviets successfully claimed their own territories. However, Germany lost the war, Poland later became independent, and the Baltics acquired their own independence, albeit half a century later. In the Protocol of Sèvres, every party failed in virtually all of their objectives (reprivatizing the canal, curbing Nasser's appeal, and occupying the Sinai), except for Israel's access to shipping via the canal. The alliance between South Africa and Swaziland resulted in South Africa's relatively modest gains—in the form of denying a haven for the ANC—but the country was unable to achieve its regional objectives and the apartheid regime eventually collapsed in the early 1990s.

First-hand accounts are used to study these cases whenever possible. However, the availability of such accounts is limited due to the secret nature of these negotiations and subsequent events. This book does not seek to provide an exhaustive explanation of the events accompanying the cases (such as World

War II and the Suez Canal Crisis), but the events are marginally addressed as direct consequences of the alliances.

Although there has been much speculation and backward-looking analysis since the Protocol of Sèvres, the accounts of US Ambassador Winthrop Aldrich (1967) and Mordechai Bar-On (2006; ון בר-א 1997), a trained historian who was present at the meeting, are particularly insightful. Bar-On's accounts are useful because they are a rare instance of a direct, first-hand account from the negotiations that happened in secret alliances. Aldrich's account provides a description of American pressure applied to the British that is similarly valuable because it illustrates the lengths to which the United States attempted to rein in its erstwhile ally to avoid being dragged into war with the Soviet Union.

By examining the data—quantitatively and qualitatively—one can better understand the processes that create secret alliances. It is impossible to know which states have ultimately chosen not to pursue secret alliances, but the same can be said of many self-selection behaviors. In other words, we cannot know what we cannot know. That does not preclude us from studying the universe of cases to better understand under what conditions such behaviors occur. To choose otherwise is to actively ignore an important mechanism that has been a precursor to some of the most devastating conflicts in human history.

NOTES

1. The only unofficial record of the Sèvres meetings was made by Mordechai Bar-On, personal assistant to IDF Chief Moshe Dayan, who accompanied the Israeli party to France. Having majored in history, Bar-On may have been the perfect (or imperfect, depending on one's perspective) choice for a personal assistant to Dayan. According to some (Shlaim 1997, p. 510), Bar-On is the best source available for what transpired at the meeting.
2. The meeting was so secret that it not only used a French plane to avoid raising suspicion, but the Israeli delegation also stayed in a Parisian hotel under false names (Bar-On 2006, pp. 173–4). Coupled with the decision to meet in a private residence rather than in a government building or official residence, the utmost secrecy was required for the meeting.
3. One scholar has noted that "due to the haste and the remaining secrecy, Sir Patrick Dean was not properly briefed and as befits a professional diplomat, he did not see anything wrong with signing a memorandum that sums up talks" (Bar-On 1997, p. 94).
4. As an example of this phenomenon, each US Congress is seen to be "sovereign" in the sense that it is not bound by laws made by prior Congresses.
5. Assuming that all formal alliances cannot be known, only a sample can be studied, not the entire population.

6. In fact, Molotov used his radio broadcast of September 17, 1939 to justify the Soviet invasion of Eastern Poland, and Soviet newspapers ran false stories claiming that ethnic Poles were repressing ethnic Ukrainians, Byelorussians, and Russians, a claim eerily mirroring the false claims made by Putin in 2022 (Roberts 1989, p. 161).
7. Vasquez later revises his claim to state that alliances increase the probability of conflict, claiming that they are a "step" on the staircase to war, though he does not make a distinction between defensive and offensive alliances (Senese and Vasquez 2008).
8. For more on this, see Leeds (2003).
9. Newman (1948) p. 9).
10. Newman (1948) likewise goes on to claim that "any American politician knows that nothing he does is secret for very long" (p. 10).

2. Nobody knows what goes on behind closed doors: targeting, division of goods, and secret alliances

Conflict literature has found that alliances are the "strategic setting of choices" (Morrow 2000) conveying signals as to the intentions, commitments, and values among alliance partners. Additionally, alliances function as coordination agreements to align future policies between states (Gibler 2008). However, if a key goal of alliances is to convey information, why are some alliances designed to be secret? While some literature has addressed the calculus involved in secret alliance formation (Carson and Yarhi-Milo 2017; McManus and Yarhi-Milo 2017; Ritter 2000; 2004), a central mechanism in secret alliances has been overlooked: coordinating the promise of a good at the expense of another.

Secret alliances warrant explanation due to their historical presence (Van Evera 1999) and their link to increased conflict (Bas and Schub 2016). While assumed to be less common in contemporary international relations, secret alliances were most prevalent between 1814 and 1914. However, just as secret diplomacy persists, secret alliances still happen and are important to understanding conflict onset[1] and contribute to the complexity of "diplomatic games" associated with diplomacy (Kann 1976). It is difficult to deny that secret alliances still occur, given the increased prevalence of secrecy within states and between states. For instance, Cassman (2015) finds that post-9/11, the US government was more likely to claim state secrets in order to avoid disclosing information in court hearings. The "Five Eyes" agreement between the United States, United Kingdom, Australia, New Zealand, and Canada serves as another example of the enduring presence of secret agreements. This intelligence-sharing agreement remained largely hidden from public view between 1955 and 2017 (Rowe-Munday 2021), indicating that secrecy remains a critical element of alliance-making.

Historically, scholars point to the Molotov–Ribbentrop Pact, the Sykes–Picot Agreement, or the Treaty of London (1915) to demonstrate the significant systemic changes that can result from secret agreements. It is also not unreasonable to assume that despite their supposed lower prevalence in the modern international system, secret alliances still exist and play an important role in interstate relations.[2] This chapter aims to contribute to this body of literature by asking: Why do states engage in secret alliance-making?

CAUSES OF ALLIANCE FORMATION

One perspective of alliances argues they offer states an opportunity to respond to threats by balancing with a new ally or bandwagoning with a rising power (Walt 1990). Schweller (1994) proposes states bandwagon with rising states to expand their influence in distant, marginally important locations rather than balance against rising powers. He goes so far as to claim that bandwagoning alliances "are at the heart of every bid for world mastery" (Schweller 1994, p. 73). Others claim that states balance against rising powers as a way to "check" potential threats (Walt 1990). Others maintain states make alliances to prepare for war or to secure interests.[3] Similarly, alliances signal to non-members what the purpose, goals, and values are for the alliance (Gibler 2008).

Likewise, scholarship has demonstrated the importance of information and signaling in preventing conflict (Fearnon 1995; Jervis 2017; Milner 1997). Alliances that reveal information about intentions and values can reduce the likelihood of conflict, while others can increase it (Leeds 2003). This is because a lack of complete information is a driving factor of war (Fearon 1995; Fey and Ramsay 2011; Meirowitz and Sartori 2008; Morrow 1989; Rider 2013). However, the informational value of alliances can convey different messages to different groups. Furthermore, if the primary objective of an alliance is to signal intentions, keeping an alliance secret negates this purpose, increasing conflict probability.

SIGNALING WHO?

Alliance formation inherently involves signaling that is independent of credible commitments between alliance partners. But the question remains: Who signals to whom? Generally, alliance-making states signal to four audiences: the domestic audience, the allying state, a "target" state, and third-party states that are not direct targets. This section first examines how alliances signal to these different audiences and then explores how secret alliances either diminish or distort those signals.

Domestic Audiences

Fearon (1994) argues that democracies are more adept at signaling due to domestic audience costs, as backing down from commitments can anger their publics. Leeds (1999) finds that jointly democratic dyads or jointly autocratic dyads are more likely to cooperate in alliances due to shared domestic institutional structures. However, Weeks (2008) contends that democracies do not necessarily have advantages in signaling in international relations unless specific conditions are met. Leeds (2003) further argues that changes in domestic policymaking can explain why states fail to uphold alliance agreements.

McManus and Yarhi-Milo (2017) posit that major powers often signal their commitments to domestically controversial states through costly signals, particularly when domestic audiences might oppose those commitments. For example, South African Prime Minister Pieter Botha's diplomatic note to King Sobhuza of Swaziland in 1982 sought to curb the influx of "terrorist" ANC incursions into South Africa, which were originating in Swaziland. Though relations between Black Swaziland and White-controlled South Africa were amicable during the Cold War, this closeness was rarely publicly acknowledged. Thus, the need to appease domestic audiences necessitated different public and private discourse.

Carson and Yarhi-Milo (2017) likewise claim that states are more likely to pursue secret alliances when the costs of public alliances are high and conflict probability is elevated. However, this dynamic is likely to vary by regime type. Autocratic regimes are often more concerned with international costs, while democracies tend to prioritize both domestic and international concerns. In fact, Yarhi-Milo (2013) previously found that private diplomacy is not simply "cheap-talk" between adversaries when domestic opposition to an alliance is high. Instead, former adversaries might engage in secret diplomacy with one another when public opinion is opposed to rapprochement because of public backlash. However, in this analysis, Yarhi-Milo only examines informal secret talks rather than formally agreed-upon secret alliances.[4] Further scholarship indicates that "private diplomacy works if the defender incurs political costs if it concedes to the challenger's demand in public" (Kurizaki and Whang 2011). Therefore, there is a cost to reneging in both public and secret alliances (Chapter 5). In the former, reneging is immediately known. In the latter, a spurned ally might publicly expose an embarrassing secret agreement.

Allies

Signaling to allies often involves expressing limits to what and how a state will defend or consult with another or implicit credible commitments. Fearon (1997) notes that leaders have two options in foreign policy when credibly committing to an ally: tying their hands through audience costs or sinking costs. In tying hands, states suffer domestic repercussions for backing down. In sinking costs, states mobilize forces and commit them to an ally's defense. Both approaches result in clearer signals to domestic audiences, allies, and third parties, demonstrating the commitment's credibility. Since states signal these high costs, they are less likely to back down, reassuring their allies.

Moreover, Horowitz, Poast, and Stam (2017) find that states with a substantial arms buildup and conscription are more attractive to alliance suitors, as they appear more capable of fulfilling their commitments.

Credibility in alliance-making also sends signals to potential alliance suitors and third parties. Previous violations of alliances during difficult times result in fewer alliances in the future, while alliance violations in easier times do not incur such costs (LeVeck and Narang 2017). To address the credibility problem, Leeds (2000) proposes that alliances can be designed to be self-enforcing, making it more difficult for allies to abandon one another, thus signaling strong commitment.

Target States

When states are specifically identified as "targets" of an alliance, secrecy benefits all signatories. Publicly declaring a state as a target could compromise the alliance's strategic advantage and "tip one's hand." If, however, an alliance is defensive in nature and the "target" state is not identified as the threat, a clear signal of deterrence is sent if credible commitment is also assured. However, it's not always obvious from an alliance's text whether a specific state is being targeted. In fact, 89 percent of observations in the ATOP data do not identify a specific state, region, or activity within a region. Instead, states often assume they are "targets" of a specific alliance and, in some cases, respond by forming countering alliances, as seen with the Warsaw Pact (Mastny 2001) or the Collective Security Treaty Organization (CSTO) agreement.

Third Parties

Morrow (2000) argues that alliances are typically formalized in writing to enhance their credibility. This public signaling demonstrates the commitment to come to an ally's aid and affects the costs and benefits of aggression. Therefore, public signaling is essential for deterrence. Carson and Yarhi-Milo (2017) demonstrate that leaders can use covert action to signal their commitment to other states. For example, President Nixon's covert bombing of Cambodia and Laos during the Vietnam War demonstrated the level of American commitment to South Vietnam. While these actions were not publicly acknowledged, the covert bombing sent a clear signal to third parties, particularly North Vietnam.

In sum, scholarship demonstrates the diverse nature of alliances and their varying effects on different audiences (Leeds 2003). If Leeds is correct that defensive alliances differ from nonaggression pacts in terms of their intentions, motivations, and outcomes, it follows that secret alliances are distinct from public alliances. The information conveyed by secret alliances is unique in the sense that secret alliances, like different types of commitment, result in different effects on conflict. This leads to a key question for scholars: Why do states choose to keep alliances secret and suppress public signaling?

WHY MAKE A SECRET ALLIANCE?

Secret alliances, while relatively uncommon (4.6 percent in the COW Formal Alliance data and 7.3 percent in the ATOP data), are significant mechanisms for state interaction.[5] Secret alliances introduce uncertainty and are associated with increased conflict due to a lack of complete information (Bas and Schub 2016). While initially secret, these agreements often become public, frequently after the alliance has dissolved or its goals have been achieved. This transparency allows scholars to draw inferences about the circumstances under which secret alliances are formed.

Bas and Schub (2016) find that secret alliances increase conflict probability. They argue that mutual optimism, or trust in alliance partners, increases conflict probability because one side holds asymmetric information. They maintain that "secret alliances produce information asymmetries by construction and consequently are an ideal indicator for the presence of optimism" (p. 553). This asymmetry in information increases the probability of conflict because those secret parties have more information, making them more confident. This aligns with Fearon's (1995) assertion that incomplete information is a primary cause of conflict. However, other scholars focus not on the informational pitfalls leading to conflict but on the commitment problem as a key driver of conflict (Powell 2006).[6]

Instead, I contend that secret alliances are fundamentally about the division and allocation of goods, and that conflict is incidental to obtaining those goods. Secrecy plays a crucial role in the bargaining process because relevant parties are excluded from discussions. And if Lake (2010) is correct that international politics is a multi-player game, then we must consider how secret alliances provide a way for one state to involve another state when bargaining fails. Since bargaining breakdowns often occur due to indivisible issues (Fearon 1995), such as over territory or regime change, defection is likely. Due to the multi-player nature of international relations, states can seek out another state to deal with the issue of indivisibility or bargaining failure.

Therefore, while past scholarship on secret alliances has focused primarily on informational asymmetries, I instead focus on how issue indivisibility and defection result in secret alliance formation. As Fearon (1995) points out, these commitment problems result in preventive war, preemptive war, or uncertainty regarding future prospects for bargaining power. Since secret alliances increase the likelihood of conflict (Bas and Schub 2016), states involved in secret alliances might be more inclined to initiate conflict rather than accommodate a target unwilling to negotiate over an indivisible good. Essentially, the issues at stake in secret alliances, if publicly known, would likely lead to conflict in the first place. Therefore, it is not information asymmetry that causes conflict, but rather the nature of the goods at stake.

To illustrate this point, consider the treaty signed between Hitler and Stalin on August 23, 1939. Had the world known the true nature of this agreement, war might have begun sooner (albeit by a matter of days). France and Britain had provided security guarantees to Poland, making such a treaty unacceptable. Similarly, during the Suez Crisis, had Egypt known about the secret alliance between Britain, France, and Israel before Israel's aggressive actions in October, Egypt might have preemptively attacked.

While I do not strictly disagree with the notion that incomplete information in alliance-making can lead to conflict, I argue that secret alliances involve bargaining over indivisible issues. This indivisibility might arise from the nature of the good itself, such as territory or regime change, or because the good is deemed "salient." State C is unwilling to grant concessions to State A because the costs are too high or the future losses to the balance of power are too great. Therefore, when State A and State B cannot reach an agreement due to indivisible issues (see Figure 2.1), secret alliances are more likely to emerge, particularly when State A, the state seeking to revise the status quo, can secure an ally (State C) who is willing to share the spoils of war.

It is crucial to remember that international relations is not a two-party game, as Lake's (2010) assessment of the 2003 Iraq War highlights. When two states cannot reach a bargain, they might turn to existing allies or forge new alliances to gain leverage in negotiations. If a state chooses to pursue a secret alliance, the risk of conflict increases significantly due to the nature of the good in

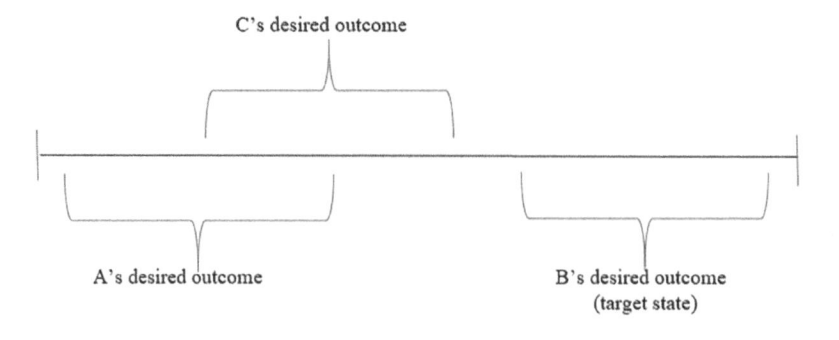

Source: Author.

Figure 2.1   Issue indivisibility, multi-player games, and secret alliances

question. Therefore, it's not a lack of complete information that leads to conflict. Rather, it is an issue of indivisibility and commitment failures resulting in defection for a specific good that results in conflict.

Secrecy itself is not inherently meaningful. Rather, secrecy conceals the true purpose of an agreement and acts as a means to an end. While states may have different goals, they can secretly bargain over those goals at the expense of State B (see Figure 2.1). Yarhi-Milo (2013) points out that, due to the costs of reneging on a secret agreement, actors might assume their partners are negotiating in good faith, which increases the likelihood of obtaining the "spoils of war."

Secret alliances are therefore more likely to be: (1) targeted; and (2) focused on securing specific goods. The allocation of goods at the expense of another is a necessary, but not sufficient, condition for a secret alliance. While secret alliances might not always involve the division of goods, it is likely that securing those goods is a primary driver, outweighing other considerations like secrecy for its own sake or audience costs. However, the situation becomes more complex when alliances are partially secret, as they convey mixed signals. While the public aspects of these alliances may serve other purposes, such as deterrence, the underlying objective remains the same: gaining something of value from another state. It's notable that, in partially secret alliances, discussions about the division of goods and the target state are often found in secret protocols.

Secret alliances can serve multiple purposes, including: (1) partitioning third-party states, (2) establishing nonaggression pacts that permit intervention in third-party states, (3) providing mutual support for one state against another, or (4) dividing goods obtained from a third-party state (or multiple third-party states) (Leeds 2003).[7]

While public alliances might be more rational for deterring or signaling to another actor, fully secret alliances and public/secret alliances have distinct logic. Public/secret alliances, or mixed alliances, likely send mixed signals because they often represent temporary policy alignments between aggressive actors. This can have multiple goals, the first of which could be to deter an opponent, while another set of goals could be the division of a good. However, given the parallels between the logic of secret portions of mixed alliances and fully secret alliances, I argue that they both share a common goal: securing an indivisible good.

Fully secret alliances are unobserved by non-signatories when they are negotiated. In fact, they are often unknown even after conflict concludes. However, the advantage of fully secret agreements is that intentions and goals are concealed from domestic publics and the international community. This secrecy ensures that states can achieve surprise and secure the good in question. While secret alliances are non-public, there is a risk of defection.

However, this secrecy gives the signatory a powerful tool to mitigate the risk. If the other party were to renege on the agreement, the signatory could publicly expose the secret agreement (Yarhi-Milo 2013). This could potentially embarrass the state domestically and internationally and would likely prevent the alliance's objectives from being achieved.

Since target states or third parties might act if secret agreements were made public, states have a strong incentive to maintain secrecy. While conflict can arise from informational asymmetries, it's more likely to be driven by indivisible issues and defection. If a secret agreement were made public, the transaction costs of extracting resources from the non-signatory would be significantly higher, making secrecy more advantageous. This leads to two propositions:

H1: States making secret alliances are more likely to identify a specific target state.

H2: States making secret alliances are more likely to address the division of some good with their alliance partner.

OTHER EXPLANATIONS

If the primary goal of signaling is to demonstrate to an opponent that another state will defend them in the event of conflict, then certain alliances should not be kept secret.[8] Defensive alliances, for example, are less likely to be secret because they signal to potential adversaries that another state has committed to their defense (Leeds 2003; Smith 1995).[9,10,11] To address this further, it's useful to distinguish between different alliance types.

Existing scholarship underscores the importance of material power in shaping conflict (Bremer 1992) and its influence on alliances and escalation (Siverson and Tennefoss 1984). The Molotov–Ribbentrop Pact serves as a prime example. Both signatories ranked high on the National Material Capabilities data (Singer, Bremer, and Stuckey 1972). In fact, a cursory glance at the data reveals that secret alliances are frequently used by powerful states like Russia, Germany, France, and the United Kingdom. However, secret alliances were also signed by Peru, Bolivia, Yugoslavia, Bulgaria, Turkey, and Bavaria. This suggests that secret alliances are beneficial to states with lower levels of relative power as measured by the CINC composite index, potentially giving them an advantage against more powerful states. In fact, Slantchev (2010) has shown that before a conflict breaks out, states wish to appear as strong as possible in hopes of attracting potential allies, but once the conflict starts, states "feign weakness" in order to gain a tactical surprise.

On the other hand, major powers are more likely than minor powers to engage in secret alliances. This likely stems from the fact that major powers often pursue different objectives than minor powers. Research on escalation (Sample 2002) and alliance formation (Krause and Singer 2001) supports the notion that major and minor powers behave differently in these contexts, suggesting similar patterns are likely to apply to secret alliances.

The secret alliance between Germany and Russia in 1887 provides a compelling example. Both states agreed to maintain neutrality if either was attacked. However, Germany also secretly pledged recognition for Russia's claims to Balkan territories in the Balkans (Article 2), a contentious issue with other Western states. This agreement was important to both states because it signaled their shared desire to prevent the Ottomans from siding with other states seeking access to the Black Sea, a move that would threaten Russia. In exchange, Germany agreed to recognize Russian influence in the Balkans as they were concerned about being drawn into a regional conflict. Maintaining secrecy was crucial to protect the balance of power and prevent war. It is therefore reasonable to assume that secret alliances are more likely to occur between major powers, as they are potentially more destabilizing.

Scholars have also posited that alliances operate under market principles, with systemic polarity and the availability of potential allies influencing the "share" of potential alliances (Kim 2010). In essence, states "shopping around" for a potential partner must carefully consider the distribution of power between states and the impact on the overall availability of alliances. Since alliance-making is more likely in a multipolar world (Walt 1990), secret alliances are also more likely in multipolar systems.

Furthermore, I assume that secret alliances are most likely in binary alliance agreements.[12] Secret alliances involving three or more states are less likely because it is more challenging to distribute the gains among multiple actors. Additionally, for a secret alliance to be successful, it must remain secret, at least until its objectives are achieved. Therefore, keeping a secret agreement "secret" is easier (and thus more likely to be successful) when the agreement involves only two states.

RESEARCH DESIGN

To address the questions outlined above, I conduct a large-n study of all ATOP alliances using the Alliance Treaty Obligations and Provisions (ATOP 4.0) data (Leeds, Ritter, Mitchell, and Long 2002). I use the alliance-member dataset, which includes one observation per alliance member, as the unit of analysis. This unit of analysis is appropriate, given that my primary focus in explaining why states choose secret alliances over public alliances. While there are certainly selection effects as to which states choose to engage in alliances, this unit of analysis cannot account for states that considered making an alliance but opted out. This limitation is endemic to all self-selection behaviors.

Therefore, any conclusions can only be extended to those states that engage in alliance-making behaviors. However, given the widespread use of the ATOP data, the fact that secret alliances eventually become public, and the use of this data elsewhere for secret alliance analysis (Bas and Schub 2016), I am confident in the models below. Furthermore, while a directed dyadic approach could be used, such an approach is less relevant to the central question of why secret alliances are chosen as a strategy, rather than focusing on specific dyadic relationships.

The ATOP dataset provides information about whether an alliance is made public or kept secret. This is coded as "0" for fully public alliances, "1" for public/secret alliances, and "2" for fully secret alliances. I also include models that make the distinction between public "0" alliances, public/secret alliances "1", and fully secret alliances "2" and present both results.

To account for the coordination aspect of secret alliances, I use the "specific threat" variable found in the ATOP data. Originally, this is coded as 1–6 for the type of threat that is addressed. This is recoded as binary, with "0" meaning that no specific threat is addressed in the alliance text and "1" meaning that a specific threat is addressed. This threat could be a particular state, a specific bloc of states, or a state acting within a region. Next, the analysis investigates whether secret alliances are primarily driven by the division of some good. I use the "division of goods" variable to indicate whether the signatories are coordinating over a specific good, with "1" corresponding to coordinating the division of some good[13] (see Table 2.1).

Then, I identify which alliances had two original signatories. I code as "1" when alliances had two members and "0" when alliances have three or more original signatories. To do this, I identify which states have the same alliance start date and member start date.

I also merge in the major powers dataset (Correlates of War Project 2016). Major power states are coded as "1" and non-major powers as "0". The total number of major powers each year is calculated to create the major power count variable. This variable captures the distribution of power within the international system and allows for an assessment of the ability of states to "shop around" for potential allies. To account for the relative power of each state in an alliance, I utilize the National Materials Capability (version 5) data to account for the power of each state (Singer 1988; Singer, Bremer, and Stuckey 1972), which measures each state's relative share of global power.

Additionally, I control for the democratic nature of states, with states having an adjusted polity score greater than or equal to 6 qualifying as democracies. Separate models include temporal dummies for World Wars I and II (see Appendix). Given that previous scholarship has noted the prevalence of secret alliances prior to 1914, this variable is appropriate to indicate whether the dynamic of secret alliance formation changed after the World Wars I and II.[14]

Table 2.1   Variables

Dependent Variable	Coding
Secret Alliance	"0" for public alliances, "1" for secret
	"0" for public alliances, "1" for partial secret, "2" for fully secret
Independent Variables	
Specific Threat	"1" if specific threat is mentioned
Division of Goods	"1" if treaty mentions a division of gains
Bilateral Alliance	"1" if alliance is bilateral
Major Power	"1" if sate is a major power
CINC	Composite Index of National Capabilities
Democracy	"1" if Polity score>=6
Major Power Count	Count of the major power states in international system
Defense	"1" if a defensive alliance
Offense	"1" if an offensive alliance
Neutrality	"1" if a neutrality alliance
Nonaggression	"1" if a nonaggression alliance
Consultation	"1" if a consultation alliance
World War I dummy	"1" if before 1914
WW II dummy	"1" if before 1939

Finally, the analysis incorporates dummy variables for different types of alliances as identified in the ATOP dataset.

RESULTS

Before turning to substantive results, a review of the descriptive statistics is warranted. The analysis utilizes the complete ATOP dataset, encompassing 2398 observations, with one observation for each member of each alliance. Of the 745 total alliances in the ATOP 4.0 dataset, 65 (9 percent) involve either full or partial secrecy. However, when examining alliances from the perspective of individual members, 7.26 percent of alliance members are associated with secret alliances (reflecting the fact that secret alliances are less likely to be multilateral) (see Table 2.2).

Separately, I examined each COW formal alliance (Gibler 2008) text to determine which alliances are secret and which were made public (these texts indicate if the alliance was to be made public or kept secret). Approximately 4 percent of COW formal alliances are secret agreements. This discrepancy stems from differences in how alliances are coded and operationalized across the datasets. Of the 68 secret alliances (as measured by alliance members) identified in the ATOP dataset, 55 are also identified in the COW dataset, leaving 13 unique secret alliances identified in ATOP but not in COW.[15] However, the COW dataset does not indicate whether the texts mention targets or division

Table 2.2 Descriptive statistics

Variable	Observations	Mean	Standard deviation	Min	Max
Public/Partial Secret/ Fully Secret	2391	.128	.470	0	1
Fully Secret Alliance	2391	.073	.260	0	1
Specific Threat	2391	.339	.473	0	1
Division of Goods	2361	.030	.171	0	1
Bilateral Alliance	2398	.0563	.496	0	1
Major Power	2398	.23	.421	0	1
CINC	2301	.028	.054	0	.378
Democracy	2122	.344	.475	0	1
Major Power Count	2398	6.028	1.111	4	8
Defense	2398	.415	.493	0	1
Offense	2398	.096	.295	0	1
Neutrality	2398	.111	.314	0	1
Nonaggression	2398	.581	.493	0	1
Consultation	2398	.506	.500	0	1

of spoils in alliances, making it inappropriate for the questions considered here (see Table 2.3).

Turning to Table 2.4, I perform rare events logit analyses on the presence or absence of a secret alliance in Models 1 and 2. Given a rare event on one of the outcomes and a relatively small sample size, utilizing a rare events approach is appropriate (King and Zeng 2001a; 2001b). While logistic regression could be used, I am of the view that rare events logistic regression is appropriate. To address concerns about potential differences between partially secret and fully secret alliances, Models 3 and 4 utilize ordered logit models with the dependent variable representing public, partially secret, and fully secret alliances.

Model 1 reveals a positive and statistically significant relationship between the mention of specific threats and the likelihood of using a secret alliance (p <= .001). In other words, secret alliances are more likely to identify a specific target. Furthermore, a positive relationship between the mention of the division of goods and the likelihood of using a secret alliance (p <= .001) suggests that secret alliances are more likely to address the allocation of specific goods than public alliances. These findings provide support for H1 and H2. As expected, secret alliances are approximately twice as likely to be bilateral (p = .004), while secret alliances are also eight times more likely to be made by

Table 2.3   Secret alliance observations

Number of Alliances	745
Number of Partially Secret Alliances	14
Number of Fully Secret Alliances	51
Number of All Secret Alliances	65
Number of Partially Secret Observations	43
Number of All Secret Observations	174
Observations	2398
Percent All Secret Observations	7.26%

major powers (p <= .001). However, a negative relationship between a state's share of global power and the likelihood of using a secret alliance (p = .003) suggests that states with a larger share of global power are less likely to engage in secret alliances. This is likely because states with greater power face fewer constraints and have less need for secrecy to advance their interests.

Additionally, the major power count variable is positive and significant (p <= .001). This suggests that the probability of a secret alliance increases as the number of major powers in the international system increases. The addition of each major power roughly doubles the likelihood of a secret alliance. In contrast, democracies are less likely to make secret alliances, with a p-value <= .001. In fact, the likelihood of secret alliances decreases by 75 percent when a state is a democracy. With a chi-squared value that is statistically significant (<= .000), there is further support for the findings presented in Model 1 (see Figure 2.2).

Model 2 tells a similar story. Moving from no mention of a specific threat to mentioning a specific threat significantly increases the likelihood of using a secret alliance (p-value <= .001).[16] This suggests that secret alliances are more likely to explicitly identify a target state. Additionally, moving from no

Table 2.4 Division of goods and targeting in secret alliances

Variables	1	2	3	4
Division of Goods/ Targeting Variables	-	-	-	-
Specific Threat	2.485*** (.257)	1.72*** (.295)	2.611*** (.255)	1.813*** (.294)
Division of Gains	2.651*** (.401)	2.311*** (.414)	2.631*** (.374)	2.239*** (.383)
Controls	-	-	-	-
Bilateral	.756*** (.259)	.556** (.27)	.838*** (.259)	.716*** (.269)
Major Power	2.109*** (.341)	1.918*** (.353)	2.045*** (.338)	1.873*** (.35)
CINC Share	-7.763*** (2.631)	-6.534** (2.612)	-7.701*** (2.612)	-6.393*** (2.598)
Major Power Count	.696*** (.113)	.647*** (.119)	.733*** (.113)	.711*** (.121)
Democracy	-1.381*** (.305)	-1.287*** (.312)	-1.409*** (.305)	-1.312*** (.314)
Defense	-	.364 (.272)	-	.403 (.272)
Offense	-	-.088 (.323)	-	.063 (.319)
Neutrality	-	1.027*** (.306)	-	.987*** (.301)
Nonaggression	-	-1.791*** (.377)	-	-1.85*** (.386)
Consultation	-	-.373 (.258)	-	-.381 (.258)
Constant	-8.976*** (.806)	-7.785*** (.861)	-	-
Cut point 1	-	-	9.331*** (.812)	8.409*** (.879)
Cut point 2	-	-	9.671*** (.82)	8.767*** (.887)
Observations	2048	2048	2048	2048
R2	-	-	.357	.402

Note: Robust standard errors are in parentheses, *** $p < .01$, ** $p < .05$, * $p < .1$.

Figure 2.2 Division of goods and targeting in secret alliances point estimates, Model 1 (95% CIs)

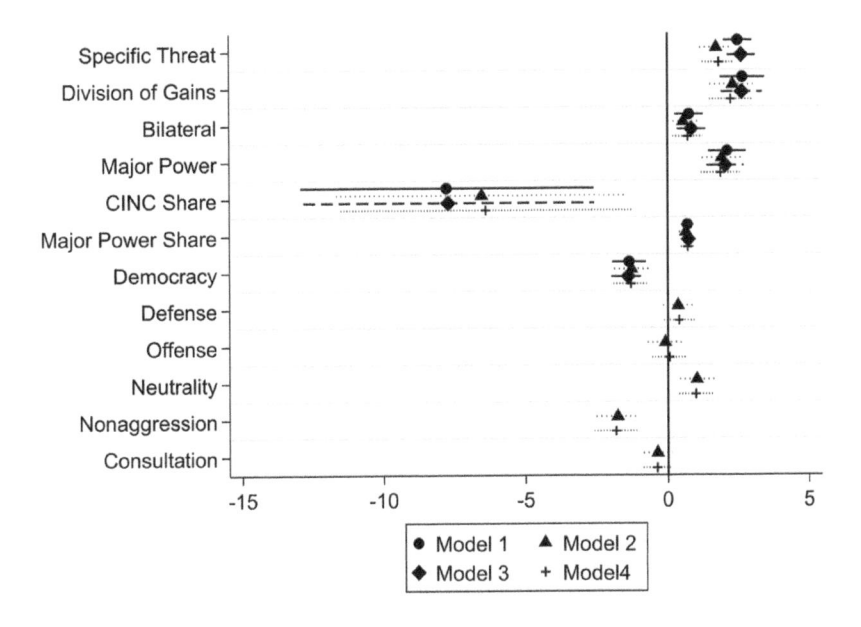

Source: Author.

mention of the division of goods to mentioning the division of goods increases the likelihood of a secret alliance (p <= .001). Likewise, the transition from a multilateral alliance to a bilateral alliance also has a positive effect (p = .04), suggesting that secret alliances are more likely to be bilateral than multilateral. Finally, the transition from minor power to major power status also significantly increases the likelihood of a secret alliance (p <= .001) (see Figure 2.3).

Next, as a state gains a larger share of global power, it is less likely to make a secret alliance, with a p-value of .012. This finding aligns with the intuition that secret alliances are more likely to be pursued by states with a smaller share of global power. The presence of more major powers in the international system significantly increases the likelihood of a secret alliance (p <= .001). Democracy, on the other hand, has a negative and statistically significant effect on the likelihood of secret alliances (p <= .001), suggesting that democracies are less likely to engage in this type of diplomacy. Additionally, secret alliances are more likely in a neutrality pact, with moving from a non-neutrality pact to a neutrality pact resulting in a positive effect with a p-value of .001.

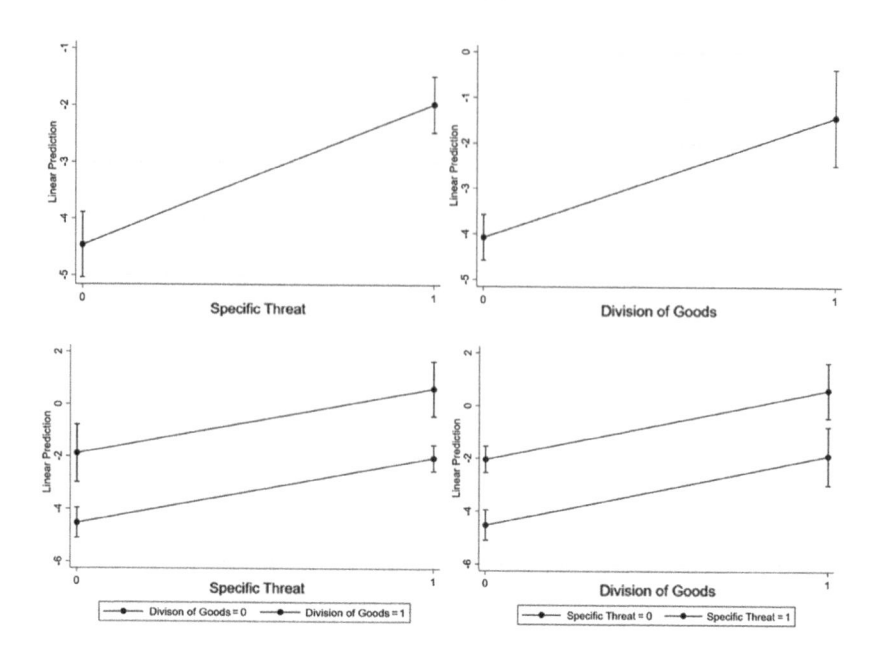

Figure 2.3 Division of goods and targeting in secret alliances marginal effects, Model 1 (99% CIs)

Similarly, the presence of a nonaggression pact results in a decreased chance of making a secret alliance (p <= .001). The chi-squared test results are statistically significant (<= .001), further supporting these findings.

Models 3 and 4 utilize ordered logistic models to account for differences between public, partially secret, and fully secret alliances. These models provide a more robust test of the hypothesis that secret alliances are more likely to address the division of goods and the identification of a target state. Model 3 shows that the mention of a specific threat is statistically significant (p-value <= .01) in predicting partially secret and fully secret alliances. This suggests that the likelihood of mentioning a specific threat increases by 2.61 times when moving from no mention of a threat to the inclusion of a threat. Additionally, Model 3 reveals a statistically significant positive relationship (p <= .01) between the mention of the division of gains and the likelihood of partially or fully secret alliances. Moving from no mention of a division of gains to the mention of a division of gains increases the likelihood of a partially or fully secret alliance by 2.63 times.

Turning to Model 4, there is a positive effect for specific threat (p <= .001), with moving from no specific threat mentioned to mentioning a specific threat resulting in a 1.8 increase in the log-odds of a secret alliance. Furthermore, the model shows a statistically significant positive relationship (p <= .001) between the mention of a division of gains and the likelihood of a secret alliance. The likelihood of a secret alliance increases by 2.24 times when moving from no mention of a division of gains to the inclusion of a division of gains.

Models 3 and 4 show similar patterns for other variables compared to Models 1 and 2. Here, bilateral alliances, major powers, major power share, and neutrality alliances are positively associated with partially and fully secret alliances. Additionally, the cut points of 1 and 2 indicate statistical significance for these latent response variables, indicating that this effect operates for both fully secret and partially secret alliances. The chi-squared test results are statistically significant (<= .001), further supporting the findings presented in these models.

Finally, I conduct approximate likelihood ratio tests to check for violations of the proportionality of odds assumption. In Model 3, with a chi-squared value of .4244, I am not able to reject the null hypothesis. This means that I cannot guarantee that the proportionality of odds assumption is not violated. However, in Model 4, I see a chi-squared value of <= .01, meaning I can reject the null hypothesis and accept that Model 4 does not violate the proportionality of odds assumption.

Robustness Checks and Confirmation

Robustness checks were conducted to assess the potential for bias and to account for the use of "mixed signals" in partially secret alliances. These checks involved running models with only public and fully secret alliances (excluding partially secret alliances). These results are consistent with the findings presented in the main analysis. Additionally, the analysis utilizes standard logistic regression specifications with robust standard errors and finds no statistically significant differences in terms of direction, magnitude, or statistical significance. Aware of Eicker-Huber-White-robust treatment of errors and the potential for standard errors to be clustered around the same states, I also ran models with clustered standard errors (by country) for variants of Models 1–4.[17] I find no significant differences between these models and the models presented in the chapter or models using fixed effects.

To address the potential problem of heteroskedastic outliers, additional tests with robust standard errors were run. These results demonstrate that all variables remain statistically significant, with the coefficients largely consistent (though larger) across the models. The analysis also includes dummy variables for the temporal domain to assess whether events preceding the World Wars have a significant impact on the results. However, the results are consistent with the main analysis, indicating no substantial difference in the relationships between the variables. As mentioned previously, I did not expect, nor did I see, any substantial differences between the ordered logistic categories (public, partially secret, secret) and Models 1 and 2. Additionally, I also ran models that excluded the various types of alliances in a step-wise fashion and saw similar results. I then excluded all secret alliances made three years prior to major war outbreaks (defined as global in scale) and found similar results, though the coefficient sizes were slightly smaller, yet still significant and in the hypothesized direction.

These findings consistently indicate that secret alliances are more likely to mention a target state and discuss the division of goods than public alliances. These findings support the proposed theory linking indivisible issues and secret alliance formation. Additionally, the results provide further evidence that democracies are less likely to engage in secret diplomacy. This suggests that keeping secrets is more difficult in democracies due to greater

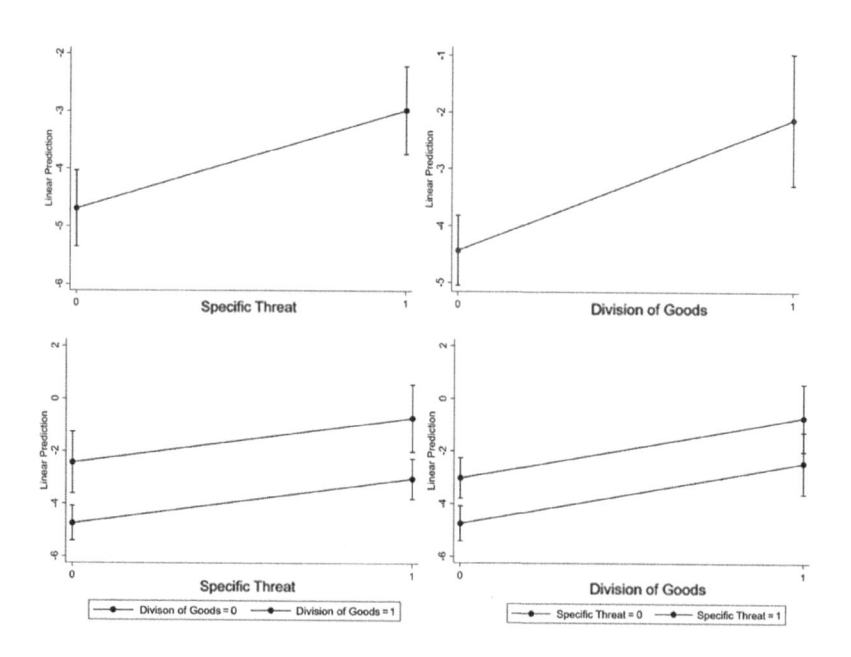

Source: Author.

Figure 2.4 Division of goods and targeting in secret alliances marginal effects, Model 2 (99% CIs)

transparency and accountability, potentially leading to greater domestic backlash (Colaresi 2014; Ritter 2000) (see Figure 2.4).

Next, given the support found for the number of major power states in the international system increasing the probability of secret alliances, I am inclined to accept the logic that secret alliances are more likely in multipolar arrangements. Specifically, as there are more states vying for power on the international stage, secret alliances are more appealing, as they give one side the advantage of surprise over a competitor (Colaresi 2014) without "tipping one's hand." I also see that secret alliances are more likely in certain types of alliances. Additionally, secret alliances are more likely among major powers than minor powers (see Table 2.5).

Table 2.5   Hypotheses confirmed/rejected

-	Model 1	Model 2	Model 3	Model 4
H1	✓	✓	✓	✓
H2	✓	✓	✓	✓

Note: ✗ = Disconfirmed, ✓ = Confirmed.

CONCLUSION

The findings presented above provide compelling evidence that the decision to form a secret alliance is primarily driven by the desire to secure a specific good at the expense of another state. First and foremost, states want something when they make a secret alliance. Secret alliances are not simply a means of concealing information, but rather a strategic tool for achieving a desired outcome while minimizing potential costs. States seeking to gain a specific good from another state are more likely to employ secrecy to shield such actions from public scrutiny, thereby reducing the risk of domestic backlash or third-party intervention. The intent of such alliances is not to start war but to get a good in the "cheapest" way possible.

While there is certainly an informational component here, if we think of general alliances as preparations for war (Senese and Vasquez 2008), secret alliances deal with indivisible goods and are more likely to result in war. This is because the nature of the goods being bargained over is indivisible, making the introduction of a secret third party into the bargaining process more likely. As Schweller (1994) notes, states will bandwagon with other states to get those goods and expand their power base. Findings here indicate a similar mechanism: states wishing to expand their base of power are more likely to make secret alliances because it allows them to get a good (political influence, expansion, or territory, etc.) that would otherwise be unobtainable. In this case, secrecy serves not as an end, but as a means to a political end that would be disadvantageous to signal publicly.

One implication of the finding that states with a larger share of global power are less likely to make secret alliances is that powerful states may not have a need for secret alliances as their share of global power increases. This is because: (1) they have enough power to suit their current policies; (2) given their overwhelming power, they do not have a need to "hide" their motives; (3) their share of global power is so large, they are more capable of "going it alone" (Patrick 2001; Skidmore 2011) and do not require a secret alliance.

As claimed, secret alliances are a different kind of alliance, in the same way that defensive and offensive alliances are different. As such, there are several reasons why scholars should take greater care to study secret alliances. First, the important role of secret alliances in the distribution of power in the international system demonstrates the role these alliances can play. Second, the role of secret alliances in war initiation (Bas and Schub 2016) demonstrates the importance of secret alliances. Third, the fact that secret alliances, particularly partially secret alliances, do not send clear signals to other states yet allow for more coordination between the states in the secret alliance has implications for international conflict (e.g., McManus and Yarhi-Milo 2017). Understanding when and why states form secret alliances is important for understanding how these "special" types of alliances matter for international conflict and the distribution of power. Since secret diplomacy has had a role to play in the initiation of World War I, World War II, the partition of the Middle East, the exit of Italy from the Triple Alliance and entry into the Triple Entente during World War I, greater understanding of the mechanism of secret diplomacy is necessary to better understand when and why states choose to keep their agreements secret. Furthermore, secret diplomacy is not confined to a particular era. Secret diplomacy and secret alliances occurred during the pre-World War I era, the interwar years, during the Cold War, and after and undoubtedly still occur today. But one of the most important questions that remains for scholars and practitioners is whether secret diplomacy has been relegated to the past.

NOTES

1. In fact, there have been four separate secret alliances made since 1956 with 14 different states. The most recent secret alliance in the ATOP data was made in 2000.
2. Furthermore, it is also not assumed by the author that all secret alliances can be known, just as not all formal alliances can be known. However, I have

no reason to assume the sample is systematically biased against the division of goods after conflict for secret alliances that are observed or unobserved. Additionally, a cursory glance at the sample demonstrates that there is a relatively equal proportion of secret alliances from "winners" and "losers" after conflict that emerges from secret alliances. Further, there is ample evidence from the data generating process that demonstrates that while sometimes secret alliance documents are unseen, scholars can still observe and infer the content of secret alliances, as with the 2000 Gulf Cooperation Council's six-party secret alliance. Additionally, the use of formal secret alliances by Bas and Schub (2016), among others, indicates that selection problems related to the study of diplomatic secrecy can be overcome, even in the case of quantitative analysis.
3. Huth and Russet even go so far as to claim that "if deterrence fails, only alliance and the military value of the state under attack are associated with the defender's willingness to go to war" (Huth and Russet 1984, p. 496).
4. One of these cases the author uses is secret talks between Nixon and Mao Zedong. However, these were not formal agreements and obviously became public once the heads of state met in public. The point of this argument is that states can extract costs on secret alliance partners by going public if the other state reneges on their agreements. However, not one case exists of this in the ATOP data. The closest case is that of the Sykes–Picot Agreement signed between the United Kingdom and France. However, it was not made public by either signatory but by Bolsheviks in Russia after the October Revolution.
5. It is worth noting that while secret alliances are rare, they are still more common than war among states in a given year in the international system and worthy of scholarly inquiry.
6. In fact, Fearon (1995) tells us there are three reasons why states might engage in war: (1) private information; (2) commitment problems; (3) issue indivisibilities. We maintain that secret alliances are formed because bargaining arrangements cannot be made over indivisibility issues and since international relations is a multi-player game, secret alliances offer an opportunity to defect, meaning there is an incentive to not commit to the bargaining partner (third party).
7. For more on how secret alliances may involve the dividing of territory, contributions, accessions, etc., see the SECRART variable in the ATOP dataset (Leeds, Ritter, Mitchell, and Long 2002).
8. For instance, Fearon (1997).
9. Leeds goes so far as to claim that "alliances provide information about the likelihood that others will intervene in a potential conflict" (Leeds 2003, p. 237).
10. Leeds (2003, Tables 1 and 2, pp. 435–6).

11. Smith (1995) similarly tells us that some alliances increase the probability of conflict, while others decrease this probability, further providing evidence that we should make a distinction between the different types of alliances and their effects on secret alliances.
12. Note that models were also run excluding this variable and they found similar effects.
13. In the ATOP coding of the division of goods, this is defined as "if there is any discussion in the alliance agreement of how gains from future conflict should be divided among the allies" (Leeds et al., 2022, p. 31).
14. Note that I also ran models with adjustments to the temporal dummy measure after 1918, 1939, and 1945. The results were virtually identical and the inclusion of the variables does not substantively impact the argument.
15. Note that this leaves 10 COW alliances identified by ATOP as secret alliances, but I am unable to identify some of those alliances as secret, based on my analysis of each available COW alliance text. One reason for the disparity in these numbers is that the ATOP dataset is updated to 2016, while the availability of COW alliance texts is only tountil 1995.
16. Odds ratios are available upon request.
17. Note that instead of using rare events logit model specifications for Models 1 and 2, I use standard logistic regression since Stata does not allow for clustered standard errors using the firthlogit command developed by Gary King. However, given the rarity of "repeat offenders" making secret alliances, I am inclined to think that this is not problematic and that the original specification of rare events logit is appropriate, given concerns that the rarity of cases may exert undue influence on the rarity of events themselves. However, with 174 observations out of 2398 total alliance observations, I am not concerned that my approach is methodologically flawed.

3. Never meant to last: violations and why secret alliances are not institutionalized

Secret alliances present a unique puzzle in international relations. While public alliances are openly acknowledged, secret alliances are not.[1] This means the role that they play is more nuanced than those of their public counterparts, despite their significant historical influence. Furthermore, the design of secret alliances is expected to differ from public alliances due to their distinct functions in global politics.

This chapter explores the reasons why secret alliances are less likely to endure and less likely to be institutionalized. Building on previous work, I argue that secret alliances are likely to have violations that occur more quickly, less likely to be formally institutionalized, and less likely to end by treaty violations. The limited scope and specific target and good at the heart of a secret alliance (Chapter 2) often render complex institutional designs unnecessary in these types of alliances. Instead, informal, ad hoc cooperation is more likely to occur within secret alliances. Additionally, institutions are less useful in bilateral arrangements due to the lower barriers to cooperation and trust in secret alliances. Furthermore, institutionalization itself often contradicts the very nature of secrecy, making it a less viable option for secret alliances. Finally, should violations occur, they are more likely to surface early in the alliance's lifespan.

LITERATURE

An ever-present threat in international relations is the risk of defection (Fearon 1994). As the adage goes, "trust is a rare commodity in international politics. To mitigate this risk, states often rely on institutional mechanisms (Jervis 1978). Repeated interactions within the confines of established structures may still lead to defection, highlighting the inherent tension between institutionalization and trust (Jervis 2017, p. 171).

Similarly, alliances can be understood in many ways. Walt (1990) begins by asking, "how do states choose their friends?" (p. 1). However, alliances can also be made not just because of friendship but also out of fear (Snyder 1984). Regardless of their motivations, states are frequently concerned about the potential for defection from alliance commitments (Morrow 2000). To address this concern, states might make credible commitments, such as stationing troops or establishing institutions to formalize their cooperation. Alliances, therefore, are deeply intertwined with reputation (Chapter 5), both for the states involved and for the alliance itself.

To deal with this, states develop reputations as reliable or unreliable partners (see Chapter 5). Reputations are inherently tied to defection and trust and must be earned, suggesting a history of repeated interactions. While some scholars emphasize the importance of reputation, others argue its impact is overstated (Mercer 2010). Mercer (2010) contends that reputation is overstated as a cause of conflict and argues "that people expect a state to behave in the future just as it behaved in the past" (p. 1).

However, Gibler (2008) distinguishes between a public and private reputation. States or leaders who fail to uphold commitments or are easily coerced are viewed as less credible (e.g., Jervis 1989; Schelling 1972; Snyder 1984). This pattern is observed in various contexts, including international loan repayments (Chan 2012), international law (Keohane 1997), domestic audience costs (Tomz 2007), and even in "national branding" (Anholt 2011).

Svolik (2006) argues that in games of cooperation, states are incentivized to lie in agreements, and this incentive affects how states design structures to minimize the problem of defection. In scenarios where states are incentivized to lie, they are less likely to create strong institutional constraints or to include robust escape clauses. In fact, because of the transparency of their system, democratic states are more likely to be trusted in international trade. Thus, openness breeds trust. When this is considered next to Bas and Schub's (2016) argument that secret alliances increase the likelihood of conflict due to the confidence derived from private information, it highlights the critical role of information in these agreements. This dynamic suggests that states engaging in private cooperation are less likely to institutionalize their agreements because their objectives are short term, and institutionalization would contradict the confidential nature of secret alliances.

Indeed, commitment problems are present throughout international relations and are not unique to alliance behavior. Acemoglu and Robinson (2001) find such behavior in civil wars, as does Fearon (1995) in international and civil conflict (Fearon 2004). Morrow (2000) highlights the use of written alliances to mitigate the risk of reneging on commitments, while other scholars contend that democracies are less prone to such violations (Gaubatz 1996). While public alliances might offer greater accountability, this does not fully explain why secret alliances often lack formal documentation.

One explanation for this phenomenon is the intended brevity of secret alliances. While the duration of an alliance can be measured by its lifespan, it can also be assessed in terms of how it terminates. This perspective offers a broader understanding of why some alliances end more quickly than others. An irregular termination signals a breach of commitment or a change in the political landscape and can negatively affect reputations. In considering how alliances terminate, Gibler (2008) examines the role of alliance reputation in both alliance formation and dispute behavior. In short, states that reneged on prior commitments are less likely to secure allies in the future (Chapter 5).

While Gibler (2008) argues that alliances generally share a common structure, he does emphasize that "alliances are written public promises" (p. 427), implying a distinction between public and private agreements. As Gibler (2008) sees it, reneging on an alliance agreement makes it less likely that a state will be able to make an alliance in the future. Thus, another way to measure alliance longevity is to measure whether they end irregularly. If alliances terminate irregularly, this implies that one side (or more) reneged on the promises within the document.[2]

Institutionalization

One strategy for mitigating the risks of defection and reneging within alliances is institutionalization. Institutionalization refers to the process of establishing formal rules, structures, and procedures between allies. These formal mechanisms facilitate cooperation and coordination between actors, making it more likely that the alliance accomplishes its goals. Institutionalization can also promote stability (Snyder 1991) and predictability (Kann 1976) by providing member states with a clear understanding of the rules, procedures, and commitments. This clarity can also dissuade potential targets from challenging the alliance, thereby reducing the likelihood of conflict (Fearon 1995; Powell 1999; 2006).

Institutionalization also facilitates the sharing of resources and expertise that a state might lack. A significant body of literature examines the specialization of forces within NATO (e.g., Christiansson 2013), even down to the level of defense industrial policy (Hartley 2006). This is also exhibited in how alliance partners distribute their military capabilities (Gannon 2023). Relatedly, states that are relatively weak allies are likely to dedicate more resources to an ally when there is room for growth within an alliance (Gannon and Kent 2021). This can further enhance the credibility and legitimacy of an alliance partner, particularly when the alliance is institutionalized, as institutionalization facilitates specialization.

This process of institutionalization can occur at both the multilateral and bilateral levels, with formal institutions being more likely to emerge within multilateral alliances. The presence of multiple actors within a multilateral organization often leads to diverse viewpoints, necessitating the creation of third-party decision-making bodies that coordinate and resolve these differences. This can, in turn, lead to the development of other external institutions that facilitate cooperation. For instance, the US-Canada Joint Defense Plan, the International Joint Commission, and other organs have fostered cooperation between long-time allies, the United States and Canada, and serve as blueprints for future cooperation.

But why might institutionalization be an attractive option? The literature indicates that institutionalization, unsurprisingly, makes coordination easier (Wallander and Keohane 2003). This is because institutions foster cooperation and trust between actors and develop the necessary organizational procedures and standard operating procedures (SOPs). Tuschhoff (1999) argues that the incorporation of a unified Germany into NATO was facilitated by the strong institutional framework of the alliance, making transparency, enforcement, and integration easier (pp. 140–1). Additionally, in multilateral institutions, this dispersal of decision-making and responsibility means that trust is optimized. Gheciu (2005) contends that a high degree of institutionalization can also act as a vehicle for socializing new members to acceptable and unacceptable behaviors and "best practices."

Institutionalization within alliance frameworks is a cornerstone of highly developed alliances. NATO, for example, has a high degree of institutionalization that is well documented by scholars (e.g., Krüger 2014; Mayer 2014). This institutionalization, professionalization, and bureaucratization are evident in the fact that approximately 4000 individuals work full time at NATO headquarters, with some 6000 meetings occurring every year (NATO 2022). The physical presence of NATO headquarters is itself a tangible indicator of institutionalization. This has enabled NATO to adapt and respond to new threats that have emerged in the post-Cold War era (Johnston 2017). While NATO itself is not independent of its member states, its existence reflects the significant role that formal organization and bureaucratization play in the most enduring alliances.

Furthermore, Weitsman (2013) argues that the United States has often pursued a strategy of forming large alliances, particularly in regions where the risk of conflict is high. While alliances offer benefits, they also have drawbacks. Allies often engage in "horse trading" to secure their desired outcomes and must cobble together solutions to placate alliance partners, a phenomenon exhibited in International Monetary Fund (IMF) loans (Dreher, Sturm, and Vreeland 2009). This dynamic is evident in the framework of the Ukraine Defense Contact Group, a loose coalition of states, both allied and non-allied, that coordinates the distribution of weapons to Ukraine. These complex trade-offs suggest that institutionalization is more likely to emerge within complex and enduring alliances, but less likely to develop within bilateral arrangements.

The US strategy in Europe, where the risk of conflict was highest during the Cold War, was heavily reliant on the centralized command structure of NATO. Political disagreements were addressed by the individual states, while NATO served as a coordinating framework for security cooperation, but everyone was allied with everyone else. On the other hand, the United States chose a decidedly "hub and spoke" alliance system in East Asia, particularly after the failure of the Southeast Asia Treaty Organization (SEATO), a looser organization characterized by less clearly defined goals, organizational structures, and internal conflicts (Buszynski 1981, p. 288). This "hub and spoke" model allowed the United States to concentrate power rather than disperse it amongst alliance partners or to an external institution. In this bilateral approach, the United States maintained a bargaining advantage over multilateral networks, meaning lesser allies were likely to have less sway in foreign policy and could make the United States less receptive to the emergence of a multilateral security institution within the region (Chen 2020).

Institutionalism, then, necessarily involves constraints. The debate about alliance institutionalization mirrors the broader discussion within international relations theory on the role of international institutions. Keohane (2005) contends that the current international hegemonic order, established by the United States after World War II, was designed to centralize authority and power, ensuring the United States could retain its influence even after its dominance waned. This informal (and occasionally formal) institutionalization of hegemony permits the United States to "punch above its weight" long after other states would have been supplanted by a rising power. By this logic, institutionalization represents a long-term solution to long-term problems. This principle can also be applied to alliance-making. If secret alliances are designed to achieve short-term objectives, then it is unlikely that they will be characterized by a high degree of institutionalization.

Furthermore, Lake (1996) maintains that the differences in the strategies pursued by the United States and the Soviet Union in Europe reflect the contrasting costs of empires and alliances. To this end, the United States institutionalized alliances in Europe, encouraging a greater say by partner states. However, the Soviets ensured that their alliance network was more heavily centralized under Moscow's control. This divergence in the degree of institutionalization stems from the different ways that power was distributed, either centrally in Moscow or across the various Western European capitals.

Questions regarding alliance termination are inherently bound up in credibility. In contract law, breach of contract outside the confines of what is explicitly detailed may result in punitive damages. In the realm of international politics, the game is a reiterated series of interactions rather than a singular game (Conybeare 1984; Jervis 1988). And in games of jointness and non-excludability at the international level (Snidal 1979), there exists an increased risk of defection. While alliances are by definition exclusive clubs, the security provided to members is equally distributed among all members. Since the benefits and requirements of an alliance can be unequal, the expectation is that negotiating states in alliances want different things. This leads to different roles, responsibilities, and payoffs. In this sense, alliances are not equal in terms of the inputs but in terms of the overall outputs that states gain equally. However, when one state thinks the cost of an alliance is no longer worth the inputs, it may be more likely to terminate the alliance early or irregularly.

States that renege on their commitments can face retaliation. While not a contract in the formal legal sense, given that there is no entity that can enforce punishment on a contracting party, sanctions may still be imposed by other actors either immediately or in the future. States that were party to the agreement can retaliate by linking the defection to other issues (Davis 2004; Haas 1980; McGinnis 1986). Additionally, defecting states will have harmed their own reputations (see Chapter 5), souring future alliance-making prospects.

While the relationship between reputation and defection has primarily focused on public alliances, the impact of reputation and defection within secret alliances remains largely unexplored. The veil of secrecy only exacerbates these problems, meaning that institutions between states in secret alliances should diminish the defection problem. Secret alliances can be either partially secret or fully secret, in which case other states are completely unaware of any agreement. Since institutions, particularly formal institutions, are highly visible, creating them would undermine the goals of secrecy. Additionally, given the private nature of secret alliances, there is an inherent selection problem. Potential alliance suitors may not be certain whether a prior secret alliance member upheld its commitments or violated the agreement. They might also lack knowledge about the degree of institutionalization in a prior secret alliance or whether it ensured compliance with the commitments. This highlights the need for further research on the likelihood of institutionalization in secret alliances to better understand the processes of formation, execution, and termination of these clandestine agreements. Ultimately, this will help to better understand the prospects for future alliance formation.

THEORY

Given the inherent secrecy surrounding secret alliances, their duration, likelihood of violation, and degree of institutionalization are likely to differ from those of public alliances. Leeds (2003) emphasizes that different alliances serve distinct purposes, leading to different probabilities of conflict. Strong signals of commitment to defend an ally, along with credible commitments (e.g., see Leeds 1999, 2000), increases the probability that a defensive alliance will deter an enemy, as this alters the cost-benefit calculus for potential aggressors (Morrow 1994).

Secret alliances are likely to endure for shorter periods before a willful violation occurs. This is because secrecy allows a state to defect without public knowledge of its actions, potentially mitigating reputational damage. Furthermore, given that secret alliances are less likely to contain provisions for renewing alliance texts, secret alliances are not likely to benefit from institutions. As a result, secret alliances are less likely to persist for extended periods. Since secret alliances do not represent long-term issue convergence (Chapter 4), institutions are less likely to emerge in these agreements.

If states lack long-term political convergence, secret alliances are likely to have a shorter duration than public alliances. This is because the goals of a secret alliance are more likely to be transactional rather than enduring. Both states entering a secret alliance are likely to anticipate the exchange of tangible goods. However, in many public alliances, long-term cooperation is more likely because states are less concerned with specific goods, suggesting a greater degree of political convergence. The lack of political convergence, coupled with the concealed nature of defection, makes it more likely that states involved in secret alliances will violate their agreements, as these violations will remain hidden from view.

Due to the nature of secret alliances, the degree of their institutionalization, the length of their existence until violation, and how they end will differ from public agreements. In short, this chapter proposes that fully and partially secret alliances are less likely to be heavily institutionalized because the nature of the good is best obtained from one-on-one cooperation. Thus, institutions are not required to formalize the relationship between states. In fact, strong institutionalization is antithetical to the idea of secret diplomacy because institutions imply a degree of public acknowledegment. Instead, given that many secret alliances are of shorter duration, secret protocols are not conducive to institutions nor do they endure long enough so that the interactions are standardized (Krasner 1972). Next, secret alliances are less likely to end irregularly after a willful violation by one of the members because of the transactional nature of such agreements.

Proposition 1

In Proposition 1, I claim that fully secret alliances are likely to experience a willful violation more quickly than other types of alliances. Given the material nature of the objectives typically pursued in secret alliances and the fact that they often come at the expense of another actor, these alliances are less likely to undergo a willful violation (H6). However, even if violations are less common, they are likely to occur more rapidly in secret alliances than in public alliances. This is due to two key factors. First, the secrecy surrounding secret alliances encourages signatories to commit a willful violation because these actions are less likely to be discovered, reducing the potential for reputational damage. Thus, their reputation is less likely to suffer than it would in public alliances. This means that at the first opportunity when a state can achieve its objectives without its partner, it is more likely to defect. Second, given that secret alliances do not represent long-term issue convergence, defection is more likely early on. This is because the signatory expects there to be fewer interactions between those states and less reputational damage to the one state. By definition, this is a transactional relationship. Additionally, the issues at stake are likely to be "salient stakes," meaning states are likely to go to extremes in order to secure them. And if a "better deal" emerges elsewhere, they are more likely to pursue that alternative. Finally, since institutions are less developed in the early stages, defection is more likely to occur when institutional constraints are nascent.

Since states defecting from a secret alliance are less likely to suffer reputational damage and secret alliances do not represent long-term issue convergence, they are more likely to defect more quickly than they would in a public alliance. This is because defection from a public alliance hinders the possibility of future side payments to other actors. With secret alliances, however, defection does not necessarily "burn a bridge" but rather damages it, making it less likely for the other state to be aware of the violation.

Consider, for example, the Molotov–Ribbentrop Pact. Nazi Germany sought to resolve the "Polish Question" and what it saw as the unjust imposition of the Treaty of Versailles. While Nazi Germany under Hitler certainly wanted to expand eastward and create lebensraum in the Soviet Union, it was willing to compromise its long-term ambitions for achieving more immediate concerns in Poland. While German-Soviet relations during the inter-war years have been widely discussed, it is important to note that Germany and the USSR did not share a common border. It was only with the invasion of Poland and its subsequent partition that the two states would share a border, ultimately facilitating the invasion of June 1941. While the pact lasted 22 months, according to Article VI, it was supposed to last for a period of ten years with a mechanism for automatic extension of another five years. However, Nazi Germany violated this pact on June 22, 1941, ending Nazi-Soviet cooperation.

Similarly, the short-lived Protocol of Sèvres, signed between the United Kingdom, France, and Israel in response to the nationalization of the Suez Canal in 1956, lasted just 13 days (October 24–November 6). These secret protocols sought to create a manufactured conflict between Israel and Egypt, ostensibly allowing "independent" French and British forces to intervene to separate the warring parties. However, the ultimate goal was to depose Gamal Abdal Nasser from office and secure control over the canal. Interestingly, the agreement did not end in a violation by any of the three signatories.

In both of these cases, the lack of strong institutional constraints likely contributed to the likelihood of defection. Were institutions present, defection may have been less likely, as a negotiated solution would have been more easily derived through institutional cooperation.

Proposition 2

Secret alliances are less likely to be highly institutionalized for a variety of reasons. These reasons stem from the very nature of secrecy and are antithetical to the logic of multi-member public alliances, particularly defensive alliances.

First, secret alliances are inherently opaque, particularly those that are fully secret. The terms of the alliance, as well as parties, are often unknown. This lack of transparency means that states are less willing or able to embed their alliances within a highly visible institutional framework. Furthermore, since institutions lend credibility to interactions, the absence of institutions makes such agreements less credible. Secrecy, particularly among democratic states, has fallen out of favor (Horn 2011). Thus, highly visible institutions in secret alliances are self-defeating in obtaining goods and a state's public reputation.

Second, if Keohane (2005) is correct in arguing that institutionalization is a long-term solution to the problems of hegemony, a similar process should be observed in alliance-making. States that share long-term convergence of interests are more likely to extend authority beyond the state itself to institutions that govern the alliance, as with NATO. Therefore, secret alliances are likely limited in scope and are less likely to develop institutions. As established elsewhere (Chapter 2), secret alliances are about getting goods at the expense of another state. These specific goods or goals are often specifically named within alliance documents and can be achieved over a short time horizon. Furthermore, institutionalization concentrates power outside of a state, dispersing authority among multiple actors. This can hinder both secrecy and increase the cost of alliance maintenance, as spoils must be shared with more actors.

Third, secret alliances are designed to insulate signatories from the costs associated with public alliances. Signatories are not held accountable for their actions and thus face lower costs when pursuing the intended goals of the secret agreement. While parties may be accountable to one another, they are not accountable in a strictly hierarchical way. They are instead accountable to one another as equals who both have private information that increases the probability of achieving their objectives (Bas and Schub 2016).

Fourth, while we should expect to see less institutionalization within secret alliances, this does not preclude informal contact and communication between states. Given the transactional nature of the alliance, we should expect to see greater military cooperation between the actors, as the good in question will most likely be a "salient stake," meaning something the target state is willing to fight for. Therefore, military coordination is more likely to be mentioned in secret alliance texts than in public alliances.

This is because, if previous claims are correct regarding the aims and scope of secret alliances (Chapter 2), they often concern the division of a specific good. To obtain that good, secret alliance-making states are likely to cooperate both politically and militarily. However, political cooperation does not necessarily imply institutional cooperation or the creation of new institutions. Furthermore, issues related to the military are generally considered highly classified, making military cooperation an effective means to secure desired outcomes without requiring public-facing institutions. Military cooperation also offers an advantage to political leaders by providing "political cover." If an alliance becomes public, either before or after the objectives are met, political leaders can attribute any failures to the other state or to the military leaders involved in the interstate discussions. When the alliance becomes public, either before or after the objectives are met, the political leadership can then blame any failures on the other state but also on those military leaders who were involved in the interstate military discussions.

For example, the Nazi–Soviet cooperation after the Molotov–Ribbentrop Pact warrants discussion. While much of the historical focus has been on the political aspects of the pact, there was a significant degree of covert military cooperation between the Soviet and Nazi occupying forces. In reality, Soviet/Nazi political and military cooperation had occurred covertly for years (for further background, see Johnson 2021; also Newman 1948). This included meetings between Soviet and Nazi representatives in 1938 regarding the fulfillment of orders from the recently captured Skoda works in Prague to the Red Army (Cienciala 2003, p. 171), as well as the training of German officers in the USSR, the development of chemical weapons and aircraft/tanks in the Soviet Union, and the extensive sharing of technology with the Soviet military.

During the occupation of Poland, the country was divided along the Narew, Vistula, and San Rivers, necessitating extensive coordination between the two militaries. During the invasion itself, Soviet forces even used radio navigation to assist Luftwaffe aircraft in targeting missions (Gross 1997, p. 63). Due to the speed of the advance, German and Soviet troops met east of the demarcation line relatively quickly in Brest-Litovsk (Johnson 2021, p. 214), requiring further communication and a German withdrawal back to the agreed-upon line. Top generals Guderian and Krivoshein even shared a reviewing stand to watch a joint Soviet-Nazi victory parade (Johnson 2021, p. 214) before the Polish campaign had concluded. Further political and military discussions were required to demarcate borders and occupation issues under the Boundary and Friendship Treaty. Political agreements and requests centered on the German need for raw materials and Soviet needs for advanced military equipment and manufacturing techniques (Johnson 2021, pp. 216–18). Military arrangements even included allowing German commercial raiders based on the Soviet coast to attack British shipping from Murmansk (Johnson 2021, p. 218), German military intelligence sharing with the Soviets regarding Finnish defenses (Edwards 2008, pp. 112–13), direct German naval assistance in Finland (Johnson 2021, p. 219), and the use of Soviet icebreakers to give the German Kriegsmarine access to the Pacific (Philbin 1994, p. 43). This extensive cooperation required political approval and close military coordination, yet it was largely ad hoc and not formally institutionalized.

Finally, and related to the third point, the risk of exposure poses a significant threat to secret alliances. States involved in such treaties are likely to face higher costs for upholding the agreement if institutional cooperation is extensive and publicly visible. This could arouse suspicion among the target state or other non-parties to the agreement, potentially leading to the formation of a counter-coalition, the discovery of the alliance's existence, or even incentivizing a preemptive strike by the target state (Benson 2011).

Proposition 3

According to Proposition 3, secret alliances are less likely to terminate through irregular means. Within the ATOP dataset, the variable "term" indicates how a treaty terminates. However, it is more insightful to consider whether a termination occurred due to a willful violation by a member state or by other means (see Proposition 1). In other words, it is important to think about whether an alliance ends in a manner consistent with treaty obligations or in an irregular manner.

The very nature of secrecy presents a significant challenge for secret alliances. Given the prevalence of defection in international relations (Gibler 2008; Majeski and Fricks 1995; Underdal 1998), the risk of defection is ever-present and may or may not be known publicly. Majeski and Fricks (1995) highlight that communication is crucial to preventing defection. Since institutions facilitate communication and foster trust, it is likely that secret alliances, which are less likely to have strong institutions, are less likely to terminate through irregular means due to the "law of thieves." This "law" directly relates to the prisoner's dilemma, where states are more or less likely to cooperate to achieve a preferential outcome.

However, this "law of thieves" assumes that only the signatories make a secret agreement, implying that no one outside the alliance would know if a signatory violated the agreement. Therefore, a state's public reputation suffers less if it defects from a secret agreement. However, the cost to a state's private reputation is likely to be much greater, as the jilted partner is less likely to achieve the goals of the secret alliance and has been betrayed by an ally. This suggests that the consequences for private reputation in a secret alliance are likely to be more significant than those for private reputation in a public alliance.

Given the likelihood of weak institutions in secret alliances, the problem of defection is compounded early on. Therefore, signatories cannot rely on support or resources in the same way as highly institutionalized alliances. Consider, for instance, the highly institutionalized framework of NATO. The alliance mitigates the risk of defection through a variety of mechanisms. First, NATO's organizational structure is such that a Secretary General acts as CEO of the organization, while the North Atlantic Council serves as the primary decision-making body, and numerous working groups handle specific areas and functions. Second, NATO has established procedures that emphasize consultation and consensus-building in reaching decisions, giving all states a say in the alliance. Third, NATO has specific membership criteria, establishing clear guidelines for joining this exclusive club. Finally, NATO has formalized relationships not only with its member and non-member states but also with other organizations, such as the European Union, the Organization for Security and Co-operation in Europe (OSCE), and even target states (e.g., the NATO-Russia Council). In turn, this promotes security and stability on a larger scale than mere individualized cooperation does. Because secret alliances lack this institutional support, it is more likely that they will end early on in an irregular manner.

Furthermore, states involved in secret alliances face the risk of "going public" during the alliance's lifespan. A notable example of this is the Sykes–Picot Agreement between France, Great Britain, and Russia during World War I. The agreement aimed to divide spheres of influence within the Middle East after the defeat of the Ottoman Empire. However, the Bolshevik Revolution in 1917 brought the text of the agreement into the public sphere, much to the embarrassment of Paris and London (Beck 2016; Saif and Al-Qaisi 2022). This incident highlights a key challenge for secret alliances: the risk of public exposure can deter states from needing strong institutions to ensure compliance with their commitments.

Morrow (2000) argues that states write down alliances to credibly commit to their partners, enhancing security both among allies and signaling to potential adversaries that they will protect their allies. By formally agreeing to secret partnerships, states similarly make commitments to one another, albeit privately. McManus and Yarhi-Milo (2017) term this "offstage signaling." The logic of offstage signaling is that these clandestine agreements can become public if one alliance partner chooses to defect, leading to a public exposure of the violation by the jilted partner. However, if the ally does not go public, the abandoned ally retains private information that their former partner is unreliable. In fact, having a written secret alliance is a two-edged sword. A partner state can always choose to go public, embarrassing both themselves and their defecting ally. Conversely, the defecting ally can also use this information as a threat against their former partner.

This dynamic highlights the critical role of domestic politics in alliance formation (see Chapters 6–8). Scholars have demonstrated that domestic politics influence the assessment of whether state interests align or if their regimes are likely to ally in the first place (e.g., Barnett and Levy 1991; Kimball 2000; Lai and Reiter 2000). Further considerations include the likelihood of allies becoming involved in conflict (Kimball 2006) or whether right-leaning parties are more likely to compromise sovereignty in favor of alliances (Rapport and Rathbun 2021).

Secret alliances are also more likely to terminate irregularly early on even if there is no "going public." If, as argued in Chapter 4, secret alliance partners are less likely to share a high degree of similarity, they are likely to have fewer areas of overlapping interests. This means that minor fissures between secret alliance partners can quickly evolve into significant differences, increasing the likelihood of an irregular termination.

Finally, the nature of secret alliances suggests that a partner state is more likely to defect if it believes it can either act independently or secure a more favorable agreement elsewhere. While public exposure can be a motivating factor in the irregular termination of a secret alliance, it could also be explained by a shift in the members' bargaining positions, the receipt of new promises from other states, or a change in their cost-benefit calculations for going it alone. These factors could increase the size of the "pie" that a state involved in a secret alliance could obtain by breaking the agreement.

OTHER EXPLANATIONS

Given that democracies are more likely to make alliances with one another (Lai and Reiter 2000), democracies should be less prone to behaviors associated with secret alliances. While previous analyses of secret alliances have concluded that democracies are less likely to engage in secret alliance-making in the first place, they should also be more likely to engage in activities not typically associated with secret diplomacy. First, democracies are more likely to be in long-term alliances because of the convergence of norms between democratic states.

Scholars have recognized that different types of alliances exhibit distinct characteristics and have different impacts (Leeds 2003). We can categorize alliances in a similar fashion to the traditional distinctions between defense, offense, neutrality, consultation, and ententes. Different alliance types serve different purposes, and just as scholars expect differences between those types, we can also anticipate differences between fully secret, partially secret, and fully public alliances. For this reason, I control for different types of alliances.

Additionally, given that secret alliances are more likely to emerge between bilateral partners rather than multilateral agreements, this analysis incorporates controls for alliance size and structure. The logic here is that coordination and trust should be mutually reinforcing in illicit conduct, suggesting that a "law of thieves" dynamic applies. This is because both states would be less likely to achieve the desired outcome, and both states possess private information about the other state that could be embarrassing if made public. Furthermore, a state involved in a secret alliance is less likely to defect because doing so would amount to an admission of the alliance's existence, potentially damaging its reputation.

I also account for a state's share of power, as in the previous chapter. As a state's total share of power in the international system increases, it is less likely to require a secret alliance to achieve its goals. Furthermore, a more powerful state is less likely to need institutions to keep its partner involved in the alliance. A count of major powers in the international system is also included as a standard control. This also captures the nature of whether the system is a bipolar, multipolar, or unipolar system. While not a perfect measure, it serves to moderate the explanatory power of the CINC variable, as it is possible that a very powerful state may have a need to make a secret alliance or institutionalize such an agreement if there are numerous major competitors in the system.

Given these propositions, I make the following hypotheses:[3]

Proposition 1: Fully secret alliances will have a shorter duration than non-secret alliances.

> *H1: Fully secret/partially secret alliances are more likely to experience a willful violation sooner than other types of alliances.*

Proposition 2: Secret alliances are not likely to have a large degree of institutionalization.

> *H2: Fully secret/partially secret alliances are less likely to have any external institutional organization associated with the alliance agreement.*

H3: Fully secret/partially secret alliances are less likely to include provisions for adding other states during the original alliance negotiations.

H4: Fully secret/partially secret alliances are less likely to specify a specific timeframe for the alliance's duration.

H5: Fully secret/partially secret alliances are more likely to involve military-to-military contact for coordination.

Proposition 3: Secret alliances are less likely to terminate due to a willful violation of the treaty by one or more members. Given the challenges of defection and the high stakes involved, a purposeful violation is less likely due to the potential costs.

H6: Fully secret/partially secret alliances are less likely to end due to a willful violation by one or more member.

RESEARCH DESIGN

To test the theory that secret alliances have shorter durations and lack robust institutional mechanisms, I begin with a time-series analysis of the Alliance Treaty Obligations and Provisions dataset (Leeds et al. 2002). I begin by using the member-level of analysis.[4] This dataset is appropriate for the propositions considered below, which are, in order: (1) violations in secret alliances occur more quickly; (2) secret alliances are less likely to be institutionalized; (3) secret alliances are less likely to terminate irregularly.

First, a distinction must be made between fully secret alliances and partially secret alliances. While there are relatively few secret alliances in the international system, evidence suggests that fully secret alliances are more common than partially secret alliances. There are 37 partially secret alliances, representing approximately 1.5 percent of alliances during this timeframe. In contrast, there are 131 fully secret alliances in the dataset, accounting for approximately 5.2 percent of the total. At 6.7 percent of all alliances, this is a borderline rare event. To account for this, this analysis employs both rare events logit models and standard logistic regression models. While the analysis reports results from both models, the primary focus is on the effects derived from the rare events models.

Furthermore, a distinction between partially secret and fully secret alliances is warranted, as the goals of these alliances are likely to differ. This mirrors Leeds's (2003) finding that alliance type influences the probability of conflict. In fully secret alliances, states are less likely to develop institutions because of the theory outlined above. The analysis should therefore expect to observe differences in alliance length and termination patterns between partially secret and fully secret alliances. Partially secret alliances share more similarities with public alliances than they do with fully secret alliances. This is because, while partially secret alliances offer a degree of signaling and public information, fully secret alliances remain completely hidden from public view, indicating that their purposes and mechanisms vary significantly. This variation underscores the need to distinguish between these degrees of secrecy.

Proposition 1

The duration of an alliance until a violation is relatively straightforward. First, the alliance end date is subtracted from the alliance start date, providing the alliance's lifespan. Next, the ATOP dataset indicates when an alliance ends due to a willful violation by a member. However, such analyses are problematic for ongoing alliances or for secret alliances that have yet to end. To address the issue of right-censoring, the analysis only includes completed alliances. In theory, including alliances that are still ongoing could affect the degree of institutionalization and how an alliance terminates, as institutionalization or irregular termination might still occur in the future. To measure this, the analysis employs Cox models with the Breslow method for ties to examine the time difference between all secret, fully secret, and partially secret alliances relative to fully public alliances, with the failure event being a willful violation. Separate models are run on any secret alliance versus public alliances and on public, partially secret, and fully secret alliances.

Proposition 2

First, it is necessary to define the concept of "institutions." Institutions have variously been defined as "formal arrangement transcending national boundaries that provides for the establishment of institutional machinery to facilitate cooperation among members in the security, economic, social, or related fields" (Plano and Olton 1979 [1988], p. 288), or as "principles, norms, rules, and decision-making procedures around which actor expectations converge in a given issue area" (Krasner 1982, p. 185). These definitions variously focus on the physical and formal to the conceptual and abstract varieties of institutions. Given these competing definitions, the analysis tests assumptions about institutionalization across both formal and informal indicators.

To that end, I first determine whether secret alliances are more or less likely to contain formal institutional arrangements with an alliance partner. ATOP codes whether an organization is formed alongside an alliance. ATOP also indicates that to qualify as an institution, "the agreement must specify required meetings within particular time periods" (ATOP Codebook 2018, p. 30).

Next, I measure institutions in a variety of indirect ways. Formal alliances have an official beginning and end date for the original signatories. States that intend to exclude future partners at a later date often codify this within the text itself, facilitating more informal cooperation between the alliance partners. This is because it assumes that the alliance agreement will only involve the signatories and does not include provisions for expansion, which would likely lead to greater institutionalization. The absence of mentions regarding the addition of other allies in the future can therefore serve as an indicator of the likelihood of future institutionalization.

Another way of measuring institutionalization is to examine the duration of the alliance. Since secret alliances often aim to secure a specific good at the expense of another, I expect that states making secret alliances are less likely to intend for the agreement to last for a long time, as it does not represent long-term issue convergence. Institutionalization is more likely to emerge in agreements that are designed to endure. Having an indeterminate alliance length tacitly acknowledges the instrumentality of the agreement. States are only involved in such an arrangement to secure the good they seek and are then more likely to "move on" from their one-time ally. With institutional constraints, this is less likely to occur because the costs of extricating oneself from an alliance and an institution are both more visible and more damaging to one's reputation.

Finally, the analysis measures the degree of alliance institutionalization with the MILCON variable in the ATOP dataset (ATOP Codebook 2018, 28). This variable indicates whether the treaty specifies contact between the militaries of the signatories. While this variable is coded categorically, with "0" corresponding to no contact between militaries and the other categories corresponding to differing levels of coordination, I collapse those categories into a single binary indicator of military institutionalization.

The Permanent Joint Board on Defense, established in 1940 between the United States and Canada, is a notable example of this. During World War II, while Canada was not involved in the war and the United States was formally neutral, this board provided the foundation for military cooperation. Later it served as a blueprint for further cooperation between the two countries and the cooperation between the United States and future allies (Stacey 1954). This suggests that measuring military cooperation is a valuable proxy for institutional cooperation, even if it does not encompass political cooperation.

Proposition 3

To assess whether an alliance ends due to a willful violation by one of the members, the analysis employs the ATOP TERM variable, which captures how an alliance terminates (ATOP Codebook 2018, pp. 39–40). The TERM variable is recoded as binary from a categorical variable. Originally, the variable is coded as "0" for alliances that were in effect by the end of 2016 or for states that lost independence, "1" for alliances that ended on time or achieved their goals, "2" for willful violation, and "3" if the alliance members negotiate a new relationship. This is recoded to "0" for all cases that do not end in a willful violation and "1" for cases that involve a willful violation.

Independent Variables

The primary explanation for the proposed dependent variables is the public/secret nature of the alliance. However, it is important to note that there are varying degrees of secrecy within these alliances. The dataset, in fact, includes alliances that are fully public, partially secret, or fully secret. In other words, some alliances have both public and secret components. While there are only 37 partially secret alliances, they do represent an interesting conundrum regarding measurement. On the one hand, these alliances send a public message but convey no message with the secret portions. This may then dilute the effect of the much more numerous fully secret alliances. One could then conduct analyses with a binary approach, with fully public alliances on the one hand and fully secret alliances on the other. However, this approach is problematic. As an alternative, one could conduct analyses with an ordered categorical approach, with fully public alliances represented by "0", partially secret alliances coded as "1", and fully secret alliances coded as "2". This final approach is preferred because it distinguishes between those alliances that contain conflicting values within the document and those that are fully secret or fully public, creating a more nuanced level of analysis.

In terms of controls, alliances are coded as bilateral if there are no more than two members to the alliance during the current phase (Leeds et al. 2002). Major power states are coded as major powers according to the Correlates of War Major Powers dataset (2016). Major powers at various times include the United States, United Kingdom, France, Germany, Austria-Hungary, Italy, Russia (Union of Soviet Socialist Republics), China, and Japan. The CINC score is taken from the Correlates of War National Material Capabilities (v 6.0) dataset (Singer, Bremer, and Stuckey 1972). This variable is a composite indicator of a state's strength in a year relative to the capabilities of all other states in the system in that year. The dummy variable for democracy is taken from the Polity IV dataset, which ranks states on a categorical scale from 10 to −10 on their degree of democracy/autocracy (Marshall et al. 2002). Then, I create a dummy variable for democracy, with states greater than or equal to 6 counted as democracies, which is consistent with general practice. States scoring less than six are considered non-democracies.

Next, in keeping with Leeds's (2003) findings regarding the different roles that various types of alliances play in the system, I consider the alliance type, which is indicated within the ATOP dataset (Leeds et al. 2002). Alliances may variously be defensive, offensive, neutral, nonaggression, or consultative. Additionally, an alliance can also be a mix of any or all of the above-mentioned categories.

The analysis excludes alliances that are still in effect from the time-series analysis. This is appropriate, as it may bias against those alliances that have endured for a long time (such as the still ongoing NATO alliance or the Gulf Cooperation alliance) or might bias against alliances that have only existed for a short period but are likely to endure. Additionally, I provide different models for this issue in the logistic models for H2–H6.

To deal with the problem of right-censored data, I am primarily concerned with alliances that have completely terminated (referred to in tables as "Terminated"). While this is problematic in some cases, such as the NATO alliance, it does not unfairly bias those alliances that are still ongoing or have been long-time features of the international system. This is particularly important for the first hypothesis, which examines whether secret alliances last longer or shorter than public alliances. Out of an abundance of caution, modeling is also conducted on all available data, including ongoing alliances (referred to in tables as "Ongoing"). Similar results were found and are presented below, though they are not extensively discussed because of the potential for bias in Hypothesis 1.

Given the relatively rare nature of secret alliances at approximately 6 percent, I conduct both rare events modeling and standard logistic regression. While the primary focus is on the rare events models, this analysis also presents results for the standard logistic regression models. Since the goal is not to explain secret alliances but rather their effect on various dependent variables, I present six dependent variables that are likely to be influenced by the public/secret nature of an agreement. These models are presented first for alliances that have terminated (to address right-censoring) and then for both terminated and ongoing alliances.

Finally, I suspect that the greatest difference between secret alliances and public alliances lies in fully secret alliances. While I expect to find overall effects for the secret alliance variable (which includes both partially and fully secret alliances), I anticipate the largest effects among fully secret alliances. This is for two reasons. First, fully secret alliances are more numerous, making up 78 percent of all secret alliances. Thus, their effect will be larger than the effect of a more evenly divided sample. Second, fully secret alliances are the alliances which are most likely to critically hinge on secrecy, meaning that the aims of the alliance and institutionalization are the most desirable and thus should be the most likely to influence the dependent variables of interest across the various hypotheses.

RESULTS

First, I begin with the results of the survival analysis, presented in Table 3.1 and Figure 3.1. Table 3.2 displays the hazard ratios for both the disaggregated and combined secret alliance variable. Figure 3.1 presents the model disaggregating the distinction between public, partially secret, and fully secret agreements. For reasons discussed previously, it is problematic to ignore this important distinction. Note that models were also run on the secret alliance variable without a distinction between fully secret and partially secret variables, and the data are presented in Model 1.

Table 3.1   Time to violation (hazard ratios)

Variables	1	2
Any Secret	.852* (.082)	-
Partially Secret	-	1.952** (.576)
Fully Secret	-	.663** (.133)
CONTROLS	-	-
Bilateral	.870 (.103)	.844 (.101)
Major Power Count	1.946*** (.354)	1.927*** (.351)
CINC Share	.157 (.217)	.145 (.201)
Democracy	.581*** (.082)	.587*** (.083)
Defense	.653*** (.074)	.661*** (.076)

Never meant to last 75

Variables	1	2
Offense	1.151	1.197
	(.191)	(.200)
Neutrality	.982	1.018
	(.173)	(.180)
Nonaggression	.529***	.538***
	(.067)	(.068)
Consultation	.915	.900
	(.106)	(.105)
Observations	1212	1212

Notes: Standard errors are in parentheses, *** p<.01, ** p<.05, * p<.1.

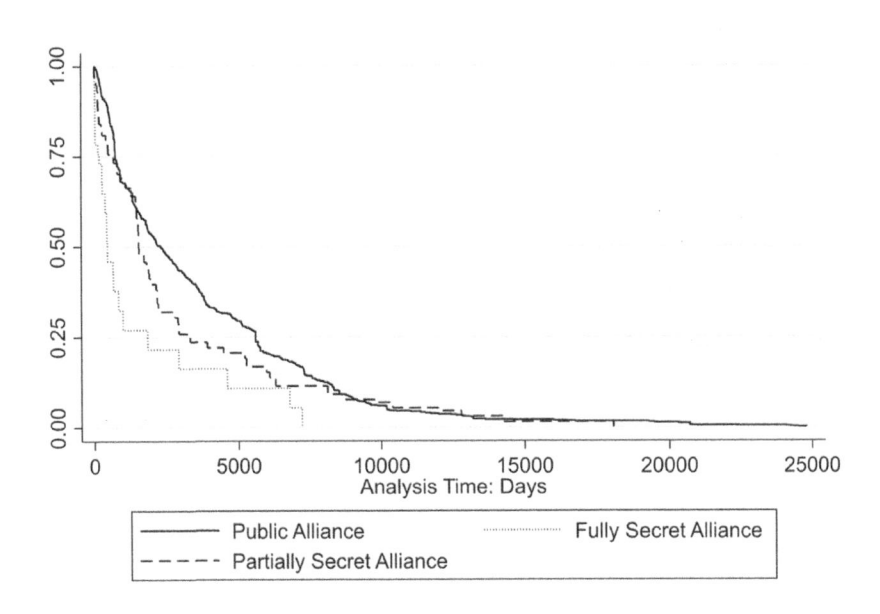

Source: Author.

Figure 3.1   Survival estimates, public/secret alliance

Table 3.2 Institutions and secret alliances (terminated and ongoing)

Variables	3	4	5	6	7	8	9	10
Any Secret	-.627** (.285)	-	-.791*** (.279)	-	-.648** (.288)	-	-.81*** (.282)	-
Partially Secret	-	1.212*** (.42)	-	1.06** (.443)	-	1.228*** (.428)	-	1.067** (.448)
Fully Secret	-	-1.685*** (.423)	-	-1.787*** (.415)	-	-1.757*** (.435)	-	-1.854*** (.427)
CONTROLS								
Bilateral	-1.098*** (.14)	-1.12*** (.142)	-1.693*** (.109)	-1.703*** (.109)	-1.107*** (.141)	-1.131*** (.143)	-1.702*** (.109)	-1.712*** (.11)
Major Power Count	-.474* (.26)	-.414 (.265)	-.563*** (.203)	-.527** (.205)	-.473* (.262)	-.412 (.267)	-.565*** (.204)	-.528** (.206)
CINC Share	-4.054** (2.03)	-4.608** (2.073)	-4.752*** (1.561)	-5.021*** (1.572)	-4.216** (2.056)	-4.79** (2.1)	-4.821*** (1.572)	-5.1*** (1.583)
Democracy	.478*** (.16)	.482*** (.162)	.753*** (.108)	.754*** (.108)	.482*** (.161)	.486*** (.163)	.757*** (.108)	.758*** (.109)
Defense	.416*** (.158)	.445*** (.161)	.498*** (.125)	.511*** (.126)	.42*** (.159)	.451*** (.162)	.5*** (.126)	.514*** (.127)
Offense	-1.327*** (.275)	-1.231*** (.278)	-1.882*** (.274)	-1.803*** (.277)	-1.356*** (.278)	-1.261*** (.282)	-1.911*** (.278)	-1.834*** (.28)

Variables	3	4	5	6	7	8	9	10
Neutrality	.454**	.582**	.068	.109	.457**	.588**	.067	.109
	(.226)	(.234)	(.16)	(.163)	(.228)	(.236)	(.161)	(.163)
Nonaggression	.885***	.938***	.725***	.754***	.895***	.948***	.729***	.758***
	(.16)	(.162)	(.122)	(.123)	(.161)	(.163)	(.122)	(.123)
Consultation	.654***	.696***	.485***	.501***	.661***	.702***	.488***	.503***
	(.147)	(.149)	(.105)	(.106)	(.148)	(.15)	(.105)	(.106)
Constant	-.703***	-.771***	.111	.078	-.709***	-.778***	.111	.079
	(.197)	(.199)	(.157)	(.157)	(.198)	(.2)	(.158)	(.158)
Observations	1229	1227	2289	2287	1229	1227	2289	2287
R^2	-	-	-	-	.182	.199	.233	.241

Notes: Standard errors are in parentheses, *** $p<.01$, ** $p<.05$, * $p<.1$.

Hypothesis 1, which posited that fully secret alliances are more likely to terminate due to a willful violation, finds support across Models 1 and 2. In Model 1, a secret alliance is likely to experience a violation more quickly than in a public alliance (p <.10). However, once the distinction is made between partially secret and fully secret alliances, the data indicate the effect is driven by fully secret alliances. Partially secret alliances, with a hazard ratio of 1.92, are less likely to experience a willful violation at the same rate as public alliances (p < .05). However, this finding is likely due to the small sample size of partially secret alliances. The hazard ratio for fully secret alliances in Model 2 is .663, meaning that fully secret alliances are likely to lead to a willful violation much more quickly than in public alliances (p <.05). In fact, the finding was so strong for the fully secret alliances that in Model 1, the combined effect of partially secret and fully secret alliances was still significant but moderated by the opposite effect for fully secret alliances (see Figure 3.2).

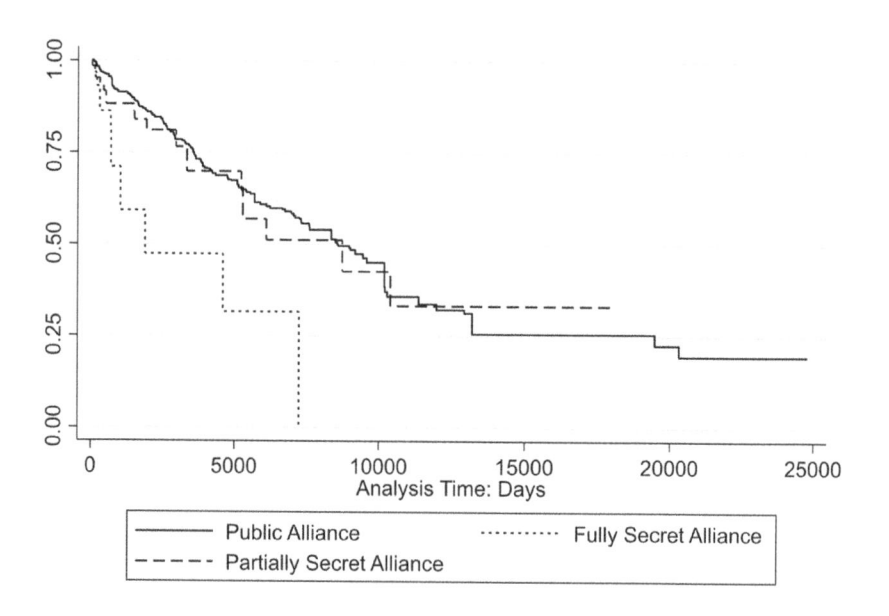

Source: Author.

Figure 3.2   *Survival estimates, public, partially secret, fully secret alliance*

Next, I turn to the models presented in Proposition 2 (H2–H5). Table 3.2 examines the presence of institutions in secret alliances, taking into account both the existence of any secret alliance and the type of secret alliance. Models 3–6 include the rare events models, while Models 7–10 present the findings for standard logistic regression models.

Turning to the substantive results, we see that in Model 3, any secret alliances are less likely to result in institutions. This is also true for fully secret alliances (Models 4 and 6). However, in partially secret alliances, institutions are more likely to occur in such arrangements (Models 4 and 6). This finding indicates that the data are being driven by fully secret alliances, which make up the largest share of secret alliances. This is an interesting finding that warrants further explanation, as it is also supported in the standard logistic model (Models 8 and 10), while in Models 6 and 8 fully secret alliances are less likely to involve institutionalization.

Unsurprisingly, across Models 3–10, democracies are more likely to create institutions in alliances ($p < .01$). On the other hand, the more powerful a state is, the less likely it is to institutionalize a secret alliance ($p < .05$ in Models 3 and 4, $p < .01$ in Models 5–10). Bilateral agreements are also less likely to feature institutionalization, consistent with the expectations above ($p < .01$). Offensive agreements are also less likely to build institutions, with a p-value of $<.01$ across all models. This is unsurprising, as offensive agreements would be the most likely to suffer from an attempt to create a forward-looking institution. Like a secret alliance, creating institutions for what is ostensibly a transactional agreement would undercut an alliance. However, defensive, neutrality, nonaggression, and consultation agreements are more likely to have institutional agreements across all models ($p < .01$ or $p < .05$). The exception to this is neutrality agreements. In Models 5, 6, 9, and 10, I am unable to reject the null hypothesis. However, the results here largely coincide with the claims made above. These types of agreements should be the most likely to have institutional arrangements. These findings allow me to find some support for H2. This support is largely driven by fully secret alliances, as it appears partially secret alliances operate under a different mechanism.

Moving to H3, I present these results in Table 3.3. This hypothesis examines whether alliances contain provisions for the additional joining of new members in the future. Results indicate support for this claim. However, again, these results are driven by the 78 percent of secret alliances that are fully secret. There are no statistically significant results for partially secret alliances, meaning I am unable to reject the null hypothesis with respect to partially secret alliances.

Table 3.3 Secret alliances and adding members

Variables	11	12	13	14	15	16	17	18
Any Secret	-.938** (.372)	-	-1.074*** (.373)	--	-.972** (.378)	-	-1.106*** (.379)	-
Partially Secret	-	.411 (.579)	-	.292 (.595)	-	.374 (.599)	-	.257 (.613)
Fully Secret	-	-1.747*** (.476)	-	-1.888*** (.477)	-	-1.822*** (.489)	-	-1.957*** (.489)
Controls								
Bilateral	-3.084*** (.217)	-3.203*** (.226)	-3.733*** (.185)	-3.828*** (.191)	-3.129*** (.22)	-3.254*** (.229)	-3.766*** (.187)	-3.865*** (.193)
Major Power Count	-1.07*** (.327)	-1.081*** (.331)	-1*** (.281)	-.997*** (.283)	-1.078*** (.331)	-1.095*** (.336)	-1.008*** (.283)	-1.008*** (.285)
CINC Share	-3.568 (2.29)	-3.584 (2.305)	-3.271* (1.881)	-3.343* (1.894)	-3.798 (2.343)	-3.801 (2.36)	-3.395* (1.913)	-3.459* (1.927)
Democracy	.193 (.2)	.233 (.203)	.116 (.14)	.142 (.142)	.195 (.202)	.235 (.205)	.118 (.141)	.143 (.142)
Defense	.672*** (.191)	.637*** (.194)	.474*** (.145)	.433*** (.146)	.681*** (.193)	.646*** (.196)	.476*** (.145)	.434*** (.147)
Offense	1.544*** (.266)	1.708*** (.279)	1.468*** (.267)	1.619*** (.279)	1.57*** (.269)	1.737*** (.282)	1.486*** (.268)	1.638*** (.281)
Neutrality	.007 (.403)	.146 (.411)	-.397 (.382)	-.33 (.39)	-.021 (.411)	.122 (.421)	-.434 (.39)	-.367 (.398)

Variables	11	12	13	14	15	16	17	18
Nonaggression	.938***	1.008***	.504***	.545***	.951***	1.021***	.506***	.547***
	(.199)	(.204)	(.157)	(.159)	(.201)	(.205)	(.158)	(.16)
Consultation	.434**	.541***	.3**	.37**	.44**	.548***	.302**	.372**
	(.189)	(.194)	(.144)	(.146)	(.191)	(.196)	(.145)	(.147)
Constant	-.79***	-.876***	-.213	-.262	-.799***	-.885***	-.213	-.261
	(.23)	(.234)	(.185)	(.187)	(.231)	(.236)	(.186)	(.188)
Observations	1216	1214	2278	2276	1216	1214	2278	2276
R2	-	-	-	-	.363	.379	.424	.433

Notes: Standard errors are in parentheses, *** $p < .01$, ** $p < .05$, * $p < .1$.

In Models 11, 13, 15, and 17, there is support for the claim that secret alliances are less likely to contain provisions for adding new members. However, this is driven by fully secret alliances. In fact, fully secret alliances are less likely to contain provisions for adding a new member to the alliance (p < .01), with moving from a public alliance and a partially secret alliance to a fully secret alliance resulting in a lower chance of adding new members. This, again, provides partial support for H3, with the reservation that this is confined to fully secret alliances.

For the other variables, moving from multilateral to bilateral agreements means states are less likely to include provisions for new members across all models (p < .01). Furthermore, across all models, the number of major powers in the international system is likely to decrease the probability of having provisions for the addition of new members (p < .01). Interestingly enough, the CINC share is only statistically significant in Models 13, 14, 17, and 18 (p < .1). Defense, offense, nonaggression, and consultation pacts are also more likely to include provisions for adding new members to varying degrees across all models. However, there are no significant findings for neutrality alliances. Furthermore, the significant findings for offensive alliances are slightly surprising, as alliances dedicated to conquest should, in theory, be less willing to welcome new members to the alliance, as this would divide up goods into smaller pieces.

Turning to H4, I claim that secret alliances are less likely to mention the length of time. These results indicate that, once again, the data are driven by fully secret alliances. Fully secret alliances are less likely to contain provisions regarding the length of time the alliance is subject to enforcement. Models 20, 22, 24, and 26 (see Table 3.4) indicate that moving from partially secret and fully public alliances results in a decreased likelihood of a specific length of time the alliance is in force (p < .1). However, there is no statistically significant effect for partially secret alliances (Models 20, 22, 24, and 26). And in Models 19, 21, 23, and 25, the "any secret" variable is significant and positive, meaning the presence of any secret alliance is likely to preclude any mention of the specific length of an alliance.

Next, moving on to the control variables, bilateral alliances are more likely to contain a clause limiting the specific length of the alliance (p < .01) across all models. The CINC share and major power count are not statistically significant across any of the models, meaning I am unable to reject the null hypothesis. Next, democracy is statistically significant only across Models 21, 22, 25, and 26 (p < .05), meaning that in those specifications, democracies are more likely to mention a specific length in their alliance agreements. Neutrality, nonaggression, and consultation are statistically significant and positive across all models, meaning that these types of alliances are more likely to include provisions regarding length. However, offensive alliances are negative and significant across all models except for Models 22 and 26, meaning that offensive alliances are less likely to mention a specific length.

Table 3.4 Secret alliances and specific length mentioned

Variables	19	20	21	22	23	24	25	26
Any Secret	-.412* (.228)	-	-.41* (.232)	-	-.416* (.23)	-	-.413* (.234)	-
Partially Secret	-	-.169 (.449)	-	-.181 (.496)	-	(.458)	-	-.151 (.503)
Fully Secret	-	-.447* (.251)	-	-.431* (.253)	-	-.452* (.253)	-	-.435* (.255)
Controls	-	-	-	-	-	-	-	-
Bilateral	1.565*** (.147)	1.567*** (.147)	2.357*** (.123)	2.359*** (.123)	1.582*** (.148)	1.586*** (.148)	2.372*** (.124)	2.375*** (.124)
Major Power Count	-.171 (.238)	-.154 (.238)	-.243 (.206)	-.232 (.206)	-.171 (.239)	-.154 (.24)	-.243 (.207)	-.232 (.207)
CINC Share	-1.548 (1.651)	-1.64 (1.653)	-1.361 (1.471)	-1.434 (1.472)	-1.582 (1.668)	-1.674 (1.67)	-1.373 (1.48)	-1.446 (1.482)
Democracy	-.111 (.164)	-.112 (.164)	.251** (.119)	.252** (.119)	-.11 (.165)	-.111 (.165)	.253** (.119)	.254** (.119)
Defense	1.328*** (.161)	1.334*** (.161)	1.139*** (.128)	1.145*** (.128)	1.343*** (.162)	1.349*** (.162)	1.148*** (.128)	1.153*** (.129)

Variables	19	20	21	22	23	24	25	26
Offense	-.594***	-.567***	-.375*	-.345	-.601***	-.573***	-.379*	-.348
	(.207)	(.209)	(.214)	(.215)	(.209)	(.21)	(.215)	(.216)
Neutrality	2.186***	2.171***	2.153***	2.136***	2.229***	2.217***	2.184***	2.169***
	(.292)	(.291)	(.261)	(.26)	(.296)	(.296)	(.264)	(.263)
Nonaggression	.997***	1.003***	.988***	.992***	1.01***	1.017***	.995***	1***
	(.173)	(.174)	(.133)	(.133)	(.175)	(.175)	(.133)	(.133)
Consultation	1.395***	1.384***	1.855***	1.848***	1.409***	1.401***	1.866***	1.861***
	(.156)	(.156)	(.124)	(.124)	(.157)	(.157)	(.125)	(.125)
Constant	-2.006***	-2.012***	-2.717***	-2.722***	-2.029***	-2.038***	-2.735***	-2.742***
	(.215)	(.215)	(.188)	(.188)	(.217)	(.217)	(.189)	(.189)
Observations	1216	1214	2280	2278	1216	1214	2280	2278
R2	-	-	-	z	.221	.221	.286	.286

Notes: Standard errors are in parentheses, *** $p < .01$, ** $p < .05$, * $p < .1$.

Next, turning to H5, which claims that secret alliances are more likely to have contact between states' militaries, there are effects in the expected direction. Again, though, this effect is driven by fully secret alliances. In Models 27, 29, 31, and 33, the effect is present in the any secret alliance variable ($p < .01$). However, upon closer inspection in Models 28, 30, 32, and 34 (see Table 3.5), this is driven by the fully secret variable ($p < .01$), meaning that fully secret alliances are more likely to establish procedures for contact between states' militaries. The effect for partially secret alliances is not significant.

As for the controls, bilateral alliances are less likely to have contact between members' militaries in Models 29, 30, 33, and 34 ($p < .01$). Similarly, as the CINC score increases, states are less likely to mandate contact between their militaries in Models 29, 30, 33, and 34 ($p < .01$). In the same models, democracies are more likely to maintain contact between their militaries ($p < .1$). Neutrality and nonaggression agreements are less likely to contain provisions for military contact ($p < .01$), while defense, offense (sometimes), and consultation pacts are more likely to contain provisions for contact in most models ($p < .01$).

Finally, H6 is considered in Table 3.6. This hypothesis claims that a willful violation by an alliance member in a secret alliance is less likely. In keeping with this "law of thieves" hypothesis, there is some support to indicate that states making secret alliances are less likely to commit a willful violation. For any secret alliance variable, there are significant negative effects in Models 35 and 39 ($p < .1$), though not in Models 37 and 41. Again, this finding is driven by the presence of fully secret alliances, which are statistically significant in Models 36 and 40 ($p < .05$), though not in Models 38 and 42. Partially secret alliances are not significant across any of the models.

Turning to the control variables, there are more mixed results here compared to the prior tables. Bilateral alliances are more likely to contain willful violations in Models 35, 36, 39, and 40 ($p < .01$). Major power count is significant and positive across all models ($p < .01$), meaning that the addition of a new major power increases the chance of a willful violation. CINC share is only moderately supported across Models 35, 36, 39, and 40, with an increase in CINC share representing a decreased probability of defecting via a willful violation ($p < .1$). Democracy is steadily negative and significant, meaning democracies are less likely to commit willful violations than non-democracies ($p < .01$). Results are mixed for alliance type, with offensive and nonaggression pacts being less likely to result in willful violations across some models but not others. On the other hand, consultation agreements are more likely to result in willful violations in Models 35, 36, 39, and 40.

Table 3.5 Secret alliances and military contact

Variables	27	28	29	30	31	32	33	34
Any Secret	.964*** (.244)	-	.629*** (.226)	-	.978*** (.247)	-	.633*** (.228)	-
Partially Secret	-	.189 (.53)	-	-.171 (.513)	-	.132 (.55)	-	-.233 (.532)
Fully Secret	-	1.122*** (.269)	-	.782*** (.247)	-	1.14*** (.272)	-	.788*** (.249)
Controls	-	-	-	-	-	-	-	-
Bilateral	.11 (.167)	.114 (.168)	-.529*** (.115)	-.531*** (.115)	.113 (.169)	.118 (.17)	-.531*** (.115)	-.533*** (.116)
Major Power Count	-.319 (.283)	-.292 (.284)	-.337 (.226)	-.327 (.227)	-.318 (.286)	-.293 (.287)	-.336 (.227)	-.326 (.228)
CINC Share	-2.407 (2.129)	-2.492 (2.134)	-5.178*** (1.86)	-5.205*** (1.861)	-2.604 (2.165)	-2.689 (2.172)	-5.356*** (1.882)	-5.385*** (1.884)
Democracy	.136 (.201)	.139 (.201)	.223* (.121)	.224* (.121)	.133 (.203)	.137 (.203)	.223* (.122)	.225* (.122)
Defense	1.331*** (.204)	1.327*** (.204)	1.224*** (.124)	1.22*** (.124)	1.352*** (.206)	1.35*** (.207)	1.23*** (.125)	1.226*** (.125)

Variables	27	28	29	30	31	32	33	34
Offense	.498**	.499**	.001	-.005	.503**	.506**	-.001	-.007
	(.204)	(.205)	(.191)	(.192)	(.206)	(.208)	(.192)	(.194)
Neutrality	-1.111***	-1.196***	-.804***	-.837***	-1.158***	-1.247***	-.824***	-.859***
	(.366)	(.376)	(.247)	(.251)	(.373)	(.384)	(.25)	(.254)
Nonaggression	-.86***	-.863***	-.423***	-.426***	-.872***	-.874***	-.424***	-.427***
	(.217)	(.217)	(.126)	(.126)	(.218)	(.219)	(.126)	(.127)
Consultation	.756***	.773***	.429***	.434***	.767***	.786***	.431***	.436***
	(.178)	(.179)	(.115)	(.115)	(.18)	(.181)	(.115)	(.116)
Constant	-2.675***	-2.686***	-1.446***	-1.444***	-2.71***	-2.725***	-1.452***	-1.45***
	(.275)	(.276)	(.173)	(.174)	(.278)	(.279)	(.174)	(.174)
Observations	1233	1229	2296	2292	1233	1229	2296	2292
R2	-	-	-	-	.16	.162	.137	.138

Notes: Standard errors are in parentheses, *** $p<.01$, ** $p<.05$, * $p<.1$.

Table 3.6 Secret alliances and military contact

Variables	27	28	29	30	31	32	33	34
Any Secret	.964*** (.244)	-	.629*** (.226)	-	.978*** (.247)	-	.633*** (.228)	-
Partially Secret	-	.189 (.53)	-	-.171 (.513)	-	.132 (.55)	-	-
Fully Secret	-	1.122*** (.269)	-	.782*** (.247)	-	1.14*** (.272)	-	-
Controls								
Bilateral	.11 (.167)	.114 (.168)	-.529*** (.115)	-.531*** (.115)	.113 (.169)	.118 (.17)	-.531*** (.115)	-
Major Power Count	-.319 (.283)	-.292 (.284)	-.337 (.226)	-.327 (.227)	-.318 (.286)	-.293 (.287)	-.336 (.227)	-.326 (.228)
CINC Share	-2.407 (2.129)	-2.492 (2.134)	-5.178*** (1.86)	-5.205*** (1.861)	-2.604 (2.165)	-2.689 (2.172)	-5.356*** (1.882)	-
Democracy	.136 (.201)	.139 (.201)	.223* (.121)	.224* (.121)	.133 (.203)	.137 (.203)	.223* (.122)	-
Defense	1.331*** (.204)	1.327*** (.204)	1.224*** (.124)	1.22*** (.124)	1.352*** (.206)	1.35*** (.207)	1.23*** (.125)	-

Variables	27	28	29	30	31	32	33	34
Offense	.498**	.499**	.001	-.005	.503**	.506**	-.001	–
	(.204)	(.205)	(.191)	(.192)	(.206)	(.208)	(.192)	
Neutrality	-1.111***	-1.196***	-.804***	-.837***	-1.158***	-1.247***	-.824***	–
	(.366)	(.376)	(.247)	(.251)	(.373)	(.384)	(.25)	
Nonaggression	-.86***	-.863***	-.423***	-.426***	-.872***	-.874***	-.424***	–
	(.217)	(.217)	(.126)	(.126)	(.218)	(.219)	(.126)	
Consultation	.756***	.773***	.429***	.434***	.767***	.786***	.431***	–
	(.178)	(.179)	(.115)	(.115)	(.18)	(.181)	(.115)	
Constant	-2.675***	-2.686***	-1.446***	-1.444***	-2.71***	-2.725***	–	–
	(.275)	(.276)	(.173)	(.174)	(.278)	(.279)		
Observations	1233	1229	2296	2292	1233	1229	2296	2292
R2	–	–	–	–	.16	.162	.137	.138

Notes: Standard errors are in parentheses, *** $p < .01$, ** $p < .05$, * $p < .1$.

CONCLUSION

The findings above generally support the hypotheses, with one important caveat: the findings are largely driven by fully secret alliances. Fully secret alliances are the most clandestine of all alliance agreements, whereas partially secret alliances have both public and private components, sending mixed or partial signals to the international community. Additionally, the relatively small sample size of partially secret alliances makes analysis problematic. Fully secret alliances, however, are likely to be the most consequential because they are most often designed to secure indivisible goods, potentially destabilizing commitments (Fearon 1995). A notable finding is that the commitment problem (Fearon 1995) in fully secret alliances appears less problematic in partially secret alliances or fully public alliances. This is because the "law of thieves" dynamic operates in such a way that secret allies are less likely to defect due to the stakes involved. Both the goals of the alliance and their broader public reputation are at risk (Chapter 5) if a party defects in a fully secret alliance. Here we can think of private reputations existing between signatories to secret alliances, while the state also has a broader public reputation with the larger international community. Defecting from a fully secret alliance, therefore, would necessarily harm both the public and private reputation of the state.

While fully secret alliances are less likely to experience a willful violation, when these violations do occur, they are more likely to happen early on during the alliance. As illustrated above, the Molotov–Ribbentrop Pact lasted for less than 20 percent of its intended duration. The explanation posed here is tied to the claims made in Chapter 1: secret alliances are transactional and, once

Table 3.7   Hypotheses confirmed/rejected

	H1	H2	H3	H4	H5	H6
All Secret Alliances	-	-	-	-	-	-
Effect	Lower	Negative	Negative	Negative	Positive	Negative
Confirmed?	✓	✓	✓	✓	✓	✓
Partially Secret Alliances	-	-	-	-	-	-
Effect	Higher	Positive	No Effect	No Effect	No Effect	No Effect
Confirmed?	×	×	×	×	×	×
Fully Secret Alliances	-	-	-	-	-	-
Effect	Lower	Negative	Negative	Negative	Positive	Negative
Confirmed?	✓	✓	✓	✓	✓	✓

Note: × = Disconfirmed, ✓ = Confirmed.

the desired objective is obtained, the secret alliance is no longer necessary. However, this does not explain why partially secret alliances are no more or less likely to experience a willful violation than public alliances. It is possible that the public component of a partially secret alliance exerts a moderating effect on the intent within the secret alliance. Additionally, the promises made in secret protocols of an otherwise public alliance might be less consequential than those made in fully secret alliances.

The analysis reveals strong evidence that fully secret alliances are less likely to have robust political institutions. Conversely, fully secret alliances are more likely to involve significant contact between militaries, a finding that aligns with the objectives of secret alliances. If secret alliances are primarily concerned with the division of spoils at the expense of another (Chapter 2), then military cooperation makes logical sense, as this form of cooperation is more effective at the military rather than the political level.

As for other forms of institutions, fully secret alliances are less likely to develop institutional structures, less likely to concern themselves with adding new members, and less likely to mention the duration of the agreement. All of these findings indicate that secret alliances are less likely to develop robust institutional structures that are likely to endure or are likely to incorporate new alliance members. Theoretically, this makes sense: secret alliances are less likely to have public-facing institutions. On the other hand, military coordination between secret alliance partners is greater, which is in keeping with this same logic. Since military matters are often closely guarded, keeping cooperation confined to military-to-military coordination makes it easier for states to conceal their true motives while still ensuring a moderate degree of cooperation with an ally.

NOTES

1. Note that secret alliances can be partially or fully secret, according to the Alliance Treaty and Obligation coding procedures. When the term "secret alliances" is referred to here, it generally means the secret portion of only partially secret alliances. In the tests below, the distinction is made between fully and partially secret alliances.
2. While some states may argue that external events changed or that a member state did not uphold its end of the bargain, in the strictest sense of the word, one of the parties has reneged on its promises. While finger-pointing may occur, if the document does not contain so-called "escape clauses" they can readily point to justify their exit, other actors are likely to see the state extricating itself from an alliance obligation in a poor light. The topic of reputation and its effect on future alliance formation is covered more thoroughly in Chapter 5.

3. Note that hypotheses explicitly say "fully/partially secret" to minimize wordiness. I expect there to be clear distinctions between fully and partially secret alliances. Therefore, finding significance for only one type of secret alliance but not the other type of secret alliance does not mean the hypothesis is rejected.
4. This unit of analysis is appropriate here because none of my questions are inherently tied to questions of a dyadic or dyadic yearly nature. Second, the argument regarding institutionalization is best viewed at the member level rather than at the individual dyadic level. Finally, the same can be said of the termination.

4. Let's just be friends: secret alliances and political similarity

A core question in the alliance literature is whether alliances occur between "like-minded" states. In other words, do states ally with states that share political similarity? Alternatively, might secret alliances be "one-off" events based on transactional interests? Regime type has often served as a proxy for similarity of interests, at least among democracies. While the literature has frequently (though not always) demonstrated that democracies are more likely to ally with one another (Gibler and Wolford 2006; Lai and Reiter 2000; Siverson and Emmons 1991), no research has yet addressed if secret alliances are more or less likely to occur between similar or dissimilar states. This is a crucial question because it helps to identify causal mechanisms that might lead a state to favor a secret alliance over a public one.

The Molotov–Ribbentrop Pact between Nazi Germany and the Soviet Union in 1939 serves as a compelling case study. Despite their profound ideological differences, the two states found common ground, culminating in an economic agreement in the spring of 1939 (Johnson 2021)—a crucial precursor to their later political agreement. Similarly, the rapprochement between Black-controlled Swaziland and White-controlled South Africa demonstrates South Africa's success in securing cooperation from a neighboring African state on a major political issue. In contrast, France and the United Kingdom shared considerable political similarity during the Protocol of Sèvres, yet their partnership with Israel, a relatively unknown entity at the time, was quite different. Given Israel's precarious security situation, formal alliances with other states may be less frequent than its security needs would dictate. This might lead to a bias in measures of alliance affinity against Israel, given its increased reliance on informal and secret agreements.

This chapter investigates the political similarity of secret alliance makers. Specifically, it examines the following questions: Are secret alliances more likely to form between states with low levels of alliance similarity? Are there meaningful differences between fully secret and partially secret alliances? Given the nature of the goods exchanged in secret alliances (Chapter 2) and the documented linkages between secret alliance partners, I propose that an inverse relationship exists between political similarity and the propensity for states to negotiate secret alliances.

LITERATURE

The decision to form an alliance is not solely determined by a single factor but rather is a complex calculation involving several key considerations: the nature of the threat, the availability of potential partners, the combination of capabilities offered by potential allies, and the nature of the commitments made. A compelling example of these incentives is the Soviet Union's decision to ally with Nazi Germany in 1939. While the Soviets were both concerned about the growing power of Germany and incentivized to spread communism to other states (Moorhouse 2014, p. 15), the USSR needed allies to accomplish both of these goals. While concerned about Germany's growing power and motivated to expand communism (Moorhouse 2014), the Soviets needed allies. In fact, the Soviets had been actively and publicly pursuing alliances with both the United Kingdom and France as early as April 1939 (Hoover Institution 2024; Kotkin 2017; Roberts 1989). However, the distance from the USSR coupled with their unwillingness to offer iron-clad security guarantees meant that the Soviets, faced with their own two-front problem between Japan and Germany, decided to ally with the Nazis (Roberts 1989, p. 136). This begs the question: Why might two publicly avowed enemies form an alliance and what does this say about scholars' measures and understanding of political similarity?

The decision to ally with another state depends upon both need (demand) and available partners (supply). One of the first metrics in assessing the supply of an alliance partner is determining another state's willingness to cooperate. Several factors might preclude a state from being considered as a potential ally: it may pose a direct security threat, it may have an alliance with a security threat, it may be unwilling to antagonize another state, it may have cultural, religious, or historical ties with an opposing state or weak ties with the alliance seeker, it may not possess the necessary capabilities, or it may be geographically distant. Furthermore, a state's prior reputation and its record of upholding commitments are also crucial considerations (Chapter 5). Before reputation is even a factor, one must consider how politically similar two potential alliance partners are with one another. After all, if states are politically dissimilar, are the security threats facing them sufficient to overcome this political dissimilarity? Are the potential allies aligned politically? If not, what factors might drive them to form an alliance?

Measuring Political Similarity

Measuring political similarity initially seems straightforward, but the literature reveals considerable debate about appropriate statistical measures and the observational building blocks for such measures. In terms of statistical measures, the debates have centered around which statistical methods offer the best evidence of what "true" political similarity looks like. Critics have argued that commonly used measures introduce bias or fail to accurately weight values based on the actors' assessments of the relationship's significance. Additionally, other scholars have debated whether proxy variables such as alliance alignment or United Nations voting scores are the best indicators of political similarity.

Altfeld and Bueno de Mesquita (1979) propose that analyzing the "thickness" of a state's alliance portfolio reveals its security preferences and its political similarity to other states. They utilize tau-b (derived from a 1938 measure) to gauge the strength of association between left-hand and right-hand variables (Altfeld and Bueno de Mesquita 1979, p. 101) and then call this "political similarity." This approach assumes that alliance data are ordinal, with ordering running from the lowest level of commitment to the highest level of commitment. A defensive alliance represents the strongest commitment, while the presence of no alliance tie is the lowest level of commitment. They argue that states are more inclined to ally with states sharing similar policy preferences, though they also account for the potential costs and benefits from a given alliance and the potential consequences from a defeat. This measure would go on to be utilized in a variety of studies purporting to measure political similarity between states (e.g., see Altfeld 1984; Altfeld and Paik 1986; Berkowitz 1983; Lalman and Newman 1991).

However, Signorino and Ritter (1999) challenge the validity of the tau-b approach as a measure of similarity, arguing that while tau-b is suitable for ranked data, it is inappropriate for measuring similarity because it focuses on the *order* of alliances rather than the *type* of alliances. They instead seek "to measure the extent to which states *I* and *J* have the same type of alliance commitments to each of the individual members of the international system" (Signorino and Ritter 1999, p. 121; see also Bennett and Stam 2000, p. 370). This critique gains significance when considered alongside Leeds's (2003) argument, published just four years later, that alliance type significantly influences the probabilities of war or peace. For them, it is the *nature* of what states promise to one another that matters more than the fact that they hold an alliance with another state. Signorino and Ritter's criticism is that there are distinct differences between the value of a defensive alliance versus, say, a neutrality pact. For example, a defensive agreement promises more to an ally than a neutrality pact does, as neutrality and consultation pacts represent the weakest forms of alliances (Chiba and Johnson 2022, p. 2). States with multiple overlapping neutrality or nonaggression pacts with other states may appear to be closer politically according to the tau-b measure than they do in an approach that rank-order weights the level of commitments between states. Such an approach directly addresses what is actually promised in the alliances. In other words, tau-b is an insufficient measure of the strength of political similarity because it does not weight the value of different types of alliance commitments appropriately. In effect, Signorino and Ritter (1999) treat alliance data as ordinal rather than nominal data. Bennett and Rupert (2003) later validate the S-score approach, documenting significant differences existing between the tau-b measures and Signorino and Ritter's (1999) approach. They maintain that tau-b measures *association* but not *similarity*. They find that the S-score approach strengthens Bueno de Mesquita and Lalman's (1992) conclusions and resolve unusual findings in Bennett and Stam's (2000) work.

Häge (2011) strongly criticizes Signorino and Ritter's (1999) operationalization, identifying methodological flaws and implausible results. One example that he gives is that the original S-score suggests that the United Kingdom and China were more closely aligned than the United Kingdom and the United States during much of the Cold War, a finding that contradicts the widely accepted "special relationship" between the United States and the United Kingdom (Andrews 2005; Reynolds 1985; Wallace and Phillips 2009). Häge argues that the S-score measure is corrupted by observations where states are not incentivized to form alliances (i.e., "non-events") or when states have different propensities to form alliances. Häge (2011) suggests that the geographic, political, historical, and cultural proximity between the United States and Canada might render a formal alliance unnecessary, even in the absence of NATO, as an attack on Canada would effectively be considered an attack on the United States. After all, do "brothers" really need an alliance if blood truly is thicker than water? Similarly, one state within a region might be inclined to make numerous alliances with other states. However, a neighboring state that does not ally with any other state would be portrayed by this measure as politically dissimilar because it refrains from the behavior altogether. In fact, this is more common than not, as alliance-making remains a relatively rare event in international relations. Prominent cases such as Austria after World War II, which is surrounded by NATO members and neutral Switzerland and Liechtenstein, are indicative of the absence of alliance ties because there simply is no need for an alliance.

As an alternative to this S-score approach, Häge advocates for Scott's π and Cohen's κ as more appropriate measures of political similarity. His concerns largely stem from his understanding of alliance data being nominal rather than ordinal, which is a departure from previous approaches. Scott's π is derived from Scott's (1955) measure of inter-observer agreement in survey experiments in nominal scale data. In data where promises can vary greatly, multiple independent coders analyze the data and keep track of the differences between the coders, allowing for a measure of reliability of confidence in any single observation. However, Scott's π assumes that coders assign values equally across categories by chance, which can create bias and inaccurate measurements if those values are not equally distributed.

Cohen's κ, on the other hand, is derived from Cohen's (1960) approach to dealing with nominal data. Again, reliability of the coding is of the utmost concern for this measure. Cohen's (1960) example assumes in decisions regarding nominal categories: (1) units are independent of one another; (2) "categories of the nominal scale are independent, mutually exclusive, and exhaustive"; (3) judges (coders) operate independently (p. 38). Scores of agreement between the ranking of categories are then determined to measure the confidence in the quality of the coding. These scores may range from −1 to 1 and the score is generally considered more robust than Scott's π because it accounts for the possibility of an agreement occurring by chance and corrects for it.

Häge (2011) argues that these measures are preferable, given that they are chance-corrected agreement indices. In fact, one of their major appeals is that they adjust for the low density of foreign policy ties in the international system, relative to the number of potential pairs of state alliances and for when different states may have different propensities to form alliances in the first place. This makes them more accurate measures of political similarity because they consider states' different roles in international relations.

Other scholars attempt to measure political similarity without relying on alliance data and ranked measures of commitment. For instance, Simon and Gartzke (1996) measure political similarity between states by utilizing United Nations voting scores and claim that the decision to seek an alliance is driven first by security concerns and then the selection of which partner can provide that security. However, they acknowledge the role of economic gains from trade in mitigating outstanding security issues. Gartzke (1998) similarly uses United Nations voting data to explain the lack of conflict between democratic states, finding that political alignment (measured through United Nation voting affinity) rather than regime type accounts for this phenomenon. Other scholars, though, are reticent to utilize United Nations voting scores to assess political similarity, claiming they are not independent of interests and what they often seek to measure in the dependent variable (Lai and Reiter 2000).

The use of United Nations voting scores to identify blocs and gauge the strength of dyadic relationships has a long history, tracing back to early studies of conflict processes (e.g., Ball 1951; Hovet 1960; Lijphart 1963; Manno 1966; Newcombe, Ross, and Newcombe 1970; Russett 1966). Scholars have employed United Nations voting scores to study bloc formation, trade and foreign policy compliance (Morrow, Siverson, and Tabares 1998; Richardson and Kegley 1980), the foreign policies of dependent states (Moon 1983), vote buying and roll call votes (Carter and Stone 2015), votes on Israel/Palestine issues (Becker et al. 2015; Mandler and Lutmar 2021), vote buying (Eldar 2008; Woo and Chung 2017) voting patterns in the United Nations Human Rights Council (Hug and Lukács 2014), and the effect of IMF and World Bank loans on United Nations voting patterns (Dreher and Sturm 2012).

The logic of using United Nations voting scores rests on the idea that states publicly stake out their positions on given issues. However, there are several limitations to using United Nations voting scores. The most obvious of these is that the United Nations has only existed since 1945.[1] States might be unwilling to vote publicly in a manner that could offend an ally or other state, leading to votes that do not reflect their true preferences. Given that these votes are non-binding, these states have no real "skin in the game." Another concern is that of the vote buying literature (Dreher and Sturm 2012; Dreher et al. 2012; Vreeland 2019; Vreeland and Dreher 2014; Woo and Chung 2017) which suggests that voting scores are corrupted by political issues and otherwise do not reveal a state's true preferences. While United Nations voting scores offer valuable insights into various questions, their utility as a measure of political similarity is more tenuous than that of other measures.

Nonetheless, similarity remains a useful concept for understanding how states converge or diverge in international politics. What is problematic is the way in which scholars have operationalized these assumptions. With an abstract concept such as political similarity, there are few good options.

Alliances and Political Similarity

A core assumption in alliance studies is that states are more likely to ally with states sharing similar regime types, implying that regime type might serve as a proxy measure for political similarity. However, this is a rather crude measure. Siverson and Emmons (1991) find that democracies were more likely to ally between 1946 and 1965, though not during other historical periods. Conversely, Simon and Gartzke (1996) argue that *dis*similar regimes tend to co-ally, a claim supported by Werner and Lemke (1997). Werner and Lemke (1997) are particularly critical of one-dimensional measures of political similarity, such as regime type, arguing that similarity may vary along several important dimensions. Political similarity also appears to matter for aid allocation (Neumayer 2003) and reduces incentives for harboring terrorists (Bapat 2007). Regime type, then, appears to not be a sufficient measure for political similarity and alliance formation.

Lai and Reiter (2000) offer a compelling framework for understanding alliance formation. They find that post-1945, both democracies and autocracies are more likely to ally with similar regime types but neither at a greater rate than the other. They also find that a common culture, learning (prior alliance experience), distance, and the level of threat increase alliance ties, while trade is no more or less likely to result in an alliance.[2] Lai and Reiter (2000) confirm that similar regimes were less likely to ally prior to World War II, but that democracies co-ally more often during the Cold War (p. 777).

Gibler and Wolford (2006) invert this process, arguing that defensive alliances precede political similarity (regime type) and provide an avenue for states to democratize, as external security threats recede. Other scholars claim that "trade follows the flag," with growing strength and political similarity emerging from mutual security interests (Long 2003). Chen (2021) argues that trade with a state's allies promotes peace and "extended dependence." Chiba, Johnson, and Leeds (2015) argue that "similarity of interests should thus be negatively related to the probability states form a consultation pact rather than a pact explicitly requiring active assistance" (p. 974).

For Gartzke and Gleditsch (2004), alliance design and the level of commitments specifically affects reliability. Intuitively, this implies that tau-b is not an accurate measure of reliability or the strength of ties between states. This is because the nature of what is promised in an alliance directly affects the reliability of allies in fulfilling those agreements. Instead, a score that more directly accounts for the nature of a state's promises is preferable to a measure that ignores level of commitment.

Using alliance data to measure political similarity offers several advantages over United Nations voting scores. First, alliance data have a much longer temporal availability. Second, states signing agreements with other states are indicating that they do have "skin in the game" and are credibly signaling to other states the importance of a relationship with an ally. However, of course, some states may make secret alliances, which means that the signaling value is inherently lost, creating an informational asymmetry (Bas and Schub 2016). Since this affects a relatively small proportion of agreements, it is unlikely such cases would play an outsized role. A third and related advantage is that alliances specifically deal with security-related issues ("Alliance Treaty Obligations and Provisions" (ATOP) Codebook 2022), which are the most salient of issues for states. As an example, the Germans and Soviets negotiated the Molotov–Ribbentrop Pact in August 1939. However, earlier agreements made in the spring of 1939 do not count as alliances because they do not expressly address security issues. Though such an agreement was a necessary precursor to the political agreement that occurred between Molotov and Ribbentrop, it is still not counted as a security agreement.

The incentive to ally is built upon the supposition that (1) such an alliance will deter an opposing state; (2) in the case of deterrence failure, the ally will be willing and able to fight against an opponent. But perhaps the most important justification for using alliances to measure political similarity is that alliances are relatively rare events, with states forming them only for dire security-related issues. As such, they indicate the most important issues and alignments for states and act as a better proxy variable of political similarity than alternative measures such as United Nations voting scores.

Some scholars claim that alliances reflect "a community of interests for [their] foundation" (Chu, Ko, and Liu 2021;Morgenthau 1985, p. 194). This shared interest and alignment on political issues allow leaders to leverage interests or shared values to shape public opinion regarding alliances (Chu, Ko, and Liu 2021). They proceed by arguing that even realists such as Morgenthau acknowledge that "alliances form based on common material interests, ideological solidarity, or both" (Chu, Ko, and Liu 2021, p. 485). They claim that if states emphasize the ties that bind states together and shared values, they will increase public opinion for two reasons: (1) shared values may generate "we-ness"; (2) they provide moral foundations for supporting an ally.

The concept of "we-ness" is also important for signaling commitment. "Patron" states can reassure "clients" through communicative actions based on shared values and common interests between the two states (Sukin and Lanoszka 2024). To measure shared values, Sukin and Lanoszka (2024) utilize regime type, the presence of common norms and ideologies measuring state rhetoric to identify political similarity. Wolford and Ritter (2016) question this notion of unity between allies, claiming that coalitions are more likely to be formed by leaders facing lower political security.[3]

However, in the context of secret alliances, the concept of "we-ness" and political affinity is largely irrelevant, except arguably in partially secret alliances precisely because the alliance itself is unobservable. For instance, the Soviets and Nazis had difficulty convincing audiences that their rapprochement in August 1939 was in their best interests. While not inherently problematic for autocratic regimes, scholars do note that some Nazi party members resigned their membership by throwing their party pins at Munich's Brown House, the party headquarters (Moorhouse 2014, p. 128). The Soviets also saw consternation among communist groups in the West, with Stalin going so far as having Soviet maps issued containing the signatures of Ribbentrop and Stalin to demonstrate his seal of approval (Moorhouse 2014, p. 41).

This suggests a difference between the need for public displays of similarity in public alliances and the need for political alignment in secret alliances. It is to this topic which I now turn.

THEORY

Given that secret alliances are primarily formed to allocate the division of some good (Chapter 2), they are likely to be more transactional rather than a long-term convergence of interests. In democracies, they can be useful when the alliance is formed with a state that is otherwise politically unacceptable to the domestic public. However, given the growing international aversion to secret diplomacy since the World Wars, this explanation requires further scrutiny.

The Molotov–Ribbentrop Pact exemplifies the potential for alliances between ideologically disparate states. Both states were extreme forms of totalitarian regimes, with Nazi Germany embracing national socialism, while the Soviet Union became the world's first communist state. The political alignments of both states throughout the 1930s reflect this dissimilarity. Between Hitler's rise to power in 1933 and the Nazi invasion of the Soviet Union in June 1941, the Soviets signed twelve alliances, and Germany signed ten. Of course, one of these was between the Soviets and Nazis. And of the other eleven and ten respective alliances, there were eight cases of alliances between the USSR and Germany and those states from 1933 to 1941. However, three of these included the Baltic states, which were imposed "alliances," while many others did not overlap or did not concern the same issues or relegate the states to the same degree of promises to one another.[4]

As established in Chapter 3, secret alliances are less likely to feature formalized institutions, less likely to mention adding future members, less likely to specify a duration, and more likely to involve military-to-military coordination. This is because these secret agreements are more likely to be transactional, reducing the need for public-facing institutions to ensure that the alliance endures. Since they are transactional, they are less likely to discuss adding other states and the timeframe in which the objective of the secret alliance is to be obtained. However, given the material nature of the objective, military-to-military coordination is more likely to be mentioned. This was evident in all three of the secret alliances detailed in Chapters 6–8. The Molotov–Ribbentrop Pact contained provisions for joint border commissions, usually staffed by NKVD and Gestapo representatives. The Protocol of Sèvres was explicitly structured to coordinate military actions against Egypt. And while the South Africa–Swaziland pact did not contain provisions for military-to-military contact, it necessitated significant cooperation between the two states' militaries in targeting rebel groups such as the African National Congress.

Given the transactional nature of secret alliances and the lack of institutional mechanisms to guarantee their longevity or expansion, one might initially assume that they are more likely to form between states exhibiting high degrees of political similarity. While convergent security interests are likely to increase the probability of alliance formation in public alliances, this is less likely in secret alliances. As Chiba, Johnson, and Leeds (2015) note, democracies are more likely to carefully design alliances so that they do not over-expose themselves to the risks that come with failing to fulfill an agreement (see also Gartzke and Gleditsch 2004). In a similar fashion, secret alliances are designed in such a way as to impose consequences on states that do not fulfill their agreements.

The inherent illicit nature of a secret alliance means that states have "blackmail" capability against their alliance partner built into the secret alliance, making secret alliances more likely to be fulfilled and less likely to terminate irregularly (Chapter 3) than in public alliances. This implied "blackmail" built into secret alliances helps states overcome the long-term issue convergence necessary for public alliances to be negotiated. Because each signatory knows that what they are doing would be reprehensible if made public, they are more likely to overcome political disagreements between the contracting parties because of the threat of damage to their public and private reputations and the loss of the good over which the alliance was made in the first place. Ben-Gurion's personal involvement in carrying the Israeli copy of the Sèvres treaty (Bar-On 2006, p. 185) exemplifies this dynamic.

As has been detailed elsewhere in this book, this was the reaction of British Prime Minister Anthony Eden when he learned of the formal documentation of the secret alliance made at Sèvres in October 1956 with France and Israel. Upon discovering that formal documents existed, Eden dispatched his foreign minister, Selwyn Lloyd, back to Paris to intercept the other copies and destroy them (Troen 1996). It is also reported that Eden personally destroyed the British copy because he was shocked to learn it had been written down (Bar-On 2006;Beck 2009). Eden had correctly predicted that the existence of such documents meant that plausible deniability was not possible if the other signatories possessed physical copies of the treaties. However, implicit in this assumption is that Eden trusted his allies France and Israel enough to have no need for a physical alliance document. However, clearly France and especially Israel did not trust the British enough to relinquish their copies.

However, the Nazis and Soviets clearly did not trust one another when they signed the Molotov–Ribbentrop Pact. While many states and the public anticipated secret protocols accompanying the August 1939 agreement, definitive proof was not uncovered until the end of World War II. Germany's physical copy of the pact had been destroyed during a bombing raid during the war (Dreifelds 1999, pp. 34–5), though microfiche copies of the agreement remained intact and were not destroyed by Nazi Foreign Office officials as instructed. These were then found by the Exploitation German Archives group of the State Department. However, the Soviet copy, the only original remaining copy, was not discovered until after the Soviet Union dissolved ("Archives Yield Soviet-German Pact" 1992). The existence of the physical document serves as a reminder of how little the two states trusted one another. As Stephen Kotkin points out, the public facing declaration of the agreement was a nonaggression pact, which are only negotiated between erstwhile enemies, not friends (Hoover Institution 2024).

Given the transactional nature of these agreements and the lack of strong institutional constraints on the signatories, the existence of formal documentation and the potential threat of losing the desired good incentivize states to form secret alliances even in the absence of the political convergence and similarity needed for public alliances. This leads me to propose two hypotheses related to political similarity:

H1: States with a high degree of political similarity will be less likely to make any type of secret alliances with one another.

H2: States with a high degree of political similarity will be least likely to make a fully secret alliance with one another.

However, given the literature covered above, there exist strong opinions in how political similarity is measured. One of the most obvious ways in which to obtain a rough approximation of political similarity is whether two states have been on the same side of a dispute against another state. While this is only a proxy measure of similarity, it does show the early stages of how states may begin to converge over security-related issues without becoming truly "politically similar" states. This lesser degree of political similarity is likely to illustrate when states find themselves on the same side of salient political issues. For Alley (2023, p. 1547), a shared threat is a key factor driving political convergence.

Disputes, representing a more frequent form of conflict than war, offer a more substantial measure of conflict between states. War, in fact, is a relatively rare event for states. For instance, King and Zeng (2001b, p. 138) find that in all dyads between World War II and the turn of the century, only 0.3 percent of states were at war. Disputes, in contrast, are a much more common occurrence and represent an opportunity to understand where states fall on important security-related issues. Logically, states that are on the same side of a dispute within a given timeframe will be more likely to have some agreement regarding security-related issues. This leads me to propose:

H3: States that have been on the same side of a MID in the previous ten years are more likely to sign a secret agreement with one another.

Next, given Chiba, Johnson, and Leeds's (2015) claim that democracies, in particular, are more likely to design agreements more carefully, one must also think about the degree of promises states make to one another. While some research suggests that alliances increase the probability of conflict (Siverson and Starr 1991; Vasquez 2009), other scholars note that conflict probability is inherently tied to the *nature* (Leeds 2003) of what alliance promises. In fact, this was very much the basis of the ATOP project. The depth of this project provides more fine-grained analysis of each alliance text, allowing scholars to more carefully measure the degree of commitment between states. While Leeds et al. (2002) note that some 53 percent of agreements contain a mix of different commitments ("Alliance Treaty Obligations and Provisions (ATOP) Codebook" 2022, p. 11), this does not mean that they are mutually exclusive. For instance, a state can promise to be both a defensive ally of another state as well as consult their ally. While these types of alliances are most likely to be the strongest, since they require states to both come to the defense of and consult with another state, it is not clear there is enough richness within the data to analyze all alliance types as if they were mutually exclusive.

The most obviously high level of alliance commitment is the defensive alliance. Given that defensive alliances promise to come to the defense of an ally, the degree of commitment and risk is greatest. This is because states making such alliances know that they will be at a disadvantage because if a defensive alliance is activated, they will be responding to the actions of an aggressor. Next, offensive alliances offer higher commitment because the nature of what is promised in such commitments often entails greater risk than other forms of alliances but since offensive alliances are less likely to be in response to another state's direct military actions, offensive alliances offer slightly less risk than a defensive alliance. Next, both neutrality and nonaggression pacts should represent much less obligation between the states than either offensive or defensive pacts. While the degree of difference between the nuance of nonaggression and neutrality may not be self-evident, both are likely to contain a higher degree of commitments than consultation agreements. Consultative alliances are likely to be the weakest, as they merely promise that some form of consultation will be required between signatories. It does not compel them to action. That NATO alliance, in fact, does mention consultation between signatories before committing the alliance to enact the defense provisions. And it is because of the concern that due to the increased likelihood of consultative agreements accompanying defensive alliances, states will be more likely to be forced to come to an ally's defense. In effect, then, consultation will be "washed" out of the sample. Instead, I am more concerned with "pure" consultative agreements that place no other requirements on signatories.

Given that "pure" consultative alliances are the weakest form of an alliance tie, I argue that consultative alliances are less likely in secret alliances because the nature of what is promised in purely consultative alliances is less problematic than the promises made in other types of alliances. In fact, a cursory glance of the incident level of alliances indicates that of the 83 purely consultative alliances, only seven are secret agreements. Thus, roughly 8 percent of purely consultative agreements are secret agreements. And given that secret alliances are more likely to concern themselves with a provision of a good (Chapter 2), it is unlikely that discussion of goods would occur within a consultative agreement. This leads me to propose:

> *H4: True consultative alliances are less likely to be secret alliances than public alliances.*

RESEARCH DESIGN

To answer these questions, I utilize a directed dyadic country year approach on all states that made an alliance from 1816 to 2016 in the first year of observation. This mimics the approach used by scholars elsewhere (Lai and Reiter 2000) in their study of alliance formation. Given that secret alliances are driven by the provision of a good at the expense of another (Chapter 2) and the consistent findings throughout this book and by scholars elsewhere, a directed dyadic design for the year an alliance is negotiated is appropriate. This allows for an analysis of the individual and joint effects of variables on a state's decision to seek an alliance.

While the analysis below is not a replication of Lai and Reiter's (2000) work, their work provides a useful framework for investigating the determinants of alliance similarity. However, in some cases, the data Lai and Reiter (2000) utilize are outdated, or have not been updated in decades. Given the questions these scholars examine, it provides a comparable framework of analysis to my own inquiries regarding secret alliances. In particular, their operationalizations of threat do an excellent job in measuring what external security threats there are to each state and captures the security relationship between those threats and the other state in the dyad. Notably, however, I do not rely on all possible state combinations in the international system. Instead, I rely on those cases where states definitively allied with one another. In other words, my analysis is concerned not with why a state chooses to make an alliance. Instead, my question is: Why does a state choose to make a formal secret alliance rather than a formal public alliance? My sample, then, is not the universe of every possible state combination.[5] My sample is, instead, the incidence of cases where alliances were made. From this, I can determine what variables affect a state's willingness to make a secret alliance.

In some cases, however, I do not utilize their variables due to lack of availability or appropriateness. For instance, the cultural variable is no longer hosted by the Correlates of War, or is not relevant to my line of inquiry. As such, in a few instances noted below, I rely upon alternative operationalizations or do not include such variables. For instance, I do not include the "learning" variable in this analysis. While an interesting potential explanation of alliance formation and the subject of valuable research (Reiter 1996), I do not include it in my analyses, given it is not a primary variable of interest or "standard" variable within conflict research.

Given concerns regarding the accuracy and potential bias in trade and GDP data (International Monetary Fund 1987; Mügge 2023) particularly for observations prior to 1950, these variables were also excluded from this analysis. This obviously has major effects on the analysis of secret formal alliances, as many of those observations fall within this earlier period. While trade has been established as an important link between states and the decision to ally (Gartzke 1998;Lai and Reiter 2000; Simon and Gartzke 1996), this data's limitations preclude its inclusion in this analysis. While some scholars maintain that this can lead to omitted variable bias, this is an often-overstated concern.[6]

An interesting discussion on political relevancy is also necessary here, as it mirrors the discussion regarding the sample of cases in this chapter. A significant body of scholarship discusses the appropriateness of utilizing politically relevant dyads or all dyads in analyses of conflict processes (Benson 2005; Cohen 1994; Green, Kim, and Yoon 2003; Erikson, Pinto, and Rader 2014; Minhas et al. 2022; Poast 2023; Lemke 1995; Siverson and Starr 1991; Starr 1978; Weede 1976; Werner and Lemke 1997; Xiang 2010). Some have maintained that in examining potential state pairs in the international system, scholars should only examine those cases where one is a major power or they are contiguous with one another. This is how political relevancy is often operationalized.

In the same way, it is difficult to imagine a world in which, say, Indonesia has a need for an alliance with Iceland. Thus, including every potential pair of states as potential alliance partners is problematic. We could, instead, build a dataset that only examines those alliances that were made between politically relevant states. However, this excludes an important and interesting subset of cases where neither state is a major power or contiguous with one another. For instance, Signorino and Ritter (1999, p. 124) do offer compelling methodological reasons why including all potential state pairs as possible allies is problematic. However, some scholars do examine all possible cases of state pairs, which drastically increases the sample size.

Given the relative paucity of secret alliances (especially partially secret alliances), a directed dyadic dataset of all possible state pairs from 1816 to 2016 yields a sample size of 1,987,950 cases, of which only 53,814 are politically relevant (less than 3 percent). Of this directed dyadic dataset, there are only 6328 observations of alliances and 178 secret alliance observations. This massive skew makes investigation of self-selection behavior (for both any type of alliance and secret alliances) in such a large sample size inherently difficult and an extremely rare event. Instead, a more appropriate approach for the questions addressed here is to direct my questions not to the sample of either all

Table 4.1   Variables

Dependent Variable	Coding
Secret Alliance	"0" for public alliances, "1" for secret
Public/Partially/Fully Secret	"0" for public alliances, "1" for partially secret, "2" for fully secret
Independent Variables	
Irregular Termination	"1" if irregular termination, "0" if regular
Bilateral Alliance	"1" if alliance is bilateral, "0" otherwise
Major Power	"1" if state is a major power
CINC	Composite Index of National Capabilities
Democracy	"1" if Polity score>=6
Major Power Count	Count of the major power states in international system Defense
Offense	"1" if an offensive alliance
Neutrality	"1" if a neutrality alliance
Nonaggression	"1" if a nonaggression alliance
Consultation	"1" if a consultation alliance
World War I dummy	"1" if before 1914

possible state pairs or all politically relevant state pairs (which further shrinks the alliance sample size to 1308 observations of alliance-making states) but to examine the self-selection behavior itself. In other words, why might a state choose to make a secret alliance instead of a public alliance and what role does political similarity play in that decision-making?

DEPENDENT VARIABLE

Alliance Type

Since I am primarily explaining the effects of similarity on determining alliance formation in H1 and H2, particularly secret alliance formation, I utilize the ATOP data to determine which pairs of states have alliances each year and the type (public/secret). To do this, I identify each alliance pair in the original year of observation and match these observations with their respective dyads. For example, the United States and the United Kingdom signed the NATO agreement in 1949 (along with other states). For the observation of the US–UK and UK–US in 1949, I note this as the initial year of an alliance and do not include each subsequent year for the dyadic pair unless they make a separate alliance with one another. In the rare event that a dyad agrees to more than one alliance each year, the values are collapsed into one observation. For instance, France and the United Kingdom made three separate alliances with one another in 1854 during the Crimean War

(ATOP IDs 1160, 1165, and 1180). Rather than generate six separate observations for the UK/France and France/UK dyads for 1854, I simply collapse these values together, as the observations are not actually independent of one another. As an example, 1160 and 1180 were defensive and consultative alliances, whereas 1165 was an offensive alliance. Thus, 1854 would count as a defensive, offensive, and consultative alliance for both dyadic country years.

To account for the degree of alliance/secret alliance, I take two approaches. First, I code as "0" those states making a public alliance within the dyad and then code as "1" those states that make any secret agreement with the dyadic pair. Those states making no alliance in a year are coded as missing and are dropped from the sample. For the next set of models, I code as "0" those states that make a public alliance with the dyadic partner, "1" for a partially secret alliance, and "2" for a fully secret alliance in the dyad.

Such an approach allows for the distinction between public and private alliance agreements and compares them against one another without the "noise" from the majority of dyads that have no alliance made within a given year. By collapsing observations that make more than one alliance each year into a single observation rather than a separate observation for each alliance negotiated between the states in a given year, I am taking into account the collective relationship of a state in that year rather than double-counting the few dyads that do have repeat alliances in a given year. The decision to code this variable for the year of negotiation/ratification helps assuage concerns about inflating the values of those states that do make alliances and those alliances that endure across many years or have many different members. And by dropping observations from the total possible sample of every state in the international system in a given year, I am concerning myself only with the dyads where states actually did make an agreement with one another in a given year.

INDEPENDENT VARIABLES

Alliance Portfolio Similarity

To assess the above hypotheses, I utilize a variety of different measurements provided by the ATOP project to assess similarity. These include an unweighted version of S-scores, weighted S-scores, Scott's π, and Cohen's κ. Such an approach is useful because it provides a variety of measures to more fully assess states' relationships with one another. Each of these measures has its advantages and disadvantages, so rather than picking a single measure, I utilize all four measures and leave the judgment call as to which is the "better" operationalization up to the reader. For more detail on the relative differences between the same observations using different similarity measures, see Häge (2011, p. 288).

First, I utilize ATOP's unweighted and weighted S-score approach (Chiba, Johnson, and Leeds 2015). While there is a rich history regarding what measures best indicate the degree of affinity between states (e.g., see Gartzke 1998; Lai and Reiter 2000; Signorino and Ritter 1999), I do not focus heavily on that literature here. While assessing a state's true preferences and issue alignment is fraught with both methodological and theoretical concerns, one must make a judgment call based on the literature and "best" available data to determine the level of unobservable abstract concepts such as "affinity." Issue alignment, often calculated with tools such as United Nations voting scores (e.g., Gartzke 1998), is one approach. Another approach that arguably has greater consequences in security-related areas is alliance portfolio similarity (Chiba, Johnson, and Leeds 2015). While not ideal, this operationalization does allow scholars to measure the degree to which two states share overlapping security partnerships with one another. This data are available in both weighted and unweighted scores.[7] Weighted scores are calculated with the National Material Capabilities index (Singer 1988; Singer, Bremer, and Stuckey 2012). However, in using this approach as my primary independent variables, one immediately runs into a methodological concern. Since I am measuring the degree to which secret alliances occur between "friends" with similar interests, this is inherently tied to a state's alliance portfolio. To deal with this methodological concern and the assumed independence between left- and right-sided variables, I add one year to each observation in the similarity score dataset. This approach is similar to the approach used by Chiba, Johnson, and Leeds (2015). This allows me to assess the level of similarity between two states *before* they ally with one another *prior to* merging it into my base dataset.

These measures are appropriate and use an updated coding scheme originally developed by Signorino and Ritter (1999) to measure affinity between states in security-related issues. While they initially used the COW alliance data, the Chiba, Johnson, and Leeds (2015) dataset utilizes the updated ATOP dataset (Leeds, Ritter, Mitchell, and Long 2002). This dataset has greater depth and coverage, as well as other variables that characterize and provide more information regarding alliances. Perhaps most importantly, it provides a distinction between public, partially secret, and fully secret agreements. Likewise, it makes the distinction between consultative, nonaggression, neutrality, offensive, and defensive alliances. While not all agreements have the same effect (e.g., see Leeds 2003), they do provide a similar degree of commitment across these different types of pacts. In fact, they lend themselves well to the level of commitment (in ascending order) that states are willing to provide to their allies.

Next, I also utilize Scott's π. This score was developed by Scott (1955, p. 321) to measure "the extent of inter-observer agreement" in survey research and has been accepted by scholars as a way to measure the degree of ties between two groups. Häge (2011) notes the utility of this measure, claiming that Scott's π is an appropriate measure of the strength of ties between two states.[8] One advantage of Scott's π is that the estimate takes into account that distributions may symmetrically balance.

Next, I utilize Cohen's κ, which was originally developed by Cohen (1960) to measure the degree of ties between two entities. For Häge, the value of Cohen's κ is that it "assumes that chance dissimilarity is equal to the sum of the variability in the two dyad members' valued tie profiles plus the difference in their means" (1960, p. 299). In any event, it is relatively straightforward to include both measures in one's assessment of the "thickness" of ties between states and their political similarity, along with weighted and unweighted S-scores.

All of these measures have in common that the higher the positive value between the pairs of states, the more politically similar they supposedly are. Thus, there is an ease of interpretation to each of these operationalizations. I take an agnostic approach and report all possible results derived from these four measures of political similarity. This permits the reader to determine which measure they find to be the most convincing.

Joint Democracy

To determine the democratic/autocratic nature of each state within the dyad, I rely upon the Polity IV scores created by Marshall and Gurr (2020). I code as "1" states that have a polity score $>= 6$ for both sides of a dyad. This is consistent with approaches elsewhere (e.g., Bennett and Stam 1996; Jaggers and Gurr 1995; Marshall et al. 2002). Then in the case that both states are democracies, I code those dyads as "1". Non-democratic or mixed dyads are coded as "0", with missing data and interregnums left as missing. This approach is similar to the approaches utilized elsewhere (Alley 2023; Lai and Reiter 2000).

Alliance Type

To account for the varying effects of alliance design type and similarity, I utilize the ATOP variables for defensive, offensive, neutrality, and nonaggression alliances (Leeds, Mitchell, and Long 2002). However, given concerns of the high degree of overlap between consultation and other alliance types, I recode the consultation variable as "1" for alliances that only make consultative agreements and no other promises, such as defensive, offensive, neutrality, or nonaggression.[9] This substantially alters the sample size of those alliances that are considered "pure" consultative agreements, which is the weakest form of an alliance. Substantively at the incident level of alliances, this takes the occurrence down from 49.18 percent of cases (388 alliances) to 10.52 percent of cases (83 alliances).

Threat

To determine the degree of threat faced by states in each dyad, I use the MID v. 5.0 dataset (Palmer et al. 2020). Since states facing threats are more likely to rely on a public-facing alliance to deter opponents, this distinction should be made. I use several approaches consistent with those utilized by Lai and Reiter (2000), among others, such as Chiba, Johnson, and Leeds (2015, p. 974) and Leeds and Savun (2007). First, I create a dummy variable to indicate if state a had a dispute within the prior ten years of the year of observation. Second, to measure the degree of threat faced by the state, I build a count variable of the number of unique disputes in the ten years prior to the year of observation. Third, I build a dummy variable to indicate whether state A and state B were on opposing sides of a MID within the past ten years. Fourth, I build a dummy variable to indicate whether state A and state B were on the same side of a dispute against a third-party state in the prior ten years. While not an ideal measure of similarity, this measure should indicate a state's willingness to be more likely to make a secret alliance with a state that it has previously had experience with. Finally, I also include a dummy variable that indicates if the alliance was made during a time of war, as those types of alliances are likely to be most pressing.

Major Power

To assess whether the dyad contains a major power on either side, I utilize the Correlates of War's major powers dataset (Correlates of War Project 2016). I then merge in these major powers and create a dummy variable to indicate major power presence on either side within the dyad.

CINC Scores

To assess whether more powerful or less powerful states in the international system are more likely to make secret alliances, I include a control for the Composite Index of National Capabilities for state A in the year of observation (Singer 1988; Singer, Bremer, and Stuckey 2012). Rather than build a variable measuring dyadic CINC scores as is often customary in dyadic analysis, I instead rely solely upon state A's CINC score (Johnson, Leeds, and Wu 2015).

Since CINC purports to measure a state's relative share of "power" in the system, it is appropriate to use only state A's score because much of the point of an alliance is to compound one's power. Thus, by measuring only state A's CINC, the reader will have a better understanding of how a state's individual CINC score exerts pressure on a state to ally.

Capital Distance and Contiguity

To measure the distance between capitals, I utilize the "capdist" dataset by Gleditsch (n.d.). Th data measures the great circle distance between capital cities. Next, to account for contiguity, I use the Correlates of War 3.2 dataset (Stinnett et al. 2002). This dataset contains a list of which states share land/river contiguity, among other forms of contiguity. I count as "1" those states that share land/river contiguity with one another and "0" for all other dyads.

Model Specification

Given the varied nature of the dependent variables analyzed here, I utilize ordered logistic regression, logistic models, and rare events logistic regression models. These models correspond to the appropriate dependent variable operationalizations. Rare events logistic models are presented along with logistic models, though the rare events models do not utilize robust standard errors. This approach is consistent with the findings made by King and Zeng (2001a; 2001b).

RESULTS

Before moving on to the substantive results, I provide a brief overview of the data. When utilizing the directed dyadic country year observation for all states that make alliances, this results in 6328 observations. More descriptive statistics may be found in Table A4.1.

In the first set of models in Table 4.2, I look at those observations where the dyadic state pair made an alliance within a given year. This set of models codes public alliances as "0" and "1" for those states making any kind of secret alliance. In this case, logistic regression is used with robust standard errors. Table 4.2 utilizes the same dyadic measure but uses rare events logistic models (Table 4.3). In the final set of models in Table 4.4, states that make a public alliance are coded as "0", partially secret alliances as "1", and fully secret alliances as "2". This then necessitates ordered logistic regression with robust standard errors.

Table 4.2 Political similarity (year prior) and any secret alliances (logistic model)

Variables	1	2	3	4
Scott's π	−.665*** (.251)	-	-	-
Cohen's κ	-	−.709*** (.263)	-	-
Unweighted Similarity	-	-	−.833* (.478)	-
Weighted Similarity	-	-	-	−.334 (.307)
Joint Democracy	−1.231*** (.392)	−1.23*** (.394)	−1.227*** (.383)	−1.249*** (.385)
Any Major	3.1*** (.278)	3.108*** (.278)	3.035*** (.284)	3.023*** (.307)
Capital Distance	0*** (0)	0*** (0)	0*** (0)	0*** (0)
Contiguity	.938*** (.227)	.944*** (.227)	.92*** (.225)	.941*** (.23)
CINC	−1.303 (1.276)	−1.32 (1.275)	−1.07 (1.243)	−1.236 (1.26)
Defensive	−.212 (.333)	−.207 (.335)	−.29 (.332)	−.294 (.339)
Offensive	.524* (.276)	.529* (.276)	.49* (.276)	.533* (.275)
Neutrality	1.684*** (.324)	1.678*** (.323)	1.726*** (.336)	1.714*** (.338)
Nonaggression	−1.912*** (.349)	−1.911*** (.351)	−1.963*** (.342)	−1.991*** (.348)
True Consultation	−.896* (.481)	−.895* (.482)	−.953** (.483)	−.955** (.486)
MID	.71 (.448)	.707 (.448)	.738 (.453)	.718 (.45)
MID Count	−.051*** (.012)	−.051*** (.012)	−.053*** (.012)	−.052*** (.012)
MID A/B	−.031 (.262)	−.032 (.262)	−.005 (.267)	.007 (.265)
MID A/B Same Side	1.116*** (.237)	1.116*** (.237)	1.041*** (.239)	1.017*** (.237)
War	.779*** (.256)	.777*** (.256)	.787*** (.258)	.767*** (.255)
Constant	−4.744*** (.574)	−4.728*** (.576)	−4.175*** (.718)	−4.606*** (.628)
Observations	6074	6074	6074	6074
Pseudo R^2	.504	.505	.502	.501

Note: Robust standard errors are in parentheses, *** $p < .01$, ** $p < .05$, * $p < .1$.

Table 4.3 *Political similarity (year prior) and any secret alliances (rare events model)*

Variables	5	6	7	8
Scott's π	−.65*** (.25)	-	-	-
Cohen's κ	-	−.693*** (.262)	-	-
Unweighted Similarity	-	-	−.837* (.503)	-
Weighted Similarity	-	-	-	−.332 (.289)
Joint Democracy	−01.181*** (.341)	−01.18*** (.341)	−1.176*** (.34)	−1.199*** (.339)
Major Power	3.04*** (.283)	3.048*** (.282)	2.976*** (.288)	2.966*** (.298)
Capital Distance	0*** (0)	0*** (0)	0*** (0)	0*** (0)
Contiguity	.926*** (.22)	.931*** (.22)	.91*** (.219)	.929*** (.221)
CINC	−1.213 (1.423)	−1.23 (1.423)	−.978 (1.411)	−1.143 (1.416)
Defensive	−.198 (.311)	−.193 (.312)	−.277 (.309)	−.281 (.311)
Offensive	.516** (.24)	.52** (.24)	.48** (.241)	.524** (.24)
Neutrality	1.658*** (.288)	1.652*** (.288)	1.699*** (.29)	1.687*** (.29)
Nonaggression	−1.869*** (.342)	−1.868*** (.342)	−1.921*** (.339)	−1.948*** (.339)
True Consultation	−.848* (.468)	−.847* (.468)	−.906* (.467)	−.908* (.468)
MID	.654 (.423)	.65 (.423)	.683 (.422)	.662 (.421)
MID Count	−.049*** (.013)	−.049*** (.013)	−.051*** (.013)	−.05*** (.013)
MID A/B	−.024 (.242)	−.025 (.242)	0 (.243)	.013 (.242)
MID A/B Same Side	1.094*** (.222)	1.094*** (.222)	1.02*** (.22)	.997*** (.218)
War	.754*** (.24)	.752*** (.24)	.764*** (.24)	.744*** (.239)
Constant	−4.642*** (.551)	−4.627*** (.552)	−4.068*** (.689)	−4.504*** (.594)
Observations	6074	6074	6074	6074

Note: Standard errors are in parentheses, *** $p < .01$, ** $p < .05$, * $p < .1$.

Table 4.4 Political similarity (year prior) and fully/partially secret alliances

Variables	9	10	11	12
Scott's π	-.627** (.254)	–	–	–
Cohen's κ	–	-.676** (.268)	–	–
Unweighted Similarity	–	–	-.684 (.473)	–
Weighted Similarity	–	–	–	-.291 (.309)
Joint Democracy	-1.243*** (.399)	-1.24*** (.401)	-1.239*** (.392)	-1.257*** (.394)
Major Power	3.074*** (.273)	3.082*** (.272)	3.023*** (.281)	3.009*** (.305)
Capital Distance	0*** (0)	0*** (0)	0*** (0)	0*** (0)
Contiguity	.951*** (.223)	.956*** (.223)	.932*** (.222)	.947*** (.227)
CINC	-1.316 (1.272)	-1.332 (1.271)	-1.083 (1.236)	-1.231 (1.262)
Defense	-.235 (.341)	-.228 (.343)	-.311 (.341)	-.312 (.347)
Offense	.647** (.268)	.653** (.268)	.622** (.268)	.659** (.267)

Variables	9	10	11	12
Neutrality	1.747***	1.742***	1.785***	1.776***
	(.326)	(.325)	(.337)	(.339)
Nonaggression	−1.932***	−1.928***	−1.984***	−2.005***
	(.343)	(.344)	(.337)	(.344)
True Consultation	−.91*	−.908*	−.962**	−.961**
	(.477)	(.477)	(.479)	(.482)
MID	.709	.705	.736	.716
	(.453)	(.452)	(.457)	(.453)
MID Count	−.051***	−.051***	−.054***	−.053***
	(.012)	(.012)	(.012)	(.012)
MID A/B	−.144	−.144	−.117	−.102
	(.257)	(.257)	(.262)	(.26)
MID A/B Same Side	1.15***	1.152***	1.076***	1.062***
	(.23)	(.231)	(.233)	(.233)
War	.68***	.679***	.682***	.67***
	(.237)	(.237)	(.237)	(.236)
Cut Point 1	4.717***	4.702***	4.27***	4.611***
	(.578)	(.58)	(.726)	(.635)
Cut Point 2	4.998***	4.983***	4.551***	4.892***
	(.581)	(.583)	(.725)	(.635)
Observations	6074	6074	6074	6074
Pseudo R^2	.466	.466	.463	.463

Note: Robust standard errors are in parentheses, *** $p < .01$, ** $p < .05$, * $p < .1$.

Model 1 indicates that as states become more politically similar, they are less likely to make secret alliances with one another. This measure, utilizing Scott's π, provides support for H1. Next, the MID A/B Same Side variable indicates that if two states have been on the same of a dispute in the past ten years, they are more likely to form a secret alliance with one another, supporting H3. In contrast, states making true consultative alliances are less likely to negotiate a secret alliance, supporting H4. Additionally, the presence of any major power, contiguity, neutrality pact, and the presence of a war all increase the chances of making a secret alliance with one another. However, jointly democratic states, nonaggression pacts, and the more MIDs a state has in the previous ten years decreases the chances that a state will make a secret alliance versus a public alliance.[10] None of these is particularly surprising, especially that democratic states should, according to the norms literature, be the more unlikely to make secret alliances than other regime types. Next, states that have an increasing number of disputes over the previous decade are likely to face real, material threats to their security. As such, they are more likely to pursue pacts that will provide them with a greater degree of defense. And these pacts are more likely to be public-facing, so as to deter a potential challenger (Slantchev 2010). In the same way, states actively engaged in war are more likely to make secret alliances. One interesting explanation of this stems from the formal theory literature. Slantchev (2010) claims that states overexaggerate their capabilities before a war begins in order to deter a potential challenger and states are likely to understate their power during conflict in order to draw them in. A secret alliance may provide evidence of attempts to gain the upper hand by compounding one state's side relative to another. For instance, the Treaty of London (1915) traded land to Italy as an inducement to get them to join the allies against the Central Powers. Similarly, the Sykes–Picot Agreement, made during World War I, sought to placate Russia and gain erstwhile Middle Eastern allies who were controlled by the Ottomans.

Turning to Model 2, Cohen's κ, states with a lower similarity score in the year prior to an alliance are more likely to make a secret alliance than those states with a higher political similarity score, supporting H1. Being on the same side of a MID previously increases the chances of forming a secret alliance (supporting H3), while true consultative pacts are less likely to result in secret alliance pacts. Joint democracies, nonaggression pacts, and more MIDs in the previous ten years are less likely to negotiate secret alliances. On the other hand, the presence of any major power state in the dyad, contiguous states, offensive and neutrality pacts, and war are more likely to make secret alliances with one another.

In Model 3, which utilizes unweighted similarity scores derived from the ATOP data, the more similar states are, the less likely they are to make secret alliances with one another. The converse of this is that the less politically similar states are, the more likely they are to negotiate secret alliances with one another. This finding supports the claim made in H1 that more politically similar states are less likely to pursue secret agreements with other states. On the other hand, true consultative pacts decrease the probability of a secret alliance (H4), whereas being on the same side of a dispute increases the probability (H3). Again, major powers, contiguous states, offensive and neutrality pacts, and a war are more likely to result in a secret alliance. Again, joint democracies, nonaggression, and more MIDs in the previous ten years are less likely to result in secret alliances being negotiated.

Model 4 tells much the same story except for the primary variable of interest regarding political similarity. In this model, the weighted similarity score is not statistically significant, meaning I am unable to reject the null hypothesis that less politically similar states are more likely to make secret alliances. On the other hand, both H3 and H4 are supported, with being on the same side of a dispute in the past decade positively associated with secret alliance formation, whereas true consultative pacts are less likely to result in a secret alliance. Likewise, the other variables that are significant in Models 1–3 are still statistically significant and in the same direction. Jointly democratic dyads, nonaggression pacts as well as more disputes in the previous ten years are less likely to result in secret alliances. However, the presence of a major power on either side, contiguity, offensive and neutrality pacts, and war are likely to increase the presence of a secret alliance being formed (see Figures 4.1a and 4.1b).

Turning to the models in Table 4.3, which contains the rare events models utilizing firth logistic regression, there is a similar story as in Table 4.2. In Model 5, the more politically similar (Scott's π) states become, the less likely they are to negotiate secret alliances with one another. This provides support for the claims made in H1. Similarly, H3 and H4 are both supported, with being on the same side of a MID positively associated with secret alliance formation (H3), but true consultation pacts being negatively associated. Next, joint democracies, nonaggression pacts as well as more MIDs in the previous ten years are less likely to result in a secret alliance being made. However, the presence of any major power, contiguity, offensive and neutrality alliances, and the presence of a war are likely to increase the probability of making a secret alliance (see Figures 4.2a and 4.2b).

Turning to the ordered logistic regression models in Table 4.4, we see some interesting diversions from the simple dichotomous operationalization of the previous models. These models make the distinction between public alliances (0), partially secret alliances (1), and fully secret alliances (2), with the understanding that this ordered operationalization represents the most secretive privacy arrangement is distinctly more restrictive than both partially secret and fully public alliances.

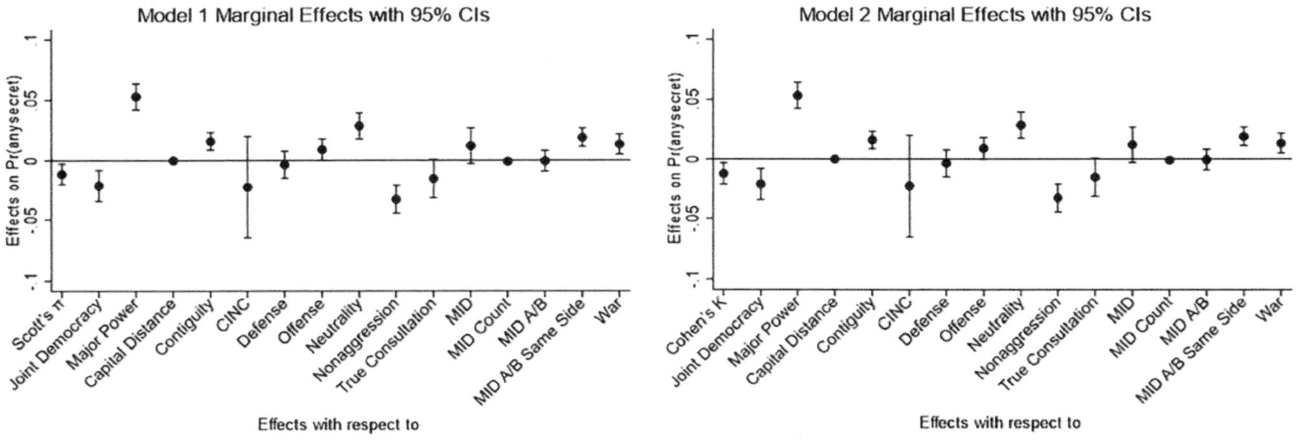

Let's just be friends 119

Figure 4.1a Marginal effects plots (Models 1–2)

Source: Author.

120   *Secret alliances*

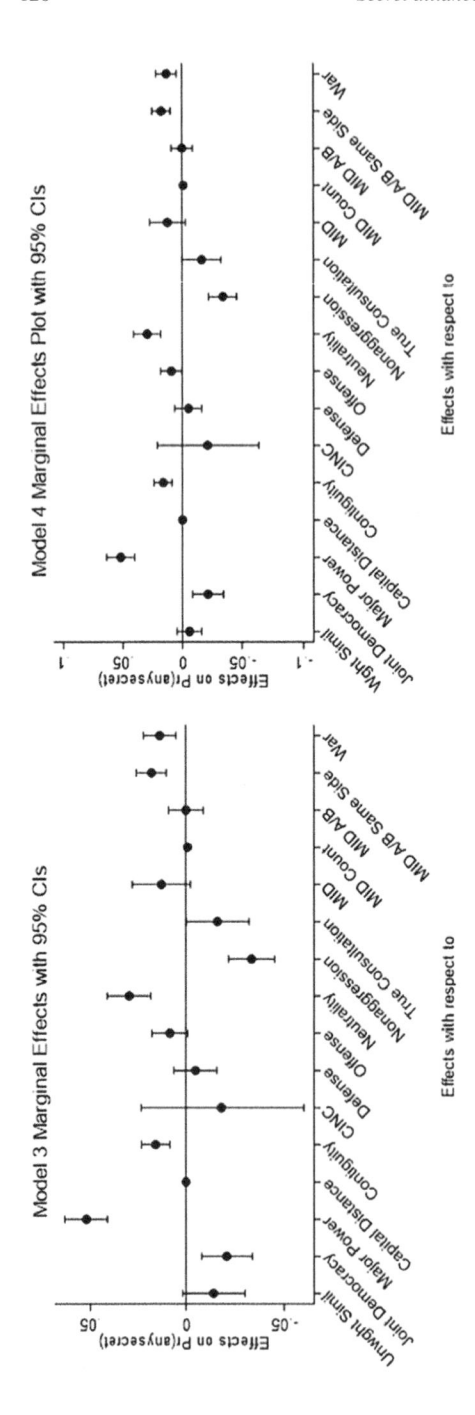

Source: Author.

Figure 4.1b   Marginal effects plots (Models 3–4)

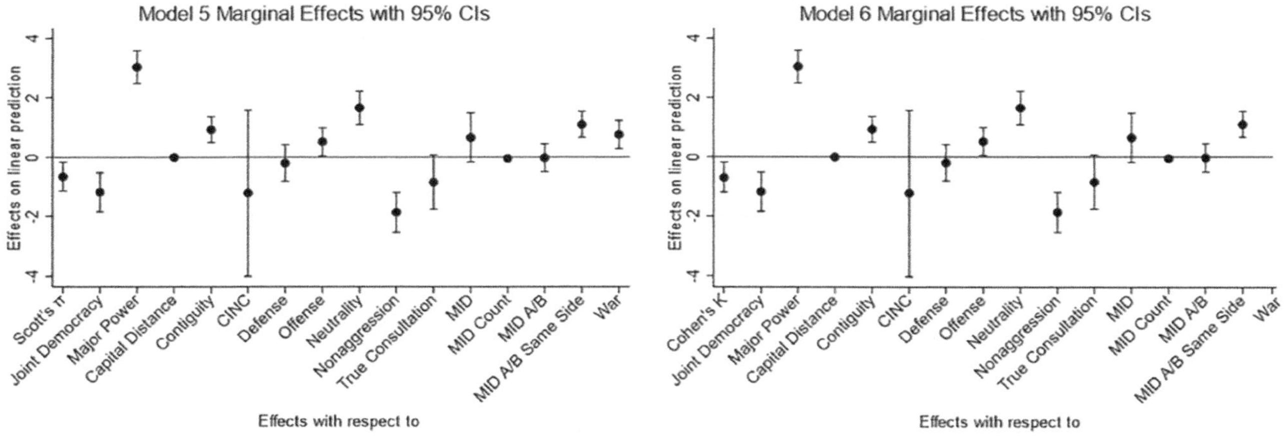

Let's just be friends 121

Figure 4.2a Marginal effects plots (Models 5–6)

Source: Author.

122 Secret alliances

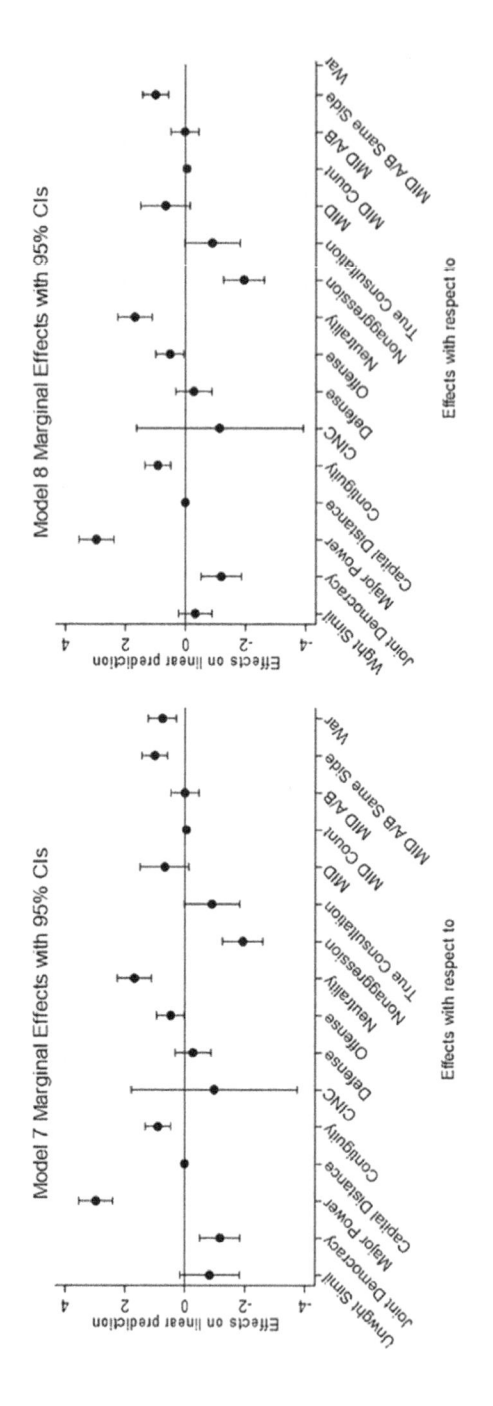

Figure 4.2b Marginal effects plots (Models 7–8)

Source: Author.

Notably, there are slightly different findings in the dichotomous operationalization, which tests the claim made in H2 that similarity is least likely in fully secret alliances. In Model 9, a one unit increase in Scott's π results in a roughly 0.63 log odds decrease in the probability of forming any type of secret alliance. Substantively, this provides support for H1: the more politically similar a state becomes to another state, the less likely it is to form a secret alliance with that state. Also, H3 and H4 are supported, with moving from no prior membership in the same MID on the same side resulting in a 1.15 increase in the log odds of forming a secret alliance. A true consultation pact, though, results in a 0.91 decrease chance in the log odds of secret alliance formation. Next, joint democracy, nonaggression alliances, and MID count are less likely to form a partially or fully secret alliance in Model 9. However, major powers, contiguous dyads, offensive and neutrality pacts, and the presence of a war are likely to result in an increased probability of forming a partially or fully secret alliance.

Model 10, like in the previous models, tells a similar story. The Cohen's κ measure indicates that a one unit increase in political similarity by this measure results in a 0.676 decrease in the log odds of forming a partially or fully secret alliance, providing support for H2. True consultation is associated with a 0.908 decrease in the log odds of secret alliance formation, supporting H4. Being on the same side of a dispute is associated with a 1.152 increase in the log odds of secret alliance formation. Likewise, joint democracy, nonaggression pacts, and MID count are less likely to form a public or fully secret alliance. On the other hand, fully secret alliances are more likely when there is a major power state, contiguity, an offensive or neutrality pact, or there is an ongoing war.

Model 11, which utilizes the unweighted similarity score, is not statistically significant. This means I am unable to reject the null hypothesis in H2. However, consistent with the findings in other models, H3 and H4 are both supported (true consultation and being on the same side of a MID). Likewise, joint democracy, nonaggression pacts, and more prior disputes are associated with a decreased probability in the log odds of making a partially or fully secret alliance. Again, major power presence, contiguity, offensive and neutrality pact, and the presence of a war increase the log odds of making a secret alliance in a given dyad.

Model 12, which utilizes the weighted similarity score, demonstrates that there is no statistically significant relationship between this measure and probability of making either a partially secret or fully secret agreement. This means I cannot accept H2. However, H3 and H4 are again supported, meaning that true consultation pacts are associated with a decreased chance of a secret alliance, whereas being on the same side of a dispute increases the probability. Joint democracy, nonaggression pacts, and MID count are significant and negative, meaning that they decrease the log odds of forming either a partially or fully secret agreement. Major power presence, contiguity, offense, neutrality, and war are all associated with an increase in the log odds of forming a partially or fully secret alliance (see Figures 4.3a and 4.3b).

The R^2 and Pseudo-R^2 across these models indicate that these models are able to predict roughly half of the variation in the dependent variable. Altogether, this is a relatively decent set of predictors for the variation between public/secret alliances and less so among public/partially secret/fully secret alliances. Alternative operationalizations were also considered and in some cases tested, such as the effect among only politically relevant alliance partners, in which case the similarity measure is not significant across any model or operationalization. However, this operationalization is problematic, as it drops the sample size down from 6074 observations to 1358 observations, thus throwing out 80 percent of all alliances negotiated and decreasing the goodness of fit. Other operationalizations also variously excluded the "threat" measures associated with past involvement in disputes over the past ten years and these likewise often resulted in models that did not do as good a job at predicting fit. Finally, operationalizations including the unaltered consultation variable cause the sign to flip, though it is still significant. However, as reported above, there is good reason to believe that the altered measure is theoretically justified.

CONCLUSION

In the post-war timeframe, states like Britain, France, and Israel were able to make a secret alliance. While all three were democracies, two were major powers in Europe and one was a newly-minted state in the Middle East. And while France and Britain shared largely similar alliance portfolios, because of Israel's position in the Middle East and ongoing conflicts with its Arab neighbors, formal alliances will always be harder for Israel. Nonetheless, while political similarity scores are not without problems in identifying the issue overlap between states, there was a good deal of ideological and issue overlap between the signatories. On the other hand, states like the Soviet Union and Nazi Germany could not be more dissimilar across a variety of measures. For instance, Germany initiated the Anti-Comintern Pact in 1936, which was specifically in response to the Soviet Union's activities in non-communist states. Nevertheless, the USSR and Germany were able to sign a secret agreement in the dying days of August 1939 in a prelude to the costliest war in human history. Though they largely had different security interests (namely, both states were either fearful of the other or hungry to expand), they were able to see where, for a time, their security interests overlapped with one another.

Let's just be friends 125

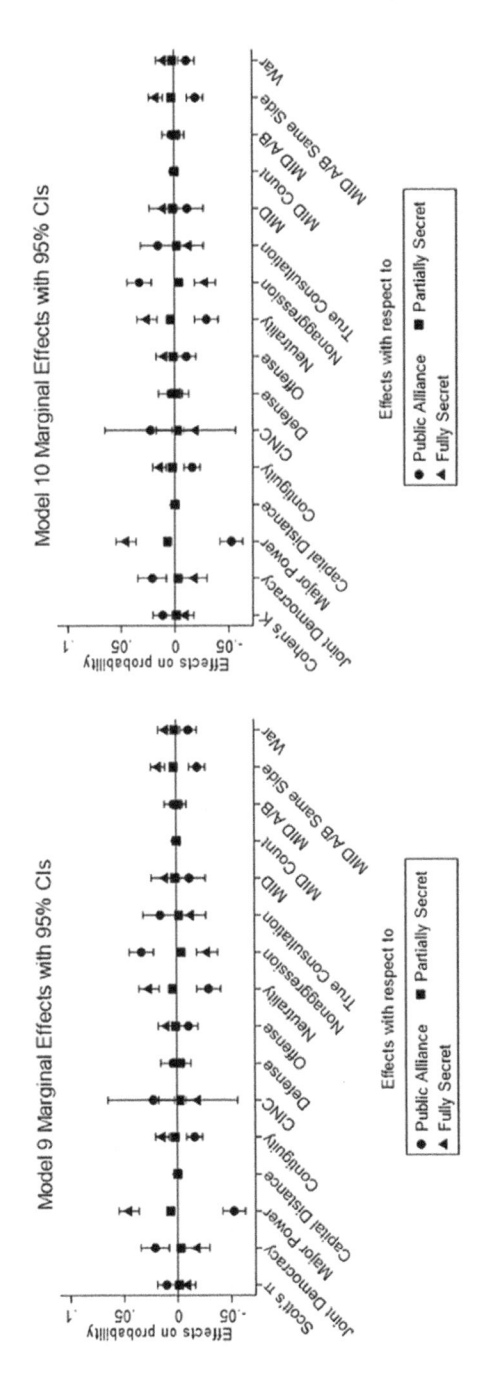

Source: Author.

Figure 4.3a   Marginal effects plots (Models 9–10)

126 Secret alliances

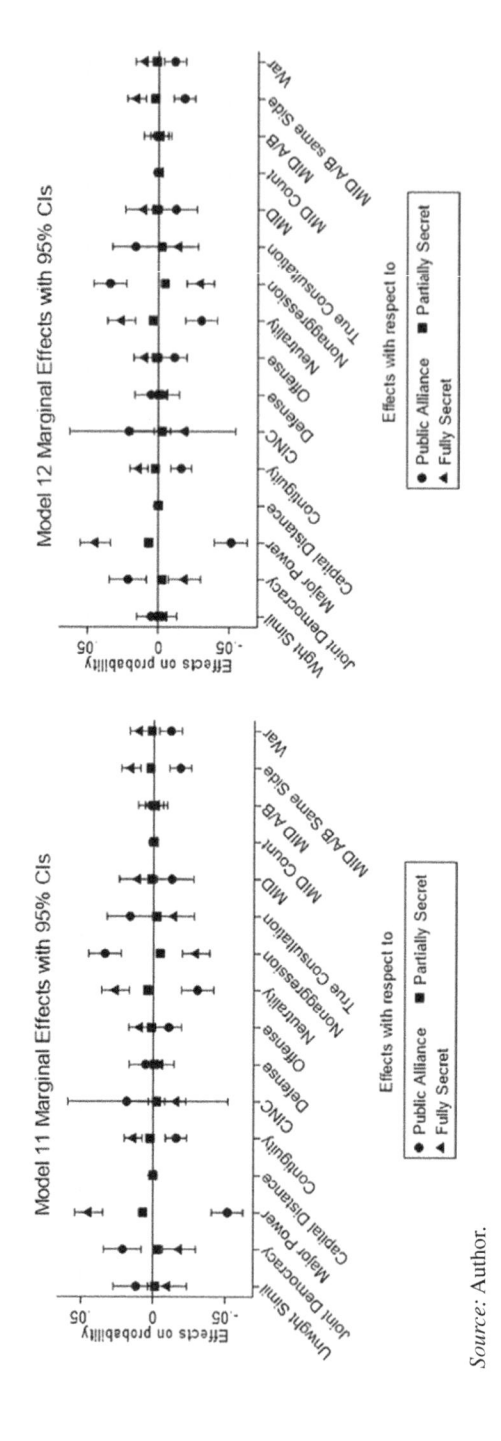

Figure 4.3b   Marginal effects plots (Models 11–12)

Source: Author.

This chapter demonstrates how secret alliances are less likely to occur between states with overlapping security interests. However, states are more likely to make a secret alliance with states that have been on the same side of a MID in the previous ten years. While partially an indictment of political similarity scores and their ability to measure "security interests," it is as much an indictment of how scholars study, conceptualize, and operationalize "interests." Nonetheless, across most models presented in this chapter, there was evidence for the claims presented in H1 and H2: states that are politically dissimilar are more likely to engage in secret alliance-making with one another. These findings are particularly true in the dichotomous measures, both in rare events logistic regression and standard logistic regression. However, the findings in the ordered logistic regression models are a bit more mixed. In two of the models, there is support for the claims made in H2. However, in the last two models, which rely on both weighted and unweighted S-scores, the hypothesis is not supported. Consistently, states that have been on the same side of a dispute in the previous ten years are more likely to make a secret alliance with one another. This seems to indicate that there is some degree of interest overlap that is not captured by the standard measures of political similarity.

Nonetheless, I am inclined to support the claims made in both H1 and H2. Given what has already been established in previous chapters within this book, states making secret alliances are more likely to engage in such behavior only because they have a temporary, transactional view of the alliance. They are distinct from public alliances in that there is a division of good at the expense of a third-party state. Thus, there is an incentive to keep the agreement quiet. To that end, states are more likely to follow through with their commitments in secret alliances, even without the presence of public-facing institutions to keep states "honest" in their agreements. The presence of higher military coordination in secret alliances is also indicative of this story: since the goals are salient stakes and are likely to result in preemptive attack by the third-party state, military coordination is more important than in public-facing agreements. The fact that these states are more likely to have been on the same side of MID previously is indicative that though they may not have a high degree of political similarity, they do have a higher degree of familiarity with one another.

The final part of this puzzle is political similarity in the year prior to a secret agreement. Since these agreements are largely transactional and the signatories are risking their public reputation on fulfilling their obligations, there is less "need" for states to be politically similar to their alliance partner. These agreements, after all, are not intended to last for a long period of time. And if defection is going to happen in these types of alliances, it will happen early on in the agreement (Chapter 3). If political similarity over a convergence of issues breeds trust in international relations, then states making secret alliances are less likely to need this trust than in public alliances. This is because states making secret alliances over the division of some good have blackmail capability over their alliance partner, making them less likely to defect due to the "law among thieves."

Table 4.5   *Hypotheses confirmed/rejected*

	H1	H2	H3	H4
Model 1	✓	-	✓	✓
Model 2	✓	-	✓	✓
Model 3	✓	-	✓	✓
Model 4	×	-	✓	✓
Model 5	✓	-	✓	✓
Model 6	✓	-	✓	✓
Model 7	✓	-	✓	✓
Model 8	×	-	✓	✓
Model 9	-	✓	✓	✓
Model 10	-	✓	✓	✓
Model 11	-	×	✓	✓
Model 12	-	×	✓	✓

Note: × = Disconfirmed, ✓ = Confirmed.

NOTES

1. For instance, see footnote 1 in Bennett and Stam (2000, p. 368).
2. Below, I discuss in greater detail the reliance on much of their framework to determine why a state is more likely to form a secret alliance over a public alliance.
3. While this analysis covers military coalitions, the same lessons may be transferable to alliances. While military coalitions are often more ad hoc and deal with more narrow, specific events, it may be worthwhile to think of alliances as potentially suffering from the same or similar effects of leader popularity.
4. For instance, Germany and Japan's alliance was formally a defensive alliance, with Hitler using that as his justification for declaring war on the United States on December 11, 1941, never mind the fact that Japan attacked the United States. On the other hand, Japan's alliance with the Soviets was a nonaggression pact.
5. While this could be a problematic approach (i.e., selecting on the dependent variable), the mixed research design of this book helps me address some of these issues. Additionally, in all self-selection behaviors, this is a concern. States can select into making an alliance in the same way that they can select into making a secret alliance. Fearon (2002) addresses similar design issues in the self-selection of states into disputes. As he describes it, scholars can never observe the cases where a state never even considered attempting to deter a more powerful state.
6. For more on this, see Clarke (2005). As he notes, scholars' fear of excluding variables is often unwarranted and frequently results in "garbage can" models in which numerous non-relevant variables are included in models. By including so many variables in an attempt to decrease bias, they may ironically increase bias. In fact, as he so eloquently puts it, "it is impossible to include all the relevant

variables in a regression equation" (p. 348). In addition to this, there is little theoretical puzzle in including every potential covariate because if every potential covariate is already known, it is likely that the question of concern the model is attempting to answer is either wholly uninteresting or already so well known it does not warrant further inquiry.
7. See the release notes accompanying the data at http://www.atopdata.org/uploads /6/9/1/3/69134503/atop_s_release_notes.pdf (Chiba and Johnson 2022). While a full explanation of the data is not provided, such an explanation of each approach can variously be found by consulting Signorino and Ritter (1999), Singer et al. (2012), Singer (1988), and Häge (2011).
8. See Häge (2011, p. 299) for the formulation of this measure.
9. Note that a separate operationalization utilizing the unaltered operationalization of the consultation variable from the ATOP dataset is also used. While the use of this variable does not affect the other variables of interest statistical significance nor direction, it does flip signs in all operationalizations, since it is the most common alliance type. Thus, separating out the distinction between the least cumbersome alliance type from other more involved forms of alliances does make sense in ensuring that scholars truly do see the effects of those types of alliance that offer only consultation and no further, deeper commitments.
10. Note that contiguity is negatively associated with secret alliance formation, meaning that the closer state capitals are to one another, the more likely states are to make a secret alliance with one another. However, the size of this effect across all models in this chapter is quite small, given that kilometers is measured on a continuous scale.

5. However it ends, it ends: reputation, norms, the long shadow of the future, and secret alliances

At the heart of secret alliances lies a fundamental contradiction. On the one hand, states seek something in the short term. Yet on the other hand, the long-term consequences, the "long shadow of the future," dictate that in pursuing short-term objectives, states may sacrifice their reputation in the reiterated game of international relations. This dynamic is particularly relevant as norms against secret diplomacy have gained wider acceptance over the past century[1] and norms, by definition, represent "the rules of proper behavior."

While reputation is considered a crucial aspect of international relations, it is not static across time or space. Reputations can ebb and flow as well as be rebuilt over time. The understanding of what constitutes a "reputation" may also change over time as values and priorities change for states. As Miller (2003) notes, defining reputation is not a straightforward task (p. 42). States can have multiple reputations, depending on the audience. For instance, Downs and Jones (2002) find this to be true in state treaty obligations. Reputation for resolve, for example, is often understood as "the extent to which a state will risk war to achieve its objectives" (Mercer 2010, p. 1). However, this is not the only way to understand reputation (e.g., Miller 2003), with competing definitions emphasizing reliability or situational reliability, particularly among states with limited experience with one another (Miller 2003, p. 43).

The alliance literature often conceptualizes reputation as a state's willingness to honor its alliance commitments. Alliances, in this sense, are not mere "scraps of paper" (Morrow 2000). States willing to write down and commit to one another risk their reputation if they do not fulfill their alliance commitments. Fearon (1997) distinguishes between "tying hands" (read commitment) and "sinking costs" (read signaling). This suggests a state is willing to risk its reputation by signaling it is committed to another state at the risk of its reputation. While the risk of reputational damage may be greatest in relation to the state with which the commitment was made, the risk can also extend to its relationships with other states. Therefore, reputation is not merely dyadic. It can also be understood as encompassing a state's broader relationship with the international community. In fact, Mercer (2010) observes that allies often view one another as irresolute, while enemies often see allies as resolute in their commitments.

Reputation has been shown to be a significant factor in various areas of international cooperation. For instance, Tomz (2007) finds that reputation influences sovereign lending and debt, affecting states' interactions with potential investors, including new states with no reputation. Simmons (1998) emphasizes the role of reputation in ensuring compliance with international agreements. Brewster (2009), as well as Guzman (2005), find that reputation matters in the context of international law. Other scholars, such as Tang (2005) claim that the "cult" of reputation in international politics gives reputation an outsized role in conflict studies.

Given the dramatic shifts in alliances and their role over time—for example, the sheer number of secret agreements between 1870 and 1914 (Kuo 2020), the post-war increase in collective defense agreements, and the decline of offensive agreements—the expectations for states to fulfill their obligations—have also changed. While the need for alliances may have changed over time, another important rationale exists for their decline. The normative shift in international relations has transformed these agreements into a political "hot potato" in a world increasingly repulsed by wars of aggression, with a growing emphasis on voluntary and universal jurisdiction in international law (Langer and Eason 2019), supplanting more "traditional" claims to "might makes right." This normative shift in international politics may explain why alliance reputations today are different than the alliance reputations of yesterday.

While norms are not always written down, particularly in the early stages of norm formation, norms against secret diplomacy (distinct from secrecy *in* diplomacy) have at least a century's worth of efforts to curb secret alliance-making. This practice has even come to be considered a vital component of international law.[2] Secrecy between states is an essential component of diplomacy, but secrecy *in* diplomacy has become a normative geopolitical faux pas for some time.

Woodrow Wilson famously declared the pitfalls of secret alliances in his Fourteen Points. In fact, so important was this in Wilson's mind that it was the first of the 14 points which he believed to be a root cause of World War I. While the incidence of secret alliances began to decline in the wake of World War I (Kuo 2020), their role in fomenting and fueling conflicts has persisted, particularly in events that relate to great power competition and the lead-up to World War II.

Kuo (2020) argues that these concerns about secret alliances assume they operate independently of one another. However, he maintains that secrecy begets secrecy. States making secret alliances are more likely to make other secret alliances in a given timeframe because of promises contained in the first secret alliance. In other words, secret alliances are not independent of one another.

The echoes of disdain for secret diplomacy after World War II mirrored those following World War I. Secret alliances would ostensibly become illegal under international law after the signing of the Vienna Convention on the Law of Treaties, proposed in 1969 and formally adopted in 1980. This treaty required that all treaties signed by signatories (of which 116 states have ratified and 15 have signed but not ratified) be submitted to the United Nations repository, meaning that secret alliances would no longer be "secret" in that they would be discoverable by any state or person. While numerous methods exist to circumvent these restrictions (Scoville 2020), these clandestine agreements rarely rise to the level of formal alliances between states.

To assess the effect of secret alliances on a state's future alliance-making prospects, this analysis considers the impact of secret alliance-making on states' reputations. Defining reputation in terms of fulfilling agreements (avoiding reneging) and avoiding the formation of secret alliances (reflecting the development of norms against such practices) enables the assessment of a state's general reputation. Chapter 3 illustrates that although secret alliances are less likely to experience a willful violation, such violations do occur periodically. States that violate both a norm of international relations (secret diplomacy) and their alliance commitments are likely to be punished more harshly, harming both their public and their private reputations. This analysis finds that a state's general reputation for upholding its alliances and avoiding secret alliances makes it more likely that a state can find future alliance suitors. Next, this analysis assesses a state's reputation for upholding its alliance commitments with its alliance partners. The findings suggest that states who renege on alliance commitments, particularly secret alliances, are less likely to make an alliance with a state they previously were secret alliance partners with.

REPUTATION: WHAT OTHERS SAY ABOUT YOU AND WHY

Reputation is complicated in that it can be associated with an individual, like heads of government (Neustadt 1991), or a group, such as states (Bernauer et al. 2010). Reputation has likewise been found to matter in states' decision-making processes (Bernauer et al. 2010). This analysis focuses on state reputation rather than leader reputation for several reasons. First, the relative paucity of secret alliances makes it challenging to study leader-specific secret alliances. Second, the recurrence of secret alliances within a leader's tenure is rare. However, given that secret alliances are more likely to occur between autocratic regimes, where leaders tend to serve longer terms, the impact of leader-specific reputations on state behavior might be more pronounced.

McGillivray and Smith (2000) and Gibler (2008) conceptualize reputations as belonging to leaders rather than states. While I do not dispute this, it is likewise fruitful to examine how states' reputations can be greater than a leader's reputation. Brewster (2009) and Crescenzi et al. (2012) similarly conceptualize reputation as belonging to the state rather than to the individual leader. Mattes (2012) employs this approach as a robustness check, though she finds the effect to be smaller (p. 702), suggesting that this is the more challenging test to find evidence for reliability. Therefore, this analysis relies on state-level reputation as a more robust measure.

Mercer's (2010) focus is on alliance reputation as a reputation for resolve, highlighting a disconnect between how allies and potential foes perceive a given alliance. However, Miller (2003) argues that reputation for reliability is more important in the study of alliances than reputation for resolve. Gibler (2008) argues that evidence for reputation is lacking in conflict studies, particularly within individual crises due to strategic self-selection. Instead, Gibler (2008) looks for evidence of reputational effects within alliances, finding that alliances do depend on a state's reputation. Specifically, he finds evidence for reputation in the leader himself. As he tells it, if a leader previously violated an alliance agreement with another state, that leader is less likely to form a future alliance. Conversely, a leader who upheld a prior alliance commitment is more likely to make an alliance in the future.

Mattes (2012) argues that alliance symmetry plays a significant role in determining whether states "trust" an alliance partner. States that are asymmetric (major-minor), where at least one state has previously reneged on an alliance, are more likely to require enhancing mechanisms to guard against potential defection. For Christensen and Snyder (1997), the risk of defection is ever-present, suggesting that reputation serves as a proxy for credibility and reliability. As established in Chapter 3, because secret alliances are increasingly seen in a poor light, the need for structures to enhance reliability is unlikely to take root in formal secret agreements. This is because a form of "insurance policy" is already built into secret agreements. Due to their secret nature and the desire to achieve the objective of the alliance, states are less likely to renege on such agreements. As such, the need for implementing costly mechanisms to guard against defection (Chapter 3) is less pronounced between secret partners. While Mattes (2012) identifies different mechanisms for symmetric versus asymmetric alliances, this analysis does not make any expectations regarding the effect of symmetry and future alliance commitments.

The study of reputation within conflict research has most often focused on a narrow conception of reputation for resolve. This is particularly the case in the deterrence literature, which often claims that a state's reputation is based upon its willingness to commit to acting when it has said or demonstrated it would be willing to defend an ally (e.g., Mercer 2010). However, this is a narrow view of reputation. Another view of reputation explored here is the reputation for upholding norms. While norms are not necessarily written down, particularly in the norm formation stage (Finnemore and Sikkink 1998), or may not even be legally binding, states generally tend to follow norms that the majority of other states have labeled as acceptable or unacceptable conduct in international relations.

NORMS: AN EVER-CHANGING WORLD AND SECRET ALLIANCE IMPLICATIONS

While the normative acceptability of secret alliances has undoubtedly shifted,[3] this shift may have potentially led to a greater prevalence of informal clandestine agreements. Defined by Finnemore and Sikkink (1998) as "a standard of appropriate behaviors for actors with a given identity" (p. 891), norms have become more important as the discipline has looked inward at methodology and normative statements and claims made in the study of peace and conflict.

Initially viewed as antithetical to the behavioral turn of the 1960s and 1970s,[4] the study of norms and the development of new norms has become a new research agenda in the study of peace and conflict. Hedley Bull's concept of an international society whereby "common interests and common values" bind states together within the framework of a "common set of rules and institutions" (2012, p. 40) highlights the role of shared norms and institutions in governing state interactions. Thus, states that consider themselves in community with one another are bound together through normative values and the institutions they establish to govern those sets of interactions.

Rather than in opposition to the quantitative or behavioral turn, these methods can be used to measure some of those normative behaviors. For instance, Mitchell (2002) finds a positive correlation between the proportion of democracies globally and the frequency of third-party dispute resolution attempts, though other arguments provide nuance to these findings (Millard 2018). Mitchell, Kadera, and Crescenzi (2008) similarly find a positive correlation between the global proportion of democracies and an increase in third-party dispute resolution attempts.

Further complicating the issue is that norms can also develop into institutions, or collections of norms that interact with one another in different ways (Finnemore and Sikkink 1998, p. 891). When formally agreed upon, alliances can exhibit a degree of institutionalization, formalizing behaviors or political objectives for the members. Some alliances, such as NATO, take on institutional forms to manage the alliance. Additionally, norms and organizations exist requiring the registration of alliances with either domestic or international bodies. As previously noted (Chapter 1), this is inherently problematic for secret alliances. To publicly acknowledge that there is a secret alliance undermines the purpose of a secret alliance.

As Finnemore and Sikkink (1998) rightly highlight, norms and values are intersubjective and likely to vary from one scenario to the next. States involved in secret alliances have three options: (1) not make a formal secret alliance; (2) not make an agreement and trust another state; (3) make a secret alliance that leans more toward informality than formality. In choosing the first option, there is a selection effect (no secret alliance), meaning that behaviors most often associated with secret diplomacy, such as wars of aggression, are less likely. Second, a state could willfully refuse to publish a secret alliance, meaning that they violate a central tenet of the post-World War II (and, arguably, World War I) norms. Third, a state could instead rely on an extreme form of an informal agreement without writing it down, trusting its partner would uphold its agreement. However, with little recourse for action, that state may lose credibility, but punishing such behavior is exceedingly difficult. Third, forming a secret agreement that is informal, possibly employing lower-ranking diplomats or government officials rather than heads of state or ministers, comes with its own risks. For instance, reneging is more likely, turnover within a cabinet or bureaucratic "churn" could affect understandings, and the proliferation of informal agreements with other states can lead to states feeling "slighted" with every transaction, increasing the likelihood of defection.

Given the fluid nature of international politics and the growing focus on normative values against conflict, with some exceptions, we should expect a decline in the number of secret agreements made globally, as these would negatively affect a state's reputation. However, the relative paucity of secret alliances in the modern era could likewise result from several other factors. First, secret alliances may have been less common since the World War II due to the bipolar nature of the era. As Kuo (2020) notes, secret alliances were more prevalent than public alliances in the lead-up to World War I and the popular notion that alliances were somehow to blame for the Great War led to their decline in the inter-war years. Second, as Jackson and Nei (2015) demonstrate, alliance networks since 1950 have become increasingly stable, with relatively little turnover among allies (p. 15278). In fact, they find a one-third chance of alliance turnover at five years prior to World War II and only a 5 percent chance post-1950 (Jackson and Nei 2015, p. 15278). States, on average, have more allies pre-1950 (Jackson and Nei 2015, pp. 15278–9). This suggests that states have been more receptive to the proposition of alliances (especially collective security arrangements) but less tolerant of states frequently shifting their alliances. This suggests that while the number of potential secret allies has increased with the increase in the number of states, the tolerance for such behavior has diminished.

Democracies tend to be less willing to tolerate deviations from norms, with a plethora of literature indicating that democratic leaders are likely to be retaliated against for engaging in norm-breaking behaviors. For instance, Tomz (2008) finds that while international commitments affect state behavior, this is largely due to reputational concerns that can be overridden by more pressing interests. Chiba, Johnson, and Leeds (2015) similarly find that democratic leaders are likely to design alliances that they are most likely to enforce and have flexible commitments.

Reiter (1994; 1996), whose work focuses on how states learn from alliances, finds that states that were victorious in prior conflicts and had alliances were more likely to use them in the future. Utilizing a learning framework, he suggests that these states "learned" that alliances could be useful in accomplishing political goals. He maintains that a state's reputation is paramount, as a failure to uphold an alliance commitment "would jeopardize the state's future reputation as an ally" (Reiter 1996, p. 59). While his analysis is confined to systemic wars (Reiter 1996, p. 60), secret alliances are likely centered around systemic wars or address issues that are both indivisible and address commitment problems. As such, secret alliances are likely to operate in a similar manner: states making secret alliances, whether they are known at the time or not, are likely to be viewed as aggressive acts by other states, making those states less likely to align themselves with secret alliance signatories in the future. As Miller (2003) points out, learning implies that states have agency to change their behavior based upon past experiences (p. 43), though he contends that reputation is exceedingly difficult to change.

In some cases, the justification for making a secret alliance is that the regime itself is already a pariah in the international community. This was the case for South Africa in its 1982 agreement with Swaziland. The apartheid regime, controlled by a strongly nationalist White Afrikaner government, was unwilling to compromise on the suppression and political disenfranchisement of native Black Africans, making it difficult to find international partners for its "total strategy" (Chan 1990, p. 15). In the same vein, Nazi Germany's expansions with the Anschluss, the Sudeten Crisis, and the eventual occupation of all Czech lands similarly hindered its ability to secure alliances with other states. Similarly, the Soviet Union found it difficult to make alliances among the major powers, due to its tensions with capitalism. Finally, Israel, as a new state in 1956, was unable to make formal alliances within its region. As a result, it sought larger states outside the region to underpin its security.

The secrecy surrounding secret alliances inherently complicates efforts to establish a state's reputation. While a state's commitment to a written formal secret alliance might seem to suggest a strong reputation, it could also be seen as a willingness to accept risks in pursuit of potential gains. Thus, the fact that a secret alliance is partially or fully secret is problematic because it does not provide a great deal of information about a state's values and commitments. Bas and Schub (2016) argue that secret alliances increase the likelihood of war due to the asymmetric information about a state's true preferences. While this information asymmetry doesn't directly cause conflict (see Chapter 2), it does have long-term implications for a state's reputation.

If reputation is built on a long-term understanding of a state's commitments and its willingness to honor those commitments, lacking full knowledge about those commitments is problematic for assessing a state's reputation. Given that reputation is something that is owned by a state but not possessed, outside states assessing another's reputation or reliability are likely to suffer with suboptimal knowledge of a state's behaviors. A state that has a private commitment to another state against a non-signatory that then fails to fulfill its commitments is likely to be shunned by its secret ally. However, if there is little to no public knowledge of the degree of cooperation between the states, then non-signatories are less likely to have a negative view of the offending state. Therefore, there is a mismatch between the perceived reputation of the maligned alliance partner and other non-members. In such scenarios, the maligned member is much less likely to make any kind of a future alliance with the state in question, whereas states unaware of such a defection are unlikely to have an increased negative view of the offending state.

THEORY

While the alliance literature frequently links reputation to a state's willingness to act decisively (i.e., to "fight") in support of its commitments, reputation in secret alliances is somewhat different. A state's decision to put pen to paper to formally show its level of commitment is a strong signal that it is willing to risk its reputation and the goals of the alliance for narrower, more immediate interests. By entering into such an agreement, a state signals its willingness to risk embarrassment, being labeled a "rogue" state, or even sanctions or retaliation to achieve its goals. This willingness to take on substantial risk suggests a state is willing to risk it all to put pen to paper. However, this very commitment could also render the state vulnerable to blackmail or accusations of infidelity from its secret ally. This raises important questions about secret alliances and reputation: How does making a secret alliance affect a state's reputation? Are states willing to mortgage their future reputation for their current political goals? What consequences are there for a state that makes a secret alliance and reneges on it?

Given that reputation in alliance-making is frequently assessed by a state's future ability to form alliances, I take a similar approach. To examine states' reactions to secret alliances, it's important to establish whether other states "knew" or suspected that a secret agreement existed. However, the only way to establish such a fact is to examine each case of secret alliance and every other state in the international system and when they came to know (or if they ever did) of the existence of a secret alliance. This presents a significant challenge, as some states may not make such knowledge publicly known, further creating a selection effect. Restricting the analysis only to politically relevant dyads (major powers and/or neighboring states) is also problematic. While a state may not directly border another state it seeks to ally with or be a major power, the state is likely to tacitly accept the view of other states with respect to one's reputation.

Two key implications emerge from this. First, a state maintains a general reputation within the larger international community. Second, it holds a more specific and tailored reputation among its allies, a reputation that encompasses both public and secret alliances. States, then, have a general reputation with the larger audience of states. And then a more tailored and specific reputation among allies.

If Bas and Schub (2016) are correct in asserting that secret alliances generate asymmetric information, then we should likewise assume that states in alliances will have different degrees of information regarding the reliability and reputation of allied states. This is likely to be true for both for public and private agreements. The inherent secrecy of secret alliances, however, introduces a further disconnect between a state's public and private reputation with its secret allies.

This analysis claims that states making partially secret alliances are less likely to be able to forge future alliances because the public knows that there is some form of agreement but may suspect there is more than is publicly presented. Next, there is an interaction effect that occurs between the degree of secrecy in an alliance and the nature of its termination. A fully secret alliance that terminates successfully is arguably the most advantageous outcome. The fully secret alliance preserves a state's public reputation, while the fulfillment of the alliance satisfies the alliance partner, thus preserving a state's private reputation.

This argument rests on several observations. First, partially secret alliances, because they are partially public, provide more information to other states than fully secret alliances. Second, states engaging in secret alliances may be seen as willing to take considerable risks, potentially making them more attractive alliance partners in the future.

Given that secret alliances are often "one-off" opportunities for a political "good," it is unlikely that states would be willing to make secret alliances with other states that have made previous secret alliances just because of their reputation. As discussed earlier, measuring reputation presents challenges because, while it characterizes the nature of a state's reliability, it may not be universally recognized. Thus, a distinction must be drawn between public and private reputation. The difficulty of measuring reputation is further exacerbated when examining secret alliances. Nonetheless, there are two ways to deal with this issue.

The first way to deal with this problem is to assess the unwillingness of states to make alliances with secret alliance signatories temporally. One should anticipate fewer alliances for states immediately after another secret alliance is formed because: (1) the alliance's existence may not be immediately known; (2) a new alliance might not be immediately needed; (3) the regime may have changed. First, determining the existence of a secret alliance can be challenging. While it is difficult to ascertain the existence of a secret alliance, they often do come to light, though this may take time. For instance, while the Western allies initially suspected a secret agreement between the USSR and Germany in September 1939, they did not have proof of such an alliance until the end of the war. Likewise, given Germany's eventual defection against its secret ally in June 1941, the Soviets became an attractive ally for both Britain and, later, the United States.

Second, a state may also not need a new alliance in the immediate aftermath of a secret alliance. The issues necessitating such alliances may be "selected out," given that secret alliances are likely to concern themselves with some material good at the expense of another (see Chapter 2). While the removal of such issues (such as the "resolution of the Polish question") may negate the need for counter-alliances, this is not often the case with political events. In fact, such "resolutions" often create as many problems internationally as they "solve," meaning that in some cases we should expect to see quick counter-alliances formed.

Third, regimes may change. Though scholars generally measure interactions at the state level, in some instances regimes may vary widely from one to the next. For instance, there is little dispute that the policies pursued by Adolf Hitler in 1945 and by Konrad Adenauer in 1949 are not remotely similar. Nonetheless, scholars often treat states, even when not interrupted by an interregnum period, as cohesive entities, which is problematic for several reasons that shall remain unaddressed here.

Reputation may thus be salvaged in the long term, as one becomes more temporally removed from an event. For instance, both West Germany and East Germany joined opposing alliances within 11 years of World War II's end. South Africa, isolated internationally due to apartheid, found formal alliances more challenging to secure than did Swaziland, which had little need for such alliances. Nonetheless, the secret pact between Pretoria and Mbabane became moot 12 years later with the election of Nelson Mandela. On the other hand, France and Britain after 1956 had little trouble making future alliances, whereas Israel did not sign another formal alliance until 1975.

To test the temporal assumption about the effect of secret alliances on reputation, I generate testable hypotheses about a state's general reputation in the larger international community and its ability to make alliances in the future. First, I propose:

> *H1: States making any kind of secret alliance will have a more difficult time making any type of alliance in the future.*

The next set of hypotheses distinguishes between fully secret and partially secret alliances. Since fully secret alliances are fully hidden from public view, the likelihood of another state knowing about such an alliance should be lower than for partially secret alliances. Given that secret alliances are at least theoretically "unobserved," I expect that states making partially secret alliances will have a more difficult time making any sort of future alliance. This is because partially secret alliances are at least partially publicly acknowledged. Because of this knowledge and the subsequent likelihood of a division of goods at the expense of another state, these states will have the most difficult chance of making a future alliance. This leads me to hypothesize that:

> *H2: States making partially secret alliances will have the hardest time making future alliances.*

Next, given that secret alliances are likely to suffer the greater "loss" to reliability, I also expect this to be compounded by the way in which an alliance ends, in keeping with Mattes (2012). States involved in secret alliances that terminate irregularly should face greater difficulty forming new alliances. This is because "reputation retaliation" is more likely when a state fails to uphold a secret alliance. Since formally writing down a secret alliance exposes a state to potential blowback were it to be publicly known, states that renege on secret alliance agreements should find it even more difficult to make alliances in the future. This leads me to propose:

> *H3: States making secret alliances that end irregularly will take longer to make an alliance in the future.*

Given the interaction between the public knowledge of an alliance and the irregular ending of a secret alliance, I expect that an interaction effect between public knowledge of an agreement and the irregular termination of an agreement leads to the greatest damage to a state's reputation. However, if an alliance is fully secret, it provides a degree of "cover" for the signatories, mitigating the likelihood of facing greater difficulty in forming future alliances. This serves to protect their public reputation with other states. While the secret alliance partner may hold a more negative view of their partner due to the defection, it is unlikely to result in long-term damage to the state's overall reputation. This is because, as discussed earlier in this book, secret alliances represent short-term issue convergence rather than long-term issue convergence. Since it is unlikely that secret alliance partners would have greater issue convergence in the future, a harmed private reputation is unlikely to affect its overall reputation. This is precisely because a jilted secret partner cannot "go public" without divulging its own involvement in the secret alliance. As such, I propose:

> *H4: States making fully secret alliances that likewise terminate irregularly will have an easier time making an alliance in the future.*

RESEARCH DESIGN

To test the hypothesis that states engaging in secret alliances experience greater difficulty in forming future alliances, I employ survival analysis tests across several model specifications to determine the amount of time until a state forms its next alliance. While these models do not include every potential variable that determines alliance formation, I maintain that scholars should have a better idea of whether the international community is more or less likely to punish a state that engages in secret alliance-making *ex post*.[5] This analysis offers a "first look" at the implications of secret alliances on future alliance-making prospects, helping to address a fundamental question: Do states making secret alliances hurt their own reputation?

To test this, I run both Cox proportional hazard models and Weibull models. Given potential violations of the proportional hazards assumption, I am inclined to favor the Cox proportional hazards model. As Wulandari, Kurnia, and Sadik note,

> if the proportional hazard assumptions are not met, which means that the linear component of the model varies depending on time, this is called non-proportional hazard. There are three options in overcoming these shortcomings, namely removing independent variables that do not meet the assumptions of the model, using the stratified Cox model, or by applying the extended Cox model. (2021, p. 2)[6]

Likewise, I use robust standard errors in the primary models and the Breslow method for ties. Tables A5.1 and A5.2 in the Appendix presents additional models with clustering at the state level, which helps to account for potential non-randomness at the treatment level.

To identify alliances that end irregularly, I consult the ATOP Codebook. I utilize the "term" variable to identify those alliances that end in an irregular manner. This is coded as "2", which is when "an alliance ends due to violation of provisions by one or more members, including willful abrogation before the scheduled termination date, the variable is coded 2" (ATOP Codebook 2022, p. 20).

Here, the unit of analysis is the country making each alliance rather than country-year or directed country-year. While alternative approaches such as yearly directed dyads or yearly non-directed dyads exist, this runs into several problems. First, these approaches vastly inflate the number of observations, potentially making it more likely to find evidence supporting the hypotheses. Second, they assume that observations from one year to the next are independent of one another when we know they are not, barring an unusual event. However, the concept of reputation explicitly assumes that observations are not independent of one another: a state making an alliance looks toward the past to determine the reputation of a potential alliance suitor. Third, one cannot observe those states that considered making an alliance but, for whatever reason, decided not to. This mirrors the logic that Fearon (2002) identifies in the deterrence literature: states selecting into crises are less likely to be deterred due to rational self-selection (e.g., see also Wolford 2015, p. 9). This also likely biases against more recent alliances, as norms have undoubtedly developed against secret diplomacy. As discussed elsewhere in this book (Chapter 1), this could explain why some states are now more likely to rely on informal agreements rather than formal agreements.

Additionally, I run tests on those alliances that have already terminated, excluding ongoing alliances. Running the models on alliances that have yet to terminate is problematic for several hypotheses presented here, though not for all. Substantively, this affects approximately half of the observations in the ATOP dataset, with many of those observations accounted for by more complex alliance networks that have proliferated since the end of World War II. Relying solely upon those alliances that have terminated results in roughly half of the observations dropping out of the sample (51.56 percent). Thus, bilateral alliances are slightly overrepresented because they tend to not last as long and are less common in the post-World War II security architecture than prior to the proliferation of collective defense agreements.

There are several reasons why ongoing alliances are not included. First, one cannot know if an alliance has ended irregularly if it is ongoing. Given my hypotheses on how an alliance ends, this is problematic for roughly half of my hypotheses. Second, terminated alliances have a definitive outcome, meaning that we have greater information regarding the potential mismatch between private and public reputations.

Furthermore, while I recognize that both states and leaders have their own reputations and that sometimes these two are indistinguishable from one another, this analysis uses the state as the unit of analysis rather than the head of government. Finally, I also make distinctions between partially and fully secret alliances and a variable that "lumps" all secret and partially secret alliances together into a single variable. This allows me to separate out the effects of fully secret alliances and partially secret alliances, as well as the interaction effects. It could be that partially secret alliances affect reputation differently because there is some degree of public visibility. On the other hand, a fully secret alliance conceals an alliance from the public, making it more difficult to quantify any effects on reputation. However, as previously mentioned, the effects of a fully secret alliance are often difficult to hide. Thus, while the alliance itself may not be immediately known, it is likely that the effects of such an alliance will become known at some point and will have some effect on the state's future public reputation. For example, Hitler could not easily conceal his invasion of Poland and the subsequent invasion by Stalin 17 days later. While their justifications may have appeared to be independent of one another, some sources at the time do indicate their belief that there was a secret agreement between the two erstwhile enemies.

Dependent Variables

The time-varying observation in this analysis is the amount of time that elapses between when a state formally joins an alliance (yrent, moent, dayent) for each observation and the amount of time that passes until its next alliance. Naturally, this means that the first observation for a state is not counted since there was no prior alliance against which to measure time. Such an approach allows me to ascertain how long a state is able to "survive" until making another alliance. While such an approach is not ideal, it does provide more information than simple binary indicators at, say, 5, 10, 15, or 20 years.[7] This extra information greatly increases my confidence in measuring the time to a state's next alliance. The continuous nature of this variable, measured in days, increases the reliability of the data until the next "success" (forming another alliance).

As an example, the United States joined its first alliance on November 30, 1908. It then joined its next alliance on December 13, 1921. This is a span of 4761 days, or 13.04 years. While one could measure an alliance's end date against the next alliance's start date, this runs into several problems. First, the alliance that came first may end after the subsequent alliance has begun, resulting in a negative value. This would unfairly bias against more "successful" alliances that last for a longer time. Second, measuring from the termination date of a prior alliance would be measuring against the success or failure of that prior alliance, which is not the objective of this analysis. Finally, while I do not expect that every state was fully aware of whether a state made an alliance in the past and whether it was reliable or not, I do assume that, as do other scholars interested in alliance reliability, states will have at least a functional knowledge of others' prior alliance commitments. In fact, the logic of alliances and reputations rests upon the logic that *one* consideration for states making alliances is another state's prior willingness to make an alliance in the first place. As this logic illustrates, non-reputable states should be "selected out" of the sample, given that as states become increasingly unreliable, other states are less likely to ally with them.

Independent Variables

Given that fully secret alliances might not be publicly known, there is a reasonable expectation that a state's public reputation may not be affected by a fully secret alliance. However, as noted earlier, since these fully secret alliances are likely to be the most salacious of agreements (thus necessitating their absolute secrecy), the effects of secret alliance-making are difficult to conceal. Therefore, while states may not "know" of the existence of a secret alliance, they may observe the outcomes of the alliance over time.

Next, to determine how an alliance ends, I consult the "termmode" variable in the ATOP dataset (Leeds et al. 2002), which codes how alliances end. I then generate a new variable and code as "1" all alliances that conclude when the alliance ends by being broken by a signatory ("3" in "termmode"). This enables the assessment of irregular termination's impact on future alliance-making prospects and is similar to the approach used elsewhere (e.g., Mattes 2012).

Next, given the claims regarding alliance termination, I code whether an alliance ends in a regular, scheduled manner or irregularly. This variable is a binary indicator, constructed from the "termmode" variable's third category, which identifies those members where "the alliance was broken before its scheduled termination date" (ATOP Codebook 2022, p. 21). Note that this variable excludes those that are right-censored or those alliances that are ongoing as of 2016. This is a conservative approach, as it increases the challenge of finding support for the hypotheses. While not directly measuring the effort put forth by an ally, the irregular termination measure generally accounts for those states that renege on their commitments. This is then likely to affect a state's private reputation.

Similarly, given the likelihood that reneging on an agreement and secret agreements are likely to have a multiplicative effect, I present models that account for both the separate and interactive effects between the type of alliance (public/partially, secret/fully secret) and the irregular termination of an alliance and its effect on future prospects. This allows me to understand the interactions between public and private reputations in alliance formation.

To account for this, I utilize the ATOP dataset (Leeds et al. 2002) to code for whether each observation is a public, partially secret, or fully secret alliance. I also run separate models with a dummy variable indicating if an alliance is public or secret. This allows me to separate out the more subtle effects of different types of secret alliances, while also illustrating the combined effects of both types of secret alliances.

Given that the hypotheses are inherently tied to many of the same questions presented throughout this book, I utilize many of the same operationalizations. Because the effects might vary depending on alliance type, the analysis controls for alliance type, mirroring Leeds's (2003) argument that alliance type influences the probability of conflict. Given the focus on the effect of secret alliances on future alliance-making behavior rather than war onset, it is appropriate to include variables representing different types of alliances.

Similarly, regime type might also affect whether a state can form alliances. Gartzke and Gledistch (2004), for instance, find that democracies are less reliable allies, suggesting that a reputation for unreliability could decrease the likelihood of forming new alliances. Conversely, Leeds and Gigliotti-Labay (2003) find that regime type does not affect reputation. While I am not assessing the regime type of a state in future observations, I am instead interested in the regime type of an alliance for each observation. So, rather than tracking the change of a state, say, five or ten years out from when it made an alliance, I am instead interested in the regime type of a state at the time it makes an alliance, not the regime type with the next alliance it makes.

As mentioned in Chapter 2, secret alliances are more likely to be bilateral. Multilateral alliances are more common today, increasing a state's reputation through greater engagement in these agreements. Thus, making bilateral alliances provides less information to both the international community (since its alliance is with only one other state) and to the allying state. Furthermore, dividing spoils is easier in a bilateral alliance than in a multilateral alliance. Since bilateral alliances should be most consequential when broken (since the costs of defection are borne by one and committed by another), I expect that states breaking such agreements likely suffer greater consequences to private reputations in the future. I code as "1" to indicate a bilateral alliance and "0" to indicate a multilateral alliance.

Major powers, while more likely to make secret alliances (Chapter 2), should be no more or less likely to make alliances in the future. This is because major powers are often seen as the "indispensable states" in alliance politics. Thus, a major power that defects should be less likely to be punished because its "services" are more likely to be needed, as they are the most enviable alliance partners, given their power. I count as "1" if a state making the alliance is a major power and "0" otherwise.

This analysis also accounts for a state's CINC score. This allows me to account for the effects of power on the ability to make alliances in the future and the effect on a state's reputation. While not measuring a state's future power, it instead measures the power of a state for the observation in the year the alliance took effect (rather than the CINC score of the next alliance a state makes).

Next, I use dummy variables for the different types of alliances coded by the ATOP dataset. This includes dummy variables for defense, offense, neutrality, nonaggression, and consultation. This allows me to separate out the effects of each type of alliance on the prospects for future alliances. This is necessary because different types of alliance necessitate different levels of commitment.

Finally, given concerns that the volume of secret alliances has decreased over time (e.g., Kuo 2020), I generate a dummy variable to indicate whether or not an alliance is signed before the outbreak of World War I. Given that norms against secret alliance-making did not emerge until the end of World War I, I code as "1" all alliances that were made prior to the end of World War I and "0" those alliances made after World War I. Given Finnemore and Sikkink's (1998) arguments regarding norm emergence, cascade, and internalization, I suspect that states making secret alliances after World War I will be less able to make alliances in the future, as prevailing attitudes change.

In keeping with Mattes (2012), I consider the role that symmetry plays in determining whether a state is likely to make an alliance with a state that makes prior alliance commitments. To account for this, I code an alliance as "1" if the alliance is asymmetric. That is to say, there is at least one major power and one minor power party to the alliance. To do this, I went through the ATOP dataset for each alliance and identified which alliances had major powers. Then, I compared this to whether another state party to the alliance was a major power. In the case of major-major or minor-major, the variable is coded as "0". In the case of major-minor alliances, it is coded as "1". If there was any asymmetry in a multilateral alliance, it was coded as "1". This is consistent with Mattes's (2012) approach.

A final note is in order. Since most of the hypotheses in this chapter concern themselves with the future after an alliance ends, I confine my analysis to those alliances that are no longer in effect. This allows me to definitively assess whether a state is more or less likely to make an alliance in the future based on its behavior in its prior alliance commitments. This leaves approximately half of the sample remaining. And, given missingness among some other variables and the obvious exclusion of each first alliance (due to no prior establishment of a reputation), this further reduces those cases considered to approximately 36 percent of the dataset. However, one cannot be certain of a state's commitments unless the alliance has ended, meaning this is the proper approach.

RESULTS

Before turning to substantive results, a visual examination of the Kaplan-Meier survival estimates of the models is presented below. In Figures 5.2a and 5.2b, one can see that the length of alliances, whether public or secret or partially or fully secret, initially looks congruent with one another. However, closer inspection by multivariate models is warranted here to tease out the effects on alliance length (see Figures 5.1a and 5.1b).

To ensure robustness, the primary analysis employs Cox proportional hazard models (reported in the main text), with additional models (reported in Tables A5.1 and A5.2 in tthe Appendix) using Weibull models.[8] This is done for simplicity's sake but also to demonstrate the robustness of the findings. Table 5.1 presents the results across four different Cox models utilizing robust standard errors. This allows me to break down the effects of two different variables. In Models 1 and 2, I make a distinction between the presence of any secret alliance and a separate operationalization that makes a distinction between the effects of partially/fully secret alliances. This allows the reader to see the nuance between a fully versus partially secret agreement. Models 3 and 4 treat the irregular termination variable as an interaction effect, allowing the reader to see the multiplicative effect of both an irregular termination and the public/private distinction of an alliance agreement. This, again, provides clarity to the effects of both variables and how they interact with one another (see Table 5.2).

Table 5.1   Variables

Dependent Variable	Coding
Secret Alliance	"0" for public alliances, "1" for secret
Public/Partially/Fully Secret	"0" for public alliances, "1" for partially secret, "2" for fully secret
Independent Variables	
Irregular Termination	"1" if irregular termination, "0" if regular
Bilateral Alliance	"1" if alliance is bilateral, "0" otherwise
Major Power	"1" if state is a major power
CINC	Composite Index of National Capabilities
Democracy	"1" if Polity score>=6
Major Power Count	Count of the major power states in international system Defense
Offense	"1" if an offensive alliance
Neutrality	"1" if a neutrality alliance
Nonaggression	"1" if a nonaggression alliance
Consultation	"1" if a consultation alliance
World War I dummy	"1" if before 1914

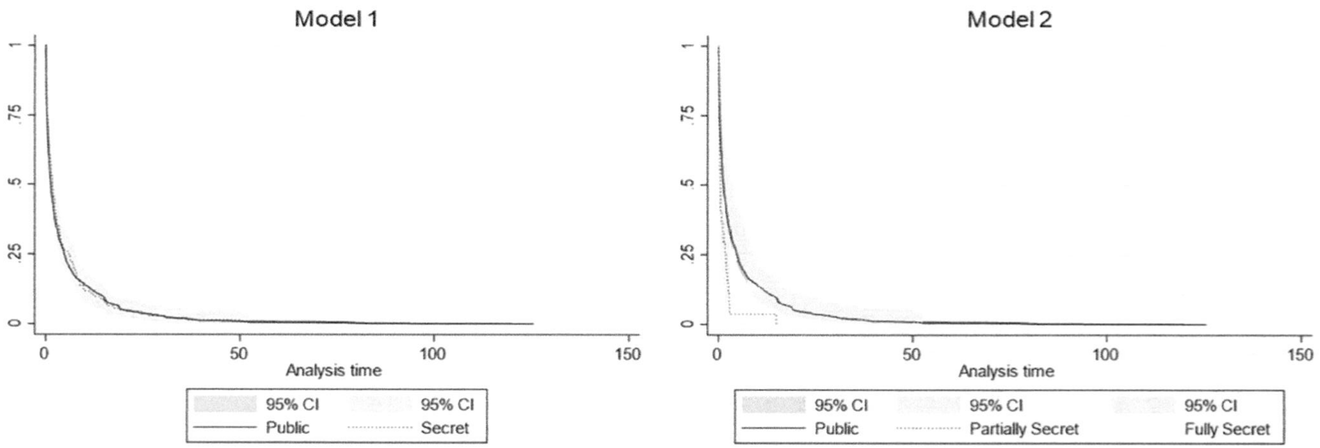

148 *Secret alliances*

Source: Author.

Figure 5.1a   Kaplan-Meyer survival estimates (Models 1–2)

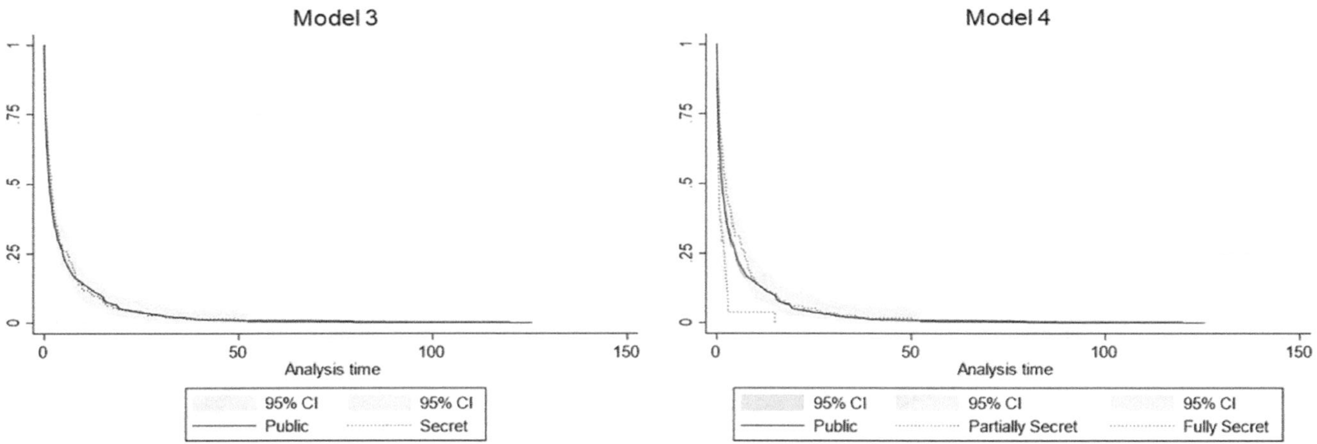

However it ends, it ends 149

Source: Author.

Figure 5.1b Kaplan-Meyer survival estimates (Models 3–4)

150 Secret alliances

Source: Author.

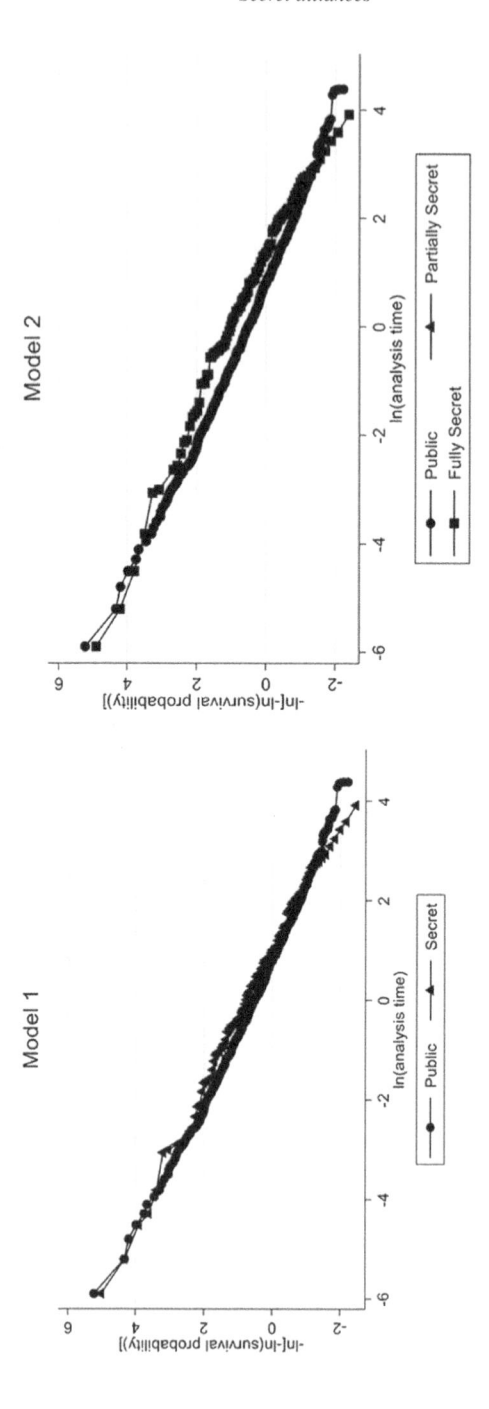

Figure 5.2a   Proportional hazards (Models 1–2)

However it ends, it ends   151

Source: Author.

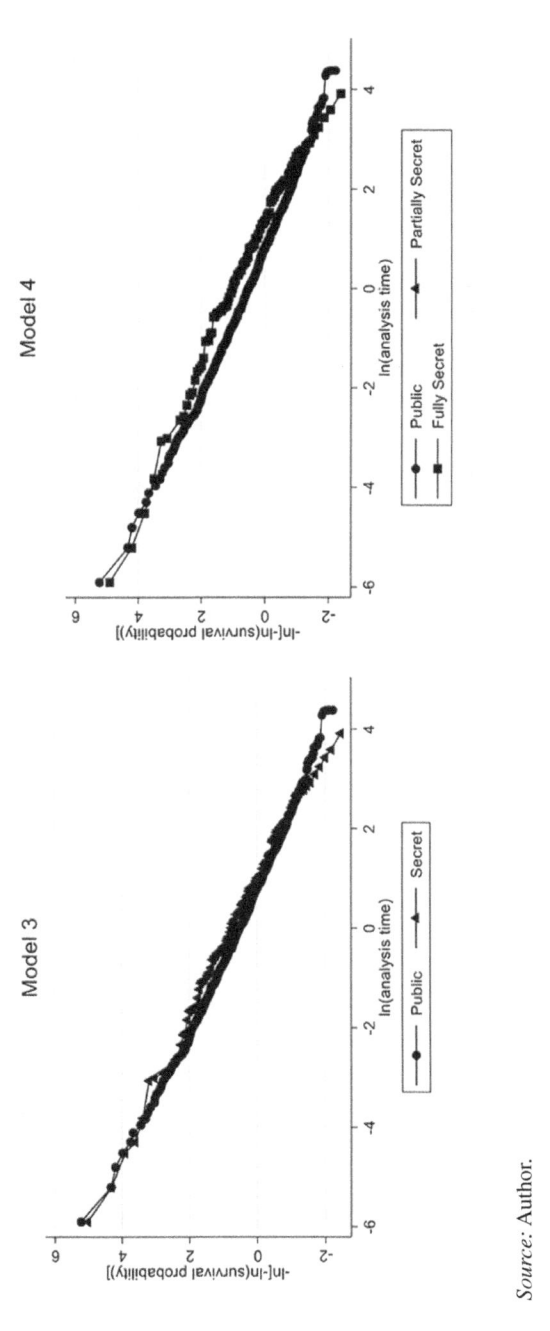

Figure 5.2b   Proportional hazards (Models 3–4)

Table 5.2 Effects of secret/termination on future alliances (Cox models)

Variables	1 Effect by Secret Alliance (0/1)	2 Effect by Secret Alliance Type (0/1/2)	3 Interaction Effect by Secret Alliance (0/1)	4 InteractionEffect by Secret Alliance Type(0/1/2)
Any Secret	1.014 (.111)	-	-	-
Public#Irregular Termination	-	-	.826** (.062)	-
Secret#Regular Termination	-	-	1.04 (.137)	-
Secret#Irregular Termination	-	-	.809 (.125)	-
Partially Secret	-	1.551** (.345)	-	-
Fully Secret	-	.890 (.107)	-	-
Public#Irregular Termination	-	-	-	.823*** (.062)
Partially Secret#Regular Termination	-	-	-	2.32*** (.364)

Variables	1 Effect by Secret Alliance (0/1)	2 Effect by Secret Alliance Type (0/1/2)	3 Interaction Effect by Secret Alliance (0/1)	4 InteractionEffect by Secret Alliance Type(0/1/2)
Partially Secret#Irregular Termination	-	-	-	.902 (.310)
Fully Secret#Regular Termination	-	-	-	.883 (.127)
Fully Secret#Irregular Termination	-	-	-	.735*** (.119)
Bilateral	1.353*** (.097)	1.385*** (.100)	1.354*** (.098)	1.376*** (.010)
Irregular Termination	.819*** (.057)	.804*** (.056)	-	-
Major Power	1.353*** (.097)	1.994*** (.230)	2.027*** (.234)	2.007*** (.231)
CINC	1.022 (.829)	.972 (.776)	1.020 (.820)	.978 (.783)
Democracy	.872 (.081)	.882 (.082)	.871 (.081)	.879 (.082)
Symmetry	.836** (.059)	.829*** (.058)	.836** (.059)	.825*** (.058)

Variables	1 Effect by Secret Alliance (0/1)	2 Effect by Secret Alliance Type (0/1/2)	3 Interaction Effect by Secret Alliance (0/1)	4 InteractionEffect by Secret Alliance Type(0/1/2)
Defense	1.166***	1.179**	1.163**	1.161**
	(.082)	(.083)	(.082)	(.083)
Offense	1.166	1.089***	1.074	1.095
	(.011)	(.102)	(.101)	(.102)
Neutrality	.938	.929	.935	.958
	(.102)	(.101)	(.102)	(.106)
Nonaggression	1.217**	1.232**	1.216**	1.229**
	(.104)	(.105)	(.104)	(.105)
Consultation	1.384***	1.390***	1.380***	1.403***
	(.104)	(.105)	(.104)	(.106)
World War I	.527***	.572***	.525	.564***
	(.050)	(.085)	(.049)	(.055)
Observations	919	919	919	919

Note: Robust standard errors are in parentheses, *** p < .01, ** p < .05, * p < .1.

Turning to Model 1, we see that any secret alliance is not statistically significant. This means I am unable to determine in this binary operationalization whether a secret alliance increases or decreases the time to the next alliance, meaning I am unable to reject the null hypothesis in H1. However, irregular termination is associated with a shorter time until the next alliance is formed. This finding is inconsistent with existing reputation literature and adds an important caveat to studies examining reputation and the prospects of future alliances. Next, we see that bilateral alliances, alliances made by major powers, defensive agreements, nonaggression and consultation pacts are likely to result in a longer period of time between one alliance and the next.

Intuitively, it is unsurprising that bilateral alliances are less likely than multilateral alliances to result in future alliance-making prospects. Several factors might contribute to this. First, information gleaned from bilateral alliances is less obvious or more confined to the singular ally. Second, an interaction effect might exist between bilateral alliances and the type of alliance a state forms. For example, a targeted multilateral offensive alliance seems less probable than a multilateral defensive alliance. Third, given the decrease in bilateral alliances relative to multilateral pacts since World War II, the sample of bilateral alliances might be less representative. Coupled with the post-World War II shift away from wars of aggression and the increase in collective defense pacts, the reasons for bilateral pacts before and after World War II have likely changed over time.

The finding that major powers take longer to make their next alliance than minor powers is surprising at face value. However, upon closer examination, the states most in need of alliances, due to the "friends" they provide, are minor power states.

Next, defensive alliances, as well as nonaggression and consultation alliances, are likely to have larger time intervals between one alliance and the next, which is not particularly surprising. The point of alliances, at least to the layman, is to provide defense against some ostensible threat. Thus, a finding above 1 (indicating a longer time to the next alliance) seems to indicate that states making such alliances are likely successful in that they do not have as much need to make another alliance. A similar logic applies to both nonaggression and consultation alliances, with both being relatively weak forms of an alliance (in contrast to defensive alliances, which are often the strongest type of alliance).

Next, the timeframe after World War I and symmetry are likely to lead to shorter times between one alliance and the next. The World War I variable indicates that alliances formed after World War I tended to have shorter timespans until the next alliance, likely due to the concentration of alliances around major wars. This aligns with Senese and Vasquez's (2008) "steps to war" hypothesis. Underlying political tensions are likely to increase the presence of alliances, as well as arms races, in the years preceding conflict. However, this does not mean that alliances cause conflict. Instead, they may be seen as effects of underlying political disagreements between states.

Symmetry is also associated with shorter time intervals until the next alliance. An interesting finding, this stands in stark contrast to the findings presented by Mattes (2012) regarding reliability-enhancing provisions. This could reflect the need for a more nuanced analysis, differentiating between major-major, major-minor, and minor-minor alliances in future research.

Model 2, which makes a distinction between fully/partially secret alliances and the independent effects of irregular termination, reveals that partially secret alliances are associated with longer intervals until the next alliance is made, supporting H2. Substantively, states making partially secret alliances are likely to find it harder to make an alliance in the future. As outlined above, this is likely due to the fact that partially secret alliances are partially known to other actors, meaning that subsequent gains from such an alliance are more difficult to hide.[9]

Next, bilateral alliances, major powers, defense, offense, nonaggression and consultation alliances are associated with an increase in the amount of time between one alliance and the next. With the exception of the finding for offensive alliances, this is consistent with the models presented in Model 1. Finally, similar to Model 1, irregular termination, symmetry, and World War I are likely to lead to shorter intervals of time between one alliance and the next.

Turning to Model 3, which incorporates an interaction effect between the public/secret variable and irregular termination, the findings are largely consistent. However, with the added interaction effect, we see that public alliances that terminate irregularly are likely to result in a shorter time until the next alliance is made. While the interaction effect between secret and regular/irregular termination is not statistically significant, the lack of statistical significance and the significant finding that public alliances that end irregularly result in a shorter time until the next alliance is noteworthy. This suggests that moving from the reference category (public, regular termination) to a public alliance that ends irregularly has a statistical effect, while secret alliances do not, regardless of how they terminate. This finding is important in that, while it does not support H3 directly, it does indicate that there is some difference between how a public alliance that ends irregularly is different from a secret alliance that ends irregularly.

Next, we see similar findings in that bilateral alliances, major powers, defense, nonaggression and consultation alliances are likely to result in a longer period of time until the formation of a new alliance. On the other hand, symmetry is likely to be of shorter duration until the next alliance forms, while the World War I dummy variable drops out of significance.

Model 4, disaggregating the variables for public/partially, secret/fully secret alliances and for regular/irregular termination, provides a more nuanced analysis. Given that this model contains the greatest amount of nuance, this is the preferred model for answering several of the hypotheses. First, partially secret alliances that end regularly are likely to result in a longer period until the next alliance is made. While not the hypothesis testing H3, it does suggest there is a difference in whether an alliance ends in a regular or unplanned manner and the prospects for future agreements. Likewise, more generally, it does support the H2 that secret alliances (devoid of the interaction effect) are likely to have a harder time making alliances in the future. Next, the finding that fully secret alliances with irregular termination results in a shorter period of time until the next alliance is statistically significant, meaning I can reject the null hypothesis for H4. Given the theory that fully secret alliances should not be publicly known and the state has not alienated its alliance partner by not following through on its commitments, I expect a shorter period of time until the next alliance.

Regarding other variables, longer periods are expected for alliances that are bilateral, involve major powers, are defensive, nonaggressven, or consultative. Shorter periods are expected for symmetrical alliances. These findings are largely consistent with the findings in the other models.

Finally, a note regarding modeling decisions is in order. As mentioned above, Cox models are preferable in this scenario, given concerns regarding potential violations of the proportional hazards assumption. However, I have presented both Weibull and Cox models to demonstrate the robustness of the findings. These models also show both robust standard errors and standard errors clustered on the member state. While clustering on the state is theoretically preferential, given the low number of states that make secret alliances and the low number that are likely to make such alliances in the future, pooling standard errors by states is problematic in that such repeat behaviors in rare events are likely to depress the overall findings.

In testing the proportional hazards assumption in Model 1, there is a χ^2 of 0.49, meaning that I am not able to reject the null hypothesis. This means that the hazards are proportional. Similarly, I fail to reject the null hypothesis of the proportional hazards assumption in Model 2 ($\chi^2 > 0.61$), Model 3 ($\chi2 > 0.59$), and Model 4 ($\chi2 > 0.76$). In Models 5–8, there is a similar story, with a $\chi2 > 0.39$ in Model 5, 0.38 in Model 6, 0.50 in Model 7, and 0.69 in Model 8. This gives me a good deal of confidence in the validity of these measures and the decision to rely primarily upon Cox specification. In Figures 5.2a and 5.2b, I present graphs of the proportional hazards assumption in Models 1–4.

CONCLUSION

While these findings only support some of the hypotheses, there is little doubt that reputation does play a secondary role in alliance formation. The results strongly support the claims made in H2 and H4. The differing operationalizations of the models (distinguishing between partially and fully secret alliances) suggest that partially secret alliances are more vulnerable to reputational damage, as at least some information about the alliance is public knowledge. However, this effect is less evident for fully secret alliances. In fact, for reasons outlined above in the theory section, fully secret alliances that terminate irregularly are likely to enjoy a shorter period of time until they make their next alliance.

Although this analysis primarily focuses on *ex ante* effects of alliance formation rather than the immediate events influencing alliance formation, alternative operationalizations could yield different findings. Nonetheless, the initial findings illustrate claims that are consistent with the presented theory. States making partially secret alliances have a harder time forming such alliances in the future because public audiences know there is some agreement, though they may not know what the entire agreement consists of. This leads other states to suspect the existence of a more extensive agreement than what has been disclosed publicly. Similarly, fully secret alliances with irregular termination enjoy two advantages. First, the concealment of the illicit agreement better safeguards a state's public reputation. Second, the fulfillment of the agreement's objectives renders a state's private reputation largely irrelevant given the generally short-term nature of many secret alliances. This means that, even while a state's private reputation may be harmed, we are unlikely to see the effects.

While it could be that reputation is affected by states making secret alliances, it must be acknowledged that there are several other unaccounted for affects that may make such reticence for secret alliance makers less capable of making alliances in the future. First, the issues that prompted the secret alliance in the first place may have been resolved by the alliance itself, rendering further alliances unnecessary. This "selecting out" of the political causes of an alliance may best be understood as a "moot point" in politics. On the other hand, things are rarely "moot points" in politics, and an alliance in the future may negate a non-signatory's willingness to make an alliance with one of the secret alliance makers in the future. Furthermore, if made relatively closely after a secret alliance, such an alliance presents an insatiable opportunity to "drive a wedge" between two allies. This case may best be illustrated by the abrupt turn of the USSR from being allies with Nazi Germany to becoming a core ally of the United States and Great Britain after its invasion by the Nazis in June 1941.

Next, it is entirely likely that states do not have reputations but that leaders do. While research on first-person images of leaders is lacking (e.g., see Horowitz, Stam, and Ellis's (2015) work on leaders and risk), this is a legitimate criticism. Nazi Germany's alliance with the Soviet Union was likely only possible because of the regimes in place by both Hitler and Stalin. Similarly, Ben-Gurion's insistence on attendance at the Sèvres meeting between the French and British made the secret alliance possible in the first place, with the British and French plausibly able to argue publicly that they were "separating" warring parties, thus giving them an air of credibility and "fairness." One would find it exceedingly difficult to argue that the current government of Germany or the government of Konrad Adenauer in 1949 bears any resemblance to the Nazi government, meaning that Germany does not have the reputation of its former Nazi rulers. Nonetheless, just as states that are sometimes in vehement opposition to their former regimes must still repay loans taken out by those regimes, they[10] are still often "politically stained" with the reputation of those regimes. And while reputation may be most obvious in the public sense, it is unclear how reputation affects individual states' decisions based on their experiences in making secret alliances.

NOTES

1. While such norms against secret diplomacy may have become more prevalent in the past several decades, states nonetheless consider diplomatic conversations to be secret. However, while states may view secret alliances as problematic and the torch-bearer of this norm has been the United States, research indicates that the United States is still willing and frequently engages in secret agreements (Scoville 2020). However, these agreements rarely rise to the level of a formal secret alliance and are instead best understood as executive agreements. Nonetheless, paradoxically, this indicates that the reliability of some states is enough to overcome the risk of embarrassment that often comes with secret agreements.
2. For instance, alliances are legally required to be deposited with the United Nations, per the Vienna Convention on the Law of Treaties, proposed in 1969 and adopted in 1980. Seemingly, this precludes secret treaties.
3. In fact, Kuo (2020) finds that 80 percent of alliances made between 1870 and 1916 were partially or fully secret. Indeed, the majority of secret alliances in the entire dataset occurred during these 46 years.
4. For instance, see Finnemore and Sikkink (1998, pp. 888–91).
5. For more discussion on the risks associated with placing too great an emphasis on omitted variable bias, see Clarke (2005). While there are sometimes legitimate reasons to include an expansive list of all variables that could potentially

impact a dependent variable, the risk must be balanced with the "kitchen sink" approach that can otherwise assign, amplify, or dilute the effects of theoretically important variables at the expense of more suspect variables.

6. See also Gartzke and Millard (forthcoming, "Throwing in the Towel").
7. Note that models were also run using this method but, for brevity's sake, are not reported here.
8. Note that models in the Appendix include both Cox models with standard errors clustered by state, as well as Weibull models with robust standard errors and similarly clustered standard errors.
9. As illustrated by examples such as the Molotov–Ribbentrop Pact, the Protocol of Sèvres, the Sykes–Picot Agreement, and the Treaty of London with Italy.
10. For instance, discussions of "collective responsibility" within German culture regarding the atrocities of World War II and the outbreak of hostilities, as well as the inability of Japan to make political inroads with some neighboring Asian states due to its aggressive foreign policy both before and during World War II.

6. The best friends are enemies: the Molotov–Ribbentrop Pact

The alliance between Nazi Germany and the Soviet Union—signed on August 23, 1939[1]—was a treaty among rivals without long-term issue convergence. Each state wanted something from the other (freedom in their spheres of influence), along with territory from third-party states. However, the provision of these goods led to the outbreak of World War II.

Both states were autocracies and repressive regimes, which meant that public knowledge of an alliance with their avowed enemies (the Soviets for the Nazis and vice versa) was unlikely to have domestic repercussions. And while the treaty had important secret components, it was immediately reported by international news sources and within Germany and the Soviet Union (NA 1939; Tolischus 1939). Many individuals and governments also suspected that a secret agreement accompanied the public declaration.

Much attention has been given to the subsequent conflict, but little notice has been paid to the coordination that occurred after the signing of the pact and before it collapsed with the invasion of the Soviet Union. This coordination tended to occur between each signatory's military or paramilitary/intelligence services. The short-term result of the pact was that both states were able to gather more allies due to the immediacy and intensity of the conflict. Over the longer term, the unified state of Germany ceased to exist for decades, and the Soviet Union's wartime alliances quickly fell apart or transformed into something else entirely as puppet regimes were established in Eastern Europe after 1945.

BACKGROUND

The Molotov–Ribbentrop Pact emerged out of the Munich Conference, during the Czech crisis. Hitler had demanded Czech territory that held a large population of ethnic Germans (Volksdeutsch) and insisted on retaining territory gained in the 1938 Austrian Anschluss. The British, French, and Soviets had alliance obligations to defend Czechoslovakia (Gibler 2009), but none of them was prepared to defend Czechoslovakia against German aggression.

The Soviets sought to draw France and the United Kingdom into an alliance that could defend against German aggression (Pons 2014). France and the United Kingdom were unwilling to commit to such an alliance because conflict was more likely to break out in the East, which would drag their countries into war. Both France and the United Kingdom were also leery of entangling alliances after the lessons they had learned in World War I (Levy 2007). Maksim Litvinov, the Soviet foreign minister, favored a collective security approach for dealing with Nazi Germany (Steiner 1999, p. 753) which involved working with the League of Nations (Roberts 1989, pp. 43–4) and drafting separate formal agreements with Western allies (Government of USSR 1977; Roberts 1989, pp. 43–4). He was abruptly fired by Stalin in 1939. Litvinov's replacement, Vyacheslav Molotov (Encyclopaedia Britannica 2018), favored an alliance with Germany that could stall for time while the Soviet military was rebuilt (Pons 2014, p. xii). Stalin's view was that the Western allies lacked resolve and would not live up to their commitments. They had not lived up to their commitments in Czechoslovakia or after the remilitarization of the Rhineland (Pons 2014, p. xii). Stalin was also hostile and suspicious of the West's motivations and ideology (Steiner 1999, p. 753). He believed that internal contradictions within the West would make alliances easy until Western capitalist states turned on one another (Moorhouse 2014; Roberts 1989, p. 36).

The Soviets also put more effort into "shopping around" for suitable allies than any other state during the inter-war years. They also frequently pursued or imposed nonaggression or neutrality pacts on neighbors and frequently broke them.[2] The Soviet distrust of Western resolve, the subsequent breakdown of negotiations with Western states (Roberts 1989, p. 5), and suspicion of Western motives led Stalin to ally with Nazi Germany, the sworn enemy of the Soviet Union. Stalin's decision to ally with Hitler was a choice to preserve the status quo and increase the Soviet Union's security while expanding its territory. The Soviets were aware of Hitler's hatred for communism, but they were willing to be practical when alliances were necessary. Khimchuk, the Soviet Ambassador to Germany in 1932, wrote that "Hitler has definitely declared his task is to fight the USSR," which was later echoed by Molotov (Roberts 1989, pp. 40 and 47). Pons (2014) states that "from August/September 1939 onwards, Stalin was committed to appeasing Hitler and to exploiting the conflict between the Western powers and Nazi Germany to create a territorial 'security system' involving expansion into eastern Europe" (p. xiii). This was accompanied by a shift in Soviet language from opposing fascism to bringing about "inter-imperialist conflict between Germany and Western states" (Pons 2014, pp. xiii–xiv). The strategy of allying with Germany created a buffer zone between European Russia and Germany (Roberts 1989, pp. 5–6) which was beneficial for the Soviet population in European Russia and Ukraine. Later Soviet leaders and historians, including Gorbachev, blamed World War II on the West's failure to ally with the Soviet Union (Roberts 1989, p. 8). Soviet Defense Minister Voroshilov blamed the West for the Soviet–Nazi alliance as early as August 27, 1939, in *Izvestia* (Roberts 1989). However, the Soviet decision to ally with Hitler enabled the conflict—claims that the lack of a Western alliance forced the Soviets into a Nazi treaty hinge on the distinction between sins of omission and those of commission. Historians such as Stephen Kotkin, on the other hand, claim that the Soviets found themselves throughout the 1930s courted by both the British and Germans, who both wanted a political upper hand and needed the other great power at the edge of Europe to either contain Germany or expand Germany (Kotkin 2017). Both Germany and the Soviets had been left out of the negotiations at Versailles, and the British desperately sought to revise the punitive treaty, for fear it would drive both the Soviets and Nazis together (Kotkin 2017).

Roberts claims that the alliance was a delay tactic, buying time to prepare the Red Army and hedge against a future Nazi attack (Roberts 1989, pp. 3–4). This meant two benefits from a Soviet–Nazi alliance: (1) an expansion of Soviet territory to provide a buffer zone; and (2) time to rebuild the army's equipment and the upper echelons of its officer ranks, which had been purged in 1936.

The Soviet decision took a "bandwagoning" approach, as outlined by Schweller (1994), to deal with its security issues. Rather than balancing against threats from other states (Walt 1985), the Soviets determined that aligning with Germany could ensure their own security while expanding their territory. Schweller (1994) states that predatory states can "bandwagon" with other predatory states to expand their political power, even in the absence of a threat. The French and British failure to uphold their agreements betrayed the Czechs to the Nazis in hopes of averting a general war. In comparison, bandwagoning seemed more appealing to the Soviets than alliances that lacked credible commitments, especially with partners who had recently damaged their reputations (Roberts 1989, p. 5).

Germany also stood to benefit from the alliance: territorial gains were assured and a temporary alliance with the Soviets would sideline its greatest threat to eastward expansion. The alliance also bought time for Germany to prepare for an invasion of the Soviet Union. Finally, when Germany was prepared to attack, it would have a common border with Soviet Russia. Before the invasion of Poland, such a shared border did not exist. On August 23, 1939, a mere nine days before the Nazi invasion of Poland, Germany and the Soviet Union publicly signed an alliance agreement. The agreement did away with their official public policies of anti-fascism and anti-communism, reaffirming the commitment to neutrality that the Soviets and the Weimar Republic reached in April 1926. However, in a secret protocol consisting of three sections, both parties agreed to designate spheres of influence (1) "in the event of a territorial and political rearrangement belonging to the Baltic States"; (2) in

Poland; and (3) a lack of "political disinterestedness [in Bessarabia]" (Gibler 2009, Document #3101). In Article I of the public Soviet–Nazi agreement, both states agreed "to desist from any act of violence, any aggressive action, and any attack on each other, either individually or jointly with other powers," pledging to not assist any third party that was belligerent to either signatory (Article II). They also agreed to remain in contact with one another (Article III) and to refrain from joining a pact aimed at either party (Article IV) (Gibler 2009, Document #3101). Additional public protocols called for peaceful arbitration (Article V), set an expiration date ten years in the future (Article VI), and required immediate enforcement (Article VII) (Gibler 2009, Document #3101).

However, it was the secret protocols that would ultimately lead to war. Poland, the primary good distributed by the alliance, was defended by its allies, France and the United Kingdom. The Baltic states and Romania would also be quite literally "up in arms" over promises that Germany and the Soviet Union had made to each other. However, neither Britain nor France would come to the aid of the Baltics or Romania because there was little they could do, and neither state had alliance obligations with those states.

In their secret protocols and other discussions, the Soviets and Nazis redrew borders in Eastern Europe at the expense of local inhabitants. Nazi forces occupied Western Poland up to the Vistula River, and the Soviets claimed the eastern half of the country. The Soviets also forced mutual defense pacts on Lithuania, Latvia, and Estonia in October 1939 and began forcibly basing Soviet troops in the Baltic states and eliminating local bureaucrats, politicians, and other opponents to Soviet rule—largely completing their work by the late spring of 1940 (Hiden and Salmon 2014). Finally, Germany had agreed not to interfere in Bessarabia—much of which is in modern-day Moldova—which was controlled by Romania in 1939. On June 28, 1940, the Soviets forced Romanian troops to withdraw from Bessarabia and occupied the area, which had a substantial population of ethnic Germans (Scurtu et al. 2002).

Extensive distrust, political acrimony, and incompatible interests between Germany and the USSR ensured that their pact would not last; it represented short- to mid-term issue convergence (e.g., Hilger and Meyer 1954; Roberts 1992; Sontag and Beddie 1948). Neither side believed that the agreement would be long-lived (Roberts 1992) but it gave them time to begin enacting their policies of extracting goods from other polities.[3]

Regardless of its duration, Germany and the Soviet Union stood to gain from this agreement. Specifically, Germany would acquire Western Poland, and the Soviets would get land in Eastern Poland, the Baltic states, and Bessarabia. If Western powers did declare war over the invasion of Poland, Germany also hoped to extract economic concessions while sidelining the Soviets, postponing the difficulties of fighting a war on two fronts. Both states were also recommitting to an agreement of nonaggression that they had signed in 1926. The previous agreement made it more likely that the two states would sign a formal secret alliance because it had been useful for Germany. Germany knew that it could obtain Soviet consent to invade Poland—Nazi Germany's immediate policy goal—by promising nonaggression for a short time. The two states did not have a long-term issue convergence, but a short-term policy overlap in the two states made a "marriage of convenience" via secret alliance more likely. As Stephen Kotkin points out, nonaggression pacts are only necessary between enemies, not among friends (Hoover Institution 2024). Though this document publicly made them appear as allies, nothing could be further from the truth. Neither state trusted the other, but both knew what the other wanted, allowing them to agree to a division of goods. What they did not know was how long that status quo would last or if either side would uphold their end of the bargain beyond the immediate agreement (Roberts 1992).

WHY A SECRET ALLIANCE?

The Molotov–Ribbentrop Pact is a classic example of predatory states setting out to obtain goods from third-party states. Both Nazi Germany and the Soviet Union were strongly autocratic regimes, which meant that public dissent and discourse were unlikely to cause problems for the rapprochement. Instead, public knowledge of their plans risked provoking a preemptive attack from stakeholders who objected to the goods they discussed in the secret alliance. This made secrecy paramount in their negotiations.

Provision of Goods and Familiarity

German evaluations in both the Weimar and Nazi eras after World War I determined that alliances would be needed for their next conflict. However, it was difficult for a vanquished Germany to find allies (Johnson 2021, pp. 23–4). Many allies from the last war had been broken up or made into independent states, creating additional difficulties. The new state of the Soviet Union was the most logical choice for a strong ally. However, the Nazis and Soviets were in no way philosophically aligned. Nonetheless, the precursor to the USSR was the first state that the Germans signed an agreement with during World War I (Johnson 2021, p. 13). Similarly, the Weimar Republic signed numerous agreements with the newly-minted Soviet Union throughout the 1920s. The various agreements included neutrality pacts, economic agreements, and more informal weapons development schemes.

Leon Trotsky, one of the USSR's earliest leaders, wrote in the mid-1920s that "Poland can be a bridge between Germany and us, or a barrier" (Eudin, Fisher, and Jones 1957). While this was before the Nazis came to power, the inter-war cooperation between any two states was perhaps greatest between Germany and the Soviets. The 1922 Treaty of Rapallo and the 1926 Treaty of Berlin were two of the most prominent agreements, but other collaborations between the two states continued throughout the inter-war years, culminating in the 1939 Molotov–Ribbentrop Pact.

Most scholars and laymen claim that the Molotov–Ribbentrop Pact represented short-term issue convergence, which is correct, but the story is more complicated. Germany, under the Weimar and Nazi governments, had a tradition of cooperation with the Soviets during the inter-war years, given that both countries were the outcasts of Europe at the time. Their cooperation was not one of friendship, but they engaged in repeated transactions until Nazi Germany ultimately turned on the Soviets. Germany's military buildup during the Weimar and Nazi eras owes much to the Soviets. The 1922 Treaty of Rapallo began a years-long cooperation between the Soviets and Germans to illicitly develop a modern military and increased trade ties.[4] As Johnson surmises, Nazi Germany only became strong because of almost 20 years of cooperation with the Soviet Union (Johnson 2021). And although Hitler renounced Rapallo in 1933, he returned to it in spirit by increased cooperation with the Soviets.

Rapallo laid the foundations for developing a modern German army. Germany was subject to arms inspections under the 1919 Versailles Treaty (Johnson 2021, p. 4).[5] The country was forbidden from developing chemical weapons, tanks, small arms, and air assets, and those prohibitions were ignored after the Nazis came to power.[6] The Soviet Army sent officers to study and attend staff colleges in Germany, and the Nazis reestablished economic, political, and military ties with the Soviet Union after Germany had cut off economic ties in 1933. In fact, Goering expanded trade with the USSR five times between 1937 and 1938 (Johnson 2021, pp. 201–2). Likewise, the Soviets demanded "four complete fighter and bomber prototypes, seven engine designs, thirteen different machine gun and bomb designs, nine types of laboratory equipment, and ten kinds of optical and electrical equipment" (Johnson 2021, p. 202).

Cooperation between Germany and the Soviets was deeper than the illicit production of military goods (Johnson 2021). It began during the Polish–Bolshevik war when the Weimar military establishment sent logistical supplies to the Soviets (Johnson 2021, pp. 37–8). General Seckt, the chief of the Reichswehr from 1920 to 1926, first proposed economic exchanges, and the cooperation increased with the formation of Sondergruppe Russland, coordinating Reichswehr activities in Russia during the Weimar era.

In the late 1930s, the strange relationship between the Soviets and Germans reached its apex. Hitler's forces had marched into the Sudetenland in October 1938, and they had occupied the remainder of the Czech lands by March 1939.

In seizing Bohemia and Moravia, Hitler had made a fatal mistake. There were few ethnic Germans in those lands, which demonstrated that Hitler's appetite for territory was not limited to specious claims of wanting to incorporate all ethnic Germans into the Reich (Moorhouse 2014, p. 10). Jozef Goebbels even wrote in his diary that the Soviet alliance was necessary because Hitler had "backed himself into a corner" (Moorhouse 2014, p. 20).

The next logical target of German aggression was Poland, where the Nazis would face greater resistance from Western powers. The 1921 Franco–Polish alliance had been strengthened by a 1939 military-to-military agreement between France and Poland.[7] Although the 1939 agreement was not a formal alliance, it did solidify ties between allies that had softened during the tough 1930s, when France was struggling to fund its military and increasingly focused on defensive means of deterring Germany. During the inter-war years, the French pursued a *cordon sanitaire* policy, hoping to isolate Germany and surround it with states that were at least unwilling to offer aid, if not openly belligerent.

The British had also made public assurances that it would defend Poland in the event of a German invasion. British Prime Minister Neville Chamberlain stated in Parliament that "in the event of any action which clearly threatened Polish independence, and which the Polish Government accordingly considered it vital to resist, His Majesty's Government would feel themselves bound at once to lend the Polish Government all support in their power" (*Parl. Debs, 5th Ser., House of Commons, Vol. 345, Col. 2415*).

Although it was not a formal alliance, Poland and the United Kingdom signed the Pact of Mutual Assistance on April 6, 1939 (Newman 1948, p. 82). It was accompanied by a hastily organized formal alliance on August 25, two days after the public signing and acknowledgement of the alliance between the Nazis and Soviets. Further additions to the pact in 1940 and 1944 included secret provisions and guarantees to the Polish government in exile. Paris had refused to fight the Germans over Czechoslovakia, but the same could not be said for Poland; the French and British now realized that Hitler was a serious threat to European security.

Poland was also pursuing "alliances" with potential aggressor states on its borders. The country experienced numerous wars during its post-World War I independence, and its domestic turmoil was largely driven by its ethnic German populations, putting Poland in a precarious position. Under Polish Chief of State Jozef Pilsudski, the country entered into nonaggression pacts with both the USSR and Nazi Germany that were supposed to be in effect in 1939. It was an attempt to delay the inevitable conflict with Germany (Newman 1948, p. 76). However, Hitler annulled the German pact in 1935 (Newman 1948, p. 79), well before his 1939 invasion. The Soviets, for their part, ended the treaty when they invaded Poland on September 17.

It was against this backdrop that Germany realized that its territorial expansion required a willing partner to counter the newly-invigorated Western allies. The most logical ally was the Soviet Union: it had vast resources, and its location made it a major threat if it went to war against Germany. With favorable trade deals, the Nazis could acquire many of the resources needed for their campaign. Germany was also hoping to avoid the challenges of a war on two fronts. There were two primary concerns here. The first was economic. Second, the Soviets were to stay out of the war until a peace deal or defeat of the Western allies could occur.

The Soviets had yet to make overtures to the British and French and instead began talking with the Nazis about a potential alliance (Newman 1948, p. 46). On April 17, 1939, German Secretary of State for Foreign Affairs Ernst von Weizsäcker and Soviet Ambassador to Berlin Alexei Merekalov met to discuss trade and had preliminary discussions for a political alliance (Newman 1948, pp. 46–7). Conversations continued throughout the summer, but their primary focus was economic rather than political (Newman 1948, pp. 46–7). A major hurdle to Soviet–German cooperation was removed in June 1939, after the Nazis dropped weapons embargoes against the Soviet Union (Johnson 2021, p. 206). Around the same time, Molotov met with the German Ambassador to Moscow and disputed the details of the recently negotiated Anglo–Polish alliance. The Nazis saw it as hostile, even though it was clearly defensive. The Soviets recognized it as defensive until it was in their best interest to see otherwise (Newman 1948, pp. 50–1).

Von Weizsäcker wrote to the Germany Ambassador to the Soviets on May 30, 1939, stating that Germany had decided to pursue an alliance with the Soviets (Sontag and Beddie 1948, p. 15), which was a policy change that is believed to have come from both Goering and Hitler (Moorhouse 2014, pp. 11–12). Throughout the spring and summer of 1939, the Germans and Soviets fell out about whether an alliance was possible. On August 12, the Soviets stated that they would sign a political alliance if the conference were held in Moscow (Johnson 2021, p. 208). On August 16, Nazi Ambassador Friedrich-Werner Graf von der Schulenburg's official telegram to Berlin stated that "Germany is ready to conclude a nonaggression pact with the Soviet Union" (Sontag and Beddie 1948, p. 58).

However, the Soviets were making simultaneous approaches to the British and French. The British had sent low-level civil servants to negotiate a potential agreement (Newman 1948, p. 58). The negotiations were quite public and openly discussed by Western newspapers (Roberts 1989). Germany's offer to send Nazi Foreign Minister Joachim von Ribbentrop ultimately made more of an impression on the Soviets, and they took the Nazi offer of rapprochement more seriously (Sontag and Beddie 1948, p. 60). Three days after the draft of the Soviet–Nazi pact was sent back to Berlin, Hitler himself accepted it

(Sontag and Beddie 1948, p. 65). In the first round of discussions, the Soviets insisted on claiming Libau and Windau, which were predominantly German towns in modern-day Latvia (Sontag and Beddie 1948, p. 71). After Hitler's assent, the negotiations continued to outline each country's spheres of influence. The Nazis would claim all of Western Poland, and the majority of the Baltics and Bessarabia went to the Soviets. There would be revisions to these negotiations before the agreement's 1941 collapse, but each side had outlined their desired territories in Poland, the Baltics, and Bessarabia.

International and Domestic Public Opinion

In theory, domestic public opinion should matter less in autocratic regimes due to the small size of their selectorates (Bueno de Mesquita et al. 2004a). In fact, both the Soviets and Nazis positively reported on each other's successes within the first few months of the campaign (Moorhouse 2014, p. 39). Moorhouse (2014) notes that "public discourse was uniformly positive about the pact, with German newspapers immediately altering the tone with which they reported Soviet current affairs or Russian culture" (p. 125). *Pravda* and *Izvestia* were even sold in Berlin after the pact was signed. Some have asserted that the Soviets attempted to appear uninterested in the disagreements between Poland, Germany, and the West by appearing neutral (Roberts 1992, pp. 8–9), despite the direct Soviet occupation of Eastern Poland and their military and economic assistance to Berlin.

In fact, German public opinion was so unimportant that German diplomat Hans von Herwath later stated that "we were able to make a deal with the Soviets because we were able without any problems with German opinion to deliver the Baltic states and eastern Poland to Russia. This the British and the French, with their public opinions, were unable to do" (Moorhouse 2014, p. 22).[8] Ribbentrop had also concluded and told the Soviets that the German public welcomed rapprochement with the Soviets (Sontag and Beddie 1948). A joke allegedly circulated in Berlin suggesting that "Stalin will yet join the 1936 Anti-Comintern Pact" (Newman 1948, p. 60). Ironically enough, Hitler later asked Molotov directly if the USSR would join the Anti-Comintern Pact (Newman 1948, p. 144). However, by the time of the Winter War in late 1939, domestic opinion in Germany was said to favor Finland over the Soviets (Moorhouse 2014, p. 76). Germany also had public detractors criticizing the Nazi–Soviet alliance when it was announced. One report indicates that Munich's Brown House, the Nazi party headquarters, was littered with discarded party badges shortly after the signing of the agreement (Moorhouse 2014, p. 128).

Unlike the Nazis, the Soviets were more concerned about potential domestic backlash. Stalin was particularly worried about such fallout, even going so far as to say to Ribbentrop after the first day of negotiations:

> Don't you think … that we have to pay a little more attention to public opinion in our two countries? For many years now, we have been pouring buckets of shit on each other's heads, and our propaganda boys could not do enough in that direction. And now, all of a sudden, are we to make our peoples believe that all is forgotten and forgiven? Things don't work so fast. Public opinion in our country, and probably in Germany too, have to be prepared slowly for the change in our relations that this treaty is to bring about. (Moorhouse 2014, pp. 27–8)

Stalin is also known to have said, "public opinion in our country will have to be prepared slowly for the change in our relations that this treaty is to bring about" (Moorhouse 2014, p. 120). To square this circle and abruptly change its public policy toward the Nazi regime, a campaign of official friendliness was launched in official Soviet pronouncements and their state-controlled press.

Nikita Khrushchev later stated that simply explaining the logic to the masses through newspapers such as *Pravda* and *Izvestia* would not be enough:

> For us to have explained our reasons for signing the treaty in straightforward newspaper language would have been offensive, and besides, nobody would have believed us. It was very hard for us—as communists—to accept the idea of joining forces with Germany. It was difficult enough for us to accept this paradox ourselves. It would have been impossible to explain it to the man in the street. (Moorhouse 2014, pp. 27–8)

The Soviets were in a more precarious position due to their extensive overseas networks and their goal of exporting communism. They not only had to deal with domestic public opinion, but also with the public opinion of "fellow travelers" abroad. The Soviet High Command took steps to address these concerns by producing maps signed by Ribbentrop and Stalin, demonstrating that both states approved the division of Poland (Moorhouse 2014, p. 41). In a report to Berlin, Schulenburg claimed that Soviet public opinion feared that the Nazis would turn on the USSR after they were done with Poland (Sontag and Beddie 1948, pp. 88–9).

Hitler also had to deal with international backlash from allies who were mortal enemies of communism (Sontag and Beddie 1948, pp. 121–2). However, Hitler was hardly one to be bothered by the feelings of others. He allegedly said of the pact, "I have given the command and I shall shoot everyone who utters one word of criticism" (Sontag and Beddie 1948, pp. 124–5). Despite this attitude, Hitler went to great lengths to accommodate Benito Mussolini. In a telegram before Germany's assault on the USSR, Hitler stated that the partnership with the Soviet Union, in spite of the complete sincerity of the efforts to bring about a final conciliation, was nevertheless often very irksome to me, for in some way or other it seemed to me to be a break with my whole origin, my concepts, and my former obligations. I am happy now to be relieved of these mental agonies. (Sontag and Beddie 1948, p. 353)

INSTITUTIONALIZATION AND MILITARY COORDINATION

The Soviet Union released the *Falsifiers of History*[9] to refute a full-length volume of captured Nazi archives published by the US Department of State in 1948. The revisionist Soviet document placed the blame on Germany and the West. The Soviets also opposed the inclusion of the Molotov–Ribbentrop Pact as evidence in the 1946 Nuremburg Trials (Newman 1948, p. 65), because it showed the depth of Nazi–Soviet cooperation in the early years of the war. In fact, Ribbentrop and Molotov spoke with one another a mere two days after the Nazi invasion of Poland, and Molotov congratulated the Nazis when they entered Warsaw (Moorhouse 2014, pp. 84–5).

Germany and the Soviet Union, and especially their military and paramilitary forces, cooperated extensively in the invasion of Poland. Soviet and Nazi troops agreed to maintain 25 kilometers of separation between their forces (Moorhouse 2014, p. 39), although closer contact occurred during events such as the joint Soviet–Nazi victory parade in Brest-Litovsk. Soviet technicians used radio equipment to guide Luftwaffe aircraft in Poland (Moorhouse 2014, p. 39). Germany's general staff also provided intelligence on Polish formations on September 9 (Newman 1948, p. 85). Some prisoners of war who fled the Nazi advances into Poland were returned by the Soviets (Moorhouse 2014, p. 58) while Volksdeutsch in the recently occupied Baltics were "repatriated" to German-controlled Poland (Moorhouse 2014, p. 68). At sea, 18 German vessels sought refuge in Murmansk, sheltering in the ostensibly neutral port to avoid British raiders (Moorhouse 2014, p. 59). Soviet icebreakers, among the best and most numerous in the world, also cleared paths for German warships (Moorhouse 2014, p. 60).

The Soviets and Nazis both insisted on an economic alliance before consenting to a political agreement (Roberts 1989, p. 101). By early 1940, Russia had supplied Germany with 300 million Reichsmarks worth of goods, including 100 million Reichsmarks of grain (Newman 1948, p. 124). Germany received raw goods such as chromium, nickel, iron, coal, and wheat that it desperately needed for the war effort. In return, the Soviets received low-interest loans and manufactured goods. However, Germany was slow to deliver finished products because it desperately needed them for its ongoing war efforts (Newman 1948, p. 124).

Trade negotiations preceded the signing of the Molotov–Ribbentrop Pact, with Hitler stating that political discussions would end if there was no economic agreement (Sontag and Beddie 1948, p. 25). Molotov later echoed that sentiment (Sontag and Beddie 1948, p. 60). After the pact had been signed, it was updated with the German–Soviet Border and Commercial Agreement signed on January 10, 1941 (Moorhouse 2014, p. 227).

After Germany claimed its Polish territory, it encouraged the Soviets to speed up their invasion.[10] A memo sent by Ribbentrop to the chancellery in Moscow ordered Ambassador Schulenburg to inform the Soviets that Germany's army would pursue fleeing Poles into the Soviet occupation zone to eliminate the threat. Schulenburg was to encourage the Soviets to invade quickly from the east (Sontag and Beddie 1948, p. 86). The Soviets likewise informed the Nazis when they called up reservists and when they planned to invade Poland, although Ribbentrop pressed Schulenburg to discover the exact day and hour (Sontag and Beddie 1948, p. 90, also pp. 92–4). However, Schulenburg was not summoned to the Kremlin until 2 am on September 16, four hours before the invasion, indicating a lack of trust between the two allies (Sontag and Beddie 1948, p. 96).

Ribbentrop proposed delegating at a lower-level meeting of Soviet and German officers in order to deconflict operational issues, suggesting that it should be in Bialystok (Sontag and Beddie 1948, p. 94). Cooperation was facilitated by Lieutenant General Ernst August Kostring, the German military attaché in Moscow, and General Kliment Voroshilov, the Soviet defense minister. Stalin personally requested that Nazi airplanes remain west of the Bialystok–Brest–Litovsk–Lemberg line to avoid an accidental downing (Sontag and Beddie 1948, p. 96). The Soviets and Nazis later issued a joint communiqué justifying their invasions of Poland; Stalin personally wrote the document that Molotov had initially refused to issue (Sontag and Beddie 1948, pp. 95, also pp. 98–100).

The Soviet–Nazi Joint Border Commission handled most of the issues arising from the division of the newly conquered Poland. Discussions began in earnest on September 23, and on September 25, Stalin proposed giving Lublin and the entire Province of Warsaw to Germany if the Nazis would give all of Lithuania to the Soviets (Sontag and Beddie 1948, pp. 102–3). This culminated in the German–Soviet Boundary and Friendship Treaty signed on September 28 (Moorhouse 2014, p. 12), which contained a secret protocol for adjusting borders between the two states (Sontag and Beddie 1948, p. 107).

Joint Border Commissions consisted of four Nazi SS officers and four Soviet NKVD officers who coordinated the "resettlement" of "undesirables" and exchanged prisoners who tried to flee communism or fascism (Moorhouse 2014, p. 56). Negotiations and coordination continued until late May 1941, weeks before Operation Barbarossa, Nazi Germany's invasion of the Soviet

Union (Sontag and Beddie 1948, p. 343). However, the first proposals to end the commissions were made on March 31, 1941 (Sontag and Beddie 1948, p. 279).

The Joint Border Commissions were the most advanced institutionalization and formalization of the Soviet–Nazi relationship. Along with informal exchanges through joint military commissions, they represented a high water mark for Nazi–Soviet relations. Other interactions included high-level exchanges through each country's foreign ministry. One such example was a change in the spheres of influence, delivering all of Lithuania to the Soviets on September 28, 1940 (Newman 1948, p. 88). Even cooperation under the 1922 Rapallo treaty was more informal, with the exchanges of relatively low-level Soviet and German officers coordinated through traditional foreign relations channels.

TERMINATION

The Soviets and Nazis cynically knew that the end of their transactional relationship was a foregone conclusion, although Stalin expected it to last longer than 669 days. One of the earliest signs of tension was the forced expulsion of Jewish people from Nazi areas into future Soviet territory (Moorhouse 2014), which occurred even before the Soviets began their invasion from the east. While the Soviets and Nazis never fully trusted one another, they initially enjoyed military, economic, and political benefits. However, tensions later arose in all three areas.

The Nazis were incensed at the Soviet annexation of Bessarabia, largely because the Soviets took a large portion of Bukovina, which was a separate territory with a large Volksdeutsch population (Sontag and Beddie 1948, p. 158). The Russian empire had ruled Bessarabia for 80 years prior to the Bolshevik Revolution, although most of its people were ethnically Romanian (Newman 1948, p. 93). Bukovina, on the other hand, had previously been an Austrian province, which Germany had not promised to the Soviets (Newman 1948, p. 93). This pushed the German-friendly Romania into the Axis camp in November 1940, even though Germany demanded that Romania acquiesce to Soviet demands (Newman 1948, p. 163). In face-to-face discussions between Molotov and Hitler, they argued that the term "sphere of influence" was not clearly defined (Newman 1948, p. 279). Moscow's annexation of the Lithuanian strip, which had a large population of Volksdeutsch, angered Berlin enough for the Soviets to offer a menial payment, which was never made (Newman 1948, p. 279). One scholar has stated that Hitler, at this stage in the war, genuinely thought he could convince the Soviets to agree to his plans for dividing up the world. When the Soviets refused, Germany was exasperated, suggesting that "the Fuhrer's primary complaint against Moscow, therefore, was not ideological; it was strategic" (Newman 1948, p. 279).

The Soviets were similarly angered that Germany mediated the dispute between Hungary and Romania over parts of Transylvania, which was subsequently divided between the two Nazi-friendly states. Failure to consult with the Soviets violated Article 3 of the pact (Newman 1948, p. 96). Molotov brushed this aside, pointing out that the Soviets did not consult Germany before occupying the Baltic states (Newman 1948, p. 96). Ribbentrop was also forced to send his ambassador to Molotov to claim that reports of German soldiers in Romania were merely there to protect supplies necessary for the war effort (Newman 1948, pp. 96–7). Similar issues arose with the Soviets protesting the presence of German troops in Finland.

When Germany's western campaign failed to subdue the United Kingdom, Hitler ordered planning for the invasion of the Soviet Union to begin in late spring 1941. After a failed visit by Molotov to Berlin in late 1940, where he met personally with Hitler, the planning for Operation Barbarossa began in earnest (Newman 1948, p. 97). The Soviets were likewise angered to learn of the new pact between Germany and Japan, though the Germans argued that they did not need to inform the Soviets because it was not directed against the USSR (Newman 1948, p. 109).

Tensions along the Soviet–Nazi border continued to increase. A flurry of diplomatic notes was exchanged regarding border incursions and the buildup of forces between the Nazis and Soviets (Moorhouse 2014, pp. 340–2). The placement of 10–15 Soviet divisions along Lithuania's newly drawn border was particularly unsettling for the Germans (Sontag and Beddie 1948, p. 156). On April 24, 1941, the Nazi embassy in Moscow reported rumors claiming that the Nazis intended to invade the USSR on June 22—ironically, that was the actual date of the invasion (Sontag and Beddie 1948, p. 330). During Ambassador Schulenburg's talk with Molotov mere hours before the invasion, he told the Soviets that the invasion was necessary "in response to the buildup of Soviet troops on the frontier" (Moorhouse 2014, p. 153).

FUTURE ALLIANCE-MAKING PROSPECTS

It is difficult to discuss how the future alliance-making prospects for Germany and the Soviet Union were affected by creating and then breaking their secret agreement. The events surrounding World War II were all related—and this discussion has been conducted elsewhere—especially when looking at event data in the militarized interstate dispute (MID) dataset. One example is Germany's invasion of the Soviet Union, which was initially set for May 15, 1941, instead of June 22. The 38-day delay occurred because Germany was assisting its Italian allies in both Yugoslavia and Greece. These events may appear to be independent in a dataset, but they are intimately connected. Later Soviet and German decisions to ally with other states must also be considered in light of the Molotov–Ribbentrop Pact and its far-reaching effects on international politics. Next, there is the simple reality of secret protocols dividing Europe into spheres of influence without consulting their inhabitants beforehand; many agreements following the Molotov–Ribbentrop Pact were imposed on the affected countries by force. This was particularly true for the Baltics, which were forced into unequal alliances with the Soviet Union in 1939 and 1940. These alliances later resulted in the Soviet military occupying those states, which were incorporated into the Soviet Union under the pretense of "free" elections that occurred only a few months later.

The devastation wrought by World War II, particularly in Eastern and Central Europe—and the imposition of friendly puppet governments in many of these states—meant that alliances made after World War II were similarly tainted with at least some degree of illegitimacy. They were not always forged by willing parties. Next, the greatest challenge in assessing the longer-term effects of the pact may be the fact that Germany ceased to exist as a state after it capitulated on May 8, 1945. First, it was occupied by the Soviet Union and the three major Western allies. Then, it was formed into two separate states: the Federal Republic of Germany in the West and the German Democratic Republic in the East. Scholars often conceptualize states as being continuous (despite their changes in government) or at least succeeded by another state, but that is not the case for Germany. In fact, West Germany's government can better be conceptualized as a continuation of the Weimar Republic than that of Hitler's Reich. After the conflict, East and West Germany joined security networks that aligned with their respective ideological blocs in the Cold War. In considering how Germany's prospects were affected, we can only look at alliances made by Nazi-dominated Germany from 1939 to 1945.

The global nature of World War II means that it is also impossible to examine every case where states considered or entered into arrangements with Germany without a formal agreement. One such example was Spain, which was nominally an ideological ally of Germany, but it neither fought nor provided any meaningful contribution to the Nazi war effort. Instead, we can only analyze formal alliances made by Germany and the Soviet Union up to the conclusion of World War II.

Nazi Germany made several subsequent alliances throughout World War II. It installed puppet regimes in most of the countries it conquered, including France, Norway, and Denmark, and it overthrew the allies of governments that had defected, such as with the deposing of Horthy in Hungary and the reinstallation of Mussolini as a puppet head of the Italian Social Republic. Slovakia became a quasi-independent state aligned with the Nazis. Germany also strengthened ties with the core Axis allies on September 27, 1940, by signing the Tripartite Pact. While Italy was already a formal Nazi ally under 1939's Pact of Steel, the inclusion of Japan particularly angered the Soviets. Japan became a formal ally of Germany, but the practical implications were abundantly unclear. World War II had two theaters on opposite sides of the world, and neither the Germans nor Japanese could effectively project power far enough to link up in a coordinated campaign against target states. Instead, the allies relied on one another to spread each opponent's forces across two different theaters.

The Alliance Treaty Obligations and Provisions (ATOP) dataset (Leeds et al. 2002) shows three more formal alliances made by the Nazis during World War II, all in 1940 or 1941. However, this does not include "alliances" with puppet regimes or states that were aligned with Nazi Germany. The most important of these was the Tripartite Pact, which was later joined by Hungary, Bulgaria, Romania, Slovakia, Yugoslavia, and Independent Croatia. Some of these "states" were puppet regimes—as with the later Italian Social Republic—but Germany was able to garner more allies after the signing of the Molotov–Ribbentrop Pact. Most of the signatories entered into agreements before the invasion of the Soviet Union.

The Soviets, for their part, also pursued other allies between the signing of the Molotov–Ribbentrop Pact and Germany's invasion in June 1941. Formal and informal alliances occurred until the end of World War II. The first such agreements were imposed on the Baltic states, beginning with Estonia (on September 28) and followed by mutual assistance pacts forced on Latvia (October 5) and Lithuania (October 10). The Soviets almost immediately stationed military forces inside the borders of all three countries, and all three states were absorbed into the USSR by summer 1940. Mass arrests and deportations soon followed.

The Soviet Union ostensibly signed 12 other formal agreements between 1940 and 1945. These included agreements with Finland (1941), Japan (1941), the formal alliance with the Western allies and others (1942), an agreement with Iran and the United Kingdom (1942), the Czech government in exile (1943), the newly-liberated French (1944), the British (1945), Yugoslavia (1945), Poland (1945), and Japan (1945) (Leeds et al. 2002). Each case could support a lengthy discussion on its own but the analysis contained here will be brief. Most agreements made by the Soviets after the June 1941 invasion were alliances of convenience. Although the vast majority of German troops fought on the Eastern front during World War II (Citino 2021), the alliance network from the West had a substantial influence on the invasion's ultimate outcome. Overland routes were vital for supplies from allies, most of which ran through Iran, but also through Eastern Russia and into Murmansk in the far north. In fact, some 78 sea-going convoys carrying 7000 airplanes, 5000 trucks, tires, fuel, raw materials, and medicine were sent to the Soviet Union

(Kasevin 2015). British General Sir David Richards described the importance of these goods:

> The Arctic convoys played a critical part in allowing our Russian allies to turn the tide of WW2 decisively in favour of the Allies. It is marvelous that British Arctic Convoy veterans are travelling to St Petersburg to celebrate with their Russian comrades-in-arms not only their role in the defeat of Nazi tyranny but also, at this troubled time, to remind us all of the deep ties between our two nations. I wish all involved a memorable and enjoyable visit. (Kasevin 2015)

While the alliance between East and West ended soon after the Nazis were defeated, ties between the Soviet Union, the United States, and the United Kingdom undoubtedly shortened World War II. Early formal and informal agreements with Japan were designed to keep the USSR from being pulled into a two-front war, which Hitler had hoped to avoid through his alliance with Stalin. Agreements with Finland were direct results of the USSR's decision to align with Hitler and invade Finland in the 1939 Winter War. Subsequent conflict saw Finland and the Soviets continuing to fight during the Continuation War and, after a separate peace had been concluded, the Finns turned on the Nazis during the Lapland War.

Antagonism between the Soviets and Yugoslavia, and with Western allies resulted in many Soviet alliances ending irregularly. Sometimes the nature of the relationship was prematurely renegotiated, as with newly-communist Poland. The Soviets were able to continue making alliances after the secret Molotov–Ribbentrop Pact failed, but many of these agreements fell apart and permanently colored the Soviet relationship not only with states within its bloc, but also with those outside the Eastern bloc.

US President Franklin D. Roosevelt may have best summarized the situation of states in unpalatable-yet-necessary alliances with the Soviets. His defense of the US alliance with the Soviet Union during World War II allegedly used an old Balkan proverb, "it is permitted you in times of grave danger to walk with the devil until you have crossed the bridge" (Schroden and Powell 2021). Reluctant allies, they were all too happy to work together if it brought down Hitler, and most were willing to overlook the hypocrisy of collaborating with one of Hitler's former allies. Similarly, Churchill famously stated that "If Hitler invaded Hell I would make at least a favourable reference to the Devil in the House of Commons" (Churchill 1950).

CONCLUSION

In the case illustrated in this chapter, Nazi Germany knew what it wanted: Poland. Invading without Soviet approval would be viewed as a threat by Moscow, and because France and the United Kingdom had already allied with

Poland, such threats could provoke a two-front war. Nazi Germany also stood to benefit from an ally that had a large reserve of raw materials for the war effort.

For some time, the USSR had sought either an alliance with Western powers or assurances from a collective security agreement via the League of Nations. However, after the failure of collective security in Abyssinia and the Czech lands (Moorhouse 2014, p. 12), the Soviets struck a different course. The United Kingdom and France were averse to alliances during the inter-war years, not wanting to antagonize Hitler, and so the Soviets felt forced into an alliance with Hitler. They also thought this could stoke conflict between Western capitalist powers, resulting in an opening for communism (Moorhouse 2014, p. 13). Hitler, who was incensed by how the Czech crisis had unfolded, looked eastward for an ally. The British and French were certain to dig in their heels after Hitler had promised no more territorial demands (Moorhouse 2014, p. 9). And while Hitler is often most closely associated with the outbreak of World War II, his actions were enabled by the offensive alliance signed between the Nazis and Soviets (Moorhouse 2014, p. 15).

The Nazi reasons for the treaty are relatively straightforward. Germany would get the Soviets to secretly agree to German expansion by (temporarily) giving them part of Poland, the Baltics, and Bessarabia. The Nazis hoped this would avoid a two-front war, allowing them to finish their conflict in the west before turning to their goals in the east. The Nazis would also gain access to goods needed for a prolonged war. In fact, befriending the Soviets early kept Germans from starving as in World War I (Moorhouse 2014, p. 168).

The Soviets were preoccupied with safety and security because of their unfavorable geography and the poor state of their military. They had begun a massive rearmament campaign on the heels of the 1922 Treaty of Rapallo, but their purging of top officers left them particularly vulnerable to the fact that the majority of their population, resources, and productive capabilities were within striking distance of invading armies. This incentivized the USSR to make a deal that expanded the periphery of its borders as a buffer zone at any cost. Cold War commentators often point to the Eastern Bloc as a manifestation of World War II, but the problem had existed long before that conflict. It was certainly on the minds of Soviet leadership throughout the 1930s when collective security failed and a triple alliance with France and the United Kingdom became impossible. The USSR's geopolitical strategy relied on the old adage to "keep your friends close but your enemies closer." Later Soviet revisionists, who began working as soon as the ink on the Molotov–Ribbentrop Pact was dry in August 1939, asserted in the *Falsifiers of History* booklet—planting beliefs that persist in many Russian minds today—that the agreement with the Nazis was purely defensive. Most Soviet citizens did not know of the secret treaty to claim Polish territory until glasnost. When a Baltic deputy controversially read the text in its entirety on a republic-level television program, it set off a firestorm of criticism in the USSR (Roberts 1989, p. xv). Attempts to revise history neglect an important fact: if Stalin had not signed his 1939 pact with Hitler, it is unlikely that tens of millions of Soviet citizens would have died the way they did (Roberts 1992, p. 10).

The Soviets and Nazis both stood to gain from their alliance, albeit temporarily. However, public disclosure of the agreement would have impaired their territorial objectives. It would also have made an alliance between the Soviets and Western powers less likely or certainly more strained.

NOTES

1. Commonly referred to as the Molotov–Ribbentrop Pact.
2. These included Turkey, Afghanistan, Lithuania, Persia, Finland, Latvia, Estonia, Italy, China, and Germany between 1925 and 1939 (Roberts 1989).
3. The alliance ended with Nazi Germany's invasion of the Soviet Union on June 22, 1941.
4. General Seeckt noted that Rapallo did not represent a political or military alliance but a political recognition of one another (Vourkoutiotis 2006, p. 151).
5. As Johnson (2021) notes, there were suspicions in the West that Rapallo contained a secret agreement to divide up Poland between the Soviets and Germans (pp. 48–49). Although it did not, the rumors eerily mirrored the cooperation that would occur 17 years later and result in the partition of Poland.
6. For more on inter-war German/Nazi–Soviet cooperation, see Johnson (2021).
7. For more, see the protocol itself. (*Protocole Franco–Polonais 1939 Gamelin-Kasprzycki: Contre-Témoignage Sur Une Catastrophe, Protokół Końcowy Francusko–Polskich Rozmów Sztabowych 15–17 Maja 1939* (1939).
8. Similarly, the US Ambassador to Germany at the time, Charles Bohlen, later claimed in his memoirs that von Herwath gave the ambassador the contents of the secret treaty the day after the alliance was signed (Bohlen 2021 [1973]).
9. It is alleged that Stalin himself edited some of this piece (Moorhouse 2014, p. 294).
10. Ribbentrop told the German Ambassador in Moscow to "discuss this at once with Molotov and see if the Soviet Union does not consider it desirable for Russian forces to move at the proper time against Polish forces in the Russian sphere of interest and, for their part, to occupy this territory" (Newman 1948, p. 65).

7. Trouble in the Suez: the British–French–Israeli plan for war

The 1956 alliance made by the United Kingdom, France, and Israel during the Suez Crisis shows how secret alliances are possible among democracies that have long-term issue convergence. This case is unusual because it occurred between more than two signatories, but in the narrower sense, the Suez Canal issue convergence was a minor part of the larger issue convergence between all three states. Each state, at a minimum, wanted to ensure continued passage through the Suez Canal after Egyptian President Gamal Abdel Nasser nationalized it on July 26, 1956. The costs to secure that access would be high, increasing the likelihood of conflict between the West and the Soviets (Shemesh and Troen 2005). The three states needed a justification for retaking the canal.

Suez Canal Company shareholders would be compensated by the Egyptian government, but nationalization meant that a vital trade route was vulnerable to Egyptian policy decisions. The seizure of the canal was also a demonstration of Nasser's increasing power for the disunited Arab world. The British were primarily concerned about the canal, but the French were wary of Egyptian interference in Algeria. Of the three allies, Israel cared the most about Nasser's growing power in the Middle East. The nationalization of the canal was about more than the canal itself: it became a symbol first of Egyptian nationalism and second of Arab nationalism.

The British, French, and Israelis colluded to undermine this symbolism and return the canal to private ownership—as an international waterway secured by European forces—checking Nasser's growing power in the Arab world. Mordecai Bar-On, the agreement's authoritative eyewitness (Shlaim 1997, p. 510) wrote that the nationalization of the canal "was totally out of place in the international realities since the Second World War" (Bar-On 2006, p. 174).

In the post-World War II reality, the United States opposed the idea of using force to reclaim the canal. The United States was frustrated by the strengthening relationship between Nasser and the Eastern bloc, his stalling of the Aswan Dam, and his refusal to broker a lasting peace between the Arab world and the newly formed state of Israel (Warner 1991, p. 304), but US policymakers were concerned that the use of force would ostracize Arab states. US President Dwight Eisenhower would only support the use of force if the flow of goods through the canal completely stopped (Richardson 1992, p. 372).

The British interpreted Eisenhower's position to mean that the United States had not fully decided on a course of action. The canal was technically a private company; even though it had been built by the French and secured by the British, the United Kingdom did not have a strong legal basis for its forcible reprivatization. However, the British government was the largest stakeholder in the Suez Canal Company (Richardson 1992, p. 372). The initial concession made to the company was a 99-year lease granted in 1869, which was supposed to last until 1968 (BBC "1956: Egypt Seizes Suez Canal" 1956).

British forces had evacuated a large military base in Egypt that was ceded to the British to guard the canal. The base had previously endured numerous attacks from the Egyptian army, some occurring as early as May 1953 (Aldrich 1967, p. 541). In 1951, the Egyptians had canceled the 1936 treaty allowing British soldiers to be stationed in Egypt (National Army Museum n.d.), though the British did not withdraw from the area surrounding the canal. Fifty-four British soldiers died in the Sinai between 1950 and 1956, with 40 Egyptians dying in 1952 after the British attempted to disarm paramilitaries in Ismalia (National Army Museum n.d.).

Nasser had insisted on a 1954 Anglo–Egyptian Agreement that would remove British troops from Egypt in less than two years. At the time, some 70,000 British soldiers remained in Egypt (National Army Museum n.d.). Under the agreement, the British retained the right to return troops to the canal zone if there was a security need for them in the following seven years (Butler 2002, p. 112). The nationalization of the canal undid all of these plans and severely threatened the economies of Europe. The economy of the United Kingdom was particularly vulnerable.

The British insisted that a return to the status quo was essential for their security interests. British Prime Minister Anthony Eden and Foreign Minister Selwyn Lloyd went on the offensive to persuade their allies. Eden wrote to Eisenhower that:

> We are all agreed that we cannot afford to allow Nasser to seize control of the canal in this way ... my colleagues and I are convinced that we must be ready, in the last resort, to use force to bring Nasser to his senses. (Warner 1991, p. 308)

The French also protested the seizure, with French Foreign Minister Charles Pineau telling the US Ambassador that it was the same as Hitler's seizure of the Rhineland (Warner 1991, p. 308). US Secretary of State John Dulles told Eisenhower that the British and French were concerned about their waning power in the Middle East; the two countries wanted to counter Nasser's growing influence and power in the Arab world (Warner 1991, p. 309). Despite these considerations, Eisenhower remained unwilling to permit the canal's recovery by force.

US dealings with Nasser had followed a consistent pattern. Before the nationalization of the canal, the United States hoped that keeping Nasser at the negotiating table would get him to see the folly of his ways. Access to US markets, with the benefits of most favored nation status, was an enticement for Nasser to cooperate on Middle East and anti-Soviet issues (Warner 1991, p. 307). However, the British had concluded that they would be unable to do business with Nasser long before the canal was seized (Warner 1991, p. 307). The United Kingdom had already resolved to induce Nasser's compliance at gunpoint.

The United States took an active diplomatic role in peacefully trying to resolve the dispute over the canal (Richardson 1992, p. 373). The canal was protected under the Covenant of 1888 as an international waterway, which led the United States to pursue an international solution (Aldrich 1967, p. 542). US pressure induced the British to host the London Conference, convening 22 nations in August 1956 to discuss a resolution. Unsurprisingly, the conference was unable to provide a solution. Eighteen of the 22 attending countries supported the British and French positions (Aldrich 1967, p. 542), but there were no solutions that could force Egypt to return the canal to private ownership. Nasser flatly rejected their plans. A second conference was held in London the following month, and it ended with predictable results (Aldrich 1967, pp. 543–4).

Dulles continued to tell the British that the United States would not support the retaking of the canal by force, fearing that such efforts would force more of the Arab world into the arms of the Soviet Union. However, the United Kingdom depended on traffic through the canal, and it had been involved in the canal's defense since the 1882 Egyptian uprising, which left it unwilling to accept the nationalization effort. As Europe's old colonial powers lost control of their colonies around the globe, it looked unlikely that the British could recover from the economic impact of having the canal closed off to British ships or goods bound for the United Kingdom.

Events moved quickly as all sides prepared for violence (Azar 1972, p. 186). France and the United Kingdom began planning military strategies for retaliation on July 27, well before the London Conference (Kunz 1991, p. 78), after UK Chancellor of the Exchequer Maurice Macmillan told Eden that the use of force was inevitable (Warner 1991, p. 309). On July 29, at a pre-scheduled meeting between Eden and Pineau, France publicly supported the United Kingdom's militant stance over the canal seizure (Kunz 1991, p. 77). Pineau again equated the seizure to Hitler's remilitarization of the Rhineland 20 years earlier (DD 1987–1476 Paris to State Department, No. 469 1956).

The United Kingdom initiated economic sanctions against Egypt on July 27 (Kunz 1991, p. 78). Although the United States was encouraged to follow suit, it only froze assets belonging to the Egyptian state; it left assets of Egyptian individuals and companies untouched (Kunz 1991, pp. 81–2). This was followed by three-party talks between the United Kingdom, the United States, and France. France and the United Kingdom unwaveringly resolved to punish Nasser, even if it meant regime change (Kunz 1991, pp. 81–2). Later in the summer of 1956, the United States agreed to cease foreign aid payments to Egypt (Kunz 1991, p. 90).

At this point, Israel and France—in conjunction with the British—began discussing an alliance to address the nationalization crisis (Troen 2005). France proposed the idea of an Israeli attack to legitimize an Anglo–French intervention (Shlaim 1997), which was presented to Eden as the "Challe Scenario." The London Conference, held between affected parties, continued through late August without any resolution to the crisis that could return the canal or restrain France and the United Kingdom. The United States was reluctant to forcibly reestablish the status quo, but the Eden government calculated that it could compel the United States to support the United Kingdom by preempting the Egyptians and escalating the conflict (Kunz 1991, p. 94). Secret discussions between France and Israel reached a fever pitch, with Ben-Gurion sending envoys for negotiations (Troen 2005). October's meeting at Sèvres was initially planned between France and the United Kingdom, but Israel secured a place at the table when Ben-Gurion personally intervened and requested that Israeli delegates be present at the meeting (Shlaim 1997, p. 513). Close ties between France and Israel made the tripartite meeting possible.

Plans took shape during October's secret meeting at Sèvres (Shlaim 1997, pp. 509–11). Israel had a poor relationship with all of its Arab neighbors, including Egypt, and it was not heavily involved in the Suez Crisis until relatively later. An incursion by Israel would make it easier for France and the United Kingdom to interject themselves into Middle Eastern politics as allegedly impartial arbiters. It is now clear that France, Israel, and the United Kingdom colluded with each other to accomplish three goals: (1) forcing Nasser into a war to give up his claim to the Suez Canal; (2) removing Nasser from power; and (3) suppressing the rise in Arab nationalism.

After intense discussions, it was agreed that Israel should attack first, followed by a joint force of French and British soldiers seizing Port Said under the auspices of intervention. Israel would attack the Suez Canal, and the other two countries would stage a false intervention several days later, ostensibly to stabilize the situation. This plan seems fantastic, but it was the more restrained option proposed by France and the United Kingdom. Ben-Gurion proposed a total reorganization of the Middle East, ending the existence of Jordan as an independent state by having it absorbed into Hashemite Iraq (Shlaim 1997, p. 515). His plan was too radical for the French and the British. The three countries settled on the more modest goal of reclaiming the canal and, if possible, toppling Nasser.

Israeli forces attacked Egypt on October 29. Egypt refused to concede to Western demands, and British and French troops mounted an attack on October 31, in accordance with the plan.[1] Israel also agreed "not to attack Jordan during the period of operations against Egypt. But in the event that during the same period Jordan should attack Israel, the British government undertakes not to come to the aid of Jordan."[2] This united the British, French, and Israelis against the Egyptians while undermining the United Kingdom's 1950 Joint Declaration on the Arab States and Israel (Tripartite Declaration).

A key assumption in the Sèvres agreement was that Egypt would relent to British and French pressure following Israeli attacks. Israel initially insisted on a joint military operation with the French because Egypt had new Soviet equipment, and the Israelis were leery of the costs of "going it alone" (Neff 1981, p. 285). France was willing to forge an alliance with Israel that could deal with Nasser, but the United Kingdom had given guarantees to other Arab states, leaving it reluctant to have Israel attack Egypt first (Neff 1981, p. 310). British Prime Minister Anthony Eden eventually relented to French pressure and agreed to the plan to ally with Israel (Varble 2008, p. 26).

The United States and the USSR were both opposed to the actions of France, Israel, and the United Kingdom. Political and economic pressure from the United States ultimately resulted in the ceasefire that ended British and French military operations around the canal (Azar 1972; Kunz 1991; Lucas 1992).[3] The scheme failed in all its objectives: the canal was not reprivatized, the Nasser regime did not collapse, and Arab nationalism continued to grow. The political retreat was a major embarrassment for France and the United Kingdom, Israel was viewed as an aggressor, and the episode strengthened ties between Egypt and the Soviets. However, the relationship between France, the United Kingdom, and the United States remained largely intact.

WHY A SECRET ALLIANCE?

The British, French, and Israelis had long-term issue convergence—their cooperation has continued into the present day—but each state also had different goals and objectives in the illicit alliance formed after Egypt's seizure of the canal. The British could not bear losing one of the few jewels remaining in their quickly fading empire. The French were incensed with the Egyptians for cutting off a vital shipping lane and for funding the Algerians. The Israelis, surrounded by hostile neighbors, feared what a united Arab world could do to their new nation. Thus, while the signatories' preferences did not align perfectly, they aligned well enough to justify a secret agreement that could create the pretense for war.

Provision of Goods and Familiarity

The roots of the crisis extend much further back than the canal's 1956 nationalization. The nationalization of the canal occurred after the US and UK withdrawal of funding for an Egyptian Aswan dam, the strengthening of ties between Egypt and the Soviets, and Egypt's diplomatic recognition of communist China (Shlaim 1997). Nasser's anti-Western and anti-imperialist rhetoric made it seem that Egypt had clearly chosen a side in the Cold War.

On a more practical level, the canal's nationalization violated the Anglo–Egyptian Treaty signed on July 27, 1954 (Karabell and Mattar 2004). While the United States was concerned with the narrow issue of the canal, the British were equally concerned about Nasser's growing influence in the region and sought to counter its emerging threat (Richardson 1992).[4]

The Israelis were concerned about the rise in pan-Arabism and the threat posed by a united Arab front that would most likely be led by Nasser. However, Israel's location exposed it to greater risks than those faced by France and the United Kingdom. World War II had taught the British and French governments that dictators must always be opposed, and so they decided on direct action to stop and remove Nasser (Richardson 1992, p. 372; Shlaim 1997).

The United Kingdom and France were concerned about nationalization because 80 percent of Western Europe's oil passed through the Suez Canal. This shortcut drastically reduced shipping time between Europe and much of the United Kingdom's diminishing empire; restricted access would have a substantial economic impact (Bowie 1974; Kunz 1991, p. 366). As Bowie (1974) notes, 28 percent of cargo through the canal was also bound for the United Kingdom (p. 366), which left the country economically vulnerable.

Israeli ships were banned from using the canal on the first day it was nationalized (BBC "1956: Egypt Seizes Suez Canal" 1956), and—in violation of the Constantinople Convention of 1888 and United Nations resolutions in 1951— from 1948 onward (Kunz 1991, p. 85). British and French ships faced similar bans after the canal was closed until the withdrawal of Israeli forces in March and April of 1957. While the Israelis were less concerned about the economic impact of the canal's closure, they feared that this represented a second round of Israeli–Arab conflict amid growing Arab nationalism. The canal's nationalization represented a security threat to Israel as much as an economic threat to France and the United Kingdom.

Under these conditions, the British, French, and Israelis met in the Parisian suburb of Sèvres to discuss what could be done to stop Nasser. Shlaim (1997) claims that the idea for an alliance to stop Nasser was first proposed by the

French (p. 511), which makes sense, given Israel's frosty relationship with the United Kingdom and the location where the agreement was signed. After learning that the French and British were to discuss the nationalization of the canal, Ben-Gurion insisted on being invited (Shlaim 1997, p. 514), and France persuaded the British to accommodate him.

The most authoritative account of the ensuing negotiations comes from Mordechai Bar-On, who served as the personal assistant to General Moshe Dayan, Chief of the Israeli Defense Forces (IDF). Bar-On was the only person known to have kept records of the secret discussions (Bar-On 2006, p. 172). Bar-On, a trained historian, witnessed the negotiations that began in earnest over three days in October 1956. In 1958, Dayan also ordered Bar-On to publish the proceedings as a book that was declassified in 1991 (Bar-On 2006, p. 178). Bar-On's insights (2006; see also Shlaim 1997) provide almost unprecedented access to the discussions occurring between states making secret alliances.

According to Bar-On (2006), French General Maurice Challe outlined the plan he had presented to Eden prior to the conference (p. 173). It called for an Israeli attack on the canal followed by a "peacekeeping" intervention from British and French forces who would demand that Egyptian and Israeli forces retreat at least ten miles from the canal (p. 173). Their actual ultimatum stated that British and French forces would move into Egypt and occupy Port Said, Ismailia, and Suez, with or without Egyptian or Israeli cooperation (Aldrich 1967, p. 547).

Bar-On (2006) wrote that "Challe assumed that the Egyptians would not accept the ultimatum and Israel would anyhow not want to reach the canal" (p. 173). This would give the British and French an excuse to start bombing Egypt under the pretense of separating two warring factions. However, it was never fully explained how European armies would be seen as impartial if they only attacked Egyptian positions. Israel would accept the ultimatum it was already prepared for, so it must be assumed that Egypt's refusal to comply would be Europe's justification.

The French had proposed this plan to Israel before the conference, but the Israelis said no (Bar-On 2006, p. 173). Bar-On (2006) explained that Ben-Gurion initially thought it was a ploy to distract Israel from its neighbor, Jordan. The Jordanian monarchy was on shaky ground at the time (p. 173). However, Ben-Gurion was also concerned about a large arms agreement between Czechoslovakia and the Egyptians (Troen 1996, p. 124) that could have been a prelude to an invasion.

Ben-Gurion decided to attend the conference, although he was highly skeptical of British involvement. The Israelis traveled to Paris aboard a French military aircraft and stayed at a Parisian hotel under false names. The talks were held in the orangery of a private residence to avoid raising suspicion (Bar-On 2006, pp. 173–4).

After exchanging pleasantries on October 22, Ben-Gurion shared his grand vision to reorganize the Middle East along lines that would benefit Israel (Bar-On 2006, p. 174). He sought a permanent, long-term solution to the problem of rising Arab sentiment. France and the United Kingdom were more concerned with the narrower issue of the canal, but the British also sought to remove Nasser from power (Bar-On 2006; Shlaim 1997, p. 528). Ultimately, the British and French did not commit to more than returning the canal to private control and addressing Nasser specifically.

Ben-Gurion declared that Israel would maintain control of the Straits of Tiran, the narrow opening between the Sinai and Arabian peninsulas, and Sharm al Sheikh, an Egyptian city close to the straits. The straits were strategic locations for any ships accessing either peninsula, and Ben-Gurion stated that it was not up for debate (Bar-On 2006, p. 184). Israel intended not only to drive Nasser out of the canal but also to seize much (if not all) of the Sinai.

Why did these signatories record their secret agreement? The canal could be returned to British control by other means, such as direct military action; the Egyptians had broken the Anglo–Egyptian treaty. The British could have easily justified the use of force to their domestic public and even to their ally, the United States. Threats from the Soviet Union contributed to the British decision to back down, but the British could have called their bluff. And while the British did want to remove Nasser[5] from power, this was not explicitly mentioned in the text of the Sèvres agreement.

The United Kingdom, as the last imperial power that had ruled much of the Arab world, was in an awkward position with other Middle Eastern states. A British attack on Egypt could be seen as an attack on all Arabs, increasing pan-Arab sentiment. The British had also signed a defense pact with Jordan that required the United Kingdom to defend Jordan against an attack from Israel. Israel's insistence on a provision that stopped the United Kingdom from aiding Jordan if it attacked Israel during the operation could create additional difficulties. Failing to react to an Israeli attack would have two effects: first, it would signal that the United Kingdom was not a reliable alliance partner; and second, it would suggest that the British had a secret understanding with Israel, simultaneously undermining UK agreements with Jordan and Israel.

The French were unhappy about the British loss of the canal, but they relied less on the oil that flowed through it. They were more concerned about Nasser's support for Algerian rebels (Troen 1996, p. 125). After recent defeats in French-Indochina—particularly France's departure from Vietnam in July 1954—the French were desperate to retain their Algerian colony. The colony's proximity to France, its valuable oil and minerals, and its large population of French citizens meant that Algeria was to France what India had been to the United Kingdom.

The uprising of Algeria's National Liberation Front (FLN) had begun in 1954 (Algeria 2023), and France had deployed 50,000 soldiers to Algeria by 1956 in an attempt to quash the rebellion. Only a few hours before the start of the Sèvres conference, the French had intercepted an Egyptian ship that was loaded with arms for the rebels in Algiers (Bar-On 2006, p. 180). Similarly, French aviators had recently forced down a plane carrying leaders of the Algerian rebellion while it was en route from Cairo to Algiers, strengthening the French conviction that Nasser was actively involved in Middle Eastern and North African conflicts (Bar-On 2006, p. 180).

France needed a quick solution to the canal issue; it could only dedicate forces to Egypt for a short period of time. Any troops used in the Suez campaign would rapidly need to be redeployed to Algeria (Bar-On 2006, p. 175). French Prime Minister Guy Mollet had argued that time was against them because Nasser was gaining more credibility in the Arab world. With the US presidential election heating up, October 1956 seemed like the most effective time for action (Bar-On 2006, p. 175).

Anglo–Israeli relations were fragile, but Franco–Israeli relations were quite warm. France was in an ideal position to mediate between its counterparts. Compared to the United Kingdom, France promised much more assistance to the Israelis, agreeing to protect Israel with naval and air assets (Bar-On 2006, p. 175). French pilots would even fly in Israeli-marked planes. Most of these planes were made in France; the French had strong arms ties with Israel. In an addendum to the protocol, the French promised to assist the Israelis in building a nuclear plant that came to be known as the Negev Nuclear plant (Shlaim 1997, p. 522). Troen (1996) also claims that Ben-Gurion had a private conversation with the French prime minister, telling him that oil had been found in Sinai (p. 522). This was a lie, but Ben-Gurion masterfully used it as an enticement to extract more concessions and promises from the French.

Ben-Gurion requested that French pilots fly two squadrons of Israeli aircraft, posing as IDF pilots, because training on the French jets had not been completed (Bar-On 2006, p. 181). This request was granted by the French, but it appears to have occurred after the British had left. During secret French and Israeli bilateral negotiations, the French promised to provide aerial and naval support for the Israelis because the IDF lacked many of those capabilities (Troen 1996, p. 128).

The British and French had a great deal of issue alignment, but the newly sovereign state of Israel was an unknown. The British were leery of trusting the Israelis too much, although they knew that Israel had to be a willing partner for the Challe Scenario to work. The United Kingdom's existing alliance with Jordan, an Israeli opponent, meant that the British could quickly find themselves forced to choose between two friends who held a deep resentment for one another. Because of these concerns, "Ben-Gurion was of the opinion that such a summary document be written and signed" (Bar-On 1997, p. 94).

The signed copy would be retained "as an extra reassurance against last-minute defection by the British" (p. 184).

We can only speculate why Ben-Gurion insisted on a written, formal copy. His demand for formal documentation, and his retention of the agreement as he walked away from the conference, demonstrates the lack of trust between Israel and the "traditional" great powers—especially the United Kingdom. The signed agreement was Ben-Gurion's insurance policy. He knew that the plot had to remain secret in order to work, but the written record was a defense against British betrayal (Bar-On 1997, p. 94). In fact, "Ben-Gurion understood this sensitivity (the Brits wanting to keep it secret) well, but it was precisely this that gave him an important card. He did not trust Britain to fulfill the commitments it had made in Sèvres. He was supported by his commitment to keep the secret of the agreement intact as long as Britain also [kept it secret]" (Bar-On 1997, p. 94).

It was actually the French who first revealed the existence of the agreement (Bar-On 1997, p. 94). Likewise, the first public participant who published a book about it was French Minister of Foreign Affairs Charles Pineau, in 1976 (Bar-On 1997, p. 94). Official public acknowledgement of the pact remained secret even 30 years later in Israel (the legal length for classified documents), primarily for diplomatic reasons (Bar-On 1997, p. 95). The press in France and the United Kingdom openly reported on the Sèvres agreement, but the Israeli press remained quiet for decades.

The French and the Israelis also coordinated beyond the immediate fiasco known as the Suez Crisis. The French promise to build a nuclear reactor was an inducement for Israel to sign the document (Shlaim 1997, pp. 522–4). Given Israel's established policy of ambiguity regarding their ownership of nuclear weapons, it is no surprise that Bar-On omits this from his unofficial account of the negotiations. It remains unclear whether the United Kingdom knew about the promise to assist Israeli nuclear research. Reports indicate that the British were the first to leave Sèvres; the Israeli and French negotiators stayed behind to enjoy champagne toasts and discuss other inducements the French were prepared to give to Israel (Shlaim 1997, p. 525).

If two separate arrangements occurred at Sèvres, leaving the British unaware of the promise of nuclear assistance, it represents a dire betrayal of one of the signatories. It is ironic that an ostensible ally was betrayed so quickly after signing the agreement, but the United Kingdom had already betrayed its Jordanian ally by agreeing to withhold military assistance in the event of conflict with Israel (Shlaim 1997, p. 524).

In any event, the wheels were quickly put in motion. Moshe Dayan ordered his troops to prepare for battle even before the Israeli delegation left France (Bar-On 2006, p. 185). As planned, Israel invaded on 29 October. The Egyptians reacted by mobilizing forces to counter Israel's incursion into the

Sinai. Next, the British and French demanded an end to hostilities and inserted themselves into the dispute, precisely as Bar-On (1997; 2006) described.

The battle began with IDF paratroopers landing deep in the Sinai, and they quickly secured the Mitla Pass (Varble 2008). These troops turned south a day later and advanced to the tip of the Sinai along with the main IDF force. The IDF quickly captured Sharm el-Sheikh, although the Egyptians resisted armored attacks for three days (Varble 2008, p. 6) before abandoning their positions. The British and French then began their bombing campaign, forcing Nasser to withdraw (Varble 2008, p. 6). Egyptian forces were at risk of being surrounded by belligerent parties on all sides, leaving the heart of Egypt open for invasion.

Unlike Israel, Egypt neither knew in advance about the ultimatum from France and the United Kingdom nor would it comply. The British and French began bombing on October 31. By November 5, France and the United Kingdom had spent 100 hours bombing Egyptian forces and emplacements, and they had committed ground forces to the Sinai (Varble 2008, p. 6). On November 6, the British and French forces that had fought Egyptians were quickly recalled due to a United Nations-brokered peace deal. International opinion and public sentiment in the United Kingdom had turned against the British government and intervention. They had described their activities as a "police action" in the interests of the international community, but "it was interpreted by many foreign statesmen as an attempt to settle the dispute over ownership of the Suez Canal Company by the use of force" (Price 1958, p. 494).

Domestic Public Opinion

All three signatories were democracies, which meant that public disclosure of their agreement was likely to have a negative effect on domestic opinion. The Eden government collapsed because of the scandal and humiliation caused by the aborted Anglo–French expedition. Consequences were less severe for the French and Israeli governments; they were more open after the plot was discovered. In Israel, the deal may have been viewed as excusable due to the precarious position of the newly minted state.

The United Kingdom presents an interesting case of a state recognizing that public knowledge of its secret plans for war would be damaging. The Eden government's actions to conceal the Sèvres agreement demonstrate its awareness of the negative domestic and international consequences that would result from disclosure. However, it is absurd that so many members in the British government thought they could plausibly deny such a plan. Given public discussions after the canal's nationalization in late July, the public would be highly suspicious even if there had not been a secret agreement at Sèvres.

Proclamations made by the British government in the House of Commons make it hard to imagine that the Suez Crisis in October and November would be linked to the nationalization of the canal in July of that same year. In a September 11 speech on the floor of Parliament, Eden said that if Nasser did not accept the plan outlined by the 18 nations at the London conference, the use of force would be acceptable (Aldrich 1967, p. 543). Other comments from the government, including ministers and backbenchers in Parliament, made it clear that the British were resolved to do something about the canal's nationalization.

Cover-up attempts began as soon as Sèvres had concluded. Troen (1996) claims that Eden himself ordered the British copy to be burned and even tried to have the French destroy their copy (p. 624), though Beck (2009) claims that some evidence exists that the Thatcher government would order the document destroyed over 20 years after it was signed (p. 616), claiming that the surviving copy was found in the British record. Bar-On (2006, p. 184) wrote:

> Sir Anthony Eden did not in his worst nightmares imagine that his representative would leave behind in writing the slightest trace of what transpired in Sèvres. But he had not had time to make his intentions clear to Dean and Logan before they left for Paris. They acted in good faith, following normal diplomatic protocol.

After learning that the agreement had been formally recorded, Eden immediately sent Foreign Secretary Selwyn Lloyd and his assistant Patrick Dean back to Paris to tell the signatories to destroy all the copies (Shlaim 1997, p. 526). However, the Israeli delegation had already left with theirs, and the French refused to comply (Shlaim 1997, p. 526).

Given Eden's efforts to have the other signatories destroy their copies of the agreement, it is unlikely that he would have allowed the British copy to remain intact. Ultimately, "the government concluded that the British copy had been 'destroyed by Sir Eden himself or by a No. 10 Private Secretary or by Sir Norman Brook'" (Beck 2009, p. 616). Eden's actions demonstrate how far he was willing to go personally to destroy copies of the agreement that could implicate all three signatories. It is likely that if he pressed the Israelis and French to give up their copies, he would have destroyed the copy already in his possession.

On the other hand, some evidence suggests that the French lost their copy of the agreement (Bar-On 1997, p. 94). Discussions between Bar-On (1997) and Abel Thomas, former Director-General of the French Ministry of Defense, confirmed that the French lost their copy instead of destroying it, although a French reporter contacted Pinot's widow in 1960, and she had a photograph of the document's final page (p. 94).

Ben-Gurion was reported to have kept the Israeli copy in his personal office before it was transferred to his library, the Ben-Gurion Heritage Institute in

Kiryat Sade Boker (Bar-On 1997, p. 94). However, this was later found to be a photographed copy and not the original. In the late 1990s, Ben-Gurion's former secretary claimed that the original document had been lost long ago (Bar-On 1997, p. 94). The contents of the agreement are now readily known, and even with its copies missing from various archives, there was at least some attempt to conceal the alliance to avoid public condemnation and to protect the international reputations of the signatories.

Apart from the original copies, each signatory was supposed to send letters to their counterparts confirming that they had ratified the agreement. The British only sent confirmation to France, justifying Ben-Gurion's decision to retain his own copy (Shlaim 1997, p. 526). France relayed the confirmation to the Israelis (Shlaim 1997, p. 526).

When the issue was brought up in Parliament, "Selwyn Lloyd, the Foreign Secretary (1955–60), had told the Commons that 'there was no prior agreement between us about it'" (Beck 2009, p. 607). Eden himself, during Prime Minister's Questions, claimed "there was not a foreknowledge that Israel would attack Egypt" (Beck 2009, p. 607). The UK Ministry of Defence told its officials that the official line was "there's nothing in the report about it" (Beck 2009, pp. 613–14). Meanwhile, diplomats rushed to salvage the international reputation of the United Kingdom. Lloyd repeated his assertions during a United Nations General Assembly meeting on November 23 (Beck 2009, p. 607).

Many in Parliament, particularly members of the opposing party, did not believe the government's story. However, a motion of censure—attempting to punish those involved with the Suez incident—failed in May 1957 (Beck 2009, p. 610). Reports from the US Ambassador to the United Kingdom explained that Parliament was not pleased with the use of force in early November 1956 (Aldrich 1967, p. 547).

The Eden government never admitted the existence of the Sèvres agreement, but it maintained that "history will prove us right" attitude (Beck 2009, p. 610). Though the Tories won the general election in 1959, the official line on Sèvres did not change. Parliamentary attempts to condemn the previous government continued, with votes to censure the Eden government coming up again in March 1960, three and a half years after the Suez Crisis (Beck 2009, p. 611).

The cover-up continued long after the dust had settled in the Sinai. Beck (2009) has noted that every successive British government refused to conduct an inquiry in Parliament; there is no official history from the British side (p. 605). It is surprising that subsequent Labour governments did not fully investigate the events surrounding the illicit agreement at Sèvres to gain a domestic political advantage. Some of this may be explained by the fact that Sèvres documents were missing from government archives, even 30 years later, when they were legally required to be declassified (Beck 2009, pp. 605–6). In the words of "Norman Brook, the Cabinet Secretary and head of the Home Civil Service at the time of Suez, ... 'Damned good care has been taken to see that the whole truth never does emerge'" (Beck 2009, p. 605).

British attempts to get the full picture failed politically, but the effects of Suez were felt decades later. UK Leader of the House of Commons Robin Cook, after resigning in 2003 over the Iraq War, warned Tony Blair "all I ask is that every morning you remember what happened to Anthony [Eden]" (Beck 2009, p. 636).

Public disclosures through unsanctioned histories or biographies continued in the decades following the Suez Crisis. The first was made by Sir Anthony Nutting, who was not in attendance at Sèvres. However, Nutting was the first "insider" with knowledge of the plot who published his memoirs of the event, followed by Moshe Dayan in Israel, Selwyn Lloyd in the United Kingdom, Abel Thomas in France, and Shimon Peres in Israel (Shlaim 1997, p. 510). These disclosures were generally reliable, but they recalled differing aspects of the final agreement. All of them agreed that the central premise was collusion between Israel, France, and the United Kingdom to start a war against Egypt in 1956.

In France, the existence of such an agreement was not as problematic. The importance of the crisis faded over time without public debate like that seen in the United Kingdom (Beck, 2009, p. 634). Foreign Minister Charles Pineau said that he hoped he would be able to say more in ten years' time, but he was unwilling to say much else during the 1950s and 1960s, hoping for the Anglo–French relationship (Beck 2009, pp. 634–5).

Troen (1996) maintains that the failure at Suez and the existence of the agreement contributed to the downfall of Prime Minister Guy Mollet's government (p. 122). The lion's share of the blame goes to French failures in Algeria, but Mollet's attempts to punish Egypt for its involvement in the Algerian independence movement would not have helped.

For the Israelis, the existence of the secret pact that instigated a war of aggression was not as controversial, perhaps given their security situation. Shlaim (1997) states that Ben-Gurion was not ashamed of the agreement, viewing it as proof that the new state of Israel had become a great power in the Middle East (p. 529). Given France's private concessions to Israel, Israel became the only state to benefit from the failed plan. The French strengthened their ties with the Israelis for the next several years, fulfilling the promise to help Israel with nuclear research.

Israel's concerns about public perception were most likely related to international venues rather than domestic ones. Ben-Gurion, desperate to avoid appearing as an aggressor on the international stage, proposed a fake air raid on an Israeli settlement. The French rejected the idea (Bar-On 2006, p. 179). The raid was never implemented, and it appears that Israel dropped its request fairly quickly, providing anecdotal evidence suggesting that of all the signatories, Israel was the least concerned with domestic public opinion.

INSTITUTIONALIZATION AND MILITARY COORDINATION

Shlaim (1997) notes that the alliance document contains several spelling and grammatical errors, suggesting the haste with which the plan had been developed (p. 524). Such errors suit one of the shortest and hastiest alliances of the 20th century, but they were not due to a lack of involvement from military leaders. The Challe Scenario was named after its creator, French Chief of Staff General Maurice Challe, who introduced it to the French government and later to Prime Minister Anthony Eden at Chequers (Shlaim 1997). Although it was predominantly envisioned as a military plan, it required political approval and coordination in its early stages to achieve goals that were sometimes contradictory. The plan called for British and French troops to publicly separate warring Egyptian and Israeli forces. Lloyd laid out the British position at the conference: British and French forces must be seen as peacekeepers, interjecting themselves into the fight between Egypt and Israel (Bar-On 1997, pp. 177–8). Their ultimatum was designed to appear impartial, but military intervention would occur shortly after the Israelis struck against the Egyptians (Bar-On 1997, p. 177). From the French and British perspective, this would preserve their reputations internationally and domestically. However, the scenario made Israel look like the aggressor, so it was agreed that no specific mention would be made of Israeli aggression (Bar-On 2006, p. 181). The signatories coordinated the exact words used in the ultimatum (Bar-On 2006, p. 176).

A key part of the agreement was for the British and the French to aid the Israelis 36 hours after the first engagement with the Egyptians (Bar-On 2006, p. 181). Lloyd initially proposed that the Israelis would be on their own for 72 hours, which was flatly rejected by Israel (Bar-On 2006, p. 177). The Israelis eventually agreed to the delay in support of the plan's plausibility.

Initial action would be a paratrooper attack on the Sinai's strategic Mitla Pass, on the approach to the canal zone. After a delay of 36 hours, the main IDF forces would advance on the ground (Bar-On 2006, p. 181). Ben-Gurion even called up IDF reserve forces in preparation for a full-scale war (Bar-On 2006, p. 184). US intelligence noticed the activation of the reserve forces in late October and worried that some use of force was in the works (Aldrich 1967, p. 545). The early mobilization of reservists suggested aggressive action would come from Israel.

The British and French did not immediately appear to be colluding with Israel, but there was no denying that they were colluding with each other. The speed with which they were deployed to the region was highly suspect; the agreement called for French and British forces to be in the canal zone in three days' time. Two of the three belligerents could claim that they were acting as peacemakers, but their response speed—and the obvious "ripeness" of the canal issue still in the mind of the public—made it unlikely that anyone would believe the events did not constitute collusion. The British, French, and Israelis deluded themselves into a *folie à trois*, thinking that anyone would believe they were not coordinating. The United Kingdom's public pronouncements, particularly by Eden in Parliament, signaled that the British were willing to use force to recover the canal (Aldrich 1967, p. 543). It suggested that at least the British were looking for a ruse that could justify an invasion of Egypt.

The coordination between Israel and France is particularly interesting. The Israelis were only willing to sign the agreement if the French (and British) provided air and naval guarantees, which were two areas in which Israel was woefully deficient. The most striking coordination was France permitting its own pilots to fly planes, made in France, with IDF markings. Given the length of time needed to train pilots, and the fact that some IDF pilots had not received full training on the new aircraft, the only option was to use pilots from either France or the United Kingdom.

Military coordination between French and British forces on the ground was fairly remarkable, considering the speed with which the plan had been developed. However, the speed and severity of international condemnation meant that none of their gains on the battlefield translated into political victories. French and British coordination with the Israelis was much less remarkable, but this likely would have changed if the plan had not fallen apart so quickly. If the British and French had withstood international pressure to withdraw, they would have needed more coordination with Israel, particularly for the canal zone's return to the status quo and the continued Israeli occupation of the Sinai.

It is unclear what this cooperation would have looked like. France's ongoing conflict in Algeria meant that French forces were desperately needed to suppress the calls for independence. British forces would most likely have had to stay on the ground in Sinai for some time, possibly reopening bases at strategic places along the eastern bank of the canal zone. Israel did not leave the Sinai until the spring of 1957, and it is likely that the plan's success would have required considerable Anglo–Israeli cooperation in and around the canal zone. If Israel maintained full control of the Sinai and granted a concession to the British to control the area around the canal, it would have meant considerable coordination for its establishment and administration. Additional cooperation would have been necessary to deal with threats from the canal's west bank and to control the 500,000 Egyptians who lived in the Sinai at the time.

The final indication of ample coordination between the French and British came from the United Nations. Because France and the United Kingdom intervened so quickly, and they vetoed a United Nations Security Council resolution demanding an Israeli withdrawal, "it was clear to everyone that this was a pre-cooked plan" (Bar-On 1997, pp. 93–4).

TERMINATION

The Sèvres agreement is the shortest secret alliance in the Alliance Treaty Obligations and Provisions (ATOP) dataset (Leeds et al. 2002), if not the shortest alliance overall. Although the treaty only lasted for a total of 13 days, it remained an official secret for a decade before any conference attendee publicly disclosed what had transpired. Military coordination and collaboration at the highest levels of the allies' governments continued until the end of the failed ruse.

The failure of the Sèvres agreement illustrates an important caveat for secret alliances: if the treaty is discovered, it can incite domestic and international backlash. It also illustrates a challenge, particularly for open, democratic societies: states can hide the *existence* of secret agreements, but hiding the *effects* of secret agreements is another matter. With the Molotov–Ribbentrop Pact, it was impossible to hide the Nazi seizure of East Poland and the Soviet seizure of West Poland; a neat division of the country would have made the international community aware of the collusion. Similarly, there was no conclusive evidence establishing that the British, French, and Israelis had conspired with one another. But US Secretary of State John Dulles summed up the public's attitude by stating that "most likely Britain and France conspired with the Israelis" (Bar-On 1997, p. 94).

All parties—particularly the British—continued to deny the existence of an agreement, but their failure to retake the canal and topple Nasser illustrates how domestic and international pressure matter in international politics. The British, French, and Israelis were not defeated in combat, but by diplomatic pressure from some of their closest allies and most ardent foes. To a lesser degree, it also illustrates how untenable such operations are in a post-World War II environment, where the Nazis (at Gleiwitz) and the Japanese (at the Marco Polo Bridge) used "false flag" operations to create a pretext for war. According to Beck (2009, p. 640):

> The Suez venture proved that a Western democracy cannot start a war on a pretext, with its Governments real motives concealed, because the result is to spread such confusion that the war cannot be carried on. If Eden had either tried to seize the Canal quite overtly or, alternatively, to overtly come to Israel's assistance as the victim of aggression, which she was, he would have had more chance of completing the operation.

The joint expedition in Sinai was defeated not by military strength, but by international criticism. The United States, perhaps the most crucial ally to both France and the United Kingdom, immediately condemned the invasion (Richardson 1992, p. 370). The US presidential election and larger tensions surrounding the Cold War left the United States unwilling to back its allies in Europe and the Middle East, particularly given the protests and threats made by the Soviet Union. US officials wanted to avoid a classic case of chain-ganging—when alliances or security guarantees drag states into wars that go against their interests—that could draw them into direct war with a Soviet Union that had allied itself with Egypt and many Middle Eastern countries.

Dulles had written earlier, in a classified memo, that the British "had made a number of mistakes in the area" and "we are most reluctant publicly to identify ourselves in the area with the UK" (Warner 1991, p. 305). The United States had tried to facilitate an Arab–Israeli settlement for some time to ease the ongoing tensions between the two groups. The United States realized that the path to solving that crisis ran through Egypt, but by early 1956, it had become clear that Nasser did not want to work with Western powers to settle the dispute (Warner 1991, p. 306).

The United States officially opposed the use of force to restore the status quo after the canal's July 26 nationalization (Richardson 1992). Instead, US officials proposed several conferences in London to resolve the impasse. Despite the official US position, Winthrop Aldrich, the US Ambassador to the United Kingdom, was invited to a British cabinet meeting that discussed seizing the canal (Aldrich 1967, pp. 541–2). This highly unusual practice clearly signaled how important the issue was for the British and how important their alliance was for the United States. The only result of the meeting was an agreement on the importance of continued consultation with the United States (Aldrich 1967, p. 542).

Aldrich (1967) later claimed that there was deep personal animosity between British Prime Minister Anthony Eden and US Secretary of State John Dulles. According to Aldrich (1967), Dulles intentionally gave Eden the impression that the United States would tolerate the use of force to retake the canal (p. 543), which was not the official US position. The misinterpretation of US support, either intentional or otherwise, aggravated tensions between the two allies.

By September 19, when the second London conference opened, the United States remained unaware of any collusion between the British and the French (Aldrich 1967, p. 544), although the use of force had been discussed between them almost from the outset. While the United States pursued a diplomatic strategy, it later appeared as if the British and French coalesced around the belief that only force would bring Nasser to heel. How that would happen was unclear.

On October 28, the day before the Israeli attack, Aldrich directly asked UK Foreign Secretary Selwyn Lloyd if Israel intended on attacking Egypt. Lloyd—who had been part of the Sèvres negotiations—maintained that the British government was equally worried about the Israeli mobilization. Lloyd stated that the United Kingdom was concerned that Israeli troops would attack Jordan, a British ally (Aldrich 1967, p. 545). After the invasion began on October 29, the British told Aldrich (1967) that they needed to consult with the French before acting. Later, when Aldrich (1967) met with Ivone Kirkpatrick, UK Permanent Under-Secretary of the Foreign Office, he was handed the pre-arranged ultimatum that France and Israel had allegedly just accepted (p. 547).

The lack of US support ensured that the pact failed. The United States began hearing rumors immediately after the canal's nationalization suggesting that the British were ready to retake the canal by force (Aldrich 1967, p. 542), a full three months before the protocol was signed. This did not implicate France and Israel directly, but it indicated a pattern of conspiracy between the three states.

The United Nations almost instantly condemned the incursion into the Sinai. Both France and the United Kingdom had permanent seats on the United Nations Security Council, but much of the condemnation came from the General Assembly via a United for Peace resolution (Price 1958) and from Soviet-aligned states. Canada proposed the creation of the United Nations Emergency Force (UNEF) under Article 22, which was deployed to the Middle East in November 1956 (Price 1958, pp. 506–7) and remained there until the 1967 outbreak of the Six Day War.

The British and French could effectively veto any substantive punishments proposed in the Security Council, but they could not deal with international backlash in the General Assembly, particularly when their closest ally, the United States, refused to rally to their support. The UNEF creation via Article 22 was a unique solution to the realities of the veto power held by permanent members of the Security Council. Criticism of France and the United Kingdom was severe and unrelenting, eventually resulting in both countries withdrawing from the Sinai. Israel was left to fend for itself. IDF forces remained in the Sinai until March 1957.

Israel, France, and the United Kingdom maintained that their actions were justified, but they endured immense pressure from the United Nations. As Price (1958) notes, there are five situations where the United Nations Charter acknowledges the use of force is appropriate: "on decision of the Security Council (Article 42), within domestic jurisdiction (Article 27), in collective self-defence (Article 51), in the exercise of a legal right, as illustrated in the Corfu Channel case, and in individual self-defence (Article 51)" (p. 494). None of these were applicable to the Suez Crisis.

After a hastily convened United Nations Security Council meeting, the Israelis maintained that they were acting in self-defense, having endured numerous attacks from the fedayeen operating on Egyptian soil. It was true that more than 1000 Israeli civilians had been harmed in cross-border raids from Egypt, but the motivation for the Israeli incursion was not retaliation. Israel's intent was clearly something more, as evidenced by the mobilization of Israeli reservists and the immediate intervention from France and the United Kingdom. The quick response indicated advance planning and suggested an alignment of British and French interests.

The British had sought to take the matter to the United Nations Security Council in late August, after the Eighteen Nations Plan from the London conference failed. The United States blocked the United Kingdom's request (Aldrich 1967, p. 543). On the day of the Israeli attack on Egypt, US Ambassador Aldrich met with Lloyd and asked what the British intended to do, to which the British foreign secretary replied, "Her Majesty's government would immediately cite Israel before the Security Council of the United Nations as an aggressor against Egypt" (Aldrich 1967, p. 546).

The French had also taken the matter to the Security Council as Dulles and his team returned from the second London conference at the end of September (Aldrich 1967, p. 544). At the time, Lloyd was also on his way to New York to speak to the United Nations and coordinate with Egyptian Foreign Minister Mahmoud Fawzi. Instead, Lloyd was recalled to London, informed of the plan, and ordered to meet with the French in Paris (Shlaim 1997, p. 511). Later, after the IDF had marched into the Sinai, the French objected that the American resolution demanding the withdrawal of Israeli forces was filed improperly. The French claimed that Chapter VI (Pacific Settlement of Disputes) was applicable, rather than Chapter VII (Price 1958, p. 503). This supported the alliance's objectives by allowing the British and French to position themselves as mediators in Middle Eastern disputes, rather than aggressors.

The French were already pressured by the ongoing independence movement in Algeria, coupled with the decay of their imperial rule in far-flung places such as Indochina. However, the British felt the heat immediately. US President Eisenhower and Secretary of State Dulles cut off all direct communication with Eden (Aldrich 1967, p. 547). The canal had been closed by the ongoing hostilities, which meant that the British and French would soon endure economic hardship. Domestic pressure from the opposition side of the UK Parliament, and even among Tory backbenchers, meant that the United Kingdom faced challenges from within and beyond its borders. There were even detractors in the British cabinet who communicated their frustrations directly with Ambassador Aldrich (1967), in violation of all diplomatic and official protocol (p. 548).

The United States cooperated with the USSR in mediating the issue before the Security Council (Aldrich 1967, p. 547). On October 30, the United States entered a resolution for debate before the Security Council that called on the IDF to remove its troops from Egyptian soil. The resolution was vetoed by both the British and French (Price 1958, p. 503).

Lester Pearson, Secretary of State for External Affairs of Canada at the time of the crisis, later stated that the United Nations and its diplomacy were responsible for ending the Suez Crisis (Price 1958, p. 503). The British and French were forced to withdraw after international and domestic pressure, although the consequences of the invasion would reverberate for years. Troen (1996, p. 122) claims that "it destroyed Eden and contributed to the downfall of the French leadership."

FUTURE ALLIANCE-MAKING PROSPECTS

The reputations of the British and French suffered enormously, but their prospects for future alliances were not greatly affected. Both countries were already members of the North Atlantic Treaty Organization (NATO), the primary security alliance framework for Europe. Given the bipolar nature of the Cold War, these two states were unlikely to be nodes of alignment on their own.

As integral and founding members of the NATO organization, France and the United Kingdom weathered the storm of international criticism over their activities in the Sinai. This may provide some contradictory evidence to the findings in Chapter 5, but it is important to remember that quantitative methods inherently speak to averages. Not every case is expected to see a decrease in future alliance-making prospects. Because the prospects for future alliances interact with other important variables, such as regime type and major power status, one must look at exceptions to better understand how these interactions can affect the outcome. Such realities support the need for case studies and quantitative evidence together as a way of providing more complete answers as to why states behave the way they do.

Israel, on the other hand, is quite different. The state of Israel was unlikely to make many formal alliances with or without the Suez fiasco. Public formal alliances were unlikely because of the potential for domestic backlash in states that would normally be allies with Israel—alliances are most likely to happen with states bordering one another (or states that have otherwise overlapping interests). Further backlash from regional organizations was also likely, given the long-standing tensions between Israel and its Arab neighbors.

According to the ATOP dataset (Leeds et al. 2002), Israel has only had seven formal alliances since its creation in 1948. Israel's first alliance after the Suez Crisis occurred in 1975, and it was made with Egypt, of all states.

Although it is coded as an alliance, it is not an "alliance" in the sense of a defensive or offensive agreement. Instead, the Sinai Interim Agreement is coded as a nonaggression pact. It remained in place for three years, until the signing of the Camp David Accords in late 1978, which was also an agreement with Egypt. Neither of these are "alliances" in the way that the general public defines them, but they were critical for Middle Eastern peace. To a large degree, they bookend the long history of conflict between the two nations.

CONCLUSION

France, the United Kingdom, and Israel secretly coordinated through the late summer and autumn of 1956 in an attempt to reclaim the Suez Canal from Egypt. Israel, which was the most militarily active player, also sought to expand into the Sinai. Although the secret alliance's primary motivation was to reclaim the canal from a specific actor (Egypt), Israel had slightly different goals. France and the United Kingdom failed to achieve their strategic and political objectives with the alliance. Israel had a marginally better outcome by gaining access to the canal for shipping. The three states were unsuccessful at suppressing the growing pan-Arabism movement led by Egyptian President Gamal Abdel Nasser.

The British and French were not sworn enemies—unlike the Soviets and Nazis signing the Molotov–Ribbentrop Pact—but there were important policy differences between them, and they both had important policy differences with Israel. The United Kingdom was growing closer to the United States, and France had begun to chart its own path under President Charles de Gaulle.

France would withdraw its troops from NATO's command structure almost a decade after the Suez Crisis; France wished to be a "third force," offering an alternative to the communist East and the US-dominated West. While France's exit from NATO's command structure was not directly tied to the Suez Crisis, it illustrates the differences between its political goals and those of the United Kingdom.

Israel had more pressing goals: curbing Arab nationalism and reshaping regional dynamics in the Middle East. Nasser's pan-Arabism had tapped into something that his Middle Eastern predecessors had been unable to accomplish, inspiring Arabs throughout the Middle East and culminating in the political union of Egypt and Syria in the United Arab Republic from 1958 to 1961.

The issues separating France, the United Kingdom, and Israel were resolved much more amicably than issues between the USSR and Nazi Germany. The Suez Crisis was a temporary issue convergence—all three states desired to keep the canal accessible to the West, even if the broader union of Arab states was less threatening to France and the United Kingdom. In their view, the only way to secure the canal was with a secret treaty coordinating the forcible reprivatization of the canal and the occupation of the surrounding land. However, the three states lacked the resolve to escalate the Suez Crisis into a full-fledged war after the Soviets communicated the costs that would be involved, and the British and French were abandoned by their US allies and the international community.

The most relevant lesson from this example may be the difficulty involved in keeping secrets. Even when signatories trust one another and their interests align in the short and long term, secrecy is not easy to maintain. And when allies do not trust one another enough to enter into an informal agreement, written documentation is necessary. When those allies suffer from an extreme lack of trust, one of the signatories may insist on leaving the discussions with a written copy of their agreement.

Rumors of a secret alliance began almost immediately after an agreement was reached, but few of the signatories, apart from British Prime Minister Anthony Eden, imagined how much domestic and public opinion would turn against them. Abel Thomas, the French Deputy-Director of Defense who was present at Sèvres, said, "one day the Sèvres conference will no doubt be publicized. It therefore depends on us whether it is remembered as the Yalta conference or the Munich conference of the Middle East" (Shlaim 1997, p. 514). While Yalta or Munich are rarely invoked in discussions of Sèvres, the word "fiasco" comes up much more frequently.

NOTES

1. Leeds et al. 2002. ATOP Codesheet 3322.
2. Ibid., section 18.
3. Kunz (1991) maintains that economic pressure by the United States on both Britain and France helped bring about a cessation in hostilities as much as political pressure from the United States and the USSR did.
4. Similarly, the British were still feeling slighted after funding for the Aswan Dam project did not receive support in Congress and was canceled by Dulles without first informing the British (Aldrich 1967, p. 541).
5. In fact, the British were worried that Nasser, through his appeals to other Arabs, might remove British influence in both Jordan and Iraq (Troen 1996, p. 125).

8. Big state, little state: apartheid, domestic opinion, and the South Africa–Swaziland agreement

Swaziland is economically and politically dependent on South Africa, even after apartheid. The country has a small population, limited resources, and no access to the sea, relying on the passage of goods through Mozambique and South Africa, a regional economic powerhouse that surrounds it on three sides. In fact, in 1982, some 90 percent of all goods from Swaziland passed through South Africa (Bischoff 1986, p. 180). In that same year, 66.6 percent of all Swazi revenue came from trade with South Africa. South African railways carried one million tons of Swazi cargo, and 23,659 Swazis—a notable segment of the tiny nation's workforce—worked in South Africa (Chan 1990, pp. 136–7).

Swaziland's isolation and overdependence may have been a blessing; relatively few outside states, particularly the West, have intervened in its internal affairs (Chan 1990, p. 42). South Africa's relationship with Swaziland, which has included direct interventions, has shaped much of Swaziland's foreign policy and international relationships.

Swaziland was in an awkward position during the Cold War. It was a country controlled by its native African majority, reliant on South Africa, and opposed to apartheid's racist underpinnings, putting it in a position similar to that of Finland after World War II. Many smaller southern African states were equally dependent on South Africa at the time, connected by interlinked transportation lines, electrical grids, trade, and the Common Customs Union (Grundy 1982, p. 170). Economic dependency was further complicated in the mid-1970s, after the Portuguese withdrew from Mozambique and made it impossible to access Mozambican ports, such as Maputo (Barber and Barratt 1990, p. 273; Price 1984, p. 11). Furthermore, the death of Swaziland's King Sobhuza II in 1982 meant that the country became a client state of South Africa as it dealt with its internal political divisions (Booth 1990, p. 333).

Many other countries in the region also relied upon South Africa. Grundy (1982) wrote that "Botswana, Lesotho, and Swaziland are the moons to the Republic's earth—their orbits may be altered by dint of prodigious sacrifice and effort, but they still remain in the economic force field of their stronger neighbor" (p. 171).

South Africa's capital, Pretoria, used three strategies to compel support from countries that depended on it (Chan 1990). First, South Africa could apply economic coercion through the South African Customs Union. Second, Pretoria's military forces intervened in Botswana and Lesotho to go after the ANC. Third, South Africa used diplomatic instruments to apply force or offer inducements for support. These policies, applied in dependent countries, were meant to support South Africa's regional policies in larger states, such as Mozambique, Zimbabwe, and Angola (Chan 1990, p. 25).

It was with this understanding that, in 1982, South Africa dangled a carrot in front of Swaziland that it was unable to ignore (Chan 1990, p. 42). South Africa hinted at territorial concessions in KaNgwane and Ingwavuma in the KwaZulu region of South Africa, offering them to Swaziland if the Swazis cooperated with South African efforts to crack down on African National Congress (ANC) forces outside of South Africa's territory. Officially, the two countries entered a nonaggression pact. There were other benefits to the agreement, and both Swaziland and South Africa saw the trade-offs as more valuable than what they gave away.

The land and the crackdown on ANC dissidents were only part of the agreement's goal. The dependency and non-confrontational relationship between Swaziland and South Africa put Swaziland in a perfect position to be the arbiter between South Africa and more militant, anti-apartheid African states. Just as Finland hosted the Conference on Security and Cooperation in Europe in 1973—and the subsequent conference in 1975 that resulted in the Helsinki Accords—Swaziland could mediate between South Africa and other states, including Mozambique.

South Africa, for its part, was also in an awkward relationship with Western democracies. Its policy of apartheid and its ill treatment of the majority of South Africans put the country at odds with Western backers and most other countries around the world (Vale 1990, p. 170). Many African nations encouraged this isolation, leading an international charge against the apartheid regime (Jaster 1988, p. 43). International hostility, an arms embargo, and the power vacuum caused by the almost immediate withdrawal of Portuguese forces from African colonies near South Africa, or South African-controlled Namibia (Jaster 1988, p. 51), left South Africa increasingly isolated. The growing Soviet and Cuban involvement in the region also meant that "South Africa has had to formulate its foreign policy with this in mind" (Chan 1990, p. 8).

South Africa needed to develop a policy that would pull southern African states closer into its orbit, push out Soviet and Cuban influence in the region, and placate Western criticism, especially from the United States (Vale 1990, p. 174). South Africa's actions in the late 1970s and 1980s can be viewed as part of the larger East–West competition, but they must also be viewed in the context of a regional security policy that South Africa hoped to develop (MacFarlane 1983, p. 53). South Africa's drive for security was informed by larger Cold War dynamics and by regional threats along and inside its borders. Sometimes these threats were communist in nature, but they were equally anti-apartheid.

Pretoria proposed what it called a "total strategy" and a Constellation of Southern African States. This total strategy hoped to link domestic and foreign politics to preserve South African primacy and continue apartheid rule (Chan 1990, p. 15). Using this strategy, a Constellation of Southern African States was designed to place South Africa at the center of regional affairs, eliminating threats to apartheid while bolstering the country's image abroad, particularly among Western states and hostile African states. The government in Pretoria saw three threats to its racial policies and efforts to preserve apartheid: liberation movements in southern Africa, conventional military threats, and international economic pressure (Price 1984, pp. 12–13). South Africa's total strategy, and the constellation created by its foreign policy, hoped to curtail liberation movements, limit threats from other militaries, and remove sanctions that had been put into place against South Africa.

The Constellation of Southern African States, which was first proposed in 1978, was bound to fail. Angola descended into chaos, White minority rule fell in Rhodesia, and the Portuguese left Mozambique. Furthermore, the surrounding states were all opposed to South Africa's White minority rule, making them unlikely to consent to South African leadership in the region. South Africa reacted to this criticism by depriving Black Africans of citizenship and doubling down on its Bantustan projects. The Bantustans were essentially reservations—in which Black Africans were forced to reside in their "homelands"—that were ostensibly autonomous but wholly dependent on Pretoria. The idea was to give Black Africans "self-ruled" homelands that could divide South Africa's Black population along ethnic lines while appearing to repair the damage done by colonialism.

South Africa's self-imposed isolation made it necessary to find an ally, or at least a state that would not oppose South African policies internationally. The country did not need a defensive ally, but it hoped that a nonaggression pact with a neighboring state could create a "domino effect" that would weakenthe united resistance against apartheid rule. Ideally, Pretoria's regional security goals could be achieved by making southern African states become less hostile to South Africa.

Although South Africa deliberately pursued a strategy of interfering in neighboring states' domestic affairs, it was also willing to cooperate with its neighbors, particularly when those countries were economically dependent on South Africa. Swaziland was one such neighbor; Swazi exports and imports depended on access to South African ports and railways (Bischoff 1986, p.

175) and still largely are in the 21st century. As an officially non-aligned state, Swaziland still had to avoid angering its larger neighbor, which surrounded it on three sides. Furthermore, given the country's small size and dependency on South Africa, Swaziland was also unable to attract much international investment (Bischoff 1986, p. 177).

Swaziland was not openly hostile to South Africa, or capitalism and the West more generally, and it did not recognize Marxist-Leninist African states. This meant that the country attracted friends such as South Africa and Taiwan that were aligned with Western interests (Bischoff 1986, p. 177). While the country had a diversified agricultural sector, and it was proximate to both Mozambique and Zimbabwe, it was problematic that any Swazi exports trying to reach markets that were hostile to South Africa would still need to pass through South African territory (Bischoff 1986, p. 180). Membership in the Southern African Customs Union also meant that Swazi industries could not find a niche for competing with South African industries that had the advantages of capital, access to cheap labor, and the ability to price out Swazi competitors (Bischoff 1986, p. 180). Mozambique, the other alternative for Swazi imports and exports, was untenable after the 1975 withdrawal of the Portuguese.

Swaziland's entire economic and political system relied on its relationship with South Africa. However, a land transfer that gave access to the sea would give the country additional options. This was what South Africa proposed in 1982.

BACKGROUND

South Africa's alliance with Swaziland was not due to the threat posed by a single other state. Instead, it was seen as a vehicle for implementing South Africa's broader regional plan while curbing the growing appeal and power of the ANC, which South Africa labeled a terrorist organization.

The ANC was formed in 1912 to promote the rights and interests of South Africa's native Black population and later became a political party. After the National Party's victory in the 1948 elections, the ANC became more active and increasingly at odds with the ruling National Party's apartheid policies. The organization was active in the 1950s and banned in 1960 after the Sharpeville massacre, in which 69 people were killed and more than 100 were wounded by police. The organization then went underground and had both political and military wings. The organization was officially banned in South Africa, but it developed bases and safe havens in surrounding countries for its operations against Pretoria.

South Africa had to maintain a delicate balance. It was surrounded by states that were indifferent to South Africa's security interests at best, and a few Marxist states were openly hostile. The country's security was threatened by three forces: liberation movements, conventional military threats, and international economic pressure. In the words of Hanlon (1986), "what South Africa would really like is sympathetic, non-socialist neighbors who would accept apartheid, support South Africa in world forums, and remain economically dependent on it. Since that is impossible, the main goal of the South African government is to have regional economic, military, and political hegemony" (p. 58). In the 1980s, South Africa alternated between wielding a very big stick and using carrots to entice states that could hardly say no.

In the 1970s, the USSR and Cuba became actively involved in various African states. This concerned Pretoria, and whenever the Soviets became involved in a southern African country, South Africa invariably followed (Price 1984). While dealing with security threats, South Africa also faced internal and external challenges to its racist apartheid policies. The country needed a strategy that could placate the international community and its domestic population while also ensuring that the National Party retained power. From its earliest days, Prime Minister P.W. Botha's premiership saw three ways to deal with these problems: (1) create a reliable constellation of Southern African states; (2) neutralize threats in neighboring states; and (3) eliminate the Soviet/Cuban presence in southern Africa (Price 1984, pp. 148–63).

Botha proposed the Constellation of South African States in 1978, hoping that it would solve several problems. First, as a regional organization, it could help secure South Africa against internal and external threats. Next, it was hoped that such cooperation would decrease the number of protests in Africa and around the world opposing the racist policies that oppressed South Africa's majority Black population. Such opposition had existed for decades, but it accelerated in earnest after the 1976 Soweto rebellion, after which South Africa faced additional sanctions blocking its access to international financial markets (Price 1984, p. 13). Finally, Botha hoped to blunt the effect of the sanctions themselves (Price 1984, p. 13). Formal and informal economic sanctions had been applied against the South African regime for years, crippling the South African economy.

The Constellation was proposed on March 7, and it hoped to draw in a few of the weaker southern African states, which could induce cooperation from larger states that were less economically beholden to Pretoria. Scholars have noted that the plan was bound to fail—it had not even been discussed privately with potential member states before the policy was made public (Jaster 1988, p. 82). Nonetheless, Botha's government pursued the strategy for several years, only admitting defeat in the 1980s. Meanwhile, South Africa cozied up to other minority-ruled southern African states, most notably Rhodesia.

After Rhodesia's failure of White minority rule and the beginning of majority rule under Mugabe, Pretoria's regional plans were in trouble. Mugabe's election victory essentially killed any hopes for the plan that might have survived under a more moderate candidate (Jaster 1988). Pretoria responded by taking a more militant stance to address its southern African security concerns in the 1980s, further isolating it from the international community. Instead of openly courting neighboring states, the Botha government adopted a divide and conquer strategy. It hoped that some majority African states could be convinced to defect from states that opposed South Africa more directly.

South Africa frequently exercised its economic power over the neighboring states that depended on it. Trade and borders with weaker neighbors—particularly Botswana, Lesotho, and Swaziland—were interrupted and closed as demonstrations of South Africa's power. However, the country also used such heavy-handed tactics against the much larger country of Zimbabwe, threatening to withdraw from a customs union and expelling 40,000 Zimbabweans who worked in South Africa in 1981 (Price 1984, pp. 158–9). South Africa also stopped rail shipments into Mozambique in 1981, forcing the new Marxist government to comply with Pretoria's regional objectives (Davis and O'Meara 1990, pp. 197–8). The country frequently exercised its military, economic, and diplomatic strength, but it also offered inducements and incentives to coerce its neighbors (Davis and O'Meara 1990, pp. 179–80).

South Africa wanted to eliminate threats from Angola and Mozambique, but also the threat posed by majority rule in the newly-renamed Zimbabwe. The country pursued a multi-pronged strategy, supporting Resistência Nacional Moçambicana (MNR) rebels in Mozambique and he National Union for the Total Independence of Angola (UNITA) rebels in Angola, making direct incursions into Angola, taking more limited actions in Zimbabwe, and trying to reconcile with select southern African states. First among those states was Swaziland in 1982, followed by Mozambique in 1984.

South Africa hoped that rapprochement would be infectious and spread through the region, bringing peace and stability to the southern cone of Africa. The country simultaneously pursued a contradictory strategy to destabilize regimes that it viewed as threatening, but Pretoria's goal was never to destabilize the entire region (Davis and O'Meara 1990, p. 181). Instead, South Africa hoped to create conditions for stability on its own terms. The inherent contradictions of its policies continued to thwart efforts at reconciliation with majority-ruled African nations.

To advance its domestic apartheid policies, South Africa created multiple Bantustans, which restricted native Africans to specific areas where they had nominal self-rule, though not in international affairs. Each Bantustan resident was the subject of a tribal king but also a nominal South African citizen. This segregated Black and White Africans in a scheme of "grand apartheid," and it was presented as South Africa's efforts to right a wrong of colonialism. However, no state recognized the purported benefits of this scheme, and it only strengthened South Africa's status as an international pariah (Chan 1990, pp. 24–5).

Bantustans concentrated Black Africans into confined areas and limited their interactions with White Africans. Because they were grouped along ethnic lines, the divided population of native Black Africans was more easily manipulated in an attempt to weaken the opposition to White rule (Chan 1990, p. 25).

Despite the government's efforts, internal opposition to apartheid continued growing; the outlawed ANC gained members and influence. In the early 1960s, the organization had begun a campaign to set up branch offices in neighboring countries. By the late 1970s, the ANC had intensified this campaign, establishing a presence in Angola, Botswana, Lesotho, Swaziland, Mozambique, and Zimbabwe by 1980 (Jaster 1988, p. 119). South Africa was eventually bordered by an arc of states that were sympathetic to the ANC. Not every ANC member was part of the group's militant wing, but South African authorities saw any member as a threat to Pretoria's security.

The degree to which the ANC could operate in each country varied greatly. Angola and Mozambique, which were Marxist-Leninist states (Chan 1990, p. 25), placed few restrictions on the activities of ANC forces inside their borders. On the other hand, Botswana, Lesotho, Swaziland, and Zimbabwe only allowed non-military forces in their countries, banning the use of their territory for attacks on South Africa (Jaster 1988, p. 119). It was no coincidence that tiny Botswana, Lesotho, and Swaziland were all economically dependent on South Africa.

Swaziland had many seasonal workers in South African mines, and Pretoria often threatened to expel them or make it harder to enter the country (Chan 1990, pp. 39–40). Such policy actions had been taken against Lesotho on several occasions, crippling its economy. Lesotho also saw numerous incursions from South African Defence Forces (SADF). Forty-two people were killed in an SADF raid in Maseru, which resulted in the expulsion of numerous South African refugees and at least 42 ANC members (Davis and O'Meara 1990, p. 201). South Africa's Botha is even rumored to have funded the Lesotho Liberation Army and condoned the Hilton bombing plot against Leabua Jonathan, Lesotho's prime minster (Davis and O'Meara 1990, p. 200). Given their small size, it was all but impossible for Botswana, Lesotho, or Swaziland to successfully police ANC activities (Jaster 1988, p. 119). Zimbabwe's efforts to regulate the ANC's activities are a bit more surprising.

In a bid to reduce the ANC's support among its neighbors, Pretoria pursued a divide and conquer strategy. The concentration of ethnic groups in different Bantustans attempted to dilute internal opposition to White rule, and externally, South Africa worked to gain international acceptance for its policies and to eliminate safe havens for the ANC. Eighty-five percent of imports to Botswana, Lesotho, and Swaziland came from South Africa, while only 25 percent of exports went to South Africa, which gave Pretoria enormous leverage (Hanlon 1986, p. 87). That leverage was applied to force Botswana, Lesotho, and Swaziland to deal more openly with South Africa. Pretoria hoped that their more moderate governments could be coerced into public support.

Swaziland's dependence on South Africa, and the fact that it was the least hostile government to apartheid rule, presented an opportunity for South Africa. Pretoria could curtail some of the influence and safe havens enjoyed by the ANC while testing a strategy that could be pursued with other dependent states, such as Botswana and Lesotho. By trading the Bantustan of KwaZulu to Swaziland, South Africa could win support against the ANC (Chan 1990, p. 25). Swaziland could also serve as a mediator with other African states, demonstrating—particularly for Lesotho and Botswana—that South Africa was willing to reward states for reconciling with Pretoria's apartheid rule.

WHY A SECRET ALLIANCE?

Swaziland feared Pretoria's economic punishments, which were regularly meted out against other southern African states. Mozambique's instability and the unrest in Zimbabwe after Rhodesia's fall gave Swaziland little choice other than to enter into an agreement with South Africa. In a deal where South Africa ceded land, including territory that had historically been claimed by Swazi kings (Price 1990, p. 151), Swaziland could gain access to the sea. Not only would this unite Swazis into a single kingdom, it would also improve the state's long-term viability by giving it an economic lifeline to the Indian Ocean (Chan 1990, p. 42). In exchange, Swaziland would cooperate with South Africa's efforts to expel ANC members from its territory, and it would serve as an intermediary with other majority-controlled African states.

However, both states were concerned about domestic public opinion and reactions from states around the world—particularly African states that were most strongly united against apartheid.

Provision of Goods and Familiarity

South Africa's total strategy is most often associated with P.K. Botha's premiership and presidency, but it originally appeared in a 1977 defense white paper, conceptualized as unity between domestic and foreign politics (Hanlon 1986, p. 7). Pretoria's National Party was concerned not only with staying in power, but also with the continuance of apartheid and White minority rule, no matter the costs. The continuance of South Africa's White minority rule was the primary goal pursued by the total strategy, and the alliance was an important component.

South Africa legitimately saw itself as surrounded by hostile, Marxist states bound together under a "total onslaught" policy led by the Soviet Union. This resulted in the Botha premiership's heavy use of military force (Pfister 2005, pp. 103–5). Under Botha's predecessor, Pretoria had instead pursued a more subtle policy, trying to purchase support from the Organization of African Unity (OAU) and individual member states (Davis and O'Meara 1990, pp. 185–6). The Botha strategy was entirely different, applying force and enticements in pursuing its goals.

South Africa saw itself leading the defense of democracy, capitalism, and Western values against the rising communist threat (Barber and Barratt 1990, p. 254).[1] Its open hostility to Marxist-Leninist ideology and liberation movements throughout Africa meant that Pretoria constantly worked to stymie movements toward full independence for native Black Africans, domestically and internationally.

This "total strategy" addressed internal and external security threats simultaneously (Jaster 1988, p. 89). Pretoria saw the external series of chaotic independence movements and the internal pushback against apartheid as connected threats to White rule in South Africa. As a result, the country frequently lashed out against ANC forces and unrelated groups in neighboring countries.

This was particularly true in Angola, which bordered Namibia. South Africa had exercised control over Namibia since World War I, and when apartheid became the formal system of racial separation for South Africa in the late 1940s, it was also applied to Namibia. As liberation movements developed across most of Africa, Namibia was no exception. Violence against South Africans in Namibia intensified in the 1960s. By 1969, United Nations Security Council Resolution 269 declared that South Africa's continued rule in Namibia was illegal, calling for Namibian independence.

In Angola, a former Portuguese colony, a vicious civil war drew in outside participants, most notably the Cubans and South Africans, with minor involvement from the Soviet Union (Price 1990, p. 145). As the domestic conflict drew intervention from outside states, South Africa inevitably became involved (Chan 1990, p. 56). The National Front for the Liberation of Angola (FNLA), the Marxist Popular Movement for the Liberation of Angola (MPLA), and the National Union for the Total Independence of Angola (UNITA)—which sometimes found itself allied with Cuba, the United States, and South Africa—all fought each other. Angola's factional violence raged from 1975 to 2002 as one of the most prominent proxy wars between communism and capitalism during the Cold War, outliving the Soviet Union itself.

While Namibia was administered by South Africa, conflict was bound to happen. Forces often launched attacks on government forces in Angola before retreating to Namibia for shelter. In 1976, South Africa decided to ally with UNITA forces under South African Prime Minister John Vorster (MacFarlane

1983), hoping to shape the Angola situation to South Africa's benefit. The SADF began conducting their own raids and incursions into Angola under the guise of ending cross-border incursions into Namibia (Jaster 1988, p. 94).

In 1981, the SADF carried out an assault deep in Angolan territory codenamed Operation Protea (Jaster 1988, pp. 94–5). It was described as a raid, but it grew into a major undertaking by SADF forces. The SADF penetrated 120 kilometers into Angola to fight South West Africa People's Organization (SWAPO) forces (Chan 1990, p. 57). This territory was jointly occupied by UNITA and SADF forces, and by the end of 1983, SADF forces were 300 kilometers into Angola (Chan 1990, p. 57). The incursion eventually ended with the 1984 Lusaka Accord, which followed on the heels of the 1982 secret agreement with Swaziland (Chan 1990, p. 57). These developments were all part of South Africa's broader strategy to set the conditions for regional peace on its own terms.

South Africa was also concerned that what happened in Rhodesia could happen inside its own borders (Chan 1990, pp. 10–11). With the fall of minority rule in Rhodesia, South Africa saw the loss of a regional ally and this demonstrated what could happen to minority rule elsewhere. It was followed by the success of revolutionary independence movements in Angola and Mozambique that provided further momentum for the ANC (Chan 1990, p. 47). The ANC had set up branch offices in every country surrounding South Africa, and Pretoria had long seen the ANC as the leading domestic challenger to its White minority rule.

Foreign Minister Pik Botha stated that unacceptable ANC activities in neighboring countries "included recruitment, planning, routing, advancing identification of targets, and methods of infiltration" (Price 1990, p. 157). Pretoria was not merely concerned with the use of physical violence against White South Africans or their government but with the ANC's mere existence as a threat to White minority rule. These concerns led to a two-pronged strategy of physical incursions eliminating ANC members in neighboring countries and pressure compelling those countries to remove the ANC on their own (Price 1990, p. 158). SADF incursions into Angola, Mozambique, and Zimbabwe all had the express goal of eliminating ANC enclaves (Price 1990, pp. 156–9). Due to its close economic ties with Botswana, Swaziland, and Lesotho, South Africa started a more formal diplomatic push to both advance its own regional goals while also addressing the ANC threat.

Local instability—and Western reluctance to get involved—allowed South Africa to carve out a regional niche for itself. The country sought alliances and agreements to establish its authority (Davis and O'Meara 1990, p. 187). Davis and O'Meara (1990) claim that South Africa engaged in "luring of regional states into non-aggression pacts with Pretoria as a first step towards promoting 'the concept of mutual defense against a common enemy'" (p. 187).

South Africa approached Swaziland in late 1981 and early 1982, hoping to sign a nonaggression pact. Prime Minister Botha announced in September 1982 that Pretoria was considering ceding land that had historically been claimed by Swaziland (Price 1990, p. 151). The land deal proposals began after South Africa backed a failed, high-profile kidnapping conducted by South Africanbacked MNR rebels from Mozambique. The failed attempt had occurred in Swaziland, and in 1981, it was followed by targeted assassinations of ANC members in Swaziland (Hanlon 1986, p. 96). While these covert activities were an embarrassment for Pretoria, they illustrated how far Botha would go to secure South Africa's interests in the region. The potential land deal, as an alternative to the violence, was an enticement that the Swazis could not ignore.

Some of the land proposed in the deal had long been claimed by the Swazis. The agreement covered the KaNgwane and KwaZulu Bantustans of South Africa, along with Ngwavuma. A late addition came in June 1982 when Nsikazi was offered up as another potential transfer (Griffiths and Funnell 1991, p. 52).

The addition of Ngwavuma lands was a bit puzzling; they had not been traditionally claimed by Swazi monarchs (Griffiths and Funnell 1991, p. 51). However, the benefits of receiving this land, especially KwaZulu, were immediately apparent to the Swazis. The territory's connection to the Indian Ocean would provide an enlarged Swaziland with direct sea access, which could reduce the country's dependency on South Africa. Richard's Bay, which was proposed as part of the land transfer, was a recently constructed port with the deepest harbor access on the African continent.

The South Africa–Swaziland agreement was originally conceptualized as a nonaggression pact, but it became much more. South Africa's concessions to Swaziland pursued regional goals by countering domestic threats to South Africa's minority rule—identified as the ANC—and reducing external criticism of the regime and its apartheid policies. Under the agreement, neither signatory would allow "any act which involves a threat or use of force against each other's territory" (Hanlon 1986, p. 96). Both sides also pledged to "'individually and jointly' combat and eliminate from their territories 'terrorism and subversion'" (Davis and O'Meara 1990, p. 199).

The agreement also permitted action "'individually and collectively ... as may be deemed necessary or expedient to eliminate this evil', leading to the suggestion that South Africa now has the right to intervene unilaterally in Swaziland" (Hanlon 1986, p. 96). The suggestion of potential SADF actions in Swazi territory was not lost on anyone. It was clearly directed at ANC activities in Swaziland, but the document made no explicit mention of the organization. It was an implicit understanding that South African forces would be allowed to act on threats to Pretoria that were using Swazi lands as a safe haven.

The land transfer furthered multiple South African regional objectives. It would create a buffer state next to revolutionary Mozambique (Price 1990,

p. 152). It would "get rid of" 750,000 South Africans who were Swazi (Price 1990, p. 152). It would create tension between Zulus and Swazis, justifying Pretoria's claim that ethnicity mattered more to Black South Africans than South African nationality (Price 1990, p. 152). Swaziland would become more indebted to South Africa and more entangled with it economically after two-thirds of Swaziland's population ended up working in South Africa (Price 1990, p. 152). South Africans and some scholars did not see it as a windfall for Swaziland's ruling elites; they saw it as an agreement binding the Swazi king to South Africa and strengthening cross-border ties.

On the other hand, the Swazis stood to gain new citizens and access to the sea, which could reduce Swaziland's economic dependence on South Africa. Such a victory could be politically advantageous for Swaziland's ruling class by uniting all ethnic Swazis under a single state for the first time in over a century. Given the economic ties between the two countries, and the fact that Swaziland's neighbors were encircling South Africa and the tumultuous Mozambique, former Swazi Prince Bhekimpi Dlamini said "that the kingdom of Swaziland had no choice but to cooperate with South Africa" (Hanlon 1986, p. 91). Swaziland's politics followed its economics.

South Africa undoubtedly recognized the long-term effects of Swaziland gaining a port, but it was likely focused on the benefits of having Swaziland as a mediator with other African states and an example of what cooperation with South Africa could look like. Overall, "the prospect of direct access to the sea has been a carrot dangled by the South Africans in front of the Swazi noses" (Chan 1990, p. 38). While it was an enticing deal, it was no free lunch.

Griffiths and Funnell (1991) summarized the deal:

> The land deal became public with the proclamation in the South African Government Gazette of 18 June 1982 of the abolition of the KaNgwane "homeland" Legislative Assembly and the excision of Ngwavuma from the KwaZulu homeland. The governments of South Africa and Swaziland were apparently on the brink of clinching a deal to transfer large tracts of South African territory to Swaziland. In return, Swaziland was to accept Swazi citizens of South Africa. The deal was the realization of a Swazi irredentist dream which had existed with more or less clarity since the British and the Boers had, in the late nineteenth century, drawn a political boundary which cut across the Swazi nation putting many people who traditionally owed allegiance to the King of Swaziland physically outside his kingdom. (p. 51)

While the existence of the land deal became public relatively quickly, the larger agreement remained secret for some time—it was not publicly revealed until after the 1984 Nkomati Accord (Chan 1990, p. 42). Because the land transfer could not be hidden from the public, it was used as a pretext to explain discussions between South Africa and Swaziland while concealing their true scope. Rather than ignore the fact that there was an agreement and obvious cooperation between the two nations, both states made news of the potential land transfer public, as public denials of a larger agreement were only likely to further inflame tensions domestically and internationally. Acknowledging the transfer allowed South Africa and Swaziland to look as if they were conducting "normal politics" while simultaneously planning to strip almost one million South Africans of their citizenship, making them Swaziland subjects without their consent.

The pact's primary objective was a classic nonaggression agreement. The land transfer was a straightforward purchase of Swazi cooperation, and the Swazis were in no position to decline (Griffiths and Funnell 1991, p. 55; Hanlon 1986, p. 96). However, given the size disparity between the two states and the related economic dependency, the pact was clearly not about state-centric aggression. Instead, it sought to constrain the actions of non-state actors, such as the ANC. At the time, the only threat to Swaziland was South Africa, making the agreement a textbook case of bandwagoning—states joining up to pursue predatory ambitions that expand their political power, even in the absence of a threat. Surrounded by an economic giant on three sides, and with a small population and a limited economy, Swaziland had few alternatives. It desperately wanted the land, so it was willing to make peace with South Africa by facilitating the destruction of ANC forces within its borders.

A transfer of Ngwavuma would also give South Africa a buffer zone between Mozambique and South Africa (Griffiths and Funnell 1991, p. 63). At the time, there was no way to know that this would become a moot point after the 1984 Nkomati Accord. South Africa was keen to keep its distance from any revolutionary government so openly opposed to its regional aims.

South Africa wanted Swaziland to recognize the Bantustans, recognize South Africa, oppose South African sanctions, and accept South Africa's activities in Mozambique (Hanlon 1986, p. 93). However, it is quite ironic that South Africa wanted Swaziland to recognize the Bantustans, because Swaziland did not extend full diplomatic recognition to Pretoria until 1985 (Bischoff 1986, p. 183). The agreement with Swaziland remained part of a larger regional security program that epitomized the Botha administration's "total strategy."

While the land would be an enormous boost for Swaziland, relieving the pressures of Finlandization, it was unclear how the transfer would occur in practice. On paper, Swaziland would expand its geographic footprint by roughly one-third, and its population would more than double in size, as ethnic Swazis were "repatriated" to the Swazi kingdom (Hanlon 1986, p. 93).

The crackdown against the ANC began shortly after the South Africa–Swaziland agreement was signed, which occurred on February 17, 1982 (Davis and O'Meara 1990, p. 200). The Swazis were not fully collaborationist, but they cooperated with Pretoria to eliminate ANC forces in their territory

(Chan 1990, p. 42). Smith (1984) asserts that at least 100 members of the ANC were expelled in the two years between the signing of the secret pact and the Nkomati Accord (also Hanlon 1986, p. 96), and the SADF conducted regular raids into Swaziland (see below).

Although the land transfer never occurred, Swaziland served as an important go-between with Marxist-led Mozambique. Mozambique was engaged in heavy conflict with Renamo rebels that were backed by South Africa, and its government eventually met with South African authorities in 1984 to sign the Nkomati Accord. Although the accord does not rise to the level of a formal treaty in either the Correlates of War (CoW) alliance dataset or the Alliance Treaty Obligations and Provisions (ATOP) dataset, it was important in reconciling South Africa with Mozambique.

Under the Nkomati Accord, Mozambique promised to expel ANC members from its territory and to cooperate with South Africa in identifying and "flushing out" elements that Pretoria felt were destabilizing to its apartheid regime. It is unlikely that rapprochement with Mozambique could have been obtained without the prior agreement between Swaziland and South Africa, and the Swazis played a vital role in bringing the two states together.

A Swazi minister without portfolio later stated that "Manzana diplomacy … brought Mozambique and South Africa together to the negotiating table" in the lead-up to the signing of Nkomati at a meeting in December 1983 (Bischoff 1986, 182). Having the non-aligned—but capitalist-inclined—Swaziland acting as a peacemaker helped moderate Mozambique's radical communist positions (Bischoff 1986, p. 182).

International and Domestic Public Opinion

South Africa and Swaziland were both concerned with domestic and international public opinion, and their secret nonaggression pact remained unknown to the public until 1984 (Chan 1990, p. 77). In fact, this partially motivated keeping the alliance secret until after the Nkomati Accord with Mozambique was signed in 1984. However, naturally, minority-ruled South Africa was largely unconcerned with what its Black population thought of the rapprochement; South Africa was only concerned with international opinion to the extent that it supported Botha's "total strategy." Meanwhile, the Swazis were concerned with the opinion of their own elites and the attitudes of other predominantly African nations.

Chan (1990) wrote about South Africa at the time, stating that "there are domestic interests which have to be preserved, but they are domestic interests of only a small section of the population" (p. 9). Given that South Africa was nominally a democracy, but a democracy for Whites only, particularly those of Afrikaner descent, it did have to appease different groups in a relatively small selectorate. The ruling class of Afrikaners, who had exercised control over the country since the National Party's victory in 1948, needed to be placated (Chan 1990, p. 10).

South Africa also planned to revoke the citizenship of almost one million native Black Africans. By redesignating these individuals as subjects of Swaziland, the White regime thought it would strengthen its hand, both domestically and internationally, particularly for its sordid justifications of apartheid (Griffiths and Funnell 1991, p. 61). The National Party expected the reassignment of one million native Africans to strengthen its performance in the polls; the elites would support their policies because they were able to get results. Internationally, South Africa hoped to argue that it was "reuniting" ethnic Swazis with their native homeland, redressing the arbitrary borders imposed by "righting" a wrong imposed by colonialism.

However, the apartheid regime had to contend with protests from native Black Africans who objected to their non-consensual change of citizenship. Barber and Barratt (1990) write that the land transfer "was met by amazement and opposition in South Africa, not least from Buthelezi and the Chief Minister of Kangwane, Enos Mabusa, neither of whom had been consulted" (p. 319). Black South Africans quickly organized their opposition to the plan. The KaNgwane Legislative Assembly opposed the idea of a transfer occurring without a plebiscite among the affected regions, and the minority government rejected their demands (Griffiths and Funnell 1991, p. 54). Further opposition came from Chief Minister Gatsha Buthelezi, the Zulu king, and the Natal Provincial Administration (Griffiths and Funnell 1991, p. 54).

Mabusa and Buthelezi united to stop the land transfer with a lawsuit filed in a South African court. The Zulus appealed to the Natal High Court, and the South African government transferred the case to the appellate court (Griffiths and Funnell 1991, p. 54). The South African government ultimately lost its court case on September 20, 1982, and was blocked from transferring land to Swaziland (Griffiths and Funnell 1991, p. 54). The government could have changed the law to permit the land transfer, and it appointed a commission to study such a plan (Griffiths and Funnell 1991, p. 54), but it decided against such a strategy.

The OAU quietly approved the land transfer, but it was not embraced internationally. This could have been because many states were reluctant to make agreements with minority-led South Africa. Other states may have suspected that an agreement in place between South Africa and Swaziland could result in regional victories for South Africa.

Many Swazis supported the land deal because it corrected a colonial wrong, but it was condemned internationally and by many Black South Africans. The plan revoked South African citizenship from close to one million ethnic Swazis without their consent (Hanlon 1986, p. 93). Some 400,000 other ethnic

Swazis also lived in South African territory, and they were excluded from the transfer to Swaziland, challenging the idea that Pretoria was correcting one of colonialism's wrongs (Hanlon 1986, p. 93).

Domestic public opinion in Swaziland was more complicated. As a monarchy with a relatively small population of native Africans, the country had an even smaller subset of Swazi elites to satisfy. However, the 1982 death of long-ruling King Sobhuza II launched Swaziland into an era of political turmoil and palace intrigue. Factions vied against each other to turn their programs into policy. Internationally, Swaziland had to strike a delicate balance by being friendly to South Africa without alienating other majority-controlled African states. Schisms between Swazi elites who favored closer relations with South Africa and those who opposed rapprochement continued to color Swaziland's politics until a new monarch took the throne in 1986.

Swaziland's Mswati III succeeded his father in 1982, and he favored closer relations with South Africa (Booth 1990, p. 333). However, he was unable to assume the throne until he turned 18, in 1986. The agreement was signed in February 1982, six months prior to Sobhuza II's death, and it is not known how actively he was involved in the agreement. Mswati knew full well that his country's economy and his own grip on the throne depended on staying in South Africa's good graces. He was not prepared to upset the status quo.

Ongoing tensions and divisions among Swazi elites—over the pact and relations with South Africa—fueled tensions within the kingdom (Davis and O'Meara 1990, p. 200). Two Swazi leaders, R.V. Dlamini and Nxumalo, favored closer ties with South Africa and enjoyed warm relations with its outgoing Foreign Minister Pik Botha (Hanlon 1986, p. 105). They fell out of favor and both were later dismissed along with the chief of police and the head of the armed forces (Smith 1984). These dismissals were ostensibly due to a customs fraud case, but relations with South Africa were damaged. Swaziland was already experiencing domestic political turmoil from the earlier dismissal of Prime Minister Mabandla Dlamini and Queen Dzeliwe (Sparks 1984). The Swazi government further alleged that Dlamini and Nxumalo were part of a group attempting to overthrow the monarchy by seizing arms from the royal armory (Sparks 1984). The ongoing uncertainty created after the alliance was made provided a perfect opportunity for South Africa to extract concessions.

The land may have been less valuable to other states, but irredentist claims to the land are a cornerstone of Swazi politics. Swazi kings lost a great deal of territory after the British divided their land in the 19th century. As one scholar puts it, "regaining ownership and occupation of this land—both inside and outside present day Swaziland—has been the dominant issue in 20th century Swazi politics" (Hanlon 1986, p. 92).

South Africa's land would have been a tremendous gain for Swaziland's monarchy, strengthening its relationship with the ruling class. However, the deal was less likely to reduce Swaziland's dependency on South Africa in the short to medium term. It would take a considerable amount of time to acquire the international funds necessary to build ports and shipping facilities on the Indian Ocean. Swaziland's hostility to communism had also ruled out any deals or investments either with Eastern bloc states or with virtually every African state under majority rule. South Africa and Western states were the only realistic sources of funding for port facilities, and it is highly likely that South African firms would have either invested at least some resources in the project or been fully responsible for such a project's completion. In that case, the Swazis could have fallen foul of sanctions placed on South Africa by other countries.

Another concern was that the sudden addition of almost one million new citizens would have exerted enormous political, social, and economic pressure on Swaziland's monarchy, even as it recovered from the death of King Sobhuza II. More Swazis would need to find jobs in South Africa, increasing their economic dependency. Many hundreds of thousands of Swazis living in KwaZulu already worked for South African firms, meaning that their transfer of citizenship would entangle Swaziland and South Africa further.

The Swazi king had the right to grant land to the public as he saw fit (Griffiths and Funnell 1991, p. 60), allowing him to distribute territory in exchange for support from his country's elites. However, the land deal fell through, and the country was ruled by two regents at the time of the agreement, making it unclear how the ruling factions would have managed the issue until Mswati was of age to rule. Had the land deal happened, it could have caused greater tensions among the winners and losers in Swaziland, exacerbating internal conflict.

Swaziland also asked the OAU to approve the deal (Griffiths and Funnell 1991, p. 60). Generally, the OAU—as a matter of principle observed in many other post-colonial regions, particularly in South America—formally opposed redrawing colonial borders. It feared that such changes would generate instability, particularly among the 14 land-locked African countries at that time (Griffiths and Funnell 1991, pp. 60-1). However, Swaziland sought OAU approval to garner further support from other African states. To that end, Daniel arap Moi, president of Kenya and outgoing OAU president, approved the plan in 1982 (Griffiths and Funnell 1991, p. 61). The ANC, which was unaware of the secret conditions attached to the agreement, did not offer any opposition, giving it further legitimacy (Griffiths and Funnell 1991, p. 61).

The secret agreement specifically focused on nonaggression, with each side promising not to interfere in one another's politics. Despite the wording of the agreement, South Africa commonly interfered in Swaziland's economic and security issues. After South Africa's 1985 bumper crop, a South African-owned firm shut down Swaziland's only grain-processing mill and forced the Swazis to import all of their grain for the year (Hanlon 1986, p. 72). In December 1986, a South African raid into Swaziland resulted in the deaths of two Swazi bystanders (Barber and Barratt 1990, p. 320). There were numerous other incursions and interventions, but the Swazis were in no position to oppose the SADF's efforts to root out anyone who had any hint of ties to the ANC. Such activities could easily cause pains for the Swazi ruling class, but public discontent was not a major consideration for the Swazi elites. Since Swaziland was not a democracy at that time (though hardly an autocracy), public discontent did not appear to rank highly in the minds of the Swazi elites, though such tensions could easily cause pains for the Swazi ruling class.

Even with the public rapprochement and public discussions of the land transfer, the full scope of the deal was kept secret for quite a long period of time. The secret pact was only made public after the 1994 deal with Mozambique (Barber and Barratt 1990, p. 295; South Africa Record 1984, pp. 3–4). And while the Nkomati Accord may get more attention than the secret agreement with Swaziland, both were integral parts of South African security in the 1980s.

INSTITUTIONALIZATION AND MILITARY COORDINATION

Barber and Barratt (1990) have stated that coordination between South Africa and Swaziland was predominantly carried out through police coordination rather than joint military action (p. 320). While this distinction is exceedingly convoluted in both South Africa and Swaziland, it speaks to the nature of the relationship between the two neighbors. The ANC was an existential security threat for South Africa's apartheid regime, but in the case of Swaziland, it could often be handled by SADF-managed police actions, rather than by the more intense skirmishes in Namibia and Angola.

Shortly after the secret South Africa–Swaziland agreement was signed, a car bomb in Swaziland killed the deputy director of the ANC and his wife (Hanlon 1986, p. 96). No one doubted who was responsible for their deaths in Swaziland, as South Africa frequently pursued the ANC into Swaziland and carried out operations in Swazi territory, but these activities were more muted than SADF and intelligence operations in other southern African states. Even after the land deal fell through, Swaziland continued cooperating with South Africa and the cross-border raids continued.

The Swazis expelled many ANC members (Hanlon 1986, p. 96). Sparks (1984) details that at least 100 ANC members were turned over to Pretoria's security services by mid-1984; the two countries cooperated on a political level and also at lower levels. Their security services coordinated with one another to identify and expel ANC members, particularly those in leadership positions.

Hanlon (1986) notes that cooperation "followed the South African raid into Maseru, when South Africa privately warned Swaziland that it would turn the country into another Lebanon if the Swazis did not tighten up on the ANC" (p. 96). The Swazis fully committed to the pact, even after South Africa reneged on the land transfer, and yet Pretoria continued to punish Swaziland for insufficient effort. South Africa believed that the Swazis were dragging their feet on the ANC, closing the border on two important holiday weekends (Hanlon 1986, p. 97).

It was clear which country was the junior partner in the nonaggression pact. Swaziland could not hide its increased cooperation with South Africa because the various high-profile events involved made plausible deniability all but impossible. When ANC members in Swaziland were kidnapped and expelled to third-party countries or repatriated back to South Africa, Swaziland could hardly claim ignorance (Hanlon 1986, p. 97). Likewise, the SADF's highly publicized efforts to help Swaziland after a February 1984 cyclone evinced a broader, covert arrangement between the two states (Hanlon 1986, p. 97).

South Africa's continued insistence upon one-sided "cooperation" by the Swazis was also not limited to the ANC and the singular issue of White rule. South Africa also worked through the Resistência Nacional Moçambicana—MNR, also known as Renamo—to carry out activities in Swaziland (Hanlon 1986, p. 97).

MNR was a Mozambican political party and militant group that resisted the control of the government. It was founded at the behest of Ian Smith's minority government in the dying days of Rhodesia, and it became an important ally opposing Marxist-Leninist forces in Mozambican politics. South Africa ultimately facilitated and funded the establishment of MNR bases in Swaziland as part of an effort to destabilize the government in Mozambique (Hanlon 1986, p. 97).

While MNR's aggression had nothing to do with Swaziland, the presence of MNR forces in Swazi lands aggravated tensions between the Swazis and other African states, particularly states aligned with the communist Eastern bloc. Confusion, and a lack of communication and acknowledgement by the SADF, meant that Swazi security forces engaged in gun battles with MNR forces in Swaziland on at least two occasions (Hanlon 1986, p. 97).

South Africa's economic isolation really began to bite during the 1980s. Some scholars have argued that Swaziland was an important conduit for South African trade, although no evidence exists to support their claims. Most of the world had placed South Africa under an embargo throughout the 1970s and 1980s, making Swaziland a valuable neighbor that could launder South African goods by presenting them as products created in an unsanctioned state. This was not a formal part of the agreement, but cooperation between

South Africa and Swaziland was often improvised and ad hoc and changed as situations developed.

Booth (1990) alleges that "Swaziland's open border with Pretoria, its preferential access to US, European, and Third World markets, and its keenness to attract African and other foreign capital, make it an ideal instrument" for evading sanctions (p. 328). In fact, Swaziland stood to gain enormously from sanctions on South Africa because of its location, its economic dependence on South Africa, and its favorable relations with Pretoria and the West. A profitable collusion could swell Swazi coffers while helping South African firms circumvent trade restrictions (Booth 1990, p. 327).

Economic forces were influential in Swaziland and other southern African states since at least the 1960s. When the Southern African Customs Union was formed in 1910, smaller colonies were wholly dependent on the much larger colony of South Africa. The enormous amount of goods imported from South Africa, and even the use of the rand as the official currency of Swaziland, intractably linked the Swazis to the economic fortunes of the apartheid regime (Booth 1990, p. 327). Although the Swazi regime did not rely on domestic support, it recognized that currency manipulation, the blocking of imports into Swaziland, or the expulsion of Swazi workers from South Africa would cripple the Swazi economy.

The customs union made it much easier for South African firms to avoid sanctions. Trade across the borders of Swaziland, South Africa, and other southern African states was inherently linked and more difficult to curtail, making sanctions avoidance commonplace. Anglin (1990) describes two approaches taken by South African firms: they could either mark South African products as "Made in Swaziland," when, in fact, they were made in South Africa, or they could set up manufacturing hubs in Swaziland and legitimately export from there to virtually anywhere in the world (p. 278). Given Swaziland's tiny population and limited resources, the latter approach was exceedingly difficult, and the former was the preferred strategy for avoiding sanctions. Political cooperation between Swaziland and South Africa was greater and longer-lasting than any other secret alliance analyzed in this study. While France, Britain, and Israel cooperated to varying degrees over the decades that followed their agreement, the cooperation between South Africa and Swaziland was truly remarkable given the vast differences between their countries.

Swaziland, a tiny, land-locked nation of approximately 650,000 people, served as a mediator between South Africa's minority government and other southern African states. This culminated in the 1984 signing of the Nkomati Accord, two years after South Africa and Swaziland signed their nonaggression pact. In fact, Swazi diplomats and intermediaries were largely responsible for the rapprochement between South Africa and Mozambique; they proposed that the Mozambicans should meet with South African emissaries in

December 1983 (Bischoff 1986, p. 182). The resulting Nkomati Accord does not constitute a formal alliance in either the COW or ATOP datasets, but it was an important step toward nonaggression between the two states, even if Mozambique was the only signatory that honored the treaty. The Nkomati Accord was a breakthrough in relations between South Africa and majority-ruled African states. The agreement required "both states to prohibit the use of their respective territories by any 'state, government, foreign military forces, organizations, or individuals which plan or prepare to commit acts of violence, terrorism, or aggression against the territorial integrity of political independence of the other or may threaten the security of its inhabitants'" (Davis and O'Meara 1990, p. 207). This ostensibly meant that Mozambique and South Africa recognized one another and that their security interests were inherently linked. Mozambique fulfilled many of its obligations under the treaty, but South Africa continued funding Renamo rebels.

Initial cooperation with Mozambique was predominantly concerned with security issues, but economic collaboration followed. The agreement established a joint security commission between South Africa and Mozambique, and it encouraged greater economic cooperation, such as supplying power from the Cabora Bassa Dam, the use of the Maputo port, and an increased number of laborers permitted to enter South Africa from Mozambique (Davis and O'Meara 1990, p. 209). This cooperation would have been impossible without Swazi involvement. Although the nonaggression pact with Swaziland bore fruit, Botha's "total strategy" was less successful. Apartheid was living on borrowed time.

TERMINATION

The agreement between South Africa and Swaziland, like the apartheid policies in South Africa itself, began unraveling as soon as majority rule took hold in South Africa. By the late 1980s, apartheid and minority rule in South Africa were hanging on by a thread. After the Soviet Union collapsed in 1991, disputes slowly settled across many African states, while new cleavages arose elsewhere, and South Africa was no longer necessary for maintaining a wall of resistance to oppose Marxist-Leninist states. The secret agreement between Swaziland and South Africa became defunct relatively quickly, although Swaziland abided by its terms until minority rule ended in South Africa in 1994.

South Africa revoked its land transfer offer on June 19, 1984 (Hanlon 1986, p. 106), a few months after the Nkomati Accord was signed with Mozambique. South Africa's domestic courts sank the deal, and Pretoria actively chose not to defy them. Land was the primary inducement for Swaziland to sign the agreement, but it was not the only motivating factor. Pretoria hinted that South

Africa would use its economic leverage over Swaziland to compel action, giving little reason to oppose South Africa's security forces sent into Swaziland to kill ANC members.

Links between the two partners remained strong throughout the 1980s, with South Africa financing the building of a Swaziland railroad in 1986. The Swazis reciprocated with repeated opposition to sanctions leveled against South Africa (Barber and Barratt 1990, p. 320).

FUTURE ALLIANCE-MAKING PROSPECTS

Minority-led South Africa, much like Israel, never had much chance for formal alliances. The country's location, its White minority rule, and its racist policies of apartheid all worked against it during the rapid period of decolonization after World War II. Even though South Africa was the richest state on the continent, it had few opportunities for alliances. This may help explain how it saw itself surrounded by enemies and developed a "total strategy" that merged domestic and international politics into a singular understanding of state survival.

Arms embargoes had been imposed on South Africa since the 1970s, and the country pursued a strategy of self-reliance, all while trying to position itself to the West as a bulwark against the spread of communism in southern Africa. However, it was unlikely that the United States—considering its position on decolonization, its own racial problems, and its support of United Nations Security Council resolutions regarding South Africa and Namibia—would fully support South Africa with a formal alliance. Agreements with other Western states were similarly improbable.

On the other hand, core Western states such as the United States, United Kingdom, and France were aligned with South Africa on a great many issues, particularly in opposition to Marxist-Leninist states. South Africa might not have been a formal ally, but by some measures, it was partnered with Western states. South Africa desperately needed Western "partners" to eliminate any hint of Soviet presence in southern Africa, but first, it needed Western states to relax their opposition to its apartheid policies (Price 1990, p. 161). Some of this occurred under the de Klerk premiership in the late 1980s, but Western states remained hesitant to openly align with the pariah state.

South Africa had also been unsuccessfully trying to make nonaggression pacts with other southern African states since the days of Prime Minister John Vorster in the early 1970s (Hanlon 1986, p. 62). In the 1980s, Botha's concept of "total strategy," in response to "total onslaught," focused efforts in ways that had not been seen under the Vorster premiership. Public alliances were highly unlikely for South Africa because of the opposition from majority African states; alliances that are supposed to protect a country should avoid agitating other states in its region.

Rumors suggested that South Africa was considering a deal with Lesotho (Price 1990, p. 152), although such an agreement never came to fruition. The hope was that Lesotho would inform on South African refugees and deport individuals at the request of Pretoria (Davis and O'Meara 1990, p. 211). Instead of being approached for a nonaggression alliance, Botswana was pressured into compliance with economic coercion (Davis and O'Meara 1990, p. 211). The agreement with Swaziland, the informal nonaggression agreement with Mozambique at Nkomati, and the rumors of seeking a similar agreement with Lesotho were all part of South Africa's "total strategy."

Swaziland's size, location, and limited value to potential aggressors have kept it relatively insulated from outside interference. Most of its external pressures have come from South Africa, particularly during the apartheid era, which partially explains Swaziland's policy of being unofficially aligned but officially non-aligned with Western states. Swaziland had been colonized, a large portion of its land and population was arbitrarily given to another state, and that state was run by descendants of Swaziland's colonizers, putting the country in a difficult position. During the era of apartheid, it had to avoid aggravating or provoking the country that literally and figuratively surrounded it. As such, any alliance with an outside power would have been wholly impractical.

Swaziland does share a border with Mozambique, which was troublesome during the latter's civil war in the 1970s and 1980s. The two countries signed a security agreement in July 1984, shortly after facilitating the Nkomati Accord (Bischoff 1986, p. 182). This meant that not only was the secret South Africa–Swaziland agreement beneficial for South Africa, it also enabled a security agreement between capitalist-oriented (though non-aligned) Swaziland and Marxist-Leninist Mozambique. This security pact is not included in the ATOP dataset, but Swaziland signed formal alliances in 2001, 2002, and 2003. These agreements were directly related to the African Union, but they represent Swaziland's greatest formal alliance commitments since its secret pact.

Even after the end of apartheid, and the resolution and reconciliation that came with it, Swaziland seeks a cordial relationship with majority-controlled South Africa. The country, now renamed Eswatini, has not made formal defensive or offensive alliances with any other state—not for fear of aggravating relations with Pretoria, but instead because it has little need for an alliance. Instead, it joined the nonaggression pact shared by members of the African Union.

With the end of South Africa's minority rule, the threat to Swaziland simply evaporated. The country need not fear domestic turmoil like that experienced in Angola or Mozambique, which means there is little need for an alliance on any practical level.

CONCLUSION

In the 1980s, Swaziland's survival depended on not angering South Africa. In a classic example of bandwagoning (Schweller 1994), Swaziland practiced a policy of "going along to get along" with South Africa. As an economic power with pariah status, South Africa was positioned to be a regional leader, but no state in the region (and many beyond) wanted to see South Africa fill such a role during its apartheid era. The incongruities of South Africa and Swaziland—along with their respective domestic opinions and the international status of the apartheid state—meant that secrecy was paramount for both to preserve domestic tranquility and maintain international relations.

However, Swaziland's mistake was to begin cooperating with South Africa before the details regarding land transfers had been finalized. If the Swazis, who were experiencing political disruption after the death of Sobhuza II, had waited until the land transfer had been finalized, Pretoria's relationship with other southern African states might have looked very different. It would have been a sea change in the apartheid regime's relationship with a majority-controlled African nation, possibly paving the way for reconciliation with other states, especially Lesotho and Botswana. However, apartheid was on borrowed time. The secret alliance that Pretoria made with Swaziland, which endured for as long as the minority-run regime, could not keep apartheid's sinking ship afloat.

NOTE

1. As Chan (1990) notes, South Africa's selling point throughout the latter parts of apartheid was its role as a bulwark against Marxism and the USSR in Africa, which neither the ANC nor other groups would commit to (p. 8).

9. Conclusion and the future of secret alliances

While knowledge of secret alliances is problematic from a research design perspective, this does not mean that empirical inquiry is impossible. Instead, as this book demonstrates, a mixed-methods approach yields a fruitful analysis. And while the incidence of formal secret alliances has undoubtedly decreased in the contemporary era, that does not diminish the need to study and understand the scientific processes surrounding secret alliance-making. Instead, scholars must ask themselves: What about the nature of norms, the international system, and informal agreements has made secret alliances less common? And, ultimately, could these structural factors see a return to a world where secret alliances become common once again?

Given that networks of secret alliances in the lead-up to World War I and World War II were central to those conflicts, it is essential that scholars better understand the life cycle of secret alliances and the implications for future conflict. Furthermore, while scholars may have concerns regarding the specification of models or the inclusion/exclusion of cases as formal or informal agreements, the point of this book has been to have a serious discussion and first-order approximation of why states make, keep, and end secret alliances. Rather than provide a complete framework for every possible covariate in the formation, termination, and duration of secret agreements, this book has provided a cohesive story of the life cycle of an important mechanism in international conflict. To date, no other volume has taken such a thorough examination of the phenomenon of secret alliances.

Since secret alliances are, by definition, secret, immediate knowledge of them may not be public. Nonetheless, as I have maintained throughout previous chapters, such formal knowledge does not exclude the suspicion that such agreements exist and that their consequences are dire to international peace and security. Instead, the most likely avenue for knowledge of formal secret alliances relies on the "success" or "failure" of such alliances in achieving their objectives. However, a cursory glance at the available sample of cases demonstrates no discernible pattern between those that can be judged as successes or failures. This complicates claims that such phenomena are unobservable.

In fact, as illustrated in the previous chapters, all three case studies were either immediately known or assumed to have involved secret agreements. Within days, if not hours, astute observers of international relations suspected a secret agreement between the Nazis and Soviets. And even from the floor of the United Nations, states suspected and openly accused France, Great Britain, and Israel of having a secret agreement. In the South Africa–Swaziland case, news of the secret arrangement leaked to the press within months of ratification. Secret agreements, between both major powers and minor powers, as well as the precursors to great wars and the unread footnotes to history, often lurk in the background of international politics, only abated by the normative turn against secret diplomacy and structural changes to the international system. Yet this begs an important question: With the return of great power competition and an increasingly multipolar world, will the world see a return to secret alliance-making?

WHAT DO WE KNOW ABOUT SECRET ALLIANCES?

Given the relative paucity of the study of secret alliances in international politics, secret alliance-making is one of the most under-studied areas of conflict and alliance-making more generally. While there have been some important areas of research, none of these have been comprehensive in their discussion of why secret alliances happen, the organization of such alliances, and what happens after they terminate. Yet the implications and risks that stem from secret alliances are crucial to understanding peace and conflict.

As demonstrated in Chapter 2 and Chapters 6–8, secret alliances occur for two reasons. First, states wanting something that is otherwise difficult to obtain are incentivized to keep secret the alliance that helps them get that good. Naturally, for a state to make public the nature of what is divided up between secret alliance partners would undercut the very reason for keeping the agreement secret. By coordinating with one another in private, it maximizes the probability that signatories will get what they are after from the target state with a minimum cost. Given that what is divided up in secret alliances has a target state and is likely to be a "salient stake," states that know or suspect there is a secret alliance are incentivized to act first to prevent the loss of the stake. Prior research has maintained that due to the informational asymmetry provided by secret agreements, conflict is more likely (Bas and Schub 2016). On the other hand, I maintain that the very nature of what is promised in secret alliances makes conflict more likely. In this view, secret alliances are commitment problems that emerge from the indivisibility of certain issues (Powell 2006). Land or regime survival, for instance, do not lend themselves very well to compromise. It is either possessed or it isn't.

As discussed more thoroughly in Chapters 7 and 8 and to a lesser extent in Chapter 6, another reason secret alliances may form is due to domestic audience considerations. As illustrated by the Molotov–Ribbentrop Pact, the level of rhetoric between the Soviets and Nazis was so severe that public pronouncements regarding reconciliation (albeit temporary) were not likely to be well received by domestic publics. Though they were autocratic regimes, when such reconciliation was made public, it did cause consternation among communist allies in the Fifth Column in Western Europe and caused angst among some Nazis, a few of whom resigned their membership over the reconciliation with the Soviet Union (Moorhouse 2014, p. 128). In a radio broadcast on September 17, 1939, Molotov even went so far as to publicly proclaim that the Soviets were invading to protect Russian and Ukrainian "brothers" in Poland (Roberts 1989, p. 6) And Soviet newspapers claimed Poland was repressing non-ethnic Poles (Roberts 1989, p. 161). This attempt to sway the masses is eerily familiar to observers of Russian propaganda during the 2022 invasion of Ukraine.

In the aftermath of the World War II, Anthony Eden was so incensed to learn that his foreign minister had allowed the agreement to be formally written down that he sent him back to Paris to retrieve the copies and destroy them. While the fiasco cost Eden his premiership, it had fewer lasting effects in France and Israel. Finally, the agreement between South Africa and Swaziland further complicated domestic politics between the minority White government and the majority Black population, who were to be "traded" to Swaziland without a say in the matter. Thus, keeping such agreements quiet serves important domestic political purposes across democratic and autocratic regimes.

As has been illustrated throughout this book, secret alliances are less likely to be multilateral than public alliances. This is because it is easier to divide spoils between two states than among multiple states. Additionally, it is easier to make bilateral agreements in the first place. The effects examined in this chapter were largely driven by fully secret alliances. This is not surprising, as fully secret alliances constitute approximately 75 percent of both types of secret alliances. However, this is equally troubling, as fully secret alliances are the most difficult to detect and have the most severe consequences for peace and conflict.

Next, this book has indicated that the relative lack of institutionalization within secret alliances is intentional. They are also less likely to contain provisions for adding members or mentioning the specific length the alliance is in force. In fact, none of the three cases studied in this book contained provisions for institutionalization or the addition of other states at a later date. Instead, the objective of such an alliance is not duration but substance: getting something out of another state that would be problematic if made public. Public-facing institutionalization is contrary to the principle of achieving surprise.

Since secret alliances are likely to be transactional in nature, institutionalization is also unlikely to occur on a large scale. While some degree of institutionalization is likely to occur, it is more likely to be ad hoc rather than formal. For example, the Molotov–Ribbentrop Pact illustrates this informal institutionalization when temporary commissions of Gestapo and NKVD officials met to trade "undesirable" individuals with one another in their occupation of Poland and the Baltics. Further adjustments to the borders and the transportation of goods needed for the war also occurred with subsequent and previous economic treaties between the two. To that end, secret alliances, particularly fully secret alliances, are more likely to mention military-to-military contact between signatories than public agreements. This is likely due to the aggressive undertones of these alliances and the need for greater military coordination to effectively divide up labor in the division of goods to be extracted from a target state. Again, to use the Molotov–Ribbentrop Pact as an example, cooperation between the Soviets and Nazis even included the use of radio direction finding for Nazi aircraft (Moorhouse 2014, p. 39) and the use of Murmansk as a port to evade British warships (Moorhouse 2014, p. 59). The attendance of Shimon Perez (Israeli Minister of Defense), Moshe Dayan (IDF Chief of Staff), Maurice Bourgès-Maunoury (French Minister of Defense), and Maurice Challe (Chief of Staff of French Armed Forces) at the Sèvres conference only serves to illustrate the emphasis placed on military cooperation in what was ostensibly a diplomatic affair.

Most importantly, Chapter 3 illustrates a central claim made by scholars: writing down formal secret alliances makes defection more difficult (Morrow 2000). As illustrated in the case of writing down the Protocol of Sèvres or the Sykes–Picot Agreement and the ascension of the Bolsheviks to power in Russia, there are real consequences when what is done in secret becomes public knowledge. Similarly, because these pacts are written down, it incentivizes states to fulfill their agreements, for fear that they will be made public if a state fails to uphold commitments. In fact, because of the consequences of "going public," secret alliances solve much of the commitment problem faced by states elsewhere in international relations (Powell 2006). Because of this leverage, secret alliances are more reliable in the sense that states are less likely to renege on their commitments. Chapter 3 also demonstrates that secret alliances are less likely to have a willful violation. However, in the event such a violation occurs, it will occur early on in the alliance. Secret alliances are also likely to endure for a shorter period of time. This is because the design of such alliances is not to be a permanent fixture between two states. Such a finding goes hand-in-hand with institutionalization. Since institutions are often designed to mitigate against defection and ensure an alliance endures, the absence of institutions likely results in shorter alliances. Likewise, such agreements represent a temporary convergence of interest between states over a material good.

Next, this book demonstrates the lack of strong issue convergence and alliance similarity between partners in secret alliances. Since secret alliances are illicit agreements, states are incentivized to keep quiet about the goals of the alliance. And while public alliances are more likely between states that have greater issue similarity, the illicit nature of what is promised in these types of alliances means states will be less likely to need strong issue convergence as is required in public alliances. Since states are less familiar with one another in making secret alliances, they are more likely to follow through with their commitments in such agreements because to not do so both threatens the loss of the good but also may harm both a state's public and private reputation. Thus, there exists a "law among thieves" that states making these agreements will both be more likely to fulfill the agreements and less likely to have a need for long-term issue convergence.

Finally, the question regarding reputation and the formation of secret alliances has been addressed in this book. As mentioned above, reputation is difficult to operationalize and theoretically analyze. Partially, this is due to disagreements within the literature. This is primarily driven by disagreements over reputations for resolve versus reputations for reliability. Similarly, in the alliance-making and deterrence literature, there is a focus on the reputations of both states and leaders. Given that time horizons are different for leaders in different types of states, I rely upon the reputation of states rather than leaders. Future inquiries may answer this question: What is the reputational reliability of leaders in making and upholding secret alliances? A particularly interesting question (with a likewise correspondingly minuscule sample size) is how willing are new leaders to uphold the secret agreements made by their predecessors?

Here, the long-term effects of making secret agreements and the long-term prospects of alliance-making are examined. In other words, what is the general reputation of states that make secret alliances (which may or may not be known), and are they more or less likely to make alliances in the future? The findings indicate that states making secret agreements are less likely to make any alliances in the future. This suggests that while secret agreements may be private, shielding other governments from the knowledge of their existence is much more difficult. This implies that as norms against secret diplomacy have grown stronger, states that do engage in secret alliance-making are more likely to be shunned by future suitors. Ostensibly, states making secret alliances do so at their own peril and mortgage their future reputations for the material gains of today.

Similarly, as supported by the literature elsewhere, reputation for upholding one's agreements matters in making future agreements. States that make secret alliances and then break them are less likely to make alliances in the future in the same way that states making public alliances and breaking them will find it tougher to make future alliances. However, there is a distinction here between those secret agreements that are partially secret versus fully secret. States making fully secret alliances are less likely to make alliances in the future, while the finding for partially secret alliances is not significant. On the other hand, partially secret alliances that end regularly are likely to result in future alliance formation.

While the sample size of these cases is small, it is also exhibited in the qualitative chapters. For instance, the Molotov-Ribbentrop Pact, broken by Nazi Germany in June 1941 with the invasion of the USSR, would prove to be one of the last major formal alliances for Germany under the Nazi regime (as recognized by the ATOP dataset). While future alliances did occur, the backdrop of World War II and the necessity of making alliances were heightened more so than before August 1939. But the fact that Germany reneged so quickly and publicly on its claimed neutrality and nonaggression pact (and the private exchange of conquered lands) illustrates the hazards of secret agreements. Since the items being secretly negotiated over are likely to be "salient stakes" but the risk of not fulfilling a secret agreement is lower than other agreements (see Chapter 3), the consequences of willful violations result in greater damage to a state's reputation. In this case, a state's public reputation may be harmed, as it breaks the norm of not engaging in secret alliances. It will also suffer private reputational damage with the jilted partner, who is less likely to trust them or make future alliances with that state.

RETURN TO THE PAST? THE FUTURE OF SECRET ALLIANCES

As Kuo (2020) points out, the appearance of secret alliances between 1870 and 1916 was greater than at any other time since 1816. One explanation for this trend is the multipolar nature of the international system during this timeframe. However, the bigger concern that Kuo (2020) notes is that secret alliances beget secret alliances. States making secret alliances often pressure their own alliance partners to not engage in public alliances with other states in the system. As such, states may be more willing to engage in other secret alliances to keep from alienating a secret alliance partner.

Given the proliferation of informal alliances in the recent past, such as between the United States and Israel and continued opacity over the "Taiwan issue," it is safe to assume an increase in secret alliances among great powers will happen in the near future. However, given trends against formal secret alliances in the past 100 years, it is likely that these formal secret alliances will be more prevalent among non-democratic regimes. This is because, since these regimes are only responsible to smaller groups within their own societies (Bueno de Mesquita and Siverson 1995; Bueno de Mesquita et al. 2002; Siverson and Bueno de Mesquita 2017), they are likely to be overrepresented in making formal secret agreements. Additionally, given increased restrictions on the press and domestic repression, formal secret agreements are less likely to be covered than in democratic regimes.

The existence of secret alliances among non-democracies has several implications. As scholars have pointed out elsewhere (Bas and Schub 2016), this increases the risk of conflict. Furthermore, since the norms against formal secret diplomacy have increased and are likely to be held most dearly by democracies, those regimes are likely to be at a disadvantage in countering non-democratic regimes. And since non-democratic regimes have less freedom of the press, etc., public knowledge of secret alliances emerging from those regimes will be less likely. This means that informational asymmetries are likely to worsen as a result of regime asymmetry.

While no one can predict the future, least of all political scientists, the costs of ignoring the past and the theoretical mechanisms that give rise to secret alliances are dire. As such, a serious inquiry into secret alliances would be remiss if an analysis of the current global order and the potentiality of future conflicts were not undertaken. Below, I cautiously endeavor a shift from the analysis of past historical cases and correlations to a discussion of the likelihood of secret alliances in the near term.

THE FUTURE OF SECRET ALLIANCES: LOOKING TO THE PAST?

As discussed in Chapter 1, the possibility of a new era of secret alliances is likely to accompany increased global tension between the United States and so-called "pacing challenges" from China and Russia. As stated previously, Russia and China have both committed to one another in a "partnership without limits." And, given the involvement of Iran and North Korea in supplying arms to Russia to aid in its fight in Ukraine, it is likely that at least some secret agreement exists between those states, whether formal or informal.

While it is unlikely that Russia has formal secret alliances with Iran or North Korea, it is likely that informal secret arrangements do exist. With the news of a new alliance made between North Korea and Russia in the summer of 2024, it is probable that secret informal agreements had existed for some time and acted as a precursor to formal, public declarations. These likely centered around weapons and other forms of support for Russia's ongoing war in Ukraine.

North Korea began supplying weapons to Russia in its ongoing war in Ukraine at some point in 2023, with news first breaking in October 2023 (Davenport 2023) when the United States publicly accused the DPRK of sending weapons to Russia for use in Ukraine. This has included, at minimum, artillery systems, artillery shells, and missiles/missile components. Evidence to support this claim was provided by the White House when pictures of shipping containers filled with arms and bound for Russia were publicly released (Davenport 2023). Further evidence emerged early in 2024, with various outlets reporting that large weapons caches of up to 13,000 shipping containers had been transferred to Russia (e.g., Jakes 2024; Rahman 2024). Such shipments were likely precursors to more formal, deeper ties. In the same way that the Soviets helped Nazi Germany after the Molotov–Ribbentrop Pact by sending unfinished goods such as minerals and food, arms are essential to Russian victory in Ukraine.

In June 2024, Russia announced a new agreement with North Korea (Cha and Kim 2024; Mi Terry and Sestanovich 2024; Smith and Park 2024). Cha and Kim (2024) note that while the full nature of the pact was initially unknown, Smith and Park (2024) report that the agreement is largely defensive in nature. North Korea, for its part, pledged "unconditional support to Russia's policies, including the war in Ukraine" (Cha and Kim 2024). And on June 20, North Korea unilaterally released the full text of the document (Hankyoreh 2024).[1] What is more, while Kim Jong-Un explicitly referred to the agreement as an alliance, Putin noticeably did not use the term "alliance" (Hankyoreh 2024). According to the text,

> in case any one of the two sides is put in a state of war by an armed invasion from an individual state or several states, the other side shall provide military and other assistance with all means in its possession without delay in accordance with Article 51 of the UN Charter and the laws of the DPRK and the Russian Federation. (Hankyoreh 2024)

Further, the signatories pledge in Article IV their "desire to protect international justice from hegemonic aspirations and attempts to impose a unipolar world order" (Sputnik International 2024). Article V then goes on to ban entering into agreements with third parties that may challenge either state, going so far in Article XVI to ban

> unilateral enforcement measures or supporting such measures of any third party if such measures affect or are directed directly or indirectly at one of the Parties, individuals and legal entities of such Party or their property under the jurisdiction of such third party, goods originating from one Party, intended for the other Party, and (or) works, services, information, results of intellectual activity, including exclusive rights to them, provided by suppliers of the other Party. (Sputnik International 2024)

In Article X, they both pledge to continue trade with one another, despite United Nations resolutions banning such trade with North Korea (Sputnik International 2024). Thus, it appears that the North Korean/Russian pact takes place within the larger context of agreements around military hardware. While it is most likely that these constitute separate agreements from what is included in the public release of the alliance, issue linkage means that the two policies are undoubtedly intertwined (Poast 2012; Tollison and Willett 1979). In fact, the weapons transfers likely made the latter alliance possible, in the same way that economic agreements between Germany and the Soviets made their later alliance possible, or the cozy relationship between France and Israel made the Protocol of Sèvres more likely.

In fact, the point of publicly releasing the document is to signal both states' support for one another rather than a monumental shift in their attitudes toward each other. Given that this alliance was made public by North Korea, its biggest contribution is not in the material goods promised between the two states, but the deterrent value of the public proclamation. Instead, what may be of more interest is the content of the secret promises between the two states. If such an informal agreement does exist, though, it is unlikely to be written down. In fact, according to Stephen Sestanovich, "what we don't know is what's been promised in secret—or will be promised over time" (Mi Terry and Sestanovich 2024). These discussions will be more likely to address concrete promises and exchanges between the two sides rather than the political niceties and promises of assurance from diplomats. As Stalin once said, "a diplomat's words have no relation to action, otherwise what kind of diplomacy is it? Words are one thing, actions another ... Sincere diplomacy is no more possible than dry water or iron wood" (Roberts 1989, p. 195).

As the case of North Korean/Russian cooperation illustrates, formal pacts (secret or otherwise) are often preceded by signals of increased cooperation between signatories. In the case of the Molotov–Ribbentrop Pact, formal commercial and economic agreements occurred in the spring of 1939, ensuring that Nazi Germany would have access to the war goods it would need in its expansion. Even prior to this formal expansion, Hermann Göring, as minister of war production, had authorized five separate trade expansions with the Soviets from 1937 to 1938 (Johnson 2021, pp. 201–2). Thus, there were clearly visible signs of rapprochement between the two sides before August 1939. And at Sèvres, Israeli Prime Minister Ben-Gurion's delegation traveled by French military aircraft and stayed under false names at a hotel in Paris to avoid raising suspicion (Bar-On 2006, pp. 173–4).

While the public declaration by Russia and North Korea does not substantively promise the division of any goods in the international system, it does foreshadow increased cooperation between the two countries. On the other hand, informal agreements between Russia and China on the eve of the February 2022 invasion of Ukraine further illustrate the increased cooperation between states opposed to the US-led international order. And while the Western world has largely condemned the invasion of Ukraine, there are numerous developing states within the Global South that are less willing to challenge or confront Russia or China as tensions with the West increase.

Given that Russia and North Korea are increasingly opposed to the current US-led global order, the incidence of secret alliances in the future is set to grow, both on the side of those states opposed to US leadership and possibly even among the United States and its partners. As a result, it is likely that the norms that developed after the World Wars are set to erode as the realities of global competition increase.

In the context of China's rise, which is seen as the greatest security challenge in the US 2022 National Security Strategy (White House 2022), there is also likely to be an increase in formal agreements between China and other states. While China has historically been reticent to make formal alliances, with some notable exceptions such as its North Korean alliance and the partnership with Albania after the Sino-Soviet split, China is incentivized to make more alliances in the future. While these alliances are unlikely to be defensive in nature, they are likely to increase military and political cooperation between signatories. The risk to China being drawn into a conflict that is not near its own shores is minimal, with China struggling to project power very far from the mainland. And were China to fail in supporting an ally it had pledged to defend, it would greatly harm China's reputation among other partners and allies. For these reasons, and China's historical unwillingness to conduct defensive alliances, the People's Republic of China is more likely to form nonaggression, neutrality, or entente agreements. Since these alliance types promise the least amount of commitment and are seen to be the least threatening and easiest to maintain, they are the most likely candidates for future Chinese alliances.

Given the previous spending by China over the past decade in the Global South and even within Europe through its "One Belt, One Road" initiative, it has bought numerous favors and friends around the globe and is part of a larger global strategy (Aoyama 2016). While China often maintains that it does not seek open confrontation with the global order, its "soft" expansion into Latin America, Africa, Eastern Europe, and other regions highlights its ability to accomplish through the funding of large-scale development projects what once would have been possible only through formal alliances. While such agreements do not constitute formal alliances, they do make cooperation between recipient states and China more likely.

While officially China only seeks repayment for loans and other development projects, the ability of many states to repay these loans is questionable (Greer 2018; Mishra 2023; Zhou 2024). And given China's enormous absorption of debt (Greer 2018) due to the One Belt, One Road initiative, it is possible that China will seek repayment in other ways. One well-documented case is the forfeiture of the Hambantota Port in Sri Lanka to China Merchants Port, a Chinese company with close ties to the Chinese Communist Party. Another example is the China-Laos Railway, which, at a cost of $6 billion, gives China enormous reach into the former French colony (VOA News 2024). However, doubts remain if the rail line will ever turn a profit (Thongnoi 2024), meaning that Laos will have a difficult time repaying China for the loans. In fact, during the Friendship Shield exercises in 2024, the railway was used to bring People's Liberation Army forces and equipment into Laos (Bartlett 2024).

The control of ports, railways, and other facilities makes it easier for China to exercise informal diplomatic and economic control with countries around the world. Similarly, it also gives China leverage via issue linkage over political issues that are important to Beijing. As such, it is likely to result in an increase in informal secret agreements between China and the governments of countries that are unable to pay back loans. While it remains to be seen if this will likewise result in more formal secret alliances, China has increasingly been able to accomplish through the purse what is impossible at the tip of a sword. To put this into perspective, according to Deng Xiaoping, "it doesn't matter if the cat is black or white, so long as it catches mice."

One benefit of secret alliance-making and public rapprochement between China and Russia is that it provides the United States with opportunities to exploit. While publicly China and Russia often lament the global order, they are frequently at odds regarding how to reverse US hegemony. In the case of Russia, it has been much more public about its opposition to US dominance, going so far as to justify its invasion of Ukraine as a "preventative war" against NATO and US "expansion." China, to its credit, has frequently lambasted US dominance but maintains that it still wants to peacefully coexist within the global order, though it disagrees with many parts of that order. China's ambitions, too, lie closer to home in the South China Sea rather than in the total revision of the international system. After all, China has perhaps benefited from the system more than any other single state. Nonetheless, China's desire to revise the international system is likely to be more incremental than Russia's more direct flaunting of international conventions and law.

These divisions between two "near peers" (White House 2022) makes it possible for the United States to further widen the gap between the two with side payments to either one or the other. However, given Russia's invasion of Ukraine and China's greater potential as a serious foe, a side deal with either is unlikely. Instead, the United States should use its vast alliance and partnership network to further make secret arrangements with tertiary states that are important to China or Russia. This may be an especially useful strategy with respect to China. Since China is the world's largest exporter (Dyvik 2024), many states are reticent to openly challenge the country for fear of retaliation. A notable example is Australia, which after publicly calling for investigations into the origins of Covid, faced a lengthy and harmful trade war with China (Walsh 2021). It is unlikely that neighbors of China that are opposed to its policies would be willing to risk angering what is likely their largest trade partner. Secrecy may provide those states with the necessary cover to confront China. But the United States' historical opposition to secret diplomacy (it is one of the only major power states to not have formal secret alliances) means that it is unlikely to embrace secret diplomacy.

While established in Chapters 1 and 2, secret defensive alliances do not make much sense if the intent is to deter aggression. However, if states are not concerned about deterring aggression, secret agreements to formally or informally cooperate provide excellent workarounds for potential retaliation by China. However, as stated above, even secret agreements will come with the tell-tale sign of rapprochement between signatories. As an example, the division of territory between the Nazis and Soviets or the transfer of Bantus to Swaziland would be difficult to explain away without first acknowledging that a secret agreement had occurred. At best, then, secret agreements between the United States and other states would only likely provide a marginal advantage in challenging a rising China. They may also prove useful to democratic states that are unwilling to be seen publicly cooperating with non-democratic states. And given there are so few full democracies in Southeast Asia, such illicit cooperation may provide an opportunity to contain China's rise.

However, given America's global role, it is unlikely that the United States would pursue a strategy of making formal secret alliances. There are several reasons for this. First, given the United States' role in stationing troops at around 800 bases in 70 different countries (O'Dell 2023; Vine 2015), the United States is less likely to need secret alliances. Because of US deployments around the world and the historical ties between many of those states and the United States, along with the existing infrastructure, it is unlikely that the United States has a need for secret allies as states did in the past. Second, given its international position and the historical calls by American presidents to oppose secret diplomacy, the United States is likely reticent to give up its moral standing in opposition to secret diplomacy. In fact, given its frequent pronouncements championing the "rules-based international order," it is unlikely that the United States would be the first state to break the norm against secret alliances. Similarly, while some research has demonstrated that democracies are less reliable allies (Gartzke and Gleditsch 2004), others claim democracies are more reliable allies (Mattes 2012). What remains to be seen, however, is whether democracies would be as reliable formal secret allies or informal secret allies as they are with public agreements. The greatest likelihood for secret alliances with democracies, then, would be with non-democracies. This is because the cost of public disclosure in a democratic country would be high, whereas, in the case of non-democracies, the greatest cost would come via retaliation short of open conflict with large autocratic regimes, such as China.

Third, given its extensive ties with so-called "partners" and not allies, the United States is also less likely to need a formal secret alliance with those states that it has strong ties with. The term "partner" (Department of Defense 2019), while defined in a regulatory and legal framework within the United States, is much less likely to draw the ire of potential foes. However, the cost is that there is no formal commitment to actual goods, such as military hardware sales, greater cooperation with the United States, or defense in the case of war. This means that there are fewer opportunities for secret allies, given that the United States is more likely to have more informal agreements with more states around the world than Russia or China.

Informal secret agreements between the United States and other states are likely to see an increase over the coming decades. However, the reasons and degrees for these increases are likely to vary by regime type and the availability or need for an informal or formal secret alliance partner. The advantages of formal secret alliances are self-evident: they are strong, often, though not always, public pronouncements about one state's commitment to another. On the other hand, the attractiveness of informal agreements is that they exist at the ministerial level, giving political cover to the leadership of both the United States and potential allies. Even though informal alliances are often attractive, they have several drawbacks that make them less appealing.

For instance, in the case of future informal agreements made by the United States, America could become over-exposed as it spreads itself thinner and thinner in attempting to contain China's influence. Additionally, these secret informal agreements are less likely to be accompanied by increased training, interoperability, and weapons sales than formal public agreements or even formal secret agreements would have. This means that in the event of conflict, the United States would be less able to operate with an informal secret partner/ally.

While the future may look different from the past, we must use theory and the knowledge of how secret alliances have operated in the past to better understand the future risks to global security emerging from a return of secret alliances. I have maintained throughout this book that it is not the secret nature of these agreements that makes conflict more likely (which runs contrary to the claims made by Bas and Shub (2016)). Instead, it is the *nature* of what is promised in these texts that increases the likelihood of conflict. What remains to be seen is if the promises in the formal or informal secret alliances of tomorrow will promise the same things that were previously promised. If so, this does not bode well for international peace.

The promise of the division of goods in the context of a secret alliance means that China can use considerable leverage, coupled with its vast economic and infrastructure investments within Asia, to drive many of its claims. China may pursue an aggressive strategy of making multiple secret agreements with other states in an attempt to divide and conquer states that oppose its claims, for instance, territorial claims in the South China Sea. However, this is outside the norm for China's traditional approach to diplomacy. Additionally, if Kuo (2020) is correct that secrecy begets secrecy, we should expect to see other secret agreements between other states within the region. However, this does not seem to be the case. One explanation for this is that the nature of what may be promised in any existing informal secret agreements differs from what is promised in formal secret alliances. Because they are informal, there are no concrete promises between governments. Another explanation could also be that the nature of what is promised in any secret agreements within the region is not a "salient stake." This means that subsequent competing secret agreements are not formed because the stakes are not high enough.

Regardless of what strategy China, the United States, or other states within the region choose, history and the theoretical reasons why states make, keep, and end secret alliances are important in understanding the power competition between the two states most likely to shape global order in the 21st century.

NOTE

1. What is odd about this public release is that North Korea chose to publicly release the document first. While there was a joint declaration of the agreement, this was not immediately accompanied by the release of the formal document. Instead, this came on the next day, with a release by the KCNA. This indicates that the formal guarantee was more sought after by North Korea. The deterrent value of publicly releasing the document would significantly benefit North Korea more than Russia, as secret agreements regarding arms transfers had obviously occurred before the defensive alliance was signed. Ironically, the decision to reach the text of the agreement with North Korea was likely the decision that Russia wanted to take after its discussions with China in February 2022. However, such public release of whatever was agreed to would likely have been to China's detriment and was most likely blocked by them. Instead, little is known about this "partnership without limits."

Appendices

CHAPTER 1 APPENDIX

Table A1.1   Secret alliance list

ATOP ID	States	Begin year	End year
1025	Austria, Two Sicilies	1815	1820
1005	UK, France, Austria, Bavaria, Hanover, Netherlands	1815	1815
1010	Austria, Hesse-Darmstadt	1815	1815
1050	Austria, Sardinia	1831	1848
1080	Austria-Hungary, Russia	1833	1853
1075	Russia, Turkey	1833	1841
1065	Austria, Prussia, Russia	1833	1839
1095	Austria, Prussia, Russia	1833	1848
1150	Brazil, Uruguay	1851	1851
1185	France, Austria	1854	1856
1210	France, Italy	1859	1859
1215	Russia, France	1859	1859
1230	Russia, Prussia	1863	1863
1255	Argenitna, Brazil, Uruguay	1865	1882
1280	Germany, Bavaria	1866	1870
1275	Germany, Baden	1866	1870
1265	Italy, Prussia	1866	1866
1270	Austria, France	1866	1866
1285	Germany, Wurrtemburg	1866	1870
1305	Bolivia, Peru	1873	1883
1310	Russia, Germany	1873	1878
1325	Russia, Austria-Hungary	1877	1878
1335	Austria-Hungary, Germany	1879	1918

ATOP ID	States	Begin year	End year
1340	Germany, Austria-Hungary, Russia	1881	1887
1345	Austria-Hungary, Serbia	1881	1895
1350	Austria-Hungary, Germany, Italy	1882	1918
1355	Austria-Hungary, Romania, Germany, Italy	1883	1918
1375	Austria-Hungary, UK, Italy	1887	1897
1365	Spain, Italy, Austria-Hungary, Germany	1887	1895
1370	Germany, Russia	1887	1890
1385	France, Russia	1893	1917
1395	China, Russia	1896	1900
1400	UK, Portugal	1899	1949
1410	Italy, Austria-Hungary	1901	1915
1420	France, Italy	1902	1918
1435	Austria-Hungary, Russia	1904	1908
1430	France, Spain	1904	1907
1425	Bulgaria, Yugoslavia	1904	1909
1440	Germany, Russia	1905	1905
1460	Russia, Italy	1909	1917
1465	Japan, Russia	1910	1916
1480	Serbia, Montenegro	1912	1915
1475	Greece, Bulgaria	1912	1913
1470	Serbia, Bulgaria	1912	1913
1490	Greece, Serbia	1913	1918
2005	Germany, Ottoman Empiure	1914	1918
2012	Austria-Hungary, Bulgaria	1914	1918
2013	Germany, Bulgaria	1914	1918
2010	Bulgaria, Ottoman Empire	1914	1918
2020	Russia, Romania	1914	1916
2025	France, Russia, UK, Italy	1915	1918
2040	France, Russia, UK, Italy, Romania	1916	1918
2035	Russia, Japan	1916	1917
2045	Japan, China	1918	1918
2060	France, Poland	1921	1939
2340	Saudi Arabia, Yemen Arab Republic	1934	Active
2350	France, Italy	1935	1935
2395	Germany, Japan, Italy, Hungary, Spain	1936	1939

ATOP ID	States	Begin year	End year
2440	Poland, UK	1939	1939
2470	USSR, Germany	1939	1941
2515	Germany, Italy, Japan, Hungary, Romania, Bulgaria	1940	1941
3322	UK, France, Italy	1956	1956
3390	France, Malagasay Republic	1960	1973
3935	South Africa, Swaziland	1982	1994
4965	Bahrain, Kuwait, Oman, Qatar, Saudi Arabia, UAE	2000	Active

CHAPTER 3 APPENDIX

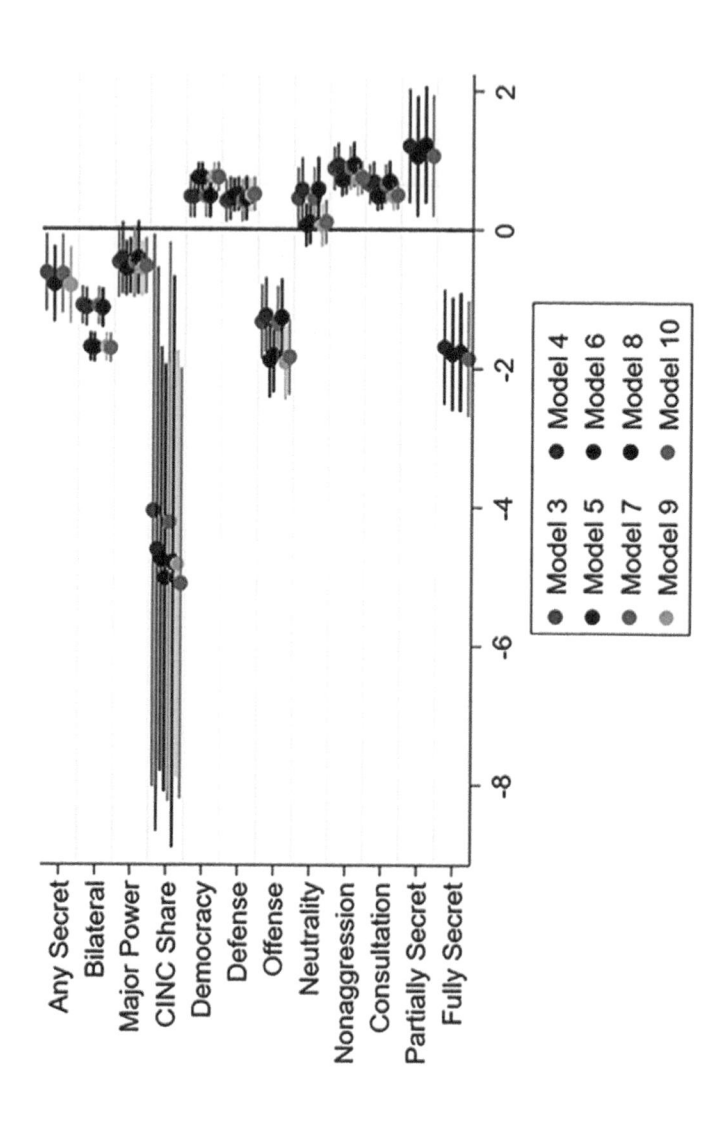

Source: Author.

Figure A3.1   Point estimates, H2 95% CIs

Appendices 245

Source: Author.

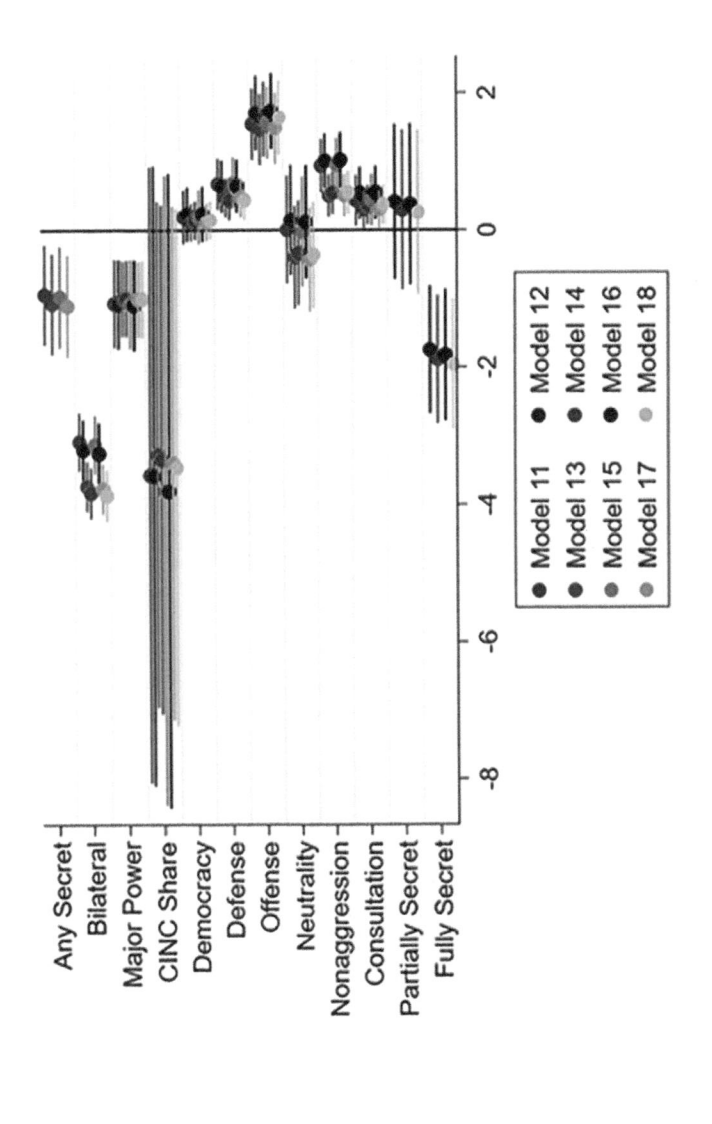

Figure A3.2 Point estimates, H3 95% CIs

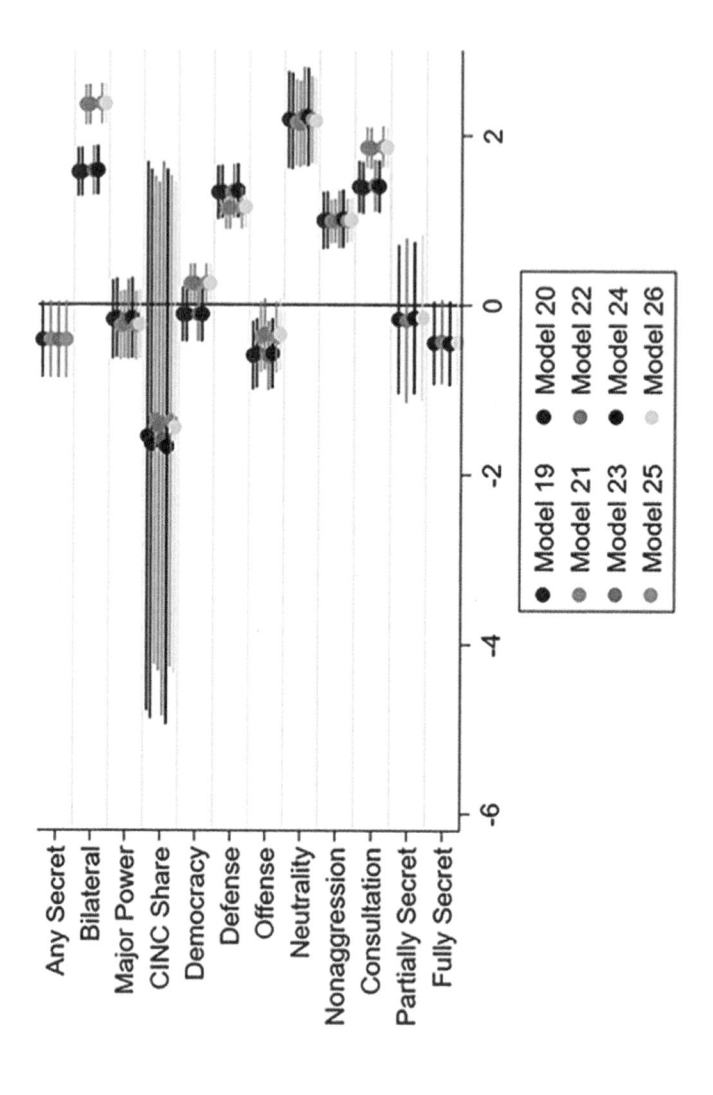

Figure A3.3   Point estimates, H4 95% CIs

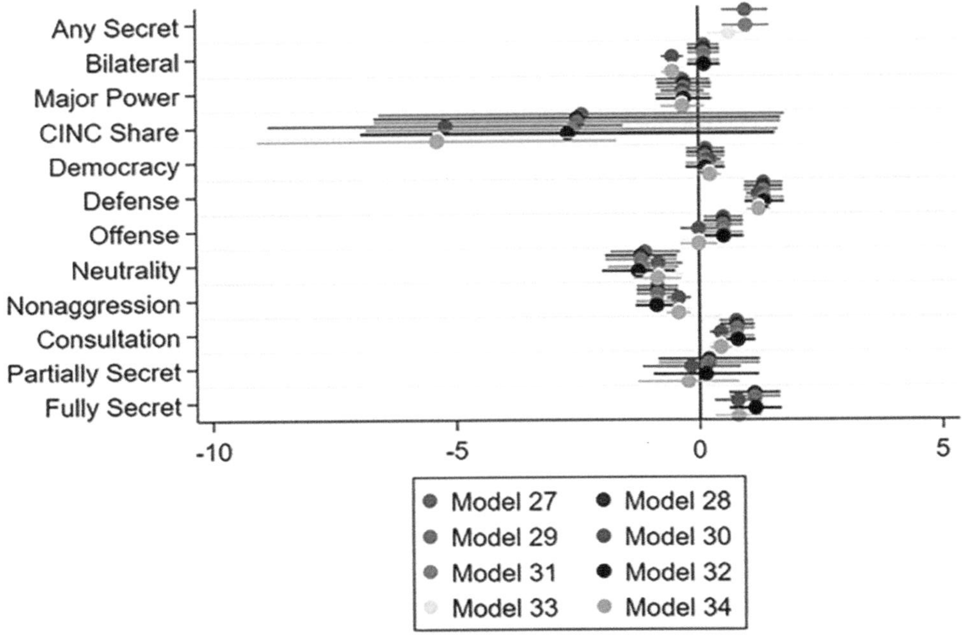

Source: Author.

Figure A3.4 Point estimates, H5 95% CIs

248 *Secret alliances*

Source: Author.

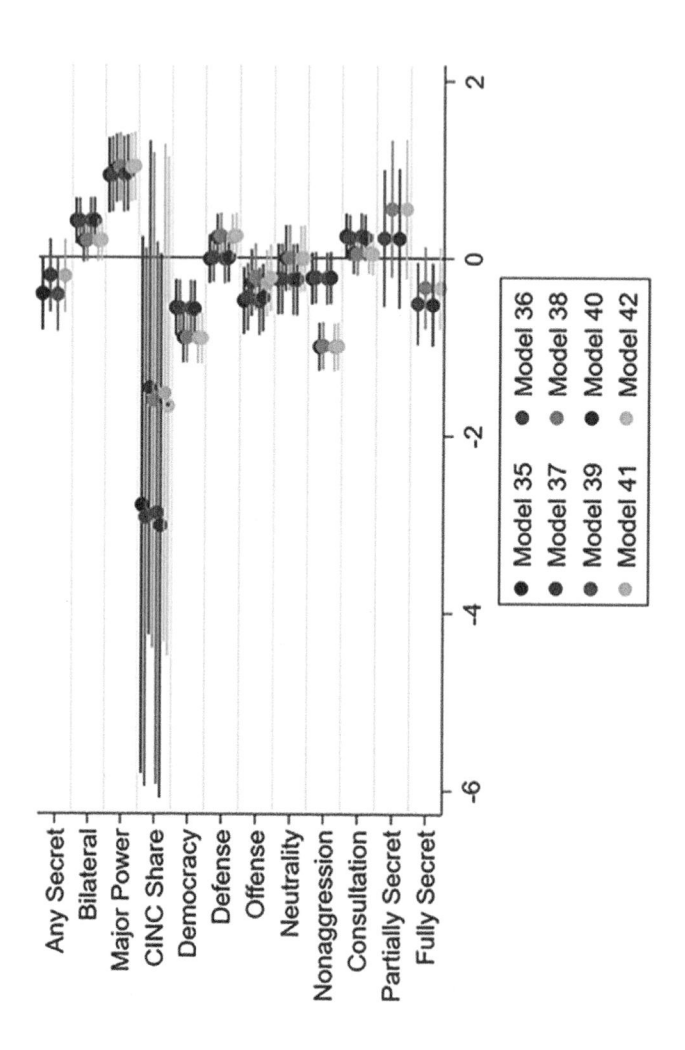

Figure A3.5 Point estimates, H6 95% CIs

CHAPTER 4 APPENDIX

Table A4.1   Descriptive statistics

Variable	Observations	Mean	Standard deviation	Min	Max
Public Alliance/Secret Alliance	6328	.028	.165	0	1
Public Alliance/Partially Secret Alliance/Fully Secret Alliance	6328	.052	.309	0	2
Scott's π	6328	.005	.316	−.594	1
Cohen's κ	6328	.039	.305	−.506	1
Unweighted Similarity	6328	.681	.219	−.469	1
Weighted Similarity	6328	.605	.285	−.882	1
Joint Democracy	6328	.133	.34	0	1
Major Power	6328	.095	.293	0	1
Capital Distance	6328	7623.452	4432.018	0	19918
Contiguity	6328	.025	.155	0	1
CINC	6328	.009	.028	0	.384
Defensive	6328	.445	.497	0	1
Offensive	6328	.089	.285	0	1
Neutrality	6328	.044	.205	0	1
Nonaggression	6328	.712	.453	0	1
True Consultation	6328	.044	.206	0	1
MID	6328	.669	.471	0	1
MID Count	6328	4.423	8.206	0	116
MID A/B	6328	.018	.134	0	1
MID A/B Same Side	6328	.032	.175	0	1
War	6328	.31	.463	0	1

CHAPTER 5 APPENDIX

Table A5.1   *Effects of secret/termination on future alliances (clustered standard errors)*

Variables	5 Effect by secret alliance (0/1)	6 Effect by secret alliance type (0/1/2)	7 Interaction effect by secret alliance (0/1)	8 Interaction effect by secret alliance type (0/1/2)
Any Secret	1.011 (.111)	-	-	-
Public#Irregular Termination	-	-	.830*** (.064)	-
Secret#Regular Termination	-	-	1.039 (.139)	-
Secret#Irregular Termination	-	-	.804 (.123)	-
Partially Secret	-	1.570** (.346)	-	-
Fully Secret	-	.883 (.107)	-	-
Public#Irregular Termination	-	-	-	.826** (.064)
Partially Secret#Regular Termination	-	-	-	2.383*** (.365)
Partially Secret#Irregular Termination	-	-	-	.909 (.306)
Fully Secret#Regular Termination	-	-	-	.882 (.128)
Fully Secret#Irregular Termination	-	-	-	.727* (.119)
Irregular Termination	.821*** (.058)	.806** (.057)	-	-
Bilateral	1.371*** (.100)	1.404*** (.103)	1.372*** (.101)	1.395*** (.103)

Variables	5 Effect by secret alliance (0/1)	6 Effect by secret alliance type (0/1/2)	7 Interaction effect by secret alliance (0/1)	8 Interaction effect by secret alliance type (0/1/2)
Major Power	2.036*** (.235)	2.007*** (.230)	2.042*** (.235)	2.020*** (.232)
CINC	1.101 (.868)	1.047 (.820)	1.100 (.867)	1.054 (.828)
Democracy	.881 (.083)	.890 (.084)	.879 (.083)	.887 (.084)
Symmetry	.819*** (.059)	.812*** (.058)	.819*** (.059)	.808*** (.058)
Defense	1.163** (.082)	1.177** (.083)	1.159** (.083)	1.157** (.083)
Offense	1.040 (.103)	1.054 (.104)	1.039 (.103)	1.059 (.103)
Neutrality	.939 (.102)	.931 (.102)	.936 (.103)	.958 (.107)
Nonaggression	1.226** (.106)	.1.24** (.108)	1.225** (.106)	1.238** (.108)
Consultation	1.398*** (.107)	1.405*** (.107)	1.394*** (.107)	1.416*** (.109)
World War I	.533*** (.327)	.580*** (.057)	.530*** (.049)	.572*** (.056)
Observations	919	919	919	919

Note: Clustered standard errors are in parentheses, *** $p < .01$, ** $p < .05$, * $p < .1$.

Table A5.2 Effects of secret/termination on future alliances (Weibull models)

Variables	9 Effect by secret alliance (0/1)	10 Effect by secret alliance type (0/1/2)	11 Interaction effect by secret alliance (0/1)	12 Interaction effect by secret alliance type (0/1/2)
Any Secret	1.011 (.111)	-	-	-
Public#Irregular Termination	-	-	.830** (.064)	-
Secret#RegularTermination	-	-	1.039 (.139)	-
Secret#Irregular Termination	-	-	.804 (.123)	-
Partially Secret	-	1.570** (.346)	-	-
Fully Secret	-	.883 (.107)	-	-
Public#Irregular Termination	-	-	-	.826** (.063)
Partially Secret#Regular Termination	-	-	-	2.383*** (.365)
Partially Secret#Irregular Termination	-	-	-	.909 (.306)
Fully Secret#Regular Termination	-	-	-	.882 (.128)

Variables	9 Effect by secret alliance (0/1)	10 Effect by secret alliance type (0/1/2)	11 Interaction effect by secret alliance (0/1)	12 Interaction effect by secret alliance type (0/1/2)
Fully Secret#Irregular Termination	-	-	-	.727* (.119)
Irregular Termination	.821*** (.058)	.806*** (.057)	-	-
Bilateral	1.371*** (.100)	1.404*** (.103)	1.372*** (.101)	1.395*** (.103)
Major Power	2.036*** (.235)	2.007*** (.230)	2.042*** (.235)	2.020*** (.232)
CINC	1.101 (.868)	1.047 (.820)	1.100 (.867)	1.054 (.828)
Democracy	.881 (.083)	.890 (.084)	.879 (.082)	.887 (.084)
Symmetry	.819*** (.059)	.812*** (.058)	.819*** (.059)	.808*** (.058)
Defense	1.163** (.082)	1.177** (.104)	1.159** (.083)	1.157** (.083)
Offense	1.040 (.103)	1.054 (.104)	1.039 (.103)	1.059** (.103)
Neutrality	.939 (.102)	.931 (.102)	.936 (.103)	.958 (.107)
Nonaggression	1.226** (.106)	1.242** (.108)	1.225** (.106)	1.238** (.108)

Variables	9 Effect by secret alliance (0/1)	10 Effect by secret alliance type (0/1/2)	11 Interaction effect by secret alliance (0/1)	12 Interaction effect by secret alliance type (0/1/2)
Consultation	1.398***	1.405***	1.394***	1.416***
	(.107)	(.107)	(.107)	(.109)
World War I	.533***	.580***	.530***	.572***
	(.050)	(.057)	(.049)	(.056)
Constant	.327***	.317***	.327***	.316***
	(.039)	(.038)	(.039)	(.038)
Observations	919	919	919	919

Note: Robust standard errors are in parentheses.

References

Acemoglu, Daron, and James A. Robinson. "A theory of political transitions." *American Economic Review* 91, no. 4 (2001): 938–63.

Aldrich, Winthrop W. "The Suez Crisis—a footnote to history." *Foreign Affairs* 45 (1967): 541.

Algeria. "Algeria—colonialism, resistance, revolution," *Britannica* (2023). https://www.britannica.com/place/Algeria/Colonial-rule.

Alley, Joshua. "Elite cues and public attitudes towards military alliances." *Journal of Conflict Resolution* 67, no. 7 (2023): 1537–63. https://doi.org/10.1177/00220027221143963.

Altfeld, Michael F. "The decision to ally: A theory and test." *Western Political Quarterly* 37 (1984): 523–44. https://doi.org/10.1177/106591298403700402.

Altfeld, Michael F., and Bruce Bueno de Mesquita. "Choosing sides in wars." *International Studies Quarterly* 23, no. 1 (1979): 87–112. https://doi.org/10.2307/2600275.

Altfeld, Michael F., and Won K. Paik. "Realignment in ITOs: A closer look." *International Studies Quarterly* 30, no. 1 (1986): 107–14. https://doi.org/10.2307/2600439.

Andrews, David M. *The Atlantic Alliance under Stress: US-European Relations after Iraq* (2005). New York, NY: Cambridge University Press.

Anglin, Douglas. "The frontline states and sanctions against South Africa." In Robert Edgar (ed.), *Sanctioning Apartheid*, pp. 255–92 (1990).

Anholt, Simon. "Beyond the nation brand: The role of image and identity in international relations." In *Brands and Branding Geographies*, (2011): 289–304. Cheltenham, UK and Northampton, MA, USA: Edward Elgar Publishing.

Aoyama, Rumi. "'One belt, one road': China's new global strategy." *Journal of Contemporary East Asia Studies* 5, no. 2 (2016): 3–22.

"Archives Yield Soviet-German Pact." *The New York Times*, sec. World (October 30, 1992). https://www.nytimes.com/1992/10/30/world/archives-yield-soviet-german-pact.html.

ATOP Codebook, "ATOP Dataset," *ATOP Data* (2018). http://www.atopdata.org/uploads/6/9/1/3/69134503/atopcodebookv4.pdf.

ATOP Codebook. "Alliance Treaty Obligations and Provisions (ATOP) Codebook" (2022). http://www.atopdata.org/uploads/6/9/1/3/69134503/atop_5_1_codebook.pdf.

Azar, Edward E. "Conflict escalation and conflict reduction in an international crisis: Suez, 1956." *Journal of Conflict Resolution* 16, no. 2 (1972): 183–201. https://doi.org/10.1177/002200277201600204.

Ball, M. Margaret. "Bloc voting in the General Assembly." *International Organization* 5, no. 1 (1951): 3–31. https://doi.org/10.1017/S0020818300029805.

Bapat, Navin. "The internationalization of terrorist campaigns." *Conflict Management and Peace Science* 24 (December 2007): 265–80. https://doi.org/10.1080/07388940701643607.

Barber, James, and John Barratt. *South Africa's Foreign Policy: The Search for Status and Security, 1945–1988*. Cambridge Studies in International Relations. Cambridge; New York: Cambridge University Press. CUP Archive (1990).

Barnett, Michael N., and Jack S. Levy. "Domestic sources of alliances and alignments: The case of Egypt, 1962–73." *International Organization* 45, no. 3 (1991): 369–95.

Bar-On, Mordechai. "Three days in Sèvres, October 1956." *History Workshop Journal* 62, no. 1 (2006): 172–86.

Bar-On, Moshe. "Where did the last copy go? The incarnations of a top-secret document." In *Studies in the Uprising of Israel*, pp. 86–102 (1997).

Bartlett, Duncan, "Laos and China use BRI-funded railway to bring their armies together." *The Diplomat* (July 19, 2024). https://thediplomat.com/2024/07/laos-and-china-use-bri-funded-railway-to-bring-their-armies-together/.

Bas, Muhammet, and Robert Schub. "Mutual optimism as a cause of conflict: Secret alliances and conflict onset." *International Studies Quarterly* 60, no. 3 (2016): 552–64.

Baum, Matthew A. "Going private: Public opinion, presidential rhetoric, and the domestic politics of audience costs in US foreign policy crises." *Journal of Conflict Resolution* 48, no. 5 (2004): 603–31. https://doi.org/10.1177/0022002704267764.

BBC, "1956: Egypt seizes Suez Canal." *BBC* (July 26, 1956). http://news.bbc.co.uk/onthisday/hi/dates/stories/july/26/newsid_2701000/2701603.stm.

Beck, Gord. "The Sykes-Picot Agreement." *Lloyd Reeds Map Collection* (2016).

Beck, Peter J. "'The less said about Suez the better': British governments and the politics of Suez's history, 1956–67." *The English Historical Review* 124, no. 508 (2009): 605–40.

Becker, Raphael N., Arye L. Hillman, Niklas Potrafke, and Alexander H. Schwemmer. "The preoccupation of the United Nations with Israel: Evidence and theory." *The Review of International Organizations* 10, no. 4 (2015): 413–37. https://doi.org/10.1007/s11558-014-9207-3.

Bennett, D. Scott. "A universal test of an expected utility theory of war." *International Studies Quarterly* 44, no. 3 (2000): 451–80. https://doi.org/10.1111/0020-8833.00167.

Bennett, D. Scott, and Matthew C. Rupert. "Comparing measures of political similarity: An empirical comparison of S versus tau b in the study of international conflict." *Journal of Conflict Resolution* 47, no. 3 (2003): 367–93. http://doi.org/10.1177/0022002703252370.

Bennett, D. Scott, and Allan C. Stam. "The duration of interstate wars, 1816–1985." *The American Political Science Review* 90, no. 2.(1996): 239–57. https://doi.org/10.2307/2082882.

Bennett, D. S., & Stam, A. C. A universal test of an expected utility theory of war. International Studies Quarterly, 44(3) (2000): 451–480.

Bennett, D.S., and Rupert, M.C. (2003). Comparing measures of political similarity: An empirical comparison of S versus τb in the study of international conflict. Journal of Conflict Resolution, 47(3), 367–393.

Benson, Brett V. "Unpacking alliances: Deterrent and compellent alliances and their relationship with conflict, 1816–2000." *The Journal of Politics* 73, no. 4 (2011): 1111–27. https://doi.org/10.1017/S0022381611000867.

Benson, Michelle A. "The relevance of politically relevant dyads in the study of interdependence and dyadic disputes." *Conflict Management and Peace Science* 22, no. 2 (2005): 113–33. https://doi.org/10.1080/07388940590948556.

Berkowitz, Bruce D. "Realignment in international treaty organizations." *International Studies Quarterly* 27, no. 1 (1983): 77–96. https://doi.org/10.2307/2600620.

Bernauer, Thomas, Anna Kalbhenn, Vally Koubi, and Gabriele Spilker. "A comparison of international and domestic sources of global governance dynamics." *British Journal of Political Science* 40, no. 3 (2010): 509–38. https://doi.org/10.1017/S0007123410000098.

Bischoff, Paul-Henri. "Swaziland: a small state in international relations." *Africa Spectrum* (1986): 175–88.

Bohlen, Charles E. *Witness to History: 1929–1969.* Plunkett Lake Press (2021).

Booth, Alan. "The frontline states and sanctions against South Africa." In *Sanctioning Apartheid*, pp. 323–38. Trenton, NJ: Africa World Press (1990).

Bowie, Robert R. *International Crises and the Role of Law: Suez 1956.* Oxford University Press (1974).

Bremer, Stuart A. "Dangerous dyads: Conditions affecting the likelihood of interstate war, 1816–1965." *Journal of Conflict Resolution* 36, no. 2 (1992): 309–41.

Brewster, Rachel. "Unpacking the state's reputation." *Harvard International Law Journal* 50 (2009): 231.

Britain, Great, Sir Ernest Llewellyn Woodward, Rohan Butler, and Margaret Esterel Lambert. *Documents on British Foreign Policy 1919–1939: Third Series. 1938–9.* London: HM Stationery Office (1950).

Bueno de Mesquita, Bruce Bueno. "Big wars, little wars: Avoiding selection bias." *International Interactions* 16, no. 3 (1990): 159–69. https://doi.org/10.1080/03050629008434753.

Bueno de Mesquita, Bruce, and David Lalman. *War and Reason: Domestic and International Imperatives.* New Haven, CT: Yale University Press (1992).

Bueno de Mesquita, Bruce Bueno, and Randolph M. Siverson. "War and the survival of political leaders: A comparative study of regime types and political accountability." *American Political Science Review* 89, no. 4 (1995): 841–55. https://doi.org/10.2307/2082512.

Bueno de Mesquita, Bruce Bueno, James D. Morrow, Randolph M. Siverson, and Alastair Smith. "Political institutions, policy choice and the survival of leaders." *British Journal of Political Science* 32, no. 4 (2002): 559–90.

Bueno de Mesquita, Bruce Bueno, James D. Morrow, Randolph M. Siverson, and Alastair Smith. "Testing novel implications from the selectorate theory of war." *World Politics* 56, no. 3 (2004a): 363–88. https://doi.org/10.1353/wp.2004.0017.

Bull, H. *The anarchical society: A study of order in world politics.* Bloomsbury Publishing (2012).

Buszynski, Leszek. "SEATO: Why it survived until 1977 and why it was abolished." *Journal of Southeast Asian Studies* 12, no. 2 (1981): 287–96.

Butler, Larry. *Britain and Empire: Adjusting to a Post-imperial World.* IB Tauris (2002).

Carson, Austin, and Keren Yarhi-Milo. "Covert communication: The intelligibility and credibility of signaling in secret." *Security Studies* 26, no. 1 (2017): 124–56.

Carson, Austin. "Facing off and saving face: Covert intervention and escalation management in the Korean War." *International Organization* 70, no. 1 (2016): 103–31.

Carter, David B., and Randall W. Stone. "Democracy and multilateralism: The case of vote buying in the UN General Assembly." *International Organization* 69, no. 1 (2015): 1–33.

Cassman, Daniel R. "Keep it secret, keep it safe: An empirical analysis of the state secrets doctrine." *Stanford Law Review* 67 (2015): 1173.

Cha, Victor, and Ellen Kim, "The New Russia-North Korea Security Alliance," *Center for Strategic and International Studies* (June 2024). https://www.csis.org/analysis/new-russia-north-korea-security-alliance.

Chan, Stephen. "Exporting apartheid: Foreign policies in Southern Africa, 1978–1988." London: Bloomsbury (1990).

Chan, Steve. "Money talks: International credit/debt as credible commitment." *The Journal of East Asian Affairs* (2012): 77–103.

Chen, Frederick R. "Extended dependence: Trade, alliances, and peace." *The Journal of Politics* 83, no. 1 (2021): 246–59. https://doi.org/10.1086/709149.

Chen, Ping-Kuei. "The prospects of the US alliance system in Asia: Managing from the hub." *Issues & Studies* 56, no. 3 (2020): 2040012. https://doi.org/10.1142/S1013251120400123.

Chiba, Daina, and Jesse C Johnson. "Release notes for ATOP Similarity Scores Dataset" (2022). http://www.atopdata.org/uploads/6/9/1/3/69134503/atop_s_release_notes.pdf.

Chiba, Daina, Jesse C. Johnson, and Brett Ashley Leeds. "Careful commitments: Democratic states and alliance design." *The Journal of Politics* 77, no. 4 (2015): 968–82. https://doi.org/10.1086/682074.

Christensen, Thomas J., and Jack Snyder. "Progressive research on degenerate alliances." *American Political Science Review* 91, no. 4 (1997): 919–22. https://doi.org/10.2307/2952174.

Christiansson, Magnus. "Pooling, sharing and specializing—NATO and international defence cooperation." In *NATO beyond 9/11: The Transformation of the Atlantic Alliance*, pp. 178–97. London: Palgrave Macmillan (2013). https://doi.org/10.1057/9780230391222_9.

Chu, Jonathan A., Jiyoung Ko, and Adam Liu. "Commanding support: Values and interests in the rhetoric of alliance politics." *International Interactions* 47, no. 3 (2021): 477–503. https://doi.org/10.1080/03050629.2021.1898955.

Churchill, Winston. *The Second World War: The Grand Alliance*. Vol. 3. Boston: Cooperation Publishing Company [by] Houghton Mifflin. (1950).

Cienciala, Anna M. "The Nazi-Soviet Pact of August 23, 1939: When did Stalin decide to align with Hitler, and was Poland the culprit?" Rochester, NY: University of Rochester Press (2003).

Citino, Robert. "Operation Barbarossa: The biggest of all time." *National WW2 Museum* (2021). https://www.nationalww2museum.org/war/articles/operation-barbarossa.

Clarke, Kevin A. "The phantom menace: Omitted variable bias in econometric research." *Conflict Management and Peace Science* 22, no. 4 (2005): 341–52.

Cohen, Jacob. "A coefficient of agreement for nominal scales." *Educational and Psychological Measurement* 20 (April 1960): 37.

Cohen, Raymond. "Pacific unions: A reappraisal of the theory that 'democracies do not go to war with each other.'" *Review of International Studies* 20, no. 3 (1994): 207–23. https://doi.org/10.1017/S0260210500118030.

Colaresi, Michael P. *Democracy Declassified: The Secrecy Dilemma in National Security*. New York: Oxford University Press (2014).

Colaresi, Michael P., and William R. Thompson. "Alliances, arms buildups and recurrent conflict: Testing a steps-to-war model." *The Journal of Politics* 67, no. 2 (2005): 345–64. https://doi.org/10.1111/j.1468-2508.2005.00320.x.

Committee on Oversight and Governmental Affairs. "Information Sharing in the Era of Wikileaks: Balancing Security and Collaboration." US Senate (2011). https://www.govinfo.gov/content/pkg/CHRG-112shrg66677/html/CHRG-112shrg66677.htm.

Conybeare, John A.C. "Public goods, prisoners' dilemmas and the international political economy." *International Studies Quarterly* 28, no. 1 (1984): 5–22. https://doi.org/10.2307/2600395.

Correlates of War Project 2016. "State System Membership List, v2016" (2017). http://correlatesofwar.org.

Crescenzi, Mark J.C., Jacob D. Kathman, Katja B. Kleinberg, and Reed M. Wood. "Reliability, reputation, and alliance formation." *International Studies Quarterly* 56, no. 2 (2012): 259–74.

Dafoe, Allan, Jonathan Renshon, and Paul Huth. "Reputation and status as motives for war." *Annual Review of Political Science* 17, no. 1 (2014): 371–93. https://doi.org/10.1146/annurev-polisci-071112-213421.

Danilovic, Vesna. "Conceptual and selection bias issues in deterrence." *Journal of Conflict Resolution* 45, no. 1 (2001): 97–125. https://doi.org/10.1177/0022002701045001005.

Das, Tushar K., and Bing-Sheng Teng. "Alliance constellations: A social exchange perspective." *Academy of Management Review* 27, no. 3 (2002): 445–56.

Davenport, Kelsey. "U.S. says North Korea shipped arms to Russia." *Arms Control Association* (November 2023). https://www.armscontrol.org/act/2023-11/news/us-says-north-korea-shipped-arms-russia.

Davis, Robert, and Dan O'Meara. "Total Strategy in Southern Africa-An Analysis of South African Regional Policy Since 1978." In Exporting Apartheid: Foreign Policies in Southern Africa, 1978–1988, 179–217. New York, NY: Palgrave Macmillan (1990).

Davis, Christina L. "International institutions and issue linkage: Building support for agricultural trade liberalization." *American Political Science Review* 98, no. 1 (2004): 153–69.

DD 1987-1476 Paris to State Department, No. 469 (July 27, 1956).

Deeks, Ashley S. "Secret reason-giving." *Yale Law Journal* 129 (2019): 612.

Diehl, Paul F. "Arms races and escalation: A closer look." *Journal of Peace Research* 20, no. 3 (1983): 205–12. https://doi.org/10.1177/002234338302000301.

Dinstein, Yoram. *War, Aggression and Self-defence*. Cambridge, UK: Cambridge University Press (2017).

Downs, George W., and Michael A. Jones. "Reputation, compliance, and international law." *The Journal of Legal Studies* 31, no. S1 (2002): S95–S114. https://doi.org/10.1086/340405.

Dreher, Axel, and Jan-Egbert Sturm. "Do the IMF and the World Bank influence voting in the UN General Assembly?" *Public Choice* 151, no. 1–2 (2012): 363–97. https://doi.org/10.1007/s11127-010-9750-2.

Dreher, Axel, Jan-Egbert Sturm, and James Raymond Vreeland. "Global horse trading: IMF loans for votes in the United Nations Security Council." *European Economic Review* 53, no. 7 (2009): 742–57. https://doi.org/10.1016/j.euroecorev.2009.03.002.

Dreifelds, Juris. *Latvia in Transition*. Transferred to digital reprinting. Cambridge: Cambridge University Press (1999).

Dyvik, Einar. "Top exporting countries 2023," *Statista* (July 4, 2024). https://www.statista.com/statistics/264623/leading-export-countries-worldwide/.

Edwards, Robert. "The Winter War: Russia's invasion of Finland," 1939–1940. New York: Pegasus Books (2008).

Eldar, O. "Vote-trading in international institutions." *European Journal of International Law* 19, no. 1 (2008): 3–41. https://doi.org/10.1093/ejil/chn001.

Encyclopedia Britannica. "German-Soviet Nonaggression Pact," *Encyclopedia Britannica* (2018). https://www.britannica.com/event/German-Soviet-Nonaggression-Pact.

Erikson, Robert S., Pablo M. Pinto, and Kelly T. Rader. "Dyadic Analysis in international relations: A cautionary tale." *Political Analysis* 22, no. 4 (2014): 457–63. https://doi.org/10.1093/pan/mpt051.

Eudin, Xenia Joukoff, Harold Henry Fisher, and Rosemary Brown Jones. *Soviet Russia and the West: A Documentary Survey. 1920–1927.* Vol. I2. Stanford, CA: Stanford University Press (1957).

Fearon, James D. "Domestic political audiences and the escalation of international disputes." *American Political Science Review* 88, no. 3 (1994): 577–92. https://doi.org/10.2307/2944796.

Fearon, James D. "Rationalist explanations for war." *International Organization* 49, no. 3 (1995): 379–414.

Fearon, James D. "Signaling foreign policy interests: Tying hands versus sinking costs." *Journal of Conflict Resolution* 41, no. 1 (1997): 68–90. https://doi.org/10.1177/0022002797041001004.

Fearon, James D. "Selection effects and deterrence." *International Interactions* 28, no. 1 (2002): 5–29. https://doi.org/10.1080/03050620210390.

Fearon, James D. "Why do some civil wars last so much longer than others?" *Journal of Peace Research* 41, no. 3 (2004): 275–301. https://doi.org/10.1177/0022343304043770.

Fenster, Mark. "Disclosure's effects: WikiLeaks and transparency." *Iowa Law Review* 97 (2011): 753.

Fey, Mark, and Kristopher W. Ramsay. "Uncertainty and incentives in crisis bargaining: Game-free analysis of international conflict." *American Journal of Political Science* 55, no. 1 (2011): 149–69.

Finnemore, Martha, and Kathryn Sikkink. "International norm dynamics and political change." *International Organization* 52, no. 4 (1998): 887–917.

Gannon, J. Andrés. "Planes, trains, and armored mobiles: Introducing a Dataset of the Global Distribution of Military Capabilities." *International Studies Quarterly* 67, no. 4 (2023): sqad081. https://doi.org/10.1093/isq/sqad081.

Gannon, J. Andrés, and Daniel Kent. "Keeping your friends close, but acquaintances closer: Why weakly allied states make committed coalition partners." *Journal of Conflict Resolution* 65, no. 5 (2021): 889–918. https://doi.org/10.1177/0022002720978800.

Gartzke, E. and Millard, M.C. (forthcoming) "Throwing in the Towel: Audience Costs, Democracy, and Acknowledgement of Defeat."

Gartzke, Erik. "Kant we all just get along? Opportunity, willingness, and the origins of the democratic peace." *American Journal of Political Science* 42, no. 1 (1998): 1–27. https://doi.org/10.2307/2991745.

Gartzke, Erik, and Kristian Skrede Gleditsch. "Why democracies may actually be less reliable allies." *American Journal of Political Science* 48, no. 4 (2004): 775–95. https://doi.org/10.1111/j.0092-5853.2004.00101.x.

Gaubatz, Kurt Taylor. "Democratic states and commitment in international relations." *International Organization* 50, no. 1 (1996): 109–39.

Gheciu, Alexandra. "Security institutions as agents of socialization? NATO and the 'New Europe'." *International Organization* 59, no. 4 (2005): 973–1012.

Gibbs, David N. "Secrecy and international relations." *Journal of Peace Research* 32, no. 2 (1995): 213–28. https://doi.org/10.1177/0022343395032002007.

Gibler, Douglas M. "The costs of reneging: Reputation and alliance formation." *Journal of Conflict Resolution* 52, no. 3 (2008): 426–54. https://doi.org/10.1177/0022002707310003.

Gibler, Douglas M. *International Military Alliances, 1648–2008*. Washington, DC: CQ Press (2009). https://doi.org/10.4135/9781604265781.

Gibler, Douglas M., and Scott Wolford. "Alliances, then democracy: An examination of the relationship between regime type and alliance formation." *Journal of Conflict Resolution* 50, no. 1 (2006): 129–53. https://doi.org/10.1177/0022002705281360.

Gibler, Douglas M., Steven V. Miller, and Erin K. Little. "An analysis of the militarized interstate dispute (MID) dataset, 1816–2001." *International Studies Quarterly* 60, no. 4 (2016): 719–30.

Gleditsch, Kristian S. "Distance between capital cities/Kristian Skrede Gleditsch" (n.d.). http://ksgleditsch.com/data-5.html.

Government of U.S.S.R. "Dokumenty Vneshnei Politiki SSSR (Documents on the Foreign Policy of the U.S.S.R.)" (XXI, doc. 82) (1977).

Green, Donald, Sooyeon Kim, and David Yoon. "Dirty pool." *International Organization* 55 (February 2003). https://doi.org/10.1162/00208180151140630.

Greer, Tanner, "One Belt, One Road, one big mistake." Foreign Policy (December 6, 2018). https://foreignpolicy.com/2018/12/06/bri-china-belt-road-initiative-blunder/.

Griffiths, Ieuan, and D.C. Funnell. "The abortive Swazi land deal." *African Affairs* 90, no. 358 (1991): 51–64.

Gross, Jan. "Sovietization of Poland's Eastern territories." In *From Peace to War: Germany, Soviet Russia, and the World, 1939–1941*, pp. 63–78. New York: Berghahn Books (1997).

Grundy, Kenneth W. "South Africa in the political economy of southern Africa." *International Politics in Southern Africa* (1982): 150.

Gulick, E.V. Europe's classical balance of power: A case history of the theory and practice of one of the great concepts of European statecraft. (No Title) (1955).

Guzman, Andrew T. "Reputation and international law." *Georgia Journal of International & Comparative Law* 34 (2005): 379. https://doi.org/10.2139/ssrn.1112064.

Haas, Ernst B. "Why collaborate? Issue-linkage and international regimes." *World Politics* 32, no. 3 (1980): 357–405.

Häge, Frank M. "Choice or circumstance? Adjusting measures of foreign policy similarity for chance agreement." *Political Analysis* 19, no. 3 (2011): 287–305. https://doi.org/10.1093/pan/mpr023.

Hajimu, Masuda. "Gentlemen's agreement." In *The Wiley Blackwell Encyclopedia of Race, Ethnicity, and Nationalism*, pp. 1–3 (2015). https://doi.org/10.1002/9781118663202.wberen529.

Hankyoreh, "North Korea's real motive for publishing the full text of new treaty with Russia," *Hankyoreh* (June 21, 2024). https://english.hani.co.kr/arti/english_edition/e_northkorea/1145928.html.

Hanlon, Joseph. *Beggar Your Neighbours: Apartheid Power in Southern Africa*. Vol. 356. Bloomington, IN: Indiana University Press (1986).

Hartley, Keith. "Defence industrial policy in a military alliance." *Journal of Peace Eesearch* 43, no. 4 (2006): 473–89. https://doi.org/10.1177/0022343306064976.

Hiden, John, and Patrick Salmon. The Baltic nations and Europe: Estonia, Latvia and Lithuania in the twentieth century (Rev. ed). Longman (1994).

Hiden, John, and Patrick Salmon. *The Baltic Nations and Europe: Estonia, Latvia and Lithuania in the Twentieth Century.* Routledge (2014).

Hilger, Gistav, and Alfred Meyer. *The Incompatible Allies. German-Soviet Relations, 1918–1941.* New York, NY: Macmillan (1954).

Hoover Institution. *Stephen Kotkin on the Hitler-Stalin Pact | Reflections* (2024). https://www.youtube.com/watch?v=6e8NHJWUbho.

Horn, Eva. "Logics of political secrecy." *Theory, Culture & Society* 28, no. 7–8 (2011): 103–22. https://doi.org/10.1177/0263276411424583.

Horowitz, Michael C., Allan C. Stam, and Cali M. Ellis. *Why Leaders Fight.* Cambridge, UK: Cambridge University Press (2015).

Horowitz, Michael C., Paul Poast, and Allan C. Stam. "Domestic signaling of commitment credibility: Military recruitment and alliance formation." *Journal of Conflict Resolution* 61, no. 8 (2017): 1682–710.

Hovet, Thomas. *Bloc Politics in the United Nations.* Cambridge, MA: Harvard University Press (1960). https://doi.org/10.4159/harvard.9780674498969.

Hug, Simon, and Richard Lukács. "Preferences or blocs? Voting in the United Nations Human Rights Council." *The Review of International Organizations* 9, no 1 (2014): 83–106. https://doi.org/10.1007/s11558-013-9172-2.

Hussein, Mohammed, and Mohammed Hadad. "Infographic: US military presence around the world" (2021). https://goo.su/bh9X3qH.

Huth, Paul K. "Extended deterrence and the outbreak of war." *American Political Science Review* 82, no. 2 (1988): 423–43. https://doi.org/10.2307/1957394.

Huth, Paul, and Bruce Russett. "What makes deterrence work? Cases from 1900 to 1980." *World Politics* 36, no. 4 (1984): 496–526.

International Monetary Fund (ed.). *Final Report of the Working Party on the Statistical Discrepancy in World Current Account Balances.* Washington, DC: IMF (1987).

Jackson, Matthew O., and Stephen Nei. "Networks of military alliances, wars, and international trade." *Proceedings of the National Academy of Sciences* 112, no. 50 (2015): 15277–84. https://doi.org/10.1073/pnas.1520970112.

Jaggers, Keith, and Ted Robert Gurr. "Tracking democracy's third wave with the Polity III data." *Journal of Peace Research* 32, no 4 (1995): 469–82. https://doi.org/10.1177/0022343395032004007.

Jakes, Lara. "What weapons is North Korea accused of supplying to Russia?" *The New York Times* (June 17, 2024). https://www.nytimes.com/2024/06/17/world/europe/russia-north-korea-weapons-ukraine.html.

Jaster, Robert Scott. *The Defence of White Power: South African Foreign Policy under Pressure.* Berlin: Springer (1988).

Jeffery, Keith. *MI6: The History of the Secret Intelligence Service 1909–1949.* A&C Black (paperback edn). Bloomsbury (2010).

Jervis, R. Cooperation under the security dilemma. World politics, 30(2), (1978): 167–214.

Jervis, Robert. "Realism, game theory, and cooperation." *World Politics* 40, no. 3 (1988): 317–49.

Jervis, Robert. *The Logic of Images in International Relations.* New York, NY: Columbia University Press (1989).

Jervis, Robert. *Perception and Misperception in International Politics: New edition.* Princeton, NJ: Princeton University Press (2017).

Johnson, Janet Buttolph, and Richard Joslyn. *Political Science Research Methods* (3rd edn). Washington, DC: CQ Press (1995).

Johnson, Jesse C., Brett Ashley Leeds, and Ahra Wu. "Capability, credibility, and extended general deterrence." *International Interactions* 41, no. 2 (2015): 309–36. https://doi.org/10.1080/03050629.2015.982115.

Johnson, Loch, and James M. McCormick. "Foreign policy by executive fiat." *Foreign Policy* 28 (1977): 117–38.

Johnson, Ian Ona. *Faustian Bargain: Soviet-German Military Cooperation in the Interwar Period*. Oxford: Oxford University Press (2021).

Johnston, Seth A. *How NATO Adapts: Strategy and Organization in the Atlantic Alliance since 1950*. Baltimore, MD: Johns Hopkins University Press (2017).

Jones, Daniel M., Stuart A. Bremer, and J. David Singer. "Militarized interstate disputes, 1816–1992: Rationale, coding rules, and empirical patterns." *Conflict Management and Peace Science* 15, no. 2 (1996): 163–213. https://doi.org/10.1177/073889429601500203.

Kann, Robert A. "Alliances versus ententes." *World Politics* 28, no. 4 (1976): 611–21. https://doi.org/10.2307/2010069.

Karabell, Zachary, and Philip Mattar. *Encyclopedia of the Modern Middle East and North Africa*. The Gale Group Inc. (2004).

Kasevin, Eugene. "Through ice and fear for Russia: The Arctic convoys." *Russia Beyond* (2015). https://www.rbth.com/longreads/arctic_convoys/.

Keohane, Robert O. "International relations and international law: two optics." *Harvard International Law Journal* 38 (1997): 487.

Keohane, Robert O. *After Hegemony: Cooperation and Discord in the World Political Economy*. Princeton, NJ: Princeton University Press (2005).

Kim, TongFi. "The alliance market: American security relations under unipolarity." PhD dissertation. The Ohio State University (2010).

Kimball, Anessa L. *Alliances from the inside out: A Theory of Domestic Politics and Alliance Behavior*. New York: State University of New York at Binghamton (2000). https://www.proquest.com/docview/304945228/abstract/843B326122841C9PQ/1.

Kimball, Anessa L. "Alliance formation and conflict initiation: The missing link." *Journal of Peace Research* 43, no. 4 (2006): 371–89.

King, Gary, and Langche Zeng. "Logistic regression in rare events data." *Political Analysis* 9, no. 2 (2001a): 137–63.

King, Gary, and Langche Zeng. "Explaining rare events in international relations." *International Organization* 55, no. 3 (2001b): 693–715.

Kotkin, Stephen. *Stalin. Vol. 2: Waiting for Hitler, 1929–1941*. New York: Penguin Press (2017).

Krasner, Stephen D. "Are bureaucracies important? (or Allison Wonderland)." *Foreign Policy* 7 (1972): 159–79. https://doi.org/10.2307/1147761.

Krasner, Stephen D. "Structural causes and regime consequences: Regimes as intervening variables." *International Organization* 36, no. 2 (1982): 185–205.

Krause, Volker, and J. David Singer. "Minor powers, alliances, and armed conflict: Some preliminary patterns." In *Small States and aAliances*, pp. 15–23. Heidelberg: Physica-Verlag HD (2001).

Krüger, Dieter. "Institutionalizing NATO's military bureaucracy: The making of an integrated chain of command." In *NATO's Post-Cold War Politics: The Changing Provision of Security*, pp. 50–68. London: Palgrave Macmillan (2014).

Kunz, Diane B. *The Economic Diplomacy of the Suez Crisis*. Chapel Hill, NC: University of North Carolina Press (1991). https://www.jstor.org/stable/10.5149/9780807862698_kunz.

Kuo, Raymond. "Secrecy among friends: Covert military alliances and portfolio consistency." *Journal of Conflict Resolution* 64, no. 1 (2020): 63–89. https://doi.org/10.1177/0022002719849676.

Kurizaki, Chuhei, and Taehee Whang. *Inferring Secret Diplomacy*. Technical Report Version 1.1, Working Paper. Texas: Texas AM University (2011).

Lai, Brian, and Dan Reiter. "Democracy, political similarity, and international alliances, 1816–1992." *Journal of Conflict Resolution* 44, no. 2 (2000): 203–27. https://doi.org/10.1177/0022002700044002003.

Lake, David A. "Anarchy, hierarchy, and the variety of international relations." *International Organization* 50, no. 1 (1996): 1–33. https://doi.org/10.2307/2991814.

Lake, David A. "Two cheers for bargaining theory: Assessing rationalist explanations of the Iraq War." *International Security* 35, no. 3 (2010): 7–52.

Lake, David A. *Hierarchy in International Relations* (Cornell paperbacks). Cornell Studies in Political Economy. Ithaca, NY: Cornell University Press (2011).

Lalman, David, and David Newman. "Alliance formation and national security." *International Interactions* 16, no. 4 (1991): 239–53. https://doi.org/10.1080/03050629108434760.

Langer, Máximo, and Mackenzie Eason. "The quiet expansion of universal jurisdiction." *European Journal of International Law* 30, no. 3 (2019): 779–817. https://doi.org/10.1093/ejil/chz050.

Leeds, Brett Ashley. "Domestic political institutions, credible commitments, and international cooperation." *American Journal of Political Science* (1999): 979–1002. https://doi.org/10.2307/2991814.

Leeds, Brett Ashley. "Credible commitments and international cooperation: Guaranteeing contracts without external enforcement." *Conflict Management and Peace Science* 18, no. 1 (2000): 49–71.

Leeds, Brett Ashley. "Do alliances deter aggression? The influence of military alliances on the initiation of militarized interstate disputes." *American Journal of Political Science* 47, no. 3 (2003): 427–39.

Leeds, Brett Ashley. "Alliance treaty obligations and provisions (ATOP) codebook." Houston, TX: Rice University (2005). http://www.atopdata.org/.

Leeds, Brett Ashley, and Jennifer Gigliotti-Labay. "You can count on me? Democracy and alliance reliability." Paper presented at the *Annual Meeting of the American Political Science Association, Philadelphia* (2003).

Leeds, Brett Ashley, and Burcu Savun. "Terminating alliances: Why do states abrogate agreements?" *The Journal of Politics* 69, no. 4 (2007): 1118–32. https://doi.org/10.1111/j.1468-2508.2007.00612.x.

Leeds, Brett Ashley, Andrew G. Long, and Sara McLaughlin Mitchell. "Reevaluating alliance reliability: Specific threats, specific promises." *Journal of Conflict Resolution* 44, no. 5 (2000): 686–99. https://doi.org/10.1177/0022002700044005006.

Leeds, Brett, Jeffrey Ritter, Sara Mitchell, and Andrew Long. "Alliance treaty obligations and provisions, 1815–1944." *International Interactions* 28, no. 3 (2002): 237–60. https://doi.org/10.1080/03050620213653.

Leeds, Brett Ashley. "Alliance Treaty Obligations and Provisions (ATOP) Codebook" (2022). http://www.atopdata.org/uploads/6/9/1/3/69134503/atop_5_1_codebook.pdf

Lemke, Douglas. "The tyranny of distance: Redefining relevant dyads." *International Interactions* 21, no. 1 (1995): 23–38. https://doi.org/10.1080/03050629508434858.

LeVeck, Brad L., and Neil Narang. "How international reputation matters: Revisiting alliance violations in context." *International Interactions* 43, no. 5 (2017): 797–821.

Levy, Jack S. "The role of necessary conditions in the outbreak of World War I." In *Explaining War and Peace: Case Studies and Necessary Condition Counterfactuals*, pp. 47–84. Abingdon, Oxfordshire: Routledge (2007).

Lijphart, Arend. "The analysis of bloc voting in the General Assembly: A critique and a proposal." *American Political Science Review* 57, no. 4 (1963): 902–17. https://doi.org/10.2307/1952608.

Lipson, Charles. "Why are some international agreements informal?" *International Organization* 45, no. 4 (1991): 495–538.

Long, Andrew G. "Defense pacts and international trade." *Journal of Peace Research* 40, no. 5 (2003): 537–52. https://doi.org/10.1177/00223433030405003.

Lucas, W. Scott. "NATO, 'Alliance' and the Suez crisis." In *Securing Peace in Europe, 1945–62: Thoughts for the Post-Cold War Era*, pp. 260–76. London: Palgrave Macmillan (1992).

MacFarlane, S. Neil. "Intervention and security in Africa." *International Affairs (Royal Institute of International Affairs 1944–)* 60, no. 1 (1983): 53–73.

Majeski, Stephen J., and Shane Fricks. "Conflict and cooperation in international relations." *Journal of Conflict Resolution* 39, no. 4 (1995): 622–45. https://doi.org/10.1177/0022002795039004002.

Mandler, Leah, and Carmela Lutmar. "Birds of a feather vote together? EU and Arab League UNGA Israel voting." In *Soft Threats to National Security*, 89–104. Routledge (2021).

Manno, Catherine Senf. "Majority decisions and minority responses in the UN General Assembly." *Journal of Conflict Resolution* 10, no. 1 (1966): 1–20. https://doi.org/10.1177/002200276601000101.

Maoz, Zeev, and Bruce Russett. "Normative and structural causes of democratic peace, 1946–1986." *American Political Science Review* 87, no. 3 (1993): 624–38.

Marshall, M. G., Gurr, T. R., Davenport, C., & Jaggers, K. Polity IV, 1800-1999: comments on Munck and Verkuilen. Comparative Political Studies, 35(1) (2002): 40–45.

Marshall, Monty G., and Ted Robert Gurr. "Polity5: Political regime characteristics and transitions, 1800–2018." *Center for Systemic Peace* 2 (2020).

Marshall, Monty G., Ted Robert Gurr, Christian Davenport, and Keith Jaggers. "Polity IV, 1800–1999: Comments on Munck and Verkuilen." *Comparative Political Studies* 35, no. 1 (2002): 40–5. https://doi.org/10.1177/001041400203500103.

Mastny, Vojtech. *Learning from the Enemy: NATO as a Model for the Warsaw Pact*. Vol. 58. Forschungsstelle für Sicherheitspolitik und Konfliktanalyse, ETH Zürich (2001).

Mattes, Michaela. "Reputation, symmetry, and alliance design." *International Organization* 66, no. 4 (2012): 679–707. https://doi.org/10.1017/S002081831200029X.

Mayer, Sebastian. "Introduction: NATO as an organization and bureaucracy." *NATO's Post-Cold War Politics: The Changing Provision of Security* (2014): 1–27.

McGillivray, Fiona, and Alastair Smith. "Trust and cooperation through agent-specific punishments." *International Organization* 54, no. 4 (2000): 809–24. https://doi.org/10.1162/002081800551370.

McGinnis, Michael D. "Issue linkage and the evolution of international cooperation." *Journal of Conflict Resolution* 30, no. 1 (1986): 141–70. https://doi.org/10.1177/0022002786030001010.

McManus, Roseanne W., and Keren Yarhi-Milo. "The logic of 'offstage' signaling: Domestic politics, regime type, and major power-protégé relations." *International Organization* 71, no. 4 (2017): 701–33.

Meirowitz, Adam, and Anne E. Sartori. "Strategic uncertainty as a cause of war." *Quarterly Journal of Political Science* 3, no. 4 (2008): 327–52.

Mercer, Jonathan. *Reputation and International Politics*. Cornell Studies in Security Affairs. Ithaca, NY: Cornell University Press (2010).

Metz, Rachel Tecott, Jason Davidson, and Zuri Linetsky. "The difference between an ally and a partner." *Instick* (blog) (February 25, 2023). https://goo.su/zW9Vdz.

Mi Terry, Sue, and Stephen Sestanovich, "Russia and North Korea signed a defense pact with each other. What does this mean?" *PBS News* (June 23, 2024). https://www.cfr.org/expert-brief/russia-struck-defense-pact-north-korea-what-does-it-mean.

Millard, Matt. "Rethinking the Kantian peace: Evidence from a liberal, moderate, and conservative measure of norm diffusion." *New Global Studies* 12, no. 3 (2018): 325–41. https://doi.org/10.1515/ngs-2018-0017.

Miller, Gregory D. "Hypotheses on reputation: alliance choices and the shadow of the past." *Security Studies* 12, no. 3 (2003): 40–78. https://doi.org/10.1080/09636410390443035.

Milner, H. *Interests, Institutions, and Information: Domestic Politics and International Relations*. Princeton, NJ: Princeton University Press (1997).

Milner, Helen V. *Interests, Institutions, and Information: Domestic Politics and International Relations*. Princeton, NJ: Princeton University Press (2020).

Minhas, Shahryar, Cassy Dorff, Max B. Gallop, Margaret Foster, Howard Liu, Juan Tellez, and Michael D. Ward. "Taking dyads seriously." *Political Science Research and Methods* 10, no. 4 (2022): 703–21. https://doi.org/10.1017/psrm.2021.56.

Mishra, Kushagra. "A review of China's Belt and Road Initiative: Debt traps, port seizure, and Malacca Strait bypass." *Medium* (November 27, 2023). https://medium.com/@imkushagramishra/a-review-of-chinas-belt-and-road-initiative-debt-traps-port-seizure-and-malacca-strait-bypass-249a8cc1cfda.

Mitchell, Sara McLaughlin. "A Kantian system? Democracy and third-party conflict resolution." *American Journal of Political Science* (2002): 749–59. https://doi.org/10.2307/3088431.

Mitchell, S.M., Kadera, K.M., and Crescenzi, M.J. 11 Practicing democratic community norms. International Conflict Mediation: New Approaches and Findings, 243 (2008).

Moon, Bruce E. "The foreign policy of the dependent state." *International Studies Quarterly* 27, no. 3 (1983): 315–40. https://doi.org/10.2307/2600686.

Moorhouse, Roger. *The Devils' Alliance: Hitler's Pact with Stalin, 1939–1941*. New York, NY: Hachette UK (2014).

Morgenthau, Hans Joachim. *Politics among Nations: The Struggle for Power and Peace* (6th edn). New York: Alfred A. Knopf (1985).

Morgenthau, H., and Nations, P.A. The struggle for power and peace. Nova York, Alfred Kopf (1948).

Morrow, James D. "On the theoretical basis of a measure of national risk attitudes." *International Studies Quarterly* 31, no. 4 (1987): 423–38. https://doi.org/10.2307/2600530.

Morrow, James D. "Capabilities, uncertainty, and resolve: A limited information model of crisis bargaining." *American Journal of Political Science* (1989): 941–72.

Morrow, James D. "Alliances and asymmetry: An alternative to the capability aggregation model of alliances." *American Journal of Political Science* (1991): 904–33. https://doi.org/10.2307/2111499.

Morrow, James D. "Alliances, credibility, and peacetime costs." *Journal of Conflict Resolution* 38, no. 2 (1994): 270–97. https://doi.org/10.1177/0022002794038002005.

Morrow, James D. "Alliances: Why write them down?" *Annual Review of Political Science* 3, no. 1 (2000): 63–83. https://doi.org/10.1146/annurev.polisci.3.1.63.

Morrow, James D., Randolph M. Siverson, and Tressa E. Tabares. "The political determinants of international trade: Tthe major powers, 1907–1990." *American Political Science Review* 92, no. 3 (1998): 649–61. https://doi.org/10.2307/2585487.

Mügge, Daniel, and Brian. "The problem with trade measurement in international relations." *International Studies Quarterly* 67, no. 2 (2023). https://doi.org/10.1093/isq/sqad020.

NA. "What will Britain do? Russian pact gives Hitler a free hand in Poland." *The Topeka Daily Capital* (August 24, 1939).

National Army Museum. "Suez Canal Zone." *National Army Museum* (n.d.). https://www.nam.ac.uk/explore/suez-canal-zone#:~:text=Between%201945%20and%201956%2C%20British,the%20most%20unpopular%20Army%20postings.

NATO. "NATO Headquarters" (2022). https://goo.su/lBFvV6.

Neff, Donald. *Warriors at Suez: Eisenhower Takes America into the Middle East*. Linden Press/Simon and Schuster (1981). https://cir.nii.ac.jp/crid/1130000796630531584.

Neumayer, Eric. "What factors determine the allocation of aid by Arab countries and multilateral agencies?" *The Journal of Development Studies* 39 (February 2003): 134–47. https://doi.org/10.1080/713869429.

Neustadt, Richard E. *Presidential Power and the Modern Presidents: The Politics of Leadership from Roosevelt to Reagan*. New York, NY: Simon and Schuster (1991).

Newcombe, Hanna, Michael Ross, and Alan G. Newcombe. "United Nations voting patterns." *International Organization* 24, no. 1 (1970): 100–21. https://doi.org/10.1017/S0020818300017422.

Newman, Bernard. "The captured archives: The story of the Nazi-Soviet documents." Latimer House, London (1948). https://cir.nii.ac.jp/crid/1130282268916332416.

O'Brien, Alexa, "The trial of Chelsea Manning." *The Cairo Review of Global Affairs* (2023). https://www.thecairoreview.com/essays/the-trial-of-chelsea-manning/.

O'Dell, Hope. "The US is sending more troops to the Middle East. Where in the world are US military deployed?" *The Chicago Council on Global Affairs* (October 25, 2023). https://globalaffairs.org/bluemarble/us-sending-more-troops-middle-east-where-world-are-us-military-deployed.

Palmer, Glenn, Roseanne W. McManus, Vito D'Orazio, Michael R. Kenwick, Mikaela Karstens, Chase Bloch, Nick Dietrich, Kayla Kahn, Kellan Ritter, and Michael J. Soules. "The MID5 Dataset, 2011–2014: Procedures, coding rules, and description." *Conflict Management and Peace Science* 39, no. 4 (2022): 470–82.

Palmer, G., D'Orazio, V., Kenwick, M.R., and McManus, R.W. Updating the militarized interstate dispute data: A response to Gibler, Miller, and Little. International Studies Quarterly, 64(2) (2020), 469–475.

Parl. Debs, 5th ser., House of Commons, vol. 345, col. 2415.

Patrick, Stewart. "Don't fence me in: The perils of going it alone." *World Policy Journal* 18, no. 3 (2001): 2–14.

Penney, Jonathon W. "Chilling effects: Online surveillance and Wikipedia use." *Berkeley Technology Law Journal* 31 (2016): 117.

Pfister, Roger. "Apartheid South Africa and African states: From pariah to middle power, 1961–1994." *International Library of African Studies* 14. London: Tauris Academic Studies (2005).

Philbin, Tobias R. *The Lure of Neptune: German-Soviet Naval Collaboration and Ambitions, 1919–1941.* Chapel Hill, NC: University of South Carolina Press (1994).

Plano, Jack C., and Roy Olton. *The International Relations Dictionary.* Kalamazoo, MI: New Issues Press (1979). 2nd edn (1988).

Poast, Paul. "Does issue linkage work? Evidence from European alliance negotiations, 1860 to 1945." *International Organization* 66, no. 2 (2012): 277–310. https://doi.org/10.1017/S0020818312000069.

Poast, Paul. "US allies vs. partners—what's the difference?" *Chicago Council on Global Affairs* (blog) (March 23, 2023). https://globalaffairs.org/commentary-and-analysis/videos/us-allies-vs-partners-whats-difference.

Pons, S. (2014). Stalin and the Inevitable War: 1936–1941 (paperback edu). Routledge.

Powell, Robert. *In the Shadow of Power: States and Strategies in International Politics.* Princeton, NJ: Princeton University Press (1999).

Powell, Robert. "War as a commitment problem." *International Organization* 60, no. 1 (2006): 169–203.

Price, David B. "The Charter of the United Nations and the Suez war." *David Davies Memorial Institute of International Studies. Annual memorial lecture* 1, no. 10 (1958): 494–511. https://doi.org/10.1177/004711785800101004.

Price, Megan, and Patrick Ball. "Big data, selection bias, and the statistical patterns of mortality in conflict." *SAIS Review of International Affairs* 34, no. 1 (2014): 9–20.

Price, Robert M. "Pretoria's southern African strategy." *African Affairs* 83, no. 330 (1984): 11–32.

Price, Robert. "Pretoria's Southern African strategy." *In Exporting Apartheid: Foreign Policies in Southern Africa, 1978–1988*, pp. 145–69. New York: Macmillian (1990).

Protocole Franco–Polonais, *Gamelin-Kasprzycki: Contre-Témoignage Sur Une Catastrophe, Protokół Końcowy Francusko–Polskich Rozmów Sztabowych*, 15–17 maja 1939.

Putnam, Robert D. "Diplomacy and domestic politics: The logic of two-level games." In *International Organization*, pp. 437–70. Routledge (2017).

Rahman, Bilal. "North Korea Allegedly Sent over 13,000 Containers Carrying Arms to Russia," *Newsweek* (August 27, 2024). https://www.newsweek.com/north-korea-sent-13000-containers-weapons-russia-report-1944858.

Ramstack, Tom. "Wikileaks case harms U.S. diplomacy, Manning sentencing told." *Reuters* (August 5, 2013). https://www.reuters.com/article/usa-wikileaks-manning/wikileaks-case-harms-u-s-diplomacy-manning-sentencing-told-idINDEE9740EL20130805.

Rapport, Aaron, and Brian Rathbun. "Parties to an alliance: Ideology and the domestic politics of international institutionalization." *Journal of Peace Research* 58, no. 2 (2021): 279–93. https://doi.org/10.1177/0022343319900916.

Reiter, Dan. "Learning, realism, and alliances: The weight of the shadow of the past." *World Politics* 46, no. 4 (1994): 490–526. https://doi.org/10.2307/2950716.

Reiter, Dan. *Crucible of Beliefs: Learning, Alliances, and World Wars.* Chapel Hill, NC: Cornell University Press (1996).

Reynolds, David. "A 'special relationship'? America, Britain and the international order since the Second World War." *International Affairs (Royal Institute of International Affairs)* 62, no. 1 (1985): 1–20. https://doi.org/10.2307/2618063.

Richardson, Louise. "Avoiding and incurring losses: Decision-making in the Suez crisis." *International Journal* 47, no. 2 (1992): 370–401. https://doi.org/10.1177/002070209204700207.

Richardson, Neil R., and Charles W. Kegley Jr. "Trade dependence and foreign policy compliance: A longitudinal analysis." *International Studies Quarterly* 24, no. 2 (1980): 191–222. https://doi.org/10.2307/2600200.

Rider, Toby J. "Uncertainty, salient stakes, and the causes of conventional arms races." *International Studies Quarterly* 57, no. 3 (2013): 580–91.

Ritter, Jeffrey M. "Know thine enemy: Information and democratic foreign policy." In *Power and Conflict in the Age of Transparency*, pp. 83–113. New York: Palgrave Macmillan (2000).

Ritter, Jeffrey Munro. *"Silent Partners" and Other Essays on Alliance Politics*. Cambridge, MA: Harvard University Press (2004).

Roberts, Geoffrey K. "The unholy alliance: Stalin's pact with Hitler." Bloomington, IN: Indiana University Press (1989).

Roberts, Geoffrey. "The Soviet decision for a pact with Nazi Germany." *Soviet Studies* 44, no. 1 (1992): 57–78. https://www.jstor.org/stable/152247.

Rowe-Munday, Sebastian, "After 75 years, the Five Eyes intelligence alliance remains a mystery," *National Interest Blog* (2021). https://nationalinterest.org/blog/buzz/after-75-years-five-eyes-intelligence-alliance-remains-mystery-180852.

Russett, Bruce M. "Discovering voting groups in the United Nations." *American Political Science Review* 60, no. 2 (1966): 327–39. https://doi.org/10.2307/1953359.

Sabaratnam, Meera. "Avatars of Eurocentrism in the critique of the liberal peace." *Security Dialogue* 44, no. 3 (2013): 259–78. https://doi.org/10.1177/0967010613485870.

Sabrosky, Alastair. "Interstate alliances: Their reliability and the expansion of war." *The Correlates of War II: Testing Some Realpolitik Models* (1980): 161–98.

Saif, Qutaiba Abdel Adhim Kadhem-Dr, and Adnan Irhayyim Al-Qaisi. "October Socialist Revolution 1917 and its impact on Iraq." *Iraqi Journal of Humanitarian, Social and Scientific Research* 2, no. 4 (2022).

Sample, Susan G. "Arms races and dispute escalation: Resolving the debate." *Journal of Peace Research* 34, no. 1 (1997): 7–22. https://doi.org/10.1177/0022343397034001002.

Sample, Susan G. "Furthering the investigation into the effects of arms buildups." *Journal of Peace Research* 35, no. 1 (1998): 122–6. https://doi.org/10.1177/0022343398035001009.

Sample, Susan G. "The outcomes of military buildups: Minor states vs. major powers." *Journal of Peace Research* 39, no. 6 (2002): 669–91.

Sample, Susan G. "Arms races." In *What Do We Know about War?* (3rd edn), pp. 63–80. Washington, DC: Rowman and Littlefield (2021).

Schachter, Oscar. "The twilight existence of nonbinding international agreements." *American Journal of International Law* 71, no. 2 (1977): 296–304. https://doi.org/10.2307/2199530.

Schelling, Thomas C. On letting a computer help with the work. John F. Kennedy School of Government, Harvard University (1972).

Schelling, Thomas C. *Arms and Influence* (Veritas paperback edn). New Haven, CT: Yale University Press (2020).

Schroden, Jonathan, and Alexander Powell. "Working with the Devil? The potential for US-Taliban cooperation against the Islamic State in Afghanistan." *War on the Rocks* (September 16, 2021). https://warontherocks.com/2021/09/working-with

-the-devil-the-potential-for-u-s-taliban-cooperation-against-the-islamic-state-in-afghanistan/.

Schuessler, John M. "The deception dividend: FDR's undeclared war." *International Security* 34, no. 4 (2010): 133–65.

Schweller, Randall L. "Bandwagoning for profit: Bringing the revisionist state back in." *International Security* 19, no. 1 (1994): 72–107.

Scott, William A. "Reliability of content analysis: The case of nominal scale coding." *The Public Opinion Quarterly* 19, no. 3 (1955): 321–5.

Scoville, Ryan, "New evidence of secret international agreements," *Lawfare Blog* (February 19, 2020). https://www.lawfaremedia.org/article/new-evidence-secret-international-agreements.

Scurtu, Ioan, Theodora Stănescu-Stanciu, and Georgiana Margareta Scurtu. "Soviet ultimata and replies of the Romanian government." *Istoria Românilor între anii 1918–1940*. Universitatea din București (2002).

Senese, Paul D., and John A. Vasquez. *The Steps to War: An Empirical Study*. Princeton, NJ: Princeton University Press (2008).

Shemesh, Moshe, and Selwyn Illan Troen. *The Suez-Sinai Crisis: A Retrospective and Reappraisal*. Abingdon, Oxfordshire, UK: Routledge (2005).

Shlaim, Avi. "The Protocol of Sévres, 1956: Anatomy of a war plot." *International Affairs* 73, no. 3 (1997): 509–30. https://doi.org/10.2307/2624270.

Signorino, Curtis S., and Jeffrey M. Ritter. "Tau-b or not Tau-b: Measuring the similarity of foreign policy positions." *International Studies Quarterly* 43, no. 1 (1999): 115–44. https://doi.org/10.1111/0020-8833.00113.

Simon, Michael W., and Erik Gartzke. "Political System Similarity and the Choice of Allies: Do democracies flock together, or do opposites attract?" *Journal of Conflict Resolution* 40, no. 4 (1996): 617–35. https://doi.org/10.1177/0022002796040004005.

Simmons, Beth A. "Compliance with international agreements." *Annual Review of Political Science* 1, no. 1 (1998): 75–93. https://doi.org/10.1146/annurev.polisci.1.1.75.

Singer, J. David. "Reconstructing the correlates of war dataset on material capabilities of states, 1816–1985." *International Interactions* 14, no. 2 (1988): 115–32.

Singer, J. David, and Melvin Small. "Formal alliances, 1815–1939: A quantitative description." *Journal of Peace Research* 3, no. 1 (1966): 1–31. https://doi.org/10.1177/002234336600300101.

Singer, J. David, Stuart Bremer, and John Stuckey. "Capability distribution, uncertainty, and major power war, 1820–1965." *Peace, War, and Numbers* 19, no. 48 (1972): 9.

Singer, J.D., Bremer, S.A., and Stuckey, J. Capability Distribution, Uncertainty, and Major Power War, 1820–1965 1. In Advancing Peace Research (pp. 161–174). Routledge (2012).

Siverson, Randolph M., and Bruce Bueno de Mesquita. "The selectorate theory and international politics." *In Oxford Research Encyclopedia of Politics* (2017). https://oxfordre.com/politics/display/10.1093/acrefore/9780190228637.001.0001/acrefore-9780190228637-e-293.

Siverson, Randolph M., and Juliann Emmons. "Birds of a feather: Democratic political systems and alliance choices in the twentieth century." *Journal of Conflict Resolution* 35, no. 2 (1991): 285–306. https://doi.org/10.1177/0022002791035002007.

Siverson, R.M., and King, J. Attributes of national alliance membership and war participation, 1815–1965. *American Journal of Political Science*, 1–15 (1980).

Siverson, Randolph M., and Harvey Starr. *The Diffusion of War: A Study of Opportunity and Willingness*. Michigan, MN: University of Michigan Press (1991).

Siverson, Randolph M., and Michael R. Tennefoss. "Power, alliance, and the escalation of international conflict, 1815–1965." *American Political Science Review* 78, no. 4 (1984): 1057–69.

Skidmore, David. *The Unilateralist Temptation in American Foreign Policy*. Abingdon, Oxfordshire, UK: Routledge (2011).

Slantchev, Branislav L. "Feigning weakness." *International Organization* 64, no. 3 (2010): 357–88.

Small, Melvin (1995). "Democracy & Diplomacy: the Impact of Domestic Politics on US Foreign Policy, 1798 - 1994." Johns Hopkins University Press. Baltimore, MD.

Smith, Allister. "Turmoil in Swaziland Disturbs South Africa." Washington Post. 16 June (1984).

Smith, Alastair. "Alliance formation and war." *International Studies Quarterly* 39, no. 4 (1995): 405–25.

Smith, Alastair. "Diversionary foreign policy in democratic systems." *International Studies Quarterly* 40, no. 1 (1996a): 133–53. https://doi.org/10.2307/2600934.

Smith, Alastair. "To intervene or not to intervene: A biased decision." *Journal of Conflict Resolution* 40, no. 1 (1996b): 16–40. https://doi.org/10.1177/0022002796040001003.

Smith, Alastair. "International crises and domestic politics." *American Political Science Review* 92, no. 3 (1998): 623–38. https://doi.org/10.2307/2585485.

Smith, Josh, and Ju-Min Park. "Russia's Putin and North Korea's Kim sign mutual defence pact." *Reuters* (June 19, 2024). https://www.reuters.com/world/asia-pacific/putin-kim-agree-develop-strategic-fortress-relations-kcna-says-2024-06-18/.

Snidal, Duncan. "Public goods, property rights, and political organizations." *International Studies Quarterly* 23, no. 4 (1979): 532–66. https://doi.org/10.2307/2600328.

Snyder, Glenn H. "The security dilemma in alliance politics." *World Politics* 36, no. 4 (1984): 461–95. https://doi.org/10.2307/2010183.

Snyder, Glenn H. "Alliances, balance, and stability." *International Organization* 45, no. 1 (1991): 121–42.

Sŏ, Chae-jŏng (ed.). *Origins of North Korea's Juche: Colonialism, War, and Development*. Lanham, MD: Lexington Books (2013).

Sontag, Raymond James, and Johnathan Beddie. *Nazi-Soviet Relations, 1939–1941: Documents from the Archives of the German Foreign Office*. Vol. 3023. Department of State (1948).

South Africa Record. South Africa Record. Pretoria, South Africa: SAIIA-South Africa Institute of International Affairs (1984). https://policycommons.net/artifacts/1452375/saiia-southern-africa-record-no-36/2084189/.

Sparks, Allister, "Turmoil in Swaziland disturbs South Africa." *Washington Post* (June 16, 1984). https://www.washingtonpost.com/archive/politics/1984/06/16/turmoil-in-swaziland-disturbs-south-africa/242e8203-e1fd-4aca-8894-7df448d37ea9/.

Springer, Simon, Heather Chi, Jeremy Crampton, Fiona McConnell, Julie Cupples, Kevin Glynn, Barney Warf, and Wes Attewell. "Leaky geopolitics: The ruptures and transgressions of WikiLeaks." *Geopolitics* 17, no. 3 (2012): 681–711. https://doi.org/10.1080/14650045.2012.698401.

Sputnik International, Sputnik, "Full Text of Russia-North Korea Strategic Agreement," *Sputnik International* (June 20, 2024). https://sputnikglobe.com/20240620/full-text-of-russia-north-korea-strategic-agreement--1119035258.html.

Stacey, Charles Perry. "The Canadian-American Permanent Joint Board on Defence, 1940–1945." *International Journal* 9, no. 2 (1954): 107–24. https://doi.org/10.1177/002070205400900204.

Starr, Harvey. "'Opportunity' and 'willingness' as ordering concepts in the study of war." *International Interactions* (June 1978). https://doi.org/10.1080/03050627808434499.

Stein, Arthur A. *Why Nations Cooperate: Circumstance and Choice in International Relations.* Chapel Hill, NC: Cornell University Press (1990).

Steiner, Zara. "The Soviet Commissariat of Foreign Affairs and the Czechoslovakian crisis in 1938: New material from the Soviet archives." *The Historical Journal* 42, no. 3 (1999): 751–79. https://doi.org/10.1017/S0018246X99008626.

Stinnett, Douglas, Jaroslav Tir, Paul Diehl, Philip Schafer, and Charles Gochman. "The Correlates of War (COW) project direct contiguity data, Version 3.0." *Conflict Management and Peace Science* 19 (September 2002): 59–67. https://doi.org/10.1177/073889420201900203.

Sukin, Lauren, and Alexander Lanoszka. "Credibility in crises: How patrons reassure their allies." *International Studies Quarterly* 68, no. 2 (2024): sqae062. https://doi.org/10.1093/isq/sqae062.

Svolik, Milan. "Lies, defection, and the pattern of international cooperation." *American Journal of Political Science* 50, no. 4 (2006): 909–25. https://doi.org/10.1111/j.1540-5907.2006.00223.x.

Tadjdini, Azin. "International Law GRRLS Blog," *Secrecy in International Agreements* (2015).

Tang, Shiping. "Reputation, cult of reputation, and international conflict." *Security Studies* 14, no. 1 (2005): 34–62. https://doi.org/10.1080/09636410591001474.

Taubman, William. *Gorbachev: His Life and Times.* New York, NY: Simon and Schuster (2017).

Thongnoi, Jitsiree. "China-Laos railway brings higher mobility, employment as profit concerns linger," *The China-Global South Project* (May 8, 2024). https://chinaglobalsouth.com/analysis/china-laos-railway-brings-higher-mobility-employment-as-profit-concerns-linger/.

Tolischus, Otto. "Nazi talks secret; Hitler lays plans with his close aides for the partition of Poland Danzig move First step 'Worthless peace phrases' of. Foreigners derided—Soviet and Reich agree on East challenge to Poland Seen Hitler's mind made up Hitler lays plans to cut up Poland. Council in Vital meeting End of encirclement seen Silent on Roosevelt appeal." *The New York Times* (25 August 1939). https://goo.su/SqR2zpO.

Tollison, Robert D., and Thomas D. Willett. "An economic theory of mutually advantageous issue linkages in international negotiations." *International Organization* 33, no. 4 (1979): 425–49. https://doi.org/10.1017/S0020818300032252.

Tomz, Michael. "Domestic audience costs in international relations: An experimental approach." *International Organization* 61, no. 4 (2007): 821–40.

Tomz, Michael. "Reputation and the effect of international law on preferences and beliefs." Unpublished manuscript (2008). https://web.stanford.edu/~tomz/working/Tomz-IntlLaw-2008-02-11a.pdf.

Toscano, Mario. *An Introduction to the History of Treaties and International Politics: The Documentary and Memoir Sources.* Baltimore, MD: Johns Hopkins University Press (1966).

Troen, S. Ilan. "The Protocol of Sèvres: British/French/Israeli collusion against Egypt, 1956." *Israel Studies* 1, no. 2 (1996): 122–39.

Troen, Selwyn Ilan. "Ben-Gurion's diary: The Suez-Sinai Campaign." In *The Suez-Sinai Crisis: A Retrospective and Reappraisal*, pp. 217–49. London: Taylor and Francis (2005).

Tuschhoff, Christian. "Alliance cohesion and peaceful change in NATO." *Imperfect Unions: Security Institutions over Time and Space* (1999): 140–61.
Underdal, Arild. "Explaining compliance and defection: Three models." *European Journal of International Relations* 4, no. 1 (1998): 5–30. https://doi.org/10.1177/1354066198004001001.
United Nations. "Vienna Convention on the Law of Treaties" (1969). https://legal.un.org/ilc/texts/instruments/english/conventions/1_1_1969.pdf.
US Department of Defense. "Alliances vs. Partnerships" (2019). https://www.defense.gov/News/Feature-Stories/story/Article/1684641/alliances-vs-partnerships/.
Vale, Peter. "The Botha Doctrine: Apartheid, Southern Africa and the West." *Exporting Apartheid: Foreign Policies in Southern Africa, 1978–1988* (1990): 170–8.
Van Evera, Stephen. *Causes of War: Power and the Roots of Conflict*. Vol. 4. Chapel Hill, NC: Cornell University Press (1999).
Varble, Derek. *The Suez Crisis*. New York, NY: The Rosen Publishing Group (2008).
Vasquez, John. *The War Puzzle Revisited*. Cambridge Studies in International Relations 110. Cambridge, UK: Cambridge University Press (2009).
Vine, David. "Where in the world Is the U.S. military?" *POLITICO Magazine* (July, 2015). https://www.politico.com/magazine/story/2015/06/us-military-bases-around-the-world-119321.
VOA News. "China-financed Laos railway expands Beijing's reach in Southeast Asia," *Voice of America* (June 29, 2024). https://www.voanews.com/a/china-financed-laos-railway-expands-beijing-s-reach-in-southeast-asia/7677853.html.
Vourkoutiotis, Vasilis. *Making Common Cause: German-Soviet Secret Relations, 1919–22*. New York, NY: Springer (2006).
Vreeland, James Raymond. "Corrupting international organizations." *Annual Review of Political Science* 22, no. 1 (2019): 205–22. https://doi.org/10.1146/annurev-polisci-050317-071031.
Vreeland, James Raymond, and Axel Dreher. *The Political Economy of the United Nations Security Council: Money and Influence* (1st edn) (2014). Long Grove, Illinois: Cambridge University Press. https://doi.org/10.1017/CBO9781139027755.
Wallace, M.D. (1979). Arms races and escalation: Some new evidence. Journal of Conflict Resolution, 23(1), 3–16.
Wallace, William, and Christopher Phillips. "Reassessing the special relationship." *International Affairs* 85, no. 2 (2009): 263–84. https://doi.org/10.1111/j.1468-2346.2009.00793.x.
Wallander, Celeste A., and Robert O. Keohane. "Risk, threat, and security institutions 1." In *Power and Governance in a Partially Globalized World*, pp. 88–114. Long Grove, Illinois: Routledge (2003).
Walsh, Michael. "Australia called for a COVID-19 probe. China responded with a trade war." *ABC News* (January 2, 2021). https://www.abc.net.au/news/2021-01-03/heres-what-happened-between-china-and-australia-in-2020/13019242.
Walt, Stephen M. "Alliance formation and the balance of world power." *International Security* 9, no. 4 (1985): 3–43.
Walt, Stephen M. *The Origins of Alliance*. Chapel Hill, NC: Cornell University Press (1990).
Waltz, K.N. Theory of international politics. Waveland Press (2010).
Warner, Geoffrey. "The United States and the Suez Crisis." *International Affairs* 67, no. 2 (1991): 303–17. https://doi.org/10.2307/2620833.

Weede, Erich. "Overwhelming preponderance as a pacifying condition among contiguous Asian dyads, 1950–1969." *Journal of Conflict Resolution* 20, no. 3 (1976): 395–411. https://doi.org/10.1177/002200277602000302.

Weeks, Jessica L. "Autocratic audience costs: Regime type and signaling resolve." *International Organization* 62, no. 1 (2008): 35–64.

Weisiger, Alex, and Keren Yarhi-Milo. "Revisiting reputation: How past actions matter in international politics." *International Organization* 69, no. 2 (2015): 473–95.

Weitsman, Patricia A. *Waging War: Alliances, Coalitions, and Institutions of Interstate Violence,* p. 191. Stanford, CA: Stanford University Press. Stanford Security Studies, an imprint of Stanford University (2013).

Werner, Suzanne, and Douglas Lemke. "Opposites do not attract: The impact of domestic institutions, power, and prior commitments on alignment choices." *International Studies Quarterly* 41, no. 3 (1997): 529–46.

White House. "National Security Strategy" (2022). https://bidenwhitehouse.archives.gov/wp-content/uploads/2022/11/8-November-Combined-PDF-for-Upload.pdf

Wolford, Scott. *The Politics of Military Coalitions.* New York, NY: Cambridge University Press (2015). https://doi.org/10.1017/CBO9781316179154.

Wolford, Scott, and Emily Hencken Ritter. "National leaders, political security, and the formation of military coalitions." *International Studies Quarterly* 60, no. 3 (2016): 540–51.

Woo, Byungwon, and Eunbin Chung. "Aid for vote? United Nations General Assembly voting and American aid allocation." *Political Studies* 66 (November 2017): 003232171773914. https://doi.org/10.1177/0032321717739144.

Wulandari, Ita, Anang Kurnia, and Kusman Sadik. "Weibull regression and stratified Cox regression in modelling exclusive breastfeeding duration." In *Journal of Physics: Conference Series.* Vol. 1940, no. 1, p. 012001. IOP Publishing (2021). https://doi.org/10.1088/1742-6596/1940/1/012001.

Xiang, Jun. "Relevance as a latent variable in dyadic analysis of conflict." *The Journal of Politics* 72, no. 2 (2010): 484–98. https://doi.org/10.1017/S0022381609990909.

Yarhi-Milo, Keren. "Tying hands behind closed doors: The logic and practice of secret reassurance." *Security Studies* 22, no. 3 (2013): 405–35.

Zhou, Cissy. "Sri Lanka's China 'debt trap' fears grow as Beijing keeps investing." *Nikkei Asia* (January 2, 2024). https://asia.nikkei.com/Spotlight/Asia-Insight/Sri-Lanka-s-China-debt-trap-fears-grow-as-Beijing-keeps-investing.

ידוס ימואל־ןיב ךמסמ לש וילוגלג ?ןורחאה קתועה סלענ סלענ ןאל" .1997 .כ ד ר מ ,וא־רב. 86–(1997) וא־רב) רתויב עיונים." 7: 86–102.

Index

alliance commitments
  and asymmetric alliances 146
  concerns about potential for defection from 56
  defensive alliance showing high levels of 104
  likelihood of future alliances 133, 146
  measuring 95–6
  punishment for violating 132
  and reputation 6–7, 24, 130, 132–3, 136
  Swaziland's greatest formal 225
alliance duration
  assessed in terms of termination 57, 156, 158
  of bilateral alliances 82
  measured by lifespan 57
  Molotov–Ribbentrop Pact 91
  results 147, 148–51, 155–7
  secret alliances
    differing from public alliances 60–61, 68, 69–70
    and specific length mentioned 69, 82–4, 91
    until violation 61, 70
    as way of measuring institutionalization 71
alliance formation
  causes of 34
  regime type as measure for 98–9
  and reliability 6
  role of domestic politics in 67
  role of reputation in 5–6, 158, 231
  signaling 34, 40
    to allies 35–6
    to domestic audiences 34–5
    to target states 36
    to third parties 36–7
  see also future alliance-making prospects; secret alliance formation

alliance institutionalization
  as antithetical to idea of secret diplomacy 61
  bilateral agreements as less likely to feature 59, 76, 79
  constraints 58–60
  as cornerstone of highly developed alliances 58–9
  definition 57
  of institutions 70
  facilitating sharing of resources 57
  formal agreements 134
  inherent tension with trust 55
  and military coordination
    Molotov–Ribbentrop Pact 171–3, 230
    South Africa and Swaziland 220–223
    Suez Crisis 194–6, 230
  need for further research on 60
  as often contradicting nature of secrecy 55, 56
  process of 57–8
  public-facing, as contrary to achieving surprise 229
  secret alliances as less likely to be institutionalized 63–5, 68–9, 70–71, 76–7, 79
  states engaging in private cooperation as less likely to engage in 56
  as strategy for mitigating risks of defection 57
  as unlikely to occur on large scale 230
alliance termination *see* secret alliance termination
alliance type
  and alliance termination 145–51
  effects on future alliances 152–4, 250–254
  in China 236

275

and conflict probability 69, 95, 104, 145
consultation as most common 129
as dependent variable 107–8
examples of 73
historical differences 27–8
as independent variable 110–111
and military contact 69, 85–6, 87, 88–9
usefulness of distinguishing between 40, 68, 69–70
and wilful violation 87
alliance violations
consequences as damaging to state reputation 232
and credibility in alliance-making 36
and defection 67
in democracies 56, 74, 87
as more likely to surface early in lifespan 55, 230
as occurring more quickly in fully secret alliances 61–3, 68, 69, 74, 78, 91
and partially secret alliances 68–9, 74, 78, 91
ratio tests to check for 49
secret alliances
as less likely to experience 87, 91, 132, 230
as likely to endure for shorter periods before violation occurs 61
states making secret alliances as less likely to commit 87
termination due to wilful 61, 69, 70, 72, 78, 142
time to violation 74–5
alliances
advantages and disadvantages 4
credible commitments 5
reputation 5–7
and China 235–40
defining 10–15
and international relations 3–7
and Russia 233–4, 235–6, 237
apartheid
advancing policies of 208–9
ANC as existential security threat for 220
collapse of regime 30

hanging on, by late 1980s 223
internal opposition to 209
isolation due to 139
putting South Africa at odds with Western backers 204–5
racist underpinnings 203
relevance to South Africa–Swaziland agreement
background 206–10
difficulty in finding partners for total strategy 136
domestic public opinion 217
future alliance-making prospects 224–6
linking Swaziland to economic fortunes brought by regime 222
provision of goods and familiarity 210–211, 213, 216
South Africa not reaching full democracy until end of 29
summary and conclusion 226
arms buildups
advantages and disadvantages 7
as one of two ways to prepare for war 3
and probability of conflict 21
and state appearance of capability 36
asymmetric information
and conflict probability 37–8, 39, 40, 137, 228
as likely to worsen due to regime symmetry 233
loss of signaling value creating 99
public disclosure decreasing problems posed by 8
and reputation of states 137, 138
secret agreements having disadvantages from 19

Bar-On, Mordechai
belief that Ben-Gurion did not trust British 2
omission of Israel's nuclear ambiguity from account 189
providing direct, first-hand account of Suez Crisis negotiations 31
view of nationalization of Suez Canal 180

Ben-Gurion, David 1–3, 20, 102, 159, 183–4, 186–9, 192–4, 235
bias 21–8, 73, 106, 129
blackmail capability 102, 128
blackmail vulnerability 137

Challe Scenario 1, 183, 188, 194
chilling effects 9
China
    alignment during Cold War 96
    alliances 235–40
    as autocratic regime 239
    commitment to Russia 233
    competing power with United States 28
    and division of goods 240
    formal secret agreement with Russia 27
    informal agreements with Russia 235–6
    major power status 72
    during Suez Canal nationalization 185
    United States attempting to contain influence of 239
commitment problem
    as driver of conflict 37
    as present throughout international relations 56
    as reason why states might engage in war 53
    secret alliances
        and issue indivisibility 136, 228
        solving 230
    varying between alliance types 90
Constellation of States 205, 207
credible commitments 5, 19, 34–6, 56, 61, 163

defection
    in asymmetric states 133
    in bilateral alliances 145
    communication for prevention of 65
    concealed nature of 61
    conflict driven by indivisible issues and 40
    disadvantages of short-term 14
    documentation as insurance policy against 19, 230
    as ever-present threat in international relations 55–6, 65, 133
    factors increasing likelihood of 135
    games of jointness and non-excludability having increased risk of 60
    Germany and Soviet Union 139
    indivisibility and commitment failures resulting in 39
    institutionalization as strategy to mitigate risks of 57, 63, 230
    as more likely in early stages 62, 66, 128
    NATO alliance mitigating risk of 66
    from public alliances 62
    and purposeful violation 69
    reputation as inherently tied to 56
    resulting in secret alliance formation 37
    secret agreements addressing 3
    from secret alliances 62
    and state lies 56
    in Suez Crisis 189
    unawareness of 137
    unrecorded agreements increasing risk of 26
diplomacy
    vs. secrecy 9
    secret alliances as riddles of international 3
    two-track 17
    see also secret diplomacy
division of goods in secret alliances
    China 240
    descriptive statistics 44
    Germany and Soviet Union agreeing to 165
    as likely to be primary driver 39
    need for greater military coordination to divide up labor in 230
    partially 39, 140
    vs. public alliances 44
    and targeting 46–50
    variable 42
domestic public opinion
    Molotov–Ribbentrop Pact 169–70, 229
    South Africa–Swaziland agreement 218–20
    Suez Crisis 190–194, 229

Eden, Anthony 1–3, 8, 26, 102, 181–4, 186, 190–200, 202, 229
Egypt *see* Nasser, Gamal Abdel; Protocol of Sèvres; Sèvres meeting; Suez Canal nationalization; Suez Crisis

familiarity
  Molotov–Ribbentrop Pact 165–9
  South Africa–Swaziland agreement 210–216
  of states making secret alliances 127
  Suez Crisis 165–9
formal alliances
  distinction with informal 8–9
  nature of 10–13
formal secret agreements
  reasons for 15–17
  and reliability 133
formal secret alliances
  agreements more likely to be recorded 19
  difficulty in hiding influence of 17
  future of 232–3, 237–40
  Germany and Soviet Union 164–5
  as likely to cover salient stakes 16
  most likely avenue for knowledge of 227
  problem with 18
  reasons for fewer 27
  and reputation 136–7
  United States 238
  as useful during crises 17
  writing down, as hindering defection 230
France
  alignment with South Africa 224
  alliances with United Kingdom during Crimean War 108
  as averse to alliances during inter-war years 178
  Franco–Polish alliance 167
  future alliance-making prospects 139
  as major power 72
  military-to-military agreement with Poland 167
  Nazi Germany's puppet regime in 175
  Poland defended by 164

provision of security guarantees to Poland 38
  secret alliances as frequently used by 40
  Soviets pursing alliances with 94
  Sykes–Picot Agreement 53, 66
  unwilling to commit to alliance with Soviets 162
  war in French Algeria and withdrawal from Indochina 2
  see also Protocol of Sèvres; Sèvres meeting; Suez Canal nationalization; Suez Crisis
future alliance-making prospects
  implication of secret alliances on 141, 147–59
  Molotov–Ribbentrop Pact 174–7, 232
  and reputation 60, 132–4, 231–2
  South Africa–Swaziland agreement 224–6
  Suez Crisis 139, 200–201
future of secret alliances
  looking to past 233–40
  returning to past 232–3

Germany
  Anglo–German alliance 6, 24
  Anti-Comintern Pact with Japan 20, 124, 169
  extension of NATO into newly unified 14, 58
  secret alliance with Russia 41
  secret alliances as frequently used by 40
  Wiemar, and Soviet Union 7, 163
  see also Molotov–Ribbentrop Pact
Great Britain
  Anglo–German alliance 6, 24
  Anglo–Polish Agreement 4, 5, 168
  USSR becoming ally of 158
  see also Protocol of Sèvres; Sèvres meeting; Suez Canal nationalization; Suez Crisis; United Kingdom
"horse trading" 58–9

informal agreements
  cooperation between partners 235–6
  democratic states 26

in international politics 14–15
Israel's increased reliance on 93
with Mozambique 225
possibly increasing risk of defection 26
secret 134, 135, 233, 235, 237, 238–40
states as more likely to rely on 142
and trust 202
United States 18
informal alliances
cooperation between partners 71, 173
distinction with formal 8–9
nature of 10–11
proliferation in recent past 232
secret 24, 28, 135
during World War II 176–7
informal contact and communication 64
informal institutionalization 230
information
alliances as mechanisms for transmitting 15
from bilateral alliances 145, 155
importance in preventing conflict 34
private 53, 56, 63, 67, 68
public 8, 70, 158
punishing those who disclose secret 27
secret alliances as means of concealing 51
see also asymmetric information
institutionalization *see* alliance institutionalization
international opinion
Molotov–Ribbentrop Pact 170–171
South Africa–Swaziland agreement 216–18
Suez Crisis 190
international relations
alliance-making as relatively rare event in 96
and alliances 3–7
alliances as important mechanisms for transmitting information in 15
and apartheid 136, 204–5, 206–9, 217, 224–5, 226
commitment problems in 56, 230
concerns over systematic bias in study of 22–4
concerns over temporal bias in studies of 25
defection as ever-present threat in 55–6, 65, 133
democracies and signalling 35
and enforceability of contracts 13
multi-player nature of 37, 38–9, 53
normative shift in 131
political similarity and trust 128
reputation considered crucial aspect of 130
secrecy in 8–9
secret alliances presenting unique puzzle in 55
states and norms 132, 134
theory on role of international institutions 59
value of formal agreements in 10
Israel
future alliance-making prospects 139
informal alliances with United States 232
seeking larger states to underpin security 136
United Nations voting scores on Israel/Palestine issues 98
see also Protocol of Sèvres; Sèvres meeting; Suez Canal nationalization; Suez Crisis
issue indivisibility 37–40, 50, 136, 228

land transfer
and acknowledgement of secret agreement 238
furthering South African regional objectives 214–15
international and domestic public opinion 217–18, 220
non-occurrence of 215–16
reneging of pact, and punishment 221
Richard's Bay as part of 213
South Africa proposing 206
South Africa revoking offer of 224
as straightforward purchase of Swazi cooperation 215
Swaziland's mistake regarding 226
"law of thieves" 65–6, 68, 87, 90
Lloyd, Selwyn 1–2, 102, 181, 191–4, 198–9

military contact and alliance type 85–6, 87, 88–9
military cooperation
  advantages 64
  and division of goods 91
  following Molotov–Ribbentrop Pact 64–5
  keeping confined to military-to-military coordination 91
  United States and Canada 71
military coordination
  and alliance institutionalization
    Molotov–Ribbentrop Pact 65, 101, 171–3, 230
    South Africa and Swaziland 220–223
    Suez Crisis 194–6, 230
  and military cooperation 91
  secret alliances as more likely to involve 64, 101, 127, 230
Molotov–Ribbentrop Pact
  agreement as precursor to 99
  alliances driving wedge between two allies 158
  background to 161–5
  context 161
  credible commitment 5
  demonstrating systemic changes resulting from secret agreements 33
  difficulties in hiding events 17
  duration 62, 91
  as example of defection from secret alliances 62, 139
  as example of importance of power in shaping conflict 40
  example of states with ideological differences finding common ground 24, 93, 101, 124, 161
  future alliance-making prospects 174–7, 232
  hiding effects of 196
  incentives of alliance 94
  institutionalization 171–3
  issues covered for case selection
    addressing of events as consequences of 30–31
    bias 29
    goods and objectives 29
    major power status 29
    regime type 29, 161
  success and failure 30
  uses of force 30
  variation of aims 30
  knowledge of secret agreements 228
  lack of trust between states on signing 102
  military cooperation following 64–5
  military coordination 65, 101, 171–3, 230
  rapprochement between two sides prior to 100, 235, 238
  reasons for secret alliance
    international and domestic public opinion 169–71, 229
    provision of goods and familiarity 165–9
  reputation and leaders 159
  salvaging of reputations in long term 139
  Soviets helping Nazis after 234
  Stag Hunt game 20
  states' difficulties securing alliances 136
  summary and conclusion 177–9
  termination 173–4
multi-player games 38

Nasser, Gamal Abdel 1–2, 30, 63, 180–188, 190, 191, 196–8, 201, 202
NATO
  discussions over extension into Germany 14
  France and UK as founding members of 200
  institutionalization 57–9, 63, 66, 134
  as long-standing alliance 73
  and need for alliances 96
  position on consultation 104
  and Russia 237
  serving as coordinating framework for security cooperation 59
  signing of agreement 107
  Suez Crisis 201
Nazi Germany see Molotov–Ribbentrop Pact
norms
  convergence of, between democratic states 67
  efforts to curb secret alliance-making 131
  measuring shared values 100

possibly set to erode due to global competition 236
representing "rules of proper behavior" 130
secret alliance implications 134–7
against secret diplomacy becoming more common 26, 130, 142, 159, 231, 233
North Korea 3–4, 27, 233–6, 240

Pineau, Christian 1, 181, 182, 189, 193
Poland
   Anglo–Polish Agreement 4, 5, 168
   becoming independent after war 30
   France and Britain providing security guarantees 38
   military-to-military agreement with France 167
   Nazi Germany hoping to obtain territory in 29
   Nazi Germany seeking to resolve "Polish Question" 62
   Nazi–Soviet annulment of pacts 167
   Pact of Mutual Assistance with Britain 167
   Polish–Bolshevik war 163–5
   Soviet Union's formal agreements with 176
Polish invasion
   background to 163–5
   date of 167
   as difficult to conceal 143, 196
   military coordination during 171–2
   Nazi–Soviet claims to territory 169
   Nazi–Soviet informal institutionalization 230
   Nazi–Soviet military cooperation during 64–5
   signed maps approving 170
   Soviet justification of 17, 32, 229
   summation 177–9
political dissimilarity
   and Cohen's k 110
   lack of research on secret alliances with 93
   and likelihood of engaging in secret alliances 127
   Molotov–Ribbentrop Pact 101, 124
   and security threats 94
   of states that do not ally with other states 96

counterargument 98
political similarity
   and alliances 98–100
   context 93–4
   dependent variable 107–8
   descriptive statistics 249
   independent variables
     alliance portfolio similarity 108–10
     alliance type 110–111
     capital distance and contiguity 112
     CINC (Composite Index of National Capabilities) scores 111–12
     joint democracy 110
     major power 111
     model specification 112
     threat 111
   literature 94–100
   measuring 95–8
   research design 105–7
   results 112–24, 125–6, 128
   S-score approach 96, 108–10, 127
   summary and conclusion 124, 127–8
   theory 100–105
prisoner's dilemma 19–20, 65
private reputation
   distinction with public reputation 56, 66, 138–9
   and fully secret alliances 90, 138, 158
   harmed, as unlikely to affect overall reputation 141, 158
   overcoming political disagreements because of threat of damage to 102
   state
     breaking bilateral agreements 145
     following through with commitments 231
     punishments harming 132
     reneging on commitments affecting 144
     short-term defection likely to harm 14
     wilful violations resulting in damage to 231
Protocol of Sèvres
   assumption of Egypt's relenting to pressure 184
   Ben-Gurion's involvement in carrying Israeli copy of 102

British governments' cover-up
    attempts 190, 191, 192–3
consequences of "going public" 230
cozy relationships making more likely
    235
democracies versus autocracies 27
demonstrating unreliability of
    defecting alliance partner 20
Eden's reaction to signing of 8, 102
failure of 196
French and British sharing political
    similarity during 93
involving two European states and
    one Middle Eastern state 29
major power status 29
Nasser's removal from power not
    explicitly mentioned in 187
objectives, and failure to achieve 30
press reportage on 189
reasons for secrecy 16
secret agreements eventually coming
    to light 18–19
seeking to reprivatize Suez Canal 29,
    30
as short-lived 62, 196
signatories as democracies 16, 19
signed in response to nationalization
    of Suez Canal 62
as structured for military coordination
    101
ultimate goal of 63
unofficial record made of 3
provision of goods
    Molotov–Ribbentrop Pact 165–9
    South Africa–Swaziland agreement
        210–216
    Suez Crisis 29, 38, 165–9
public reputation
    distinction with private reputation 56,
        66, 138–9
    and fully secret alliances 90, 138, 141,
        143, 144, 158
    overcoming political disagreements
        because of threat of damage to
        102
    and political similarity in year prior to
        secret agreement 128
state
    concealment of illicit agreement
        safeguarding 158

following through with
    commitments 231
and highly visible institutions in
    secret alliances 63
possibly not affected by fully secret
    alliance 144
punishments harming 132
short-term defection likely to harm
    14
suffering less on defection from
    secret agreement 66
wilful violations resulting in
    greater damage to 232
and terminated alliances 142

qualitative data, case selection 28–31
quantitative analysis 19–20

regime type
    democracies, autocracies, and
        defensive alliances 98–9
    vs. democratic states 117
    impacting on states forming alliances
        35, 145
    and informal secret agreements 239
    as not affecting reputation 145
    serving as proxy for political
        similarity 93, 98
    used to measure shared values 100
    variation across 29
reputation
    alliances as deeply intertwined with
        56
    alliances kept secret to protect 16
    China 236
    for commitment 6–7
        ability to adhere to 24
        alliances as deeply intertwined
            with 56–7
        assessing state's reputation for
            upholding its alliance
            commitments 132–4, 136–7
        conceptualization 130–131
        irregular termination measure 144
        punishments for violations 133
        record of upholding 94
    defining 6, 130, 132
    different perspectives on 56
    as difficult to measure 23–4

and formation of future alliances 60, 132–4, 231–2
imposing long-term cost of states reneging on agreements 13
as inherently tied to defection and trust, and must be earned 56
and institutional constraints 71
irregular termination negatively affecting 57
literature 5–7
Molotov–Ribbentrop Pact 163
overcoming political disagreements 102
"politically stained" 159
relationship with defection 60, 62, 68
for reliability 133, 231
research design 141–3
   dependent variables 143–4, 147
   independent variables 144–6, 147
for resolve 6, 130, 133–4, 231
results 155, 158–9
revelation of secret agreements affecting 14
role in alliance formation 6–7, 158
and secrecy 61, 62
secret alliances risk losing 19
as significant factor in international cooperation arena 131
Suez Crisis 192, 194, 200
theory 137–41
for upholding norms 134–7
see also private reputation; public reputation
reputational case studies 24
Russia
   alliances 233–4, 235–6, 237
   Bolshevik Revolution 18, 53, 230
   competing power with European Union 28
   formal secret agreement with China 27
   invasion of Ukraine 27, 229, 233–4, 236, 237
   major power status 72
   and North Korea 4, 27, 233–4, 235–6, 240
   salient stake 27
   secret alliance with Germany 41
   secret alliances as frequently used by 40

Sykes–Picot Agreement 66, 117, 230
see also Molotov–Ribbentrop Pact

S-score approach 96, 108–10, 127
salient stakes
   autocrats most likely to make secret alliances over 27
   examples 16
   illustrating hazards of secret agreements 232
   in international relations arena 8
   and military cooperation 64, 127
   as reason for states wanting to classify agreements as secret 16
   secret agreements not formed when stakes are not high enough 240
   states incentivized to act first to secure 228
   states likely to take extreme measures to secure 62
   written formal agreements as vital for 20
secrecy
   begetting secrecy 131, 240
   as critical element of alliance-making 33
   in diplomacy vs secret diplomacy 131
   diplomatic 24
   as having fallen out of favor 63
   institutionalization often contradicting very nature of 55
   in international relations 8–9, 19
   as not easy to maintain 202
   as not inherently meaningful 39
   as problem with knowing about secret alliances 17–18, 24
   and reputation 136, 138
   role in bargaining process 37
   as sometimes beneficial 16, 36
   and systematic bias 22
   and temporal bias 25
secret alliance formation
   alliance type as dependent variable 107–8
   context 93–4
   contiguity as negatively associated with 129
   independent variables 108–12
   issue indivisibility and defection resulting in 37–40, 50

literature 94–100
partially secret alliances 232
reasons for 37–41, 228–9
research design 105–7
results 112–24
summary and conclusion 124–5
theory 100–105
see also alliance formation; future alliance-making prospects
secret alliance termination
completely terminated 73, 76, 142
and credibility 59–60
effects on future alliances
clustered standard errors 250–251
Cox models 152–4
Weibull models 252–4
interaction effects 138, 147
irregular
advantages 158
and "blackmail" capability 102
explanation 57
independent variables 144–5
and institutionalization 70
intervals of time between alliances 155, 156–7, 158
and "law of thieves" 65–6
in research design 69–70, 142
role of reputation in 57, 140–141, 158
regular 156–7
and reliability 6
South Africa and Swaziland 223–4
Soviet–Nazi 173–4
Suez Crisis 196–200
and wilful violation 65, 69, 72, 78, 142
secret alliances
adding new members 79, 80–82, 91
explanation 33–4
findings summary 228–32
future of
looking to past 233–40
returning to past 232–3
knowledge of 227–8
as less likely to be institutionalized 63–5, 68–9, 70–71, 76–7, 79
list of 241–3
as never meant to last
context 55
literature 55–60
other explanations 67–9

research design 69–74
results 74–89, 244–8
summary and conclusion 90–91
theory 60–67
as one of two ways to prepare for war 3
and political similarity
context 93–4
dependent variable 107–8
descriptive statistics 249
independent variables 108–12
literature 94–100
research design 105–7
results 112–24, 125–6, 128
summary and conclusion 124, 127–8
theory 100–105
problem with 17–19
quantitative analysis 20–21
reasons for states recording 19–20
reputation and norms
context 130–132
norms 134–7
reputation 132–4
research design 141–6
results 147–57
summary and conclusion 158–9
theory 137–41
research design 41–3
results 43–9
robustness checks and confirmation 49–51
selection effects and bias 21–8
as significant mechanisms for state interaction 37
as successes or failures 26–8, 227
Suez Crisis as introductory example 1–3
summary and conclusion 51–2
targeting in 41–3
and United States 17–18, 25, 159, 233, 236, 237–40
see also division of goods in secret alliances; Molotov–Ribbentrop Pact; South Africa–Swaziland agreement; Suez Crisis
secret diplomacy
consequences of normative turn against 26, 130, 131–2, 142, 228, 231, 233

democracies less likely to engage in 50, 67
and diplomatic conversations 159
growing international aversion to 101
as international relations norm 132
issues addressed by being "selected out" by democratization 27
persistence of 33
question of relegation to the past 52
role in initiation of wars 52
selection effect 135
strong institutionalization as antithetical to idea of 61
United States position on 238
selection effects 22, 24–5, 41
Sèvres agreement *see* Protocol of Sèvres
Sèvres meeting
  action of Ben-Gurion before leaving 2
  Ben-Gurion's insistence on attendance 159
  British as first to leave 189
  cover-up attempts on conclusion 191
  French action prior to 188
  insightful accounts 31
  legacy 202
  October (1956) attendees 1
  plans taking shape at 183
  possibility of two separate arrangement occurring at 189
  proposal to stop Nasser taking place during 185–6
  signs of rapprochement between two sides 235
signaling
  alliance formation 34
  to allies 35–6
  and concept of "we-ness" 100
  credible commitments 19
    and reputation 7, 130, 137
    writing down alliances 66–7, 130, 137
  in defensive alliances 40, 61
  to domestic audiences 34–5
  explanation 15
  importance in preventing conflict 34
  in North Korea/Russia pact 235
  offstage 66–7
  in partially secret alliances 39, 49, 52, 70, 90
  in public alliances 39, 52

sinking costs 130
  in Suez Crisis 187, 195, 197
  to target states 36, 99, 100
  to third parties 36–7
South Africa
  in awkward relationship with Western democracies 204–5
  Constellation of States 205, 207
  cooperation with neighbors 205–6
  other countries' dependence on 203–4
  Swaziland's dependence on 203, 205–6
  total strategy 136, 205, 210–211, 215, 216, 223, 224–5
  see also apartheid
South Africa–Swaziland agreement
  acknowledgement of secret agreement 238
  apartheid as relevant to 29, 136
  background to 206–10
  as example of collusion ahead of time 17
  future alliance-making prospects 224–6
  institutionalization and military coordination 220–223
  issues covered for case selection
    bias 29
    goods and objectives 29
    major power status 29
    regime type 29
    success and failure 30, 93
    uses of force 30
    variation of aims 30
  justification for making secret alliance 136
  knowledge of secret agreements 228
  land transfer 22, 206, 213–18, 220, 221, 224
  reason for secrecy surrounding 16
  reasons for secret alliance
    international and domestic public opinion 216–20, 229
    provision of goods and familiarity 210–216
  salvaging of reputations in long term 139
  signaling commitments through costly signals 35
  summary and conclusion 226

termination 223–4
Soviet Union
  alliance with Japan as nonaggression pact 129
  centralized alliance network 59
  false claims made by leaders 32
  implications of Suez Crisis 180, 182, 184, 185, 187, 197, 202
  informal agreements not always honored example 14
  Sino–Soviet split 236
  and South Africa 204, 207, 211, 224
  United States avoiding war with 31
  and Wiemar Germany 7
  see also Molotov–Ribbentrop Pact
Stag Hunt game 19–20
Suez Canal nationalization
  British, French and Israeli concerns over 185–8
  domestic public opinion on 190–194
  events leading up to 185
  failure to seize canal 196–7
  issue convergence over 184–5
  military coordination 194–6
  opposition to 1–2
  outcome of secret alliance against 201–2
  overview 180–184
  Protocol of Sèvres
    seeking to reprivatize 29, 30
    signed in response to 62
    ultimate goal of 63
  US position on 197–8
Suez Crisis
  as example of collusion ahead of time 17
  future alliance-making prospects 139, 200–201
  institutionalization 194–6
  as introductory example of secret alliances 1–3
  issues covered for case selection
    bias 29
    goods and objectives 29
    insightful accounts 31
    major power status 29
    regime type 29
    success and failure 30
    uses of force 30
    variation of aims 30
  knowledge of secret agreements 228
  manufactured conflict 62–3
  military coordination 101, 194–6
  overview 180–184
  reasons for secret alliance
    domestic public opinion 190–194, 229
    familiarity 185–90
    long-term issue convergence 184–5
    provision of goods 29, 38, 185–90
  summary and conclusion 201–2
  termination 196–200
Swaziland
  attracting friends aligned in Western interests 206
  cooperation with South Africa 205–6
  dependence on South Africa 203, 205–6
  see also South Africa–Swaziland agreement
Sykes–Picot Agreement 16, 18, 20, 33, 53, 66, 117, 230

target states
  discussions about as often found in secret protocols 39
  and military coordination 230
  and presence of allies 21
  and risk of exposure 65
  and salient stakes 64, 228
  secret alliances as more likely to identify 40, 45, 47, 48, 50
  signaling 101
targeting
  in Polish invasion 64
  in secret alliances 39, 46–50
  South Africa–Swaziland 101
total strategy see South Africa: total strategy

Ukraine
  and commitments to peace in Europe 14
  Russia's invasion of 27, 229, 233–4, 236, 237
  and Soviet Union's strategy of allying with Germany 162
  Ukraine Defense Contact Group 58–9
United Kingdom
  alignment with South Africa 224

alliances
  during Cold War 96
  during inter-war years, averse to 178
  with France during Crimean War 108
  "Five Eyes" agreement 33
  Germany's western campaign failing to subdue 174
  as major power 72
  Pact of Mutual Assistance with Poland 167
  Poland defended by 164
  secret alliances as frequently used by 40
  signing NATO agreement 107
  Soviets pursing alliances with 94
  Sykes–Picot Agreement 53, 66
  ties with Soviet Union and United States shortening World War II 177
  unwilling to commit to alliance with Soviets 162
  see also Great Britain; Protocol of Sèvres; Sèvres meeting; Suez Canal nationalization; Suez Crisis
United States
  and Canada 58, 71, 96
  chilling effects 9
  competing power with China 28
  confusion surrounding terms "allies" and "partners" impacting 12–13
  "Five Eyes" agreement 33
  and formal alliances 13
  informal agreements with Soviet Union during Cold War 10
  informal alliance with Israel 232
  and Japan 4, 14, 129
  major power status 72
  mixed approach to commitments 5
  publicly accusing North Korea of sending weapons to Russia for use in Ukraine 234
  and secret alliances
    as best understood as executive agreements 159
    future of 233, 236, 237–40
    problem with 17–18
    temporal bias 25
  signing NATO agreement 107
  and South Africa 204, 211, 224
  Soviet Union becoming ally of 139, 158
  "special relationship" with United Kingdom 96
  strategy in Europe 59
  strategy of forming large alliances 58–9
  in Suez Crisis 16, 31, 180–184, 185, 187, 197–200, 201, 202
  ties with United Kingdom and Soviet Union shortening World War II 177
  time between first and next alliance 143

violations *see* alliance violations

World War II
  and allyship 99
  bilateral alliances since 142, 155
  impact on alliances 175–7, 232
  impact on Suez Crisis 180–181, 185, 196
  Japan's aggressive foreign policy 160
  Permanent Joint Board on Defense providing foundation for military cooperation 71
  and physical documentation 3, 229
  prevalence of secret alliances 135, 142
  provision of goods leading to outbreak of 161
  and secret diplomacy 52, 101, 132